SOCIAL PSYCHOLOGY

ROBERT E. L. FARIS

PROFESSOR OF SOCIOLOGY
UNIVERSITY OF WASHINGTON

THE RONALD PRESS COMPANY ⸓ NEW YORK

Library of Congress Catalog Card Number: 52–6203

PREFACE

This book has been written for use as a text in college courses in social psychology. Basically, the field is conceived to be the study of those aspects of human personal behavior which are developed and controlled by the interaction which takes place between the individual and his small intimate circle of associations known as the primary group.

Recent years have witnessed a significant expansion of the content of social psychology. Because of the diverse views of experimenters and the contribution of different fields of study, the increase in knowledge has sometimes proved to be an embarrassment of riches. A major purpose of this book is to show the essential unity of the knowledge that has been acquired and to emphasize the areas of fundamental agreement in the field rather than one particular school of thought. Moreover, materials from the subject fields of either sociology or psychology which do not bear directly on this conception of the subject have been excluded in the interest of a clear and integral organization.

Our knowledge of the processes of social psychology today is not static and completed; rather, it is constantly subject to revision and modification by further experiment and investigation. Although designed primarily as an introduction to social psychology, this discussion also includes a review of the latest scholarship in the field and an analysis of the methods by which new knowledge has been acquired. The constant emphasis on the experimental background should lead the student to an understanding of the present research frontiers of social psychology.

It has been intended, finally, that the discussion of human behavior presented here will admit of a direct and meaningful application by the reader to situations encountered in everyday living. It is recommended as a valuable exercise, in fact, that the student analyze his own life history or the experiences of the subject of a good fictional or biographical work in the light of the principles brought out in this volume.

The author has obligations to more people than can be listed here, for he has drawn upon all his former teachers, on the knowledge provided by many of his colleagues and friends, and on a large amount of research literature. For much of the point of view and content of this work, he is indebted to his father, Ellsworth Faris, who has given a lifetime of study to the organization of the science of social psychology.

The author is also indebted to Professor Ralph H. Turner who read and criticized the manuscript.

ROBERT E. L. FARIS

University of Washington
January, 1952

CONTENTS

CHAPTER PAGE

1   HUMAN NATURE AND THE SOCIAL ORDER   3

The Incompleteness of Man Apart from Social Organization. The Relation of the Individual to a Social Order: The General Relation of Parts to a Whole; The Concept of Emergence; The Relation of the Human Animal to Social Organization; Consequences of Long Dependence on Social Organization. Summary.

2   INADEQUACY OF BIOLOGICAL MOTIVATION   11

The Concept of Instinct as Applied to Lower Animals. The Instinct Theory in Human Behavior: The Classical Notion of Instinct; Substitutes for the Instinct Concept in the Human; Acquired Physiological Drives; The Concept of Libido as a General Drive; Objective Evidence Opposed to the Concept of Libido; The Catharsis Concept and Instinct. Summary.

3   MOTIVATION: THE INDIVIDUAL ASPECT   34

The General Tendency of Living Things to Function. The Physiological Bases of General Activity. The Completion Tendency. Emergence of Specific Wishes—The Process of Canalization. The Appeal of Novelty, Complexity, Progress. Summary.

4   MOTIVATION: SOCIAL SOURCES   49

The Role of Culture in Canalization. Generalization of Motives —Currency and Storage Aspects. Institutional Integration of Motives: Institutional Roles; Elaboration of Biological Elements; The Rigidity of Institutional Motivation; Life Organization. Morale as Social Dominance of Motivation. Summary.

5   THE EMERGENCE OF CONSCIOUSNESS   77

Inadequacy of the Concept of Conditioning. The Nature and Function of Consciousness: The Automatic Character of Habit; Consciousness as Adaptation to Crises; The Muscular Aspect of Consciousness; Conscious Behavior and the Operation of Processes Which Insure Orientation; Complex and Hypothetical Crises; Wishes, Dreads, Dreams, and Daydreams as Trial Solutions to Hypothetical or Imaginary Crises; The Relation of Emotion to Action. Mental Organization Resulting from the Process of Intercommunication. Summary.

CHAPTER   PAGE

6   THE CONCEPT OF UNCONSCIOUS MIND 114

Popular and Technical Uses of the Concepts of Unconsciousness
and Unconscious Mind. Insightless Behavior. Repression, Suppression, Sublimation. Differential Memory and Unpleasantness. Memory and Context. Further Methodological Difficulties
in the Concept of Unconscious Mind: Alternative Interpretations
of Reports of Subjects; Hypnosis as Evidence for the Repression
Hypothesis; Regression and Unconsciousness; Automatic Writing as Operation of Unconsciousness Mind. Summary.

7   THE EMERGENCE OF SELF-CONSCIOUSNESS IN SOCIAL
    INTERACTION 149

The Genesis of the Self. Internalization of the Social Process.
The Social Function of Self-Consciousness. Uncertainty and
Fluctuations in the Self-Concept: Consistent Underestimation of
Status; Unstable Conceptions of Status. Summary.

8   SOCIAL DETERMINATION OF LEARNING, PERCEPTION, AND
    MEMORY 172

The Acquisition of New Behavior: Individual Problem Solving;
"Expedient Learning" and "Proper Learning"; Learning from
Social Patterns—Unwitting Imitation; Acquisition of Speech
Through Role-Taking. The Social Factor in Perception: Per-
ception as an Active Process; Perception as Learned Behavior;
Orientation and Perception; Social Contexts of Perception. The
Structure of Memory: The Relation of Memory to Wish and
Attitude; The Dependence of Memory on Relationships. Sum-
mary.

9   SOCIAL DETERMINATION OF ATTITUDES AND BELIEFS . . 200

The Concept of Social Attitudes: Definition of Social Attitudes;
The Defining Function of Social Attitudes; The Authority of
Group and Culture; Social Influences in the Alteration of Atti-
tudes. The Social Basis of Belief: Folk Knowledge; Rumors—
Transitory Beliefs. Summary.

10   THE SOCIAL FACTOR IN ABILITY 223

The Nature of Intelligence: Aspiration and Competition; The
Organic Character of Knowledge and Ability; Cultural Nutrition
of Intelligence; Socioeconomic Differences in Intelligence; Social Factors in the Generation of Exceptional Ability. Summary.

11   THE CHARACTER OF PRIMARY INTERACTION 250

The Nature of Primary Groups. Primary Group Processes: The
Tendency to Form Groups; Differentiation of Status in Primary
Groups; Functions of Status Differentiation in Primary Rela-
tions; The Defensive Function of Status Distinction. Exclusive-
ness in the Clique. The Character of Informal Social Control.
The Power of Informal Social Control. Informal Control in

CHAPTER   PAGE

Opposition to Formal Control. Assimilation to New Primary Relations. Summary.

12 THE DIFFERENTIATION OF PERSONS BY VARIATIONS OF ROLES   281

The Nature of Role and Status: Sex Roles; Age Roles; Popularity; Leadership and Primary Relations. Contradictions, Inconsistencies, and Dilemmas of Status: Conflicts in Sex Roles of Women; Role Conflicts in a Polygynous Society; Other Types of Role Conflict. Summary.

13 THE NEUROTIC ROLE 309

The Relation of Neurosis to Conflict: Animal "Neurosis." The Relation of Neurosis to Fear. Neurosis as a Career. Character Patterns—Reactions to Crises. Summary.

14 PERSONALITY DISORGANIZATION 329

Physiological Defect: Brain Impairment; Effects of Brain Impairment on Processes of Self-consciousness; Effects of Age, Fatigue, Malnutrition, Alcohol, and Lack of Oxygen on Complex Mental Functions and Personality. Isolation and Personality Disorganization: General Effects of Isolation; Eccentricity Without Dementia; Isolation and Mental Disorganization; Isolation, Unconventionality, and the Schizophrenic Symptoms. Collapse of the Life Organization. Summary.

15 TRENDS AND PROBLEMS IN SOCIAL PSYCHOLOGY . . . 370

Backgrounds of Contemporary Social Psychology: Nineteenth-Century Individual Psychology; The Departure from Pure Individualistic Psychology; The Emphasis on Modifiability Through Environmental and Social Influences; The Emphasis on Interaction; Emergence of an Organic Viewpoint; The Gestalt and Topological Approaches; Applied Social Psychologies; Applications of Social Psychology to "Social Issues"; The Decline of Schools of Thought and Emergence of the Mature Scientific Stage. Basic Research Problems: The Definition of Physiological Essentials to Normal Behavior; Abilities; The Formation and Rigidity of Character; Empathy; Personal Disorganization; Emerging Research Problems. Contemporary Research Methods: The Clinical Method; The Life-History Method; Testing and Scaling; Statistical and Mathematical Techniques; Experiment. Summary.

INDEX OF NAMES 409

INDEX OF SUBJECTS 415

SOCIAL PSYCHOLOGY

Chapter 1

HUMAN NATURE AND THE
SOCIAL ORDER

THE IMPORTANCE of social psychology in contrast to individual psychology lies in the fact that the complex behavior of daily life is not fully explained by an inventory of the physiological system of man. Our deeds are not entirely determined from within. While a complete explanation of behavior cannot omit a treatment of internal factors, the more valuable part of the account will come from a consideration of the influences of interaction in social processes. Social processes are responsible for human nature and personality as we recognize them. Without interaction with other human beings there is a physiological shell of possibilities but no human personality.

THE INCOMPLETENESS OF MAN APART FROM
SOCIAL ORGANIZATION

Man, in comparison with other vertebrates, is the least complete and most helpless animal when separated from organized relations with other individuals of his species. He is the most dependent at birth and has the longest period of infancy, both in absolute number of years and in relation to his normal life span. All that is distinctly human in the behavior of man results from his participation in organized social life. It is only within such social processes that he acquires a mind and a conception of self. The social groups in which he has membership define for him the meaning of common objects and situations, saving him the trouble of having to figure them out for himself, and providing for all a set of uniform standards which facilitates teamwork. In addition to forming human nature in each of its members, a society continues to guide and control them throughout their lives. The internal organization of habits, attitudes, and self-conception is thus preserved in each

3

person. In prolonged isolation these human characteristics deteriorate.[1]

It is idle to speculate on the character a human individual might have apart from the influence of social life. There are no cases on record of humans reaching maturity in isolation. Observations of newborn infants give no hint of the complexity and versatility that is to be acquired by them during the growing years. The potentialities which distinguish them so greatly from all other living nonhuman creatures do not become evident until after a rich and lengthy experience in primary group interaction has been achieved.

Human psychology, then, is social psychology. Physiological processes can be studied with profit, but little in this realm of knowledge is distinctly human. A large part of physiological psychology, in fact, is based on research with lower animals. This is an efficient approach in view of the similarity of animal and human physiology and in view of the greater convenience of research with animals. But the more complex and distinctly human behavior is completely inaccessible to purely physiological research. The only avenue to knowledge of this aspect of man is through the more difficult, inconvenient, and sometimes bafflling study of the processes of social interaction. The field of social psychology may be briefly defined as the organization and control of behavior in primary interaction.

Primary interaction is that type of reciprocal social behavior which is intimate, sympathetic, and personal in character, such as the behavior of the members of a family, or close group of friends, toward one another. It is distinguished from institutional relations which are more formal in character, and which are illustrated by the relation we have with persons who, like a judge on the bench, are acting in the capacity of a formal office. The emphasis in the study of social psychology, and of personality, is on primary interaction because it is in this type of process that the earlier and more important aspects of internal organization are achieved, and because for most persons throughout their lives the most effective instruments of social control are those that operate through primary social relations.

Our inquiry, therefore, is to discover how the social process operates to transform the helpless human infant into a skillful, cooperative, and dependable person.

---

[1] See Chapter 14 for a discussion of isolation and personality disorganization.

The Relation of the Individual to a Social Order

The General Relation of Parts to a Whole.—In his interaction with other persons, each human experiences not merely a sequence of experiences with one person after another, but an organized pattern of experiences. This pattern reflects the well-known fact that men are organized into groups, institutions, and societies.

An issue of almost perpetual concern is the extent to which these social organizations can properly be regarded as being real things. To some who have been interested in the problem, the only reality is the individual. The group or society is viewed by these observers as only unreal abstractions, not capable of being the cause of any phenomenon of social psychology.[2] The phenomena which appear to be organized social groups are viewed as nothing more than the sums of traits and actions which exist only in the separate minds and persons.

On the other hand there may be found an insistence, on the part of others, that it is scientifically justifiable and profitable to consider that an organization of human individuals may form a whole which is just as real as other things made of organized parts. Cooley wrote, "There is an organization, a life-process, in any social whole that you cannot see in the individuals separately. To study them one by one and attempt to understand society by putting them together will lead you astray."[3]

In defense of the latter view it is pointed out by many that a society has greater extent and duration than any of its members. It cannot accurately be considered a sum of its members, for a mere addition of individual traits would be insufficient to produce the characteristics of a society, as a pile of bricks would fail to constitute a house. It is the arrangement of functioning interrelations which produces an organization. The parts can be replaced without disturbing the integrity of the organization and new parts may be brought in to take their place in the pattern. The organization or whole can precede any one of its replacement parts—human society already exists as each person is born and comes to take his place in it and, in this sense, is prior to the individual. It is also exterior to the individual in the sense that it contains character-

[2] The most prominent representative of this point of view at present is Floyd H. Allport. See his article "The Group Fallacy in Relation to Social Science," *American Journal of Sociology,* XXIX, No. 6 (1924), 897-921.

[3] Charles H. Cooley, *Human Nature and the Social Order* (New York: Chas. Scribner's Sons, 1902), p. 48.

istics which are not present in its members originally, or in all of its members at any one time, and that it endures over generation after generation of members. Furthermore, as has been pointed out, the whole exercises a dominance over its parts, affecting or controlling their behavior and, in some cases, even forming their internal nature.

In general these properties of the social organization and the relations of the social organization to its constituent parts—separate persons—are those of organizations in general. In fact, the same problem concerning elements and organizations, or individuals and societies, exists at other levels of science. The large jellyfish known as the *Portuguese man-of-war* appears to an untrained observer as an individual organism, but is referred to in biology as a *colony* consisting of a medusa and a number of polyps differentiated according to their various functions of feeding, protection, and reproduction. A biologist has recently described an amoeba, *Dictyostelium discoideum,* as an organism which spends a part of its life cycle as an individual and a part as a member of an organization which itself is so unified as to be readily identified as an individual of a higher order. When the individual amoeba takes its place in the organization, its internal nature is changed *according to where it is in the structure of the whole.* The life cycle begins with a spore which splits down the side to form an amoeba of the characteristic fluctuating, amorphous shape. Its behavior is like that of other amoebae; it feeds by extending pseudopods to engulf bacteria and divides by binary fission. At certain periods, however, these independent and unorganized individual amoebae congregate to form a crowd, then a sausage-shaped mass which can crawl in caterpillar fashion. After a varying amount of migration, the mass takes an upright position and a pointed tip thrusts upward. The component cells of this mass change their shapes and differentiate into two types: stalk cells and spore cells. The former are elongated and serve to support the now rounded head of spore cells, which alone perform the reproductive function. No feeding is done by cells when the organism is in the upright stage. The cycle is completed when the head of the organism disperses its spores.[4]

Organization in biochemistry has a similar relation of parts to a whole. A cell is an organization of chemical components which are only temporarily in the life process. A research scientist writes:

[4] From John Tyler Bonner, "The Social Amoebae," *Scientific American,* June, 1949, pp. 44-47.

The substances of cells are constantly being built up and broken down from a "metabolic pool" of chemically active fragments of molecules that circulate in the organism. Schoenheimer aptly likened the adult organism to a military regiment: "[It has] a size which fluctuates only within . . . limits, and a well-defined highly organized structure. *The individuals of which it is composed are continually changing.* Men join up, are broken, and ultimately leave after varying lengths of service. The incoming and outgoing streams of men are numerically equal, but they differ in composition. . . . Recruits may be likened to the diet; their retirement and death correspond to excretion." [5]

In the words of another writer:

. . . living things must work ceaselessly to exist. So life is more like a whirlpool than a machine. There is nothing machinelike about the vortex formed when water spirals downward. In one sense, an entirely new whirlpool comes into being every few seconds as the rotating center replenishes itself from the surrounding waters. But through it all the form does not change. The position of the vortex, the space it occupies, the shape of the spinning funnel, preserve their integrity over long periods of time; the system has an identity and structure of its own. Similarly the human body and every other organism known to be is a vortex of continual change.[6]

Thus it is apparent that the characteristics of a social organization are not entirely unlike those of a biological organism. Among the characteristics of an organism are (1) a pattern of interaction which gives unity to differentiated parts, (2) a purpose or function which is served by the interaction, (3) a tendency to maintain constancy of operation, (4) ability to endure longer than its component parts, and (5) ability to assimilate new materials, altering them if necessary so that they fit into the interaction pattern. All these are also characteristics of a social organization, which, therefore, has as much claim to reality as does the organization of parts on any of the lower levels—atomic, chemical, or biological. There need be no logical or scientific difficulty in studying the effects of social interaction, or the influence of a group, on persons.[7]

[5] Martin D. Kamen, "Tracers," *Scientific American*, February, 1949, pp. 31-44.
[6] John E. Pfeiffer, "Enzymes," *Scientific American*, December, 1948, pp. 29-39.
[7] This is not to deny differences between organisms and societies. One important difference is that societies can be separated into component parts and new units formed, as is done when an army is reorganized. In general, when an organism is taken apart the whole dies and the parts die with it. This, however, is not an absolute difference. Simple sponges have been pressed through fine bolting cloth, separating the cells, some of which have reassembled and reorganized, forming another sponge organism. For an excellent discussion of the reality of a whole organism, with illustrative examples, see Gardner Murphy, *Personality: A Biosocial Approach to Origins and Structure* (New York: Harper & Bros., 1947), chap. ii.
For a vigorous statement that no "group fallacy" is committed in recognizing the

The Concept of Emergence.—When parts become organized into wholes, new characteristics are observed which are not observable in the parts when they are outside the organization. These new properties are said to emerge from the whole, and may be referred to as emergent properties. The wetness of water, and its tendency to freeze and boil at certain temperatures, are not observable in hydrogen and oxygen separately. Mere mixture of hydrogen and oxygen will not form water—the elements of any organization or organism must be joined in certain proportions and in a structure of relations.

It must be recognized that the nature of the parts is not irrelevant to the properties of the organization. In a sense it is proper to say that the parts have the potentialities to behave as they do in the organized whole. Different kinds of elements lacking these potentialities will not form a successful organization—other gases will not form water; animals other than man are incapable of forming social institutions.

It will be seen in the chapters to follow that many emergent properties of human society have reacted upon the psychological nature of its members, giving them properties which would not be able to occur solely as a result of man's physiological nature.

The Relation of the Human Animal to Social Organization.—The outstanding characteristic of man's relation to his society is the degree of his dependence upon it. The necessity for care during the long, helpless infancy has been pointed out. But far more than that is involved in this dependence. Throughout his life, most of man's activities are performed in cooperation with other persons, and most of his satisfactions come through the instrumentality of social organization. Our social processes not only provide us with goods to satisfy our wants, but to a considerable extent they create the desires to be satisfied. As future discussion will indicate, the self and attitudes, habits, skills, and even many defects of behavior are attributable to the operation of organized systems of social interaction. To a considerable extent, the psychological structure of man is the creation of his social organization.[8]

organic nature of a social group, see George A. Lundberg, *Foundations of Sociology* (New York: The Macmillan Co., 1939), pp. 163-73.

[8] There is an obvious problem concerning the possibility of a social organization to create something which had to exist before there could be a social organization. Prehistory leaves no record of the details of the emergence of human society, but the only conceivable way of development was that social organizations emerged slowly, allowing the evolutionary biological development of man to furnish the gradual adaptation. Presumably any instinctive self-sufficiency, which must have

Consequences of Long Dependence on Social Organization.—
The loss of useful instincts in the process of evolution has been
compensated by a gain in versatility. Instinct gives lower animals
valuable independence and self-sufficiency but these animals lack
the advantage of the almost unlimited modifiability of the psychological nature of man. The modest repertoire of functions of even
the most advanced lower animals matures relatively early in their
lives, but the human infant faces many years of learning before he
is socially mature and ready to carry his load in the work of society.
These facts indicate the depth and irrevocability of man's commitment to existence in social organization.

Because he lives with a learned culture, man has a capacity for
adaptation to changing conditions far superior to that of other animals. Animal adaptation is achieved mainly through the extremely
slow process of biological evolution. Cultures, however, while
normally tending to be stable, have the possibility of undergoing
radical changes in a single generation, as well as the possibility
of adapting to torrid deserts, humid jungles, high altitudes, and
arctic environments.

In the pages ahead the formative and controlling influences of
society on its members are shown to be so powerful that one might
tend to conceive of the social process as a kind of slavery. Organization does in fact restrict freedom to some extent—behavior must
stay within the required pattern if teamwork is to be effective. But
organization, by virtue of the power it yields for all who belong
to it, produces a much greater quantity of freedom than is lost by
membership. To be exposed by membership in a society to any
particular language is virtually to be forced to speak it, and involves a reduction of the probability of ever speaking another
language fluently or of devising a new language. At the same time
it provides a tool which makes it possible to communicate desires,
manipulate persons, and avoid various troubles.

The extreme of freedom from social control—complete solitude
—provides escape from many cultural restrictions and social pressures, but leaves a person with the necessity of providing for his
own survival—a requirement of such continuous activity as to leave
little time for the actual exercise of freedom. On the other hand,
a successful member of an industrial society and its component
organizations has before him an enormous range of choices which

been present in the prehuman and presocial animal ancestral to modern man, remained for some time during the transition. Archeological evidence suggests that
man may have been thoroughly social for a million years or so—a time probably long
enough for unneeded instincts to be lost.

are not available to the dweller in solitude. Thus, while societies may on occasion appear to oppress persons, oppression is not the essence of society. Society is an essential basis of our existence, a creator of our desires, and the provider of our satisfactions. We can enlarge, improve, or alter it, but we cannot destroy or desert it and survive.

Summary

Other advanced animals, and some simple forms of life, are social in varying degrees, but none to the extent that man is, and none are social on the same basis. Man's behavior is acquired rather than inherited, and his society is built upon an interaction pattern of this learned behavior. In turn, each new member learns from and is continually guided by the various organized sets of social relations to which he belongs or with which he has contact.

The social organization of man is no less real and no less a thing than is a biological organism, though the two are not identical. It is real and has real effects. While social organization restricts freedom in one sense, it provides, in other ways, far more freedom than it destroys, and in fact has evolved, in the course of unknown millennia, into an absolute necessity to man.

The study of the complex and distinctively human behavior of man is therefore not a biological or individualistic inquiry, but must be a *social* psychology and a sociology. The explanation of such behavior is to be found in structures of social relations and in the history of the interaction of each person with others in his social world. This field of inquiry is less convenient than that of the study of rats in mazes, but is the only fruitful direction of inquiry into human behavior.

Selected References

Cooley, Charles H. *Human Nature and the Social Order.* New York: Chas. Scribner's Sons, 1902. A classic which remains essentially sound today.

Dewey, John. *Human Nature and Conduct.* New York: Henry Holt & Co., 1922. An important statement.

Faris, Ellsworth. *The Nature of Human Nature.* New York: McGraw-Hill Book Co., Inc., 1937. See chaps. i and ii.

Murphy, Gardner. *Personality: A Biosocial Approach to Origins and Structure.* New York: Harper & Bros., 1947. See chap. ii.

Chapter 2

INADEQUACY OF BIOLOGICAL MOTIVATION

As INDICATED in the preceding chapter, man at birth is among the most helpless of living creatures and requires the longest time to outgrow his helplessness. But more than that, there never does mature in man any efficient set of innate mechanisms which tell him how to perform the necessary actions of life. It has been suspected that innate motivation of a less definite sort may provide some rather vague and general direction to human behavior, but the evidence for this is not clear enough to prevent controversy. In the present chapter the contemporary knowledge of the nature of biological motivation in man is reviewed. Even with the uncertainties that go with incomplete knowledge it seems indisputable that biological motivation by itself is not adequate to account for any of the detail of man's complex social life.

As shown below, the instinct concept has been given a full trial and has been found to be inadequate. This was followed by a series of substitute concepts, some of which differed from the previous ideas of instincts in little more than name. Among the substitutes may be found the attempt to base a theory of human motivation on biological needs of the organism which must be satisfied in order to preserve the life of the individual or the species. It will be evident from the material in the present chapter that this theory is also inadequate. There is no question that such necessities exist, but it is also true that the human animal lacks any innate equipment to insure that he will provide for the satisfaction of these necessities. The provision is made through conscious learning, nearly all of it from social influences, and it is only after the needs are learned, and the actions necessary to their satisfaction are also learned, that an adequate motive exists.

The evidence here indicates that physiological processes contribute to motivation by supplying varying amounts of general energy or restlessness, and by supplying a few types of undefined sensations—vague cravings that have no meaning and result in no coordination activity until there has been some learning. In gen-

11

eral, then, nearly all the motivation for specific activity in the human is acquired from social sources, and while some of this motivation is directed toward the satisfaction of biological needs, most of it is in fact physiologically arbitrary. For almost all persons, the pursuit of food, water, sex, and other biological needs and gratifications require only a small proportion of the time spent in activity. The remaining time is spent in pursuit of goals which are in no sense physiological or necessary to life, although the motivation for this may be as powerful as it is for activity directed toward physiological goals.

The Concept of Instinct as Applied to Lower Animals

In general the concept of instinct is used to designate innate motives of some complexity—not such immediate reflexes as the sneeze or the knee jerk but actions comparable to the nest-building behavior of birds. A model illustration would be that of a Baltimore oriole, hatched artificially out of its nest and away from other birds, reared without opportunity to see another nest, which at the appropriate age and without any example or tutoring will build the characteristic dangling nest of its species.

While the mechanisms of instinct in this sense are not known, there are observations which support the concept of a rather blind biological process which compels an animal to act even if the goal cannot be achieved. A frequently cited example is that of the nest-building activity of the parturient female rat. In cases where insufficient material for nests is available, the rat has been observed to pick up its own tail in its mouth, return to the nest, and push the tail into the structure of the nest. This useless routine may be repeated for as much as a half hour or more, and in one case was carried on for a twelve-hour period.[1] It is clear that this kind of activity is a result of some internal biological motivation, and that the rat has no foresight or comprehension of its purpose.

Certain limitations of the instinct concept, even as applied to simple animals, have been recognized for some time. Internal biological motivation should not be conceived of as pure determination of behavior by material which is independent of environment and experience. Cell material itself, in the early period of the life of the cell, is in part determined by its environment within the

[1] From M. Sturman-Hulbe and C. P. Stone, "Maternal Behavior in the Albino Rat," *Journal of Comparative Psychology*, IX (1920), 208-9.

organism—a fact shown by repeated experiments in the transplantation of cells from one part of an organism to another.[2] There is no biological character which is completely independent of its history, and if instinct is defined as absolute internal determination of behavior it does not exist and there is no use for the term.[3]

The role of experience in such a simple and necessary activity as food-getting has been extensively shown. The relative strength of the hunger drive and thirst drive in the rat depends on which of the necessities of food or water have been most lacking. Which foods are preferred, however, and the order of preference, depend on dietary experience. In a new environment the drive to explore will take precedence over eating, drinking, and sex. It has been concluded that the relative dominance of behavior patterns in the rat is not fixed but dependent upon circumstances, and that there is no immutable hierarchy of drives.[4] Investigations of the food drive in the chicken have shown that here also it is not merely a matter of physiological need. In addition to hunger as a stimulus, the sight of a pile of grain, the novelty of it, the presence of other chickens eating, and other factors enter into the stimulation.[5]

Evidence of the modifiability of the behavior of lower animals is abundant. The concept of instinct, if it is to be used at all, may serve to designate a greater degree of internal motivation than appears to be present in man, but it is not impossible that future research may provide superior explanations of the behavior of simple animals and thereby make even this concept obsolete.

THE INSTINCT THEORY IN HUMAN BEHAVIOR

The Classical Notion of Instinct.—Until the latter part of the nineteenth century it was generally believed that animals had instincts and man did not, but rather conducted himself on the basis of reason. The influence of Darwin and the evolutionary hypothesis led to the concept of man as essentially similar to other animals, and to a search for human instincts. The definitions of instinct and the lists of human instincts varied, but the vogue

[2] See Gardner Murphy, *Personality: A Biosocial Approach to Origins and Structure* (New York: Harper & Bros., 1947), pp. 53-54.

[3] Some investigators do recommend its discard, for example Z. Y. Kuo, "A Psychology Without Heredity," *Psychological Review*, XXXI (1924), 427-28.

[4] See P. T. Young, *Motivation of Behavior* (New York: John Wiley & Sons, Inc., 1936), p. 152.

[5] Edwin G. Boring, Herbert S. Langfeld, and Harry P. Weld, (eds.), *Foundations of Psychology* (New York: John Wiley & Sons, Inc., 1948), pp. 115-16.

stood almost unchallenged in the science of psychology for a quarter of a century.[6]

The hunting instinct of man, as described by Thorndike, provides a representative example of the concept and the method. The following is his description not of a cat or gorilla, but of the supposed behavior of the human being.

To a small escaping object, man, especially if hungry, responds, apart from training, by pursuit, being satisfied when he draws nearer to it. When within pouncing distance, he pounces upon it, grasping at it. If it is not seized he is annoyed. If it is seized, he examines, manipulates and dismembers it, unless some contrary tendency is brought into action by its sliminess, sting or the like. To an object of moderate size and not offensive mien moving away from or past him man originally responds much as noted above, save that in seizing the object chased, he is likely to throw himself upon it, bear it to the ground, choke and maul it until it is completely subdued, giving then a cry of triumph.[7]

William McDougall defined instinct as "an innate disposition which determines the organism to perceive any object of a certain class, and to experience in its presence a certain emotional excitement and an impulse to action which find expression in a specific mode of behavior in relation to that object." He listed thirteen major instincts: parental or protective, combative, curiosity, food-seeking, repulsion, escape, gregariousness, self-assertion, submission, mating, acquisitiveness, constructiveness, and instinct of appeal.[8]

Other authorities have presented theories based on one instinct, two instincts, and various longer lists reaching forty and over and including such behavior as home construction, ownership, secretiveness, imitation, licking sugar, domineering, curiosity, and play.[9] This whole approach to the explanation of human motivation came under severe criticism in the early 1920's and soon after the absurdities were pointed out, toppled of its own weight. By the end of the decade, little use was made in social psychology of the concept of instinct for the explanation of human behavior.

In other fields of study, however, as well as in popular knowl-

[6] The history is thoroughly reviewed by Ellsworth Faris, *The Nature of Human Nature* (New York: McGraw-Hill Book Co., Inc., 1937). See chaps. vi and xv.

[7] Edward L. Thorndike, quoted in Ellsworth Faris, *op. cit.*, p. 43, by permission of McGraw-Hill Book Co., Inc.

[8] William McDougall, *Outline of Psychology* (New York: Chas. Scribner's Sons, 1923).

[9] See Kimball Young, *Source Book for Social Psychology* (New York: Appleton-Century-Crofts, Inc., 1927), chap. viii.

edge, the concept remains popular. There is a lag in the process of diffusion of knowledge from the research frontier of a science to other sciences, to secondary education, and to public information. Thus it happens that there can appear, as late as 1942, a completely classical application of the instinct theory to human behavior, in which application each of the major institutional divisions of activity is based on specified instincts. Protoplasmic activities (needs) of nutrition, reproduction, rivalry, and protection are linked in this theoretical presentation with the primary drives (instincts) of food, sex, dominance, and defense. Through secondary drives (also innate), tertiary drives and rationalizations, and "rationalisms," they provide the foundation for the "rationalities" (institutional divisions) of economy, sociality, religion, and polity. The theory is presented dogmatically and entirely without support of modern experimental or statistical research, and furnishes a good example of anachronism in psychological theory.[10] Other examples may be seen daily in various popular writings, and will no doubt be available for years to come.

Substitutes for the Instinct Concept in the Human.—With the passing of the above conceptions of complex, fixed, innate types of motivation there remained the problem of accounting for the direction and the power of many standard human activities, and there remained also the disposition to look internally, in the biological nature of man, for the sources. There thus arose, in rapid succession, a number of concepts which were offered to replace the rejected idea of instincts, but which, in many cases, were essentially the same thing in all but name. The list of such substitutes is too long to justify complete presentation, but representative examples are presented here to show that in general these rest on foundations little better than those of the instinct theory.

Innate "emotions" were described by Watson on the basis of observations on infants. He described a *fear* response—such as a catching of breath, blinking, clutching, puckering of lips and crying —caused by sudden removal of support or by a loud sound or other startling situation. The *rage* response of crying and struggling was said to be caused by a hampering of the infant's movements—Watson stated that "almost any child from birth can be thrown into a rage if its arms are held tightly to its sides. . . ." The *love* emotion is revealed by smiling, cooing, and extension of arms as if to em-

[10] The example is from the distinguished work by Quincy Wright, *A Study of War* (Chicago: University of Chicago Press, 1942), p. 1457. It is not an important aspect of the findings on causes of war, and does not reflect on the worth of the book.

brace, and was said to be produced by stroking, patting, rocking, and like stimulation.[11]

These observations were accepted and published without challenge in textbooks of psychology for more than twenty years, with little thought given to the desirability of repeating the observations. Obvious contradictory facts, such as the reactions of the confined infants of some of the American Indians, went unnoticed.[12] Eventually, however, these conceptions were overthrown. Various observers failed to elicit some of the responses described by Watson. It was found that the type of emotion was not identifiable from motion pictures in which the stimulus was not shown. Photographs of adult subjects as they were experiencing laboratory-induced emotions yielded a diversity of muscular response patterns which could not reliably be identified in terms of specific emotions.[13]

As is pointed out more fully in Chapter 5, emotion is an aspect of the experience of blocked activity. It involves physiological mechanisms of some complexity, but it is doubtful whether or not the types of emotion or content of emotional thought can usefully be separated or classified on the basis of physiological processes. Physiologically, pleasant excitement and fear, for example, may be little differentiated. The differentiation may be, in fact, largely or entirely a matter of attitude. If further research bears this out, the classification of emotions will be as elaborate as any classification of attitudes, and will have about the same value in the explanation of behavior.

A second prominent substitute for the instinct concept is that of the prepotent reflex, which is assumed to be an innate tendency but subject to alteration by the process of "conditioning." [14] In 1924, Allport proposed six important classes of human prepotent

[11] John B. Watson, *Psychology from the Standpoint of a Behaviorist* (Philadelphia: J. B. Lippincott Co., 1919), pp. 199-202.

[12] The Hopi and Navajo infants are, during early months, kept strapped to a cradle board most of the time. They seldom cry. This does not mean that they have lost the desire to move, for when they are released from the board their legs flex, their hands go to their mouths, and they act in general like infants elsewhere. See Wayne Dennis, "Does Culture Appreciably Affect Patterns of Infant Behavior?" *Journal of Social Psychology*, XXX (1940), 305-17.

[13] See Leonard Carmichael (ed.), *Manual of Child Psychology* (New York: John Wiley & Sons, Inc., 1946), chapter on "The Neonate" by K. C. Pratt. Also Boring, Langfeld and Weld, *op. cit.*, p. 98. The present author has made repeated observations to compare with those of Watson and generally finds little resemblance to the behavior Watson described.

[14] See Chapter 5 for a discussion of the inadequacy of the concept of "conditioning" as a basis of learning.

reflexes: starting and withdrawing, rejecting, struggling, hunger reactions, sensitive zone reactions, and sex reactions.[15] These were stated to be fundamental both in original potency and in the control which they exert over habit formation throughout life. They appear to be little more than flexible instincts which, theoretically, are modified by a process of conditioning—a process which in fact is incapable of modifying an innate reflex. This theory became widely known, but did not have a long period of wide acceptance.

A third set of substitutes were the concepts of interests, fundamental wishes, and desires. Small, under the influence of German scholars, early had offered a list of six classes of "interests": health, wealth, sociability, beauty, knowledge, and rightness.[16] His colleague, Thomas, proposed a list of fundamental wishes: recognition, response, new experience, and security.[17] Dunlap, in rejecting both instinct and emotion as fundamental sources of motivation, published the following classification of "desires": alimentary desire, excretory desire, desire of rest, desire of activity, desire of shelter, amatory desire, parental desire, desire of preeminence, and desire of conformity.[18] All three of these theories were based on the assumption that the power for the motives, and to some extent the distinction between them, had an innate basis. They thus were subject to all the difficulties of the instinct notion, and were in fact somewhat vague instinct theories without the use of the word. Nevertheless they offered a convenient way of holding on to a prejudice in favor of innate mainsprings of action, and thus remained popular for many years.[19]

Still another substitute conception for instinct is that of *drive*— which is assumed to be innate, distinct, and a powerful motivating force—or its close relative *need*. The concept of drive is widely used in the field of animal research where it is possible to arrange

[15] Floyd H. Allport, *Social Psychology* (Boston: Houghton Mifflin Co., 1924), p. 50.

[16] Albion Small, *General Sociology* (Chicago: University of Chicago Press, 1905), pp. 425 ff.

[17] William I. Thomas, *The Unadjusted Girl* (Boston: Little, Brown & Co., 1923).

[18] Knight Dunlap, "The Foundations of Social Psychology," *Psychological Review*, XXX (1923), 92-97.

[19] Although abandoning the attempt to link the classes of wishes with a concept of physiological or instinctive motivation, the authors of a distinguished book on family sociology made use of the Thomas classification as late as 1945. Claiming, however, that it is not "feasible" to substitute, for the satisfaction of a desire in the field of one of the fundamental wishes, the opportunity to achieve a different desire in the field of another wish, they appear to indicate a recognition of an instinctive character in the classes of wishes. See E. W. Burgess and Harvey Locke, *The Family* (New York: American Book Co., 1945), pp. 307-18.

experimental manipulations that are impractical in research on human beings. The relative strength of the food drive and the maternal drive in the rat, for example, has been measured by the use of an electrified grill across which the animal must go to get food, or to reach offspring. The strength of shock the rat will endure is considered to be a measure of the drive.[20]

In general it is conceived that there is an urgency or necessity to satisfy a drive, and that any physiological necessity—"need"—involves an impulsion to seek satisfaction; in short, a need is a drive and a drive is a need. To an extent, this may appear to be so, but knowledge is incomplete and it remains controversial whether all needs (biological necessities for survival or health) become motives and whether all motives are based on biological necessity. Also controversial are the extent to which human needs may directly create human drives, in the fashion of the functional instincts of lower animals, and the necessity that man indirectly learn and become conscious of the relation between his actions and his physiological well-being in order to satisfy physiological needs.

The interpretation that a need does not always stimulate a drive seems to apply better in the case of the need for salt in the human diet. Not until a scientific discovery was made in recent times did people learn to take extra quantities of salt in hot weather. The distress of extreme fatigue and muscle cramps after excessive loss of salt through perspiration was never sufficient to impel persons to add salt to their diets. In hot factories workers have to be informed or trained to consume extra salt. The physiological discomfort is by itself meaningless and motivates no behavior other than a general restlessness until it is consciously defined. It sometimes occurs that the unrecognized craving for salt, for example, becomes erroneously interpreted so that it motivates behavior that aggravates rather than relieves the biochemical imbalance. Investigators have recently discovered that chronic alcoholics with delirium tremens have low levels of chlorides in the blood, a condition which produces a discomfort the investigators call "physiological thirst." The alcoholic interprets this as a need for more liquor, but the effect of the alcohol is to make the condition worse and to perpetuate his craving. There is thus developed a kind of vicious circle of addiction, based on a misinterpretation of the discomfort resulting from a deficiency of salt.

[20] See for example Carl J. Warden, *Animal Motivation: Experimental Studies on the Albino Rat* (New York: Columbia University Press, 1931). The difficulty of setting up an experiment in which deprived human mothers walk barefoot across an electrified grill to retrieve and feed their infants will be apparent to the reader.

A modern example of a classification of human needs, tentatively stated, is that offered by Rosenzweig, who lists: "needs concerned with protection against loss or impairment of structures or functions; needs dealing with the maintenance of the individual's growth level; needs concerned with the reproduction of the organism and thus involving a certain degree of self-expansion; and needs in which such expansion is carried to creative as well as procreative activities and involves symbolical as well as concrete behavior." [21] Commitment to a physiological basis of necessity is avoided, but the selection of particular needs suggests that it is this kind of necessity the proponents of "need" theories have in mind. If "need" is nothing more than an acquired wish, the list would be unlimited, and certain prominent persons could be said to possess a "need" to become President of the United States.

Some evidence supporting the view that the need for food produces an adequate drive in the human is furnished by the studies of self-selection of diets by infants and small children. In a typical experiment, fourteen newly weaned infants chose their diets from an assorted offering for periods of from six months to four and three-quarters years. Some tendency was noted in children with dietary deficiencies or special needs to choose spontaneously the proper diet. At the end of the experiment the children "seemed healthy." [22]

A report of a trial of self-selection of diet by two girl children in their own home is on record. Beginning when the girls were fifteen and eighteen months old respectively and continuing for about five years, the children were given an unconventional amount of freedom in their choice of foods. Three meals a day were provided at regular hours. The children ate by themselves in the kitchen. Small portions of a variety of foods were put on their plates. The mother stayed nearby and gave help when asked. The children were allowed to eat any quantity, or nothing at all, or ask for food not in view. Certain foods were also available between meals—potato chips, peanuts, raw carrots, apples, and orange juice.

Although the parents involved in this experiment, both physi-

[21] Saul Rosenzweig, "An Outline of Frustration Theory," chap. xi in J. McV. Hunt, *Personality and the Behavior Disorders* (New York: The Ronald Press Co., 1944), p. 381. For a greatly contrasting and longer list, not widely followed, see Henry A. Murray, *Explorations in Personality* (New York: Oxford University Press, 1938).

[22] Clara M. Davis, "Self-regulation of Diet in Childhood," *Health Education Journal,* V (1947), 37-40. See also two other papers by the same author: "Self-selection of Diet by Newly-weaned Infants," *American Journal of Diseases of Children,* XXXVI (1928), 651-79; and "Self-selection of Diets: an Experiment with Infants," *Trained Nurse and Hospital Review,* LXXXVI (1931), 5.

cians, concluded that the trial was a "success" and reported that the children were normal and healthy at the conclusion of the period, certain details prevent the experiment from being considered a conclusive matter. At one time, one of the children ate little and would take an hour to eat one meal, causing the parents to resort to games and tricks to persuade her to eat. "Food jags" during which were consumed large amounts of single items—six eggs, three cucumbers, seven bananas, two large cans of evaporated milk—occurred from time to time. Desserts were arbitrarily limited—an important departure from self-selection—and processed foods, particularly those containing sugar or white flour, were avoided as much as possible. Sweets were severely limited, consisted only of homemade concoctions, and were not allowed at all between meals. Finally, another important departure from the experimental assumption was made by the daily administering of 400 I.U. of vitamin D supplement.[23]

In short, the above trial was not a real trial at all. A complete reliance on the ability of children to select what is good for them, and only that, would involve the inclusion of a dangerous variety of temptations without any of the protective restrictions involved in the above trial. There is abundant evidence that young children can readily become addicted to alcohol, tobacco and opiates, as well as habituated to severely unbalanced diets if the choice of foods is left to them. Nothing in the experimental evidence proves that the uncontrolled disposition of the child is a safe guide to his dietary needs.

Nor is the adult any more safe in obeying his impulses of appetite. It is not rare for persons to happen to prefer the kinds of food that are best for them, but it is also extremely common for persons to eat too much or too little, or not to eat enough protective foods, or to distort the diet by excessive use of alcohol and drugs. In extreme cases this tendency ruins health and may cause death directly or indirectly. In less extreme cases it contributes to marked abnormality. Saul describes a case of a young woman who left home when only twelve because of unhappy family conditions, and began to support herself by working. With her first week's salary she bought all the ice cream she could eat. Whenever she felt lonely and frustrated she indulged in orgies of eating. The sight of a hearty meal on the table would sometimes cause her

[23] Catherine Mackenzie, "Eating by Choice," New York Times Magazine, November 9, 1947, p. 48.

to quiver with anticipation. As a consequence of her dietary abnormality she became excessively fat.[24]

The concept of the "wisdom of the body" implies to some persons that the physiological mechanism somehow knows what is best for it, and is provided with adequate drives to select what it should have. There are observations that give support to this concept—many poisonous foods are violently repulsive to the sense of taste—but in the human it is clear that this concept is not a safe guide in all circumstances. It is distinctly not a wise policy to trust all our impulses on the belief that these derive from drives that express the "wisdom of the body."

There is much reason to doubt the value of applying the concept of a food drive or hunger drive to human behavior. In the ordinary sense of the word "need," there is a need for food, and for food of the right kind, to the extent that there is a need to stay healthy and to live. But the character of eating behavior is not at all determined by internal requirements. Habits and cultural standards greatly influence not only what is eaten, but how often and how much is eaten, and virtually all the other details of the obtaining and consumption of food.[25] If, in a prehuman stage of evolutionary development, the species ancestral to man did possess adequate food drives, these drives presumably deteriorated during the time that he has lived in organized societies. Today his physiology can make him restless and uncomfortable when he needs food, but unless he learns consciously the meaning of his symptoms, or is provided with acquired habits which automatically link his eating behavior with the symptoms of food deprivation, the sensations of discomfort do not motivate behavior of eating. Also, physiology rewards eating with a relief of discomfort, and rewards correct dietary balance with relief from deficiency diseases. Where the rewards follow immediately, as in the relief of hunger following a meal, few persons can escape the recognition of the

[24] Leon J. Saul, "Physiological Effects of Emotional Tension," chap. viii in Hunt, op. cit., p. 273.

[25] Physiological research has connected hunger pangs with contraction of the stomach, but these pangs do not regulate eating behavior. We eat by the clock rather than by the schedule of pangs, which may in fact begin soon after a full meal. Nor is the generalized weakness and discontent of hunger in all cases an adequate motive for eating. In many cases the discomfort attendant on hunger is not realized by the person experiencing the hunger to be related to his need for food. A recent comprehensive research project has produced the conclusion that the physiological processes do not furnish a full explanation of the food behavior in man, and that "another word than 'hunger' is needed to describe the drive for food." See Ancel Keys et al., The Biology of Human Starvation (University of Minnesota, 1950).

connection between the activity and the feeling. Where the rewards are slower, as in the benefits of vitamins, discovery is difficult to make, and is generally a collective discovery of science rather than an inescapable inference by an individual.

Acquired Physiological Drives.—The physiological restlessness and discomfort, and the sense of comfort, stimulation, or normality that follows behavior which terminates the cause of the discomfort, can both occur in relation to bodily demands which are clearly not innate. The examples of addiction to opiates, alcohol, tobacco, and other drugs may be offered.

Lindesmith has shown impressively that opiate addiction, powerful as it is, is not an adequate drive on the physiological basis alone—physiological habituation cannot by itself either impel a man to seek for and administer more of the drug or inform him consciously that his discomfort is a result of withdrawal of the drug.[26] Persons who become habituated in the course of medical treatment, or by any other accident, experience the same extreme discomfort as does the addict on withdrawal of the opiate. The symptoms involve persistent nausea, general weakness, aching joints and pains in the legs, diarrhea, and extreme insomnia. According to Lindesmith, there were no individuals among those he observed who learned by themselves the connection between these severe discomforts and the absence of the drug. Those who were not consciously informed of this connection by other persons did not become addicted. The shortage of the drug in these persons is not, therefore, an adequate drive since a necessary aspect of the adequate motive is the conscious recognition of the results to be obtained by further use of the drug. Furthermore, no physiological guidance of any kind is supplied as to the methods of obtaining or administering the drug. This is always learned from experienced persons.

Addiction to alcohol is in some respects similar to opiate addiction—that is, it is an acquired type of motivation. For most persons, the first taste of alcoholic beverages is without appeal, and the motivation for taking it is social motivation—the pressure from other persons to conform to conventional standards, the desire to assume adult status, and the like. The phenomenon of habituation without addiction is not reported in connection with the use of alcohol, but the role of withdrawal distress in the advanced

[26] Alfred R. Lindesmith, *Opiate Addiction* (Bloomington, Indiana: The Principia Press, Inc., 1947).

alcohol addict is similar. The withdrawal distress associated with opiate addiction is a delayed reaction beginning a few days after withdrawal and reaching its peak sometimes two weeks later. The appearance of withdrawal distress in the hangover, however, is temporally closer to, and thereby more easily associated with, the deprivation of liquor.

Once established, the desire for alcohol appears very much like a physiological drive, even though it is acquired. But it is observed that the impulse to drink is often dependent on time and place, availability of liquor, and other circumstances. There are contexts in which the desire flourishes, producing week-end drinkers, payday drinkers, celebration drinkers, and crisis drinkers. Some addicts report no impulse to drink when they have no money, or when liquor is unavailable, but experience irresistible impulses when money and liquor can be obtained.[27] A sailor may live a normal life at sea free from any desire to drink, but experience a compulsion to become drunk when the ship reaches a port.

Such milder types of addiction as that for tobacco have some of the same characteristics. There is the artificial acquisition of the taste, the withdrawal distress, the reward of relief on resumption of usage. The rich supporting context is also a part of the motivation—in this case the presence of other smokers, the standard smoking occasions, the manual habits involved in smoking, and so forth.

In somewhat similar fashion one may become addicted to almost any kind of behavior—gambling, motion pictures and radio, reading, or work. In a sense any acquired habit is in part a drive, but it is never a purely physiological drive, nor an adequate drive physiologically. Physiology can cause restlessness and discomfort of various kinds, which may be too intrusive to be overlooked, and can call attention to relief, stimulation, and pleasant sensation as consequences of activity. But we have to learn what to do in dealing with these sensations, and we are always guided to a large extent by context. The concept of "drive" is thus inadequate for an explanation of human motivation, and provides at most for a crude differentiation of certain classes of physiological discomfort and pleasantness.

The Concept of Libido as a General Drive.—Freud's concept of libido has had wide acceptance as a theoretical explanation of a

[27] See Joel V. Berreman, "The Escape Motive in Alcoholic Addiction," *Proceedings of the Pacific Sociological Society*, XVIII, No. 3, pp. 139-43.

large part of human motivation.[28]   The notion in general was that
the source of energy for affectional and cooperative behavior is
sexual in a very broad sense of the word, and that the impulse to
sexual behavior is present in the child at as early an age as is the
capacity to love.[29]

Freud conceived of the libido as an insistent innate drive which
provides gratification in the first few years of life in the oral zone,
then in the anal zone, and finally in the genital zone, while at the
same time spreading into a generalized motivation for all behavior
of a social character. It is held that to deny or frustrate the impulses of libido results in complications that produce severe abnormalities. In general the influence of this vestige of the instinct
theory has been to cause its advocates to adhere to a policy of
granting infants and small children all their wants as immediately
as possible. Every cry or indication of desire is thus to be answered with feeding, warming, rocking, stroking, drying, and other
care. This not only is said to allow the libidinal sequence to develop normally but, according to some theorists, improves gastro-
intestinal functioning, a sense of confidence in a predictable world,
social responsiveness, and love of parents. By virtue of this treatment the child may escape the "maiming and traumatic experiences from the imposition of human culture." [30]

A concept that in some cases accompanies the above notions of
libidinal drive is that of the recapitulation of the evolutionary development of the species in the life cycle of each individual. This
is a theory adopted by analogy from the evidence of biology concerning the recapitulation, in certain structural details, of the
growth of the human body. In the process of embryonic development of the higher vertebrates, including man, each individual
develops gill slits and an arterial system capable of supplying blood
to them. These disappear before birth, but give evidence of a fish
and amphibian stage in prehuman evolution. The extension of
the concept into the behavior of man was natural enough in the

[28] Sigmund Freud, "Three Contributions to the Theory of Sex," 4th ed. ("Nervous
and Mental Disease Monograph Series," No. 7 [Social Science Research Council,
1930]). The theory was first published in 1905.
[29] See Robert R. Sears, *Survey of Objective Studies of Psychoanalytic Concepts,*
Social Science Research Council, Bulletin No. 51, New York, 1943. Sears states,
"This impulse is instinctual in origin and its systematic aspects are badly tangled in
the complexities of Freudian metapsychology."
[30] O. H. Mowrer and Clyde Kluckhohn, "Dynamic Theory of Personality,"
chap. iii in Hunt, *op. cit.,* pp. 88 ff. The point is made in Chapter 1 of the present
work, and developed throughout the book, that the conception of society and
culture as essentially restrictive is the great error contributed by the instinct theory.

period when human behavior was conceived to be founded on instinct. G. Stanley Hall, in his influential work on adolescence, did much to popularize the notion in stating that in childhood the human is a savage and has a disposition toward active outdoor pursuits such as hunting, fishing, fighting, roving, as well as toward play, idleness, and predatory activity. In adolescent years man passes through a barbaric stage, with appropriate interests, until reaching adulthood and the ways of civilization.

Some followers of Freud have similarly presented the infant as actively brutal in motivation. There is a recapitulation aspect also to the stages of psychosexual development, and to Freud's conception of the repetition in each lifetime of the Oedipus drama.

Objective Evidence Opposed to the Concept of Libido.—Important in the theory of libido is the conception by Freud that small children have strong sexual desire and intense interest in sex organs. Girls are said to possess a sense of humiliation and jealousy of the male because of the lack of external male organs. Boys are said to presuppose in all persons a set of organs like their own, to hold to this conviction against contrary evidence, and to give it up only after severe internal struggles. "Clinical" evidence—observations unchecked by others and unsupported by formal experimental method—is frequently offered in support of this, along with anecdotal materials showing an interest in sex by certain small children.

Objective research, however, gives little support to the notion of a strong natural childhood interest in sexuality. Such an interest can be socially generated, often producing persistent curiosity and obsessive pursuit of information by the child, but unselected samples of children give little indication of special awareness of sex. Conn and Kanner investigated the matter in a sample of 200 children by asking how they differentiated the sexes. The most frequent methods of distinction were made on the basis of clothing, and some of the younger children—under the age of seven—said that removal of clothes made a distinction impossible. Between the ages of twelve and fourteen this basis of differentiation disappeared, but the observation is distinctly contrary to the Freudian notion of an intense interest by children in sex organs.[31] Only 116 of the children, slightly more than half, mentioned genital differences at all.

[31] J. H. Conn and L. Kanner, "Children's Awareness of Sex Differences," *Journal of Child Psychiatry*, I (1947), 3-57.

In another study, a large sample of mothers was questioned about the sex questions their children had asked. Many mothers remembered no questions of this sort, but a large number of mothers had remembered being asked about sex. The most common first question, however, was not on the matter of sex organs or sex activity, but on the origin of babies. In a sense, this is not in the usual case a sex question at all, for the small child has no reason to foresee what kind of answer will be given. The most interesting finding of this study, relating to the Freudian conceptions, bears on the female envy of male organs. Only three of the 137 questions asked by children two to five years old suggested that boys thought girls' lack of male organs was the result of injury. Nor was there any evidence that girls envied the male organs or wished to be boys. This study, concludes Sears, in his sympathetic review of psychoanalytic concepts, does not disprove the possibility of such reactions as Freud has described but their universality is not only not demonstrable, but is flatly disproved.[32]

Other research shows that children of preschool and early school years have an undifferentiated relationship with the opposite sex, and from about eight to adolescent years a preference for their own sex, and after that a period of increasing preference for the opposite sex.[33] This, however, is not a result of biological unfolding of instincts or drives, but a reflection of the pattern of the culture in which these children live. The development of the interest in sex behavior by children varies greatly according to the standards of various cultures.

Objective research concerning the alleged oral eroticism of infants and children involves mainly an examination of the thumb- and finger-sucking behavior, nail-biting, and manipulating some part of the mouth. These are found to be related to various conditions. Thumb-sucking, for example, is shown to vary according to degree of hunger, condition of nutrition, to teething, age, activity, position, the presence of observers, and other matters.[34] This is typical of the findings concerning other types of oral manipulating. Sears concludes that "oral movements are by no means

[32] Sears, op. cit., p. 30. The study is by K. W. Hattendorf, "A Study of the Questions of Young Children Concerning Sex: a Phase of an Experimental Approach to Parent Education." Journal of Social Psychology, III (1932), 37-65.

[33] E. H. Campbell, "The Social-sex Development of Children," Genetic Psychology Monographs, XXI (1939), 461-552, and C. M. Tryon, "Evaluations of Adolescent Personality by Adolescents," Monographs of the Society for Research in Child Development, Vol. 4, No. 4 (1939).

[34] Mary S. Kunst, A Study of Thumb- and Finger-sucking in Infants. ("Psychological Monographs," No. 3 [American Psychological Association, 1948]).

uniquely symptomatic of inherent oral eroticism" and that the objective research data are meager and insufficient to throw light on the notions that thumb-sucking has strong orgastic effect or that it has an autoerotic quality.[35] The libidinal interpretation thus gains little or no objective support.

A review of objective evidence concerning the object choice—the natural objects toward which libido is directed—gives little support to the Freudian formulation.

One conclusion stands out above all others: emotional development, as couched in terms of successive object choices, is far more variable than Freud supposed. This is not to say that none of the classical elements appears. They do; but with too many exceptions to be accepted as typical. The conditions under which object choice is made explain why this is. Object choice is essentially a function of learning and what is learned is a function of the environment in which the learning occurs. Since there is no universal culture pattern for intrafamilial relationships, there can be no universal pattern of learned object choices.[36]

Thus the concept of libido appears to be of little help in accounting for the actual details of cooperative or even of sexual behavior. There is a hormonal component involved in sexual activity, but it is not an adequate drive for impelling sex behavior without the aid of other influences, or for providing the style of action or its details. As Boring has pointed out:

The hormonal basis of the sex drive can vary tremendously, but sexual need and behavior are not related in any simple manner to the amount of this variation. Just as frigidity is not always caused by a deficiency of hormones, so an abnormally strong sexual desire in women is not always the result of an excessive secretion of hormones. In fact, nymphomania is often an attempt of a woman to compensate for a real or an imagined sexual inadequacy. Impotence in males, and its opposite, though sometimes correlated with low and high levels of hormonal secretion, are in other cases entirely unrelated to physical and structural factors.

Man's sexual need and behavior are, then, no more completely determined by the level of hormones in his blood than is his eating determined solely by his stomach's hunger contractions. Both appetite and sexual desire also depend upon habits and attitudes that are learned. . . .[37]

The Catharsis Concept and Instinct.—The catharsis notion, at least as old as Aristotle, is essentially instinctive in conception. Certain emotions are conceived to exist in man, located in definite

[35] Sears, *op. cit.*, pp. 8-11.
[36] *Ibid.*, p. 57.
[37] Boring, Langfeld, and Weld, *op. cit.*, pp. 117-18. By permission of John Wiley & Sons, Inc.

quantities. A man, for example, is believed to have so much anger somewhere inside him; if expressed in overt action, the anger is believed to have "come out" and no longer to exist. If it is not expressed in any way, it remains within him for an indefinite time, threatening to seek expression in various indirect ways. From Aristotle down to many present theorists, the recommended policy has been to give free expression to emotions when it can be done conveniently, in order to discharge them and relieve the nervous system.

An illustration is furnished by a recent publication on married life.[38] The theorists recommend to married couples an occasional frank quarrel, on the ground that it allows the members to discharge safely on one another the anger accumulated through a number of small daily irritations. Another experimenter actually provides opportunities for such catharsis experiences in a "spontaneity theater," where couples having trouble with marriage may freely act out their quarrels before the experimenter, and so resume their married life in relaxed harmony.[39] A writer on science topics advocates the use of toy guns by children, on the ground that these guns are instruments of a desirable type of catharsis. He quotes Benjamin Spock in support: "The child who can play at hurting and killing is able, as a result, to be more friendly than the child who bottles up his hostile feelings." [40]

[38] Evelyn M. Duvall and Reuben Hill, *When You Marry* (Boston: D. C. Heath & Co., 1945).

[39] J. L. Moreno, "Mental Catharsis and the Psychodrama," *Sociometry*, III (1940), No. 3. In the case of Mr. and Mrs. T., used by Moreno for illustration of the catharsis effect, the couple did not regain a harmonious married life, but were divorced. Moreno's pronouncement was that "A full catharsis for a separation and a divorce was attained" by virtue of the three months of expensive treatment. No evidence is presented, however, to show that the persons were less tense and unhappy after the divorce.

[40] Laird S. Goldsborough, "Better Toys for Your Child," *Reader's Digest*, December, 1949, p. 66. Spock, however, neglects dangers of another kind—the building of habits so automatic that real loaded guns, for example, are frequently discharged unthinkingly, with fatal results. This kind of avoidable accident is particularly common among children, but, as the following account shows, is found also in adult behavior. A Seattle newspaper story, dated August 30, 1950, relates, with the accompaniment of heart-rending photographs, the experience of a twenty-two-year-old father who killed his two-year-old son in just such fashion. The father had frequently pretended to shoot the boy with an air pistol, to the amusement of both of them, and on this day had brought home a new small rifle and entertained the child by pointing the unloaded rifle at him and snapping the trigger. After tiring of this game, the father went to the kitchen and his eye lit on a 16-gauge shotgun. In a later statement to police he said, "I decided to have more fun with Mike and picked up the shotgun. I didn't remember it had been loaded as a protective measure for my wife while I had gone to school on Tuesday nights. I called Mike, and pointed the gun at the location where I knew he'd be coming through the

A further illustration of the catharsis assumption is provided by a well-known psychiatrist, D. A. Slight, who is reported to have explained a presumed high rate of ulcers and high blood pressure among business executives as a consequence of accumulated aggression without the relief of a catharsis outlet. Unlike the high-handed executive of former years, the modern business leader is expected to be a diplomat and compromiser, according to Slight, and therefore "a great deal of his *innate drive* cannot be expressed outwardly." He must "listen to a lot of claptrap from union stewards who are riding him, and face pressure from government officials. After that, the executive must express benign, gentle, persuasive attitudes." As a consequence, "the *aggressive vitality drive* that makes the executive ambitious is thwarted, and *it must go somewhere*, so it goes inside. . . ." [41]

In the course of an experience in teaching race relations to a group of public officials, a psychologist has described what he believes to be a successful application of catharsis. The officials had been ordered by their superiors to take the course and were therefore angry. The lecturer encouraged their emotional outbursts at the start, allowing the officials to discharge their accumulated emotions in his direction. He reported that in time they appeared to have exhausted the supply of anger, and that they then became more friendly. [42]

There are, of course, a number of investigators and experts who hold the contrary belief and advocate the policy opposite to that of the catharsis theory—that is, that expression of anger tends to create more rather than less tension, that interpersonal resentment increases rather than decreases as a result of quarrels, and that the wise policy is essentially one of keeping calm and relaxed, thereby allowing the tension to die out by itself. Tension here is conceived as a process or set of relations rather than as a fixed quantity of material, and as such can be thought to disappear without "coming out." A physician of a Wisconsin clinic, John A. Schindler, has pro-

door. I was ready for him. When he came through the door, I yelled 'bang' and pulled the trigger."

[41] *Time*, November 28, 1949. Italics by the present author.

[42] Gordon W. Allport, "Catharsis and the Reduction of Prejudice," *Journal of Social Issues*, I, No. 3 (1945), 3-10. This trial was, of course, not a controlled experiment. To make it so would at least require a division of the officials into two equal groups, giving only the experimental group the opportunity to blow off steam, and measuring the difference in the amount of antagonism with some kind of objective technique applied to each group before and after the trial. The above incident, then, can be used only to illustrate Allport's conception of how he thinks catharsis should work.

posed a set of rules intended to promote mental normality, several of which bear on the catharsis issue and follow along these lines. Instead of giving vent to feelings, pretending to kill imaginary persons, having open quarrels, and the like, he advises that each person adopt policies such as learning to like other persons and avoiding dislikes and grudges, learning to be satisfied when a situation cannot be changed (he advised a woman who hated her life in a trailer, for example, to read *Pollyanna* with the consequence that she came to like trailer life), learning to accept adversity, learning to avoid sharp retorts and to employ cheerful or humorous reactions to provoking situations, and learning to make a decision firmly and then stop thinking about the issue. In general Schindler's key principle is that one should keep attitudes and thinking as cheerful as possible—a clear opposite to the notion of catharsis through open conflict.[43]

A similar point of view is offered by Walter C. Alvarez, professor of medicine at the Mayo Foundation. He finds the result of conflict to be not one of beneficial catharsis, but of damaging strain, illustrating his point by reference to a woman who woke with a feeling of strangling because she had spent the previous evening in an angry argument over money. (If the angry argument had been fully overt, according to the catharsis principle she would be expected to have been relaxed and at ease.) He advocates adequate sleep, rest and recreation, and, in addition, the cultivation of an attitude of serenity. In situations of stress it is better not to break out into hostile or irritated reactions, but to keep the trouble to oneself—"burning one's own smoke" in Osler's figure of speech. He mentions with approval an unwritten rule of a western society of mountain climbers—that they must "never utter the least word of complaint if it rains all day and all night, or if the pack train is late and food does not arrive. . . ." To "crab" is the unpardonable sin, not a beneficial catharsis.[44]

Thus there are two clearly opposite views of the catharsis concept, with numerous "experts" and "authorities" to support each. It is an odd characteristic of the literature on this subject that most writers who have something to say on it never seem to have heard of a point of view opposite to their own. On each side there is an abundance of plausible anecdotal support of a character which

[43] John A. Schindler, "Your Mind Can Keep You Well," *Reader's Digest,* December, 1949, pp. 52-55.
[44] Walter C. Alvarez, "How to Live With Your Nerves," *Reader's Digest,* April, 1951, pp. 103-5.

can be used to prove almost anything and which has no scientific value. What is needed here, of course, is some effective application of the experimental method to a variety of situations in which it is believed that catharsis may occur. Until this is done, the popular and influential theory of catharsis, resting fundamentally on a discarded instinct theory, must be considered an unproved and somewhat implausible notion.

One relevant experiment has in fact been reported. During the Second World War, investigators divided a sample of soldiers into random halves, and gave the first group a list of questions deliberately intended to call forth a maximum of aggression against officers. These questions were followed by a set of standard questions on personal adjustment and general attitudes toward the army. The second group was not given the questions producing antagonism, but some neutral questions in their place. It was assumed that if the catharsis process operated, the scores on the latter parts of the questionnaires should reveal some benefits of the catharsis for the first group. The experimenters state: "Actually, there were no significant differences; nor were there on other studies in which a time interval of several days elapsed between present questions about officers and a subsequent questionnaire." [45]

An even more recent study, perhaps not explicitly designed as an experiment in catharsis, yielded similar negative results.[46] A summer camp for boys was specifically designed for the experimental purpose, the subjects being twenty-four boys, averaging about twelve years old, from the New Haven area. They were all American, lower middle class, Protestant, and were homogeneous with respect to educational and family backgrounds. During the first three days of the camping period the boys were allowed to form their own spontaneous groupings and friendships, and these were recorded. During the next stage, the campers were divided arbitrarily into two rival groups, purposely arranged so as to separate as much as possible the spontaneous friendships that had formed in the earlier period. The two groups, which took the names "Red Devils" and "Bull Dogs," were encouraged to choose their own activities. A competitive situation developed rapidly and spontaneously, breaking up former patterns of friendship and re-

[45] Samuel A. Stouffer *et al.*, *The American Soldier: Adjustment During Army Life* ("Studies in Social Psychology in World War II," Vol. I, [Princeton: Princeton University Press, 1949]), p. 362, footnote.

[46] Muzafer Sherif, "A Preliminary Experimental Study of Intergroup Relations," *Social Psychology at the Crossroads*, ed. John H. Rohrer and M. Sherif (New York: Harper & Bros., 1951). A full report is planned with the title *Group Relations*.

placing them with animosity. This increased throughout the period until a destructive fight between the groups broke out, necessi-
tating the arbitrary termination of this phase of the experiment.
All the free and spontaneous competition, rivalry, and athletic
contests might have been expected to yield a harmony-producing
catharsis, but the opposite occurred.

If repetition of experiments of these types similarly continue failing to show a catharsis effect, the catharsis theory will eventually
take its place in the list of historic errors.

Summary

Following the discovery that man is an animal and closely related in the evolutionary series to other animals, there began an
effort to relate the processes governing human behavior to those
regulating the behavior of lower animals. The instinct conception,
which appeared to be of such obvious utility in accounting for animal behavior, was quickly adopted in human psychology. During
the 1920's, at about the same time the value of the instinct concept for animal behavior began to be questioned, its application to
man was so severely attacked that within about a decade the
approach was virtually abandoned in psychology. The defects of
the instinct theory then seemed obvious; hardly any two observers
could agree on the number of instincts or their character and the
very definition of instinct varied among the writers on the subject.

There remained for a time, however, a general disposition to
find certain determining principles of human behavior somehow
rooted in biological processes. Thus there grew up a large number
of proposed theories which were essentially substitutes for the
instinct theory—innate emotions, prepotent reflexes, interests,
wishes, drives, needs, and the like. As the foregoing examination
has shown, these theories in general suffer from all the defects of
the instinct theory and are of no more use in the explanation of
behavior.

In recent years it has been proposed that the entire approach is
fruitless. It does no good to search for the elements of behavior
in the physiological nature of man, because the elements are not
there. "Perhaps the disagreements of the past three hundred years
may be explained by assuming that the differences were due to the
impossibility of the problem. Men could not agree on the elements
because they do not exist." [47] The heart of the difficulty, it is

[47] Ellsworth Faris, *op. cit.*, p. 187.

pointed out further, lies in the assumption that biological individuals constitute society. But with the more modern conception that society produces personalities, it follows that the elements of human behavior will be found not in the biological organism but in the social processes.

Murphy, in an examination of the biology of human motivation, arrives at a similar conclusion. Motivation does not consist of internal initiation of action; rather, human action is a continuous process involving constant relations between organism and environment and between parts of the organism. He states:

> If this modern biological view is essentially sound, it does curious things to the catalogues of motives which in one form or another still beset us. But it is hard to tell whether we are more misled by the crisp itemizations which used to be presented as keys to the "fundamental" human motives, or by those pseudo-modest lists which define four or five obvious visceral drives and then summarize all the other life energies under the term "socially acquired drives" or some other conventional abstraction, implying that motivation is forced into the organism from without, like air into a football.[48]

At the present time, it appears to be most fruitful to conceive of the biological mechanism as active and energetic, but unprovided with original tendencies which guide and direct the action. In the process of interaction, in experience and particularly in social experience, man acquires organization in his behavior.

SELECTED REFERENCES

FARIS, ELLSWORTH. *The Nature of Human Nature.* New York: McGraw-Hill Book Co., Inc., 1937. Chaps. vi and xv.
YOUNG, KIMBALL. *Source Book for Social Psychology.* New York: Alfred A. Knopf, Inc., 1930. Contains a review of the leading instinct theories.

[48] Murphy, *op. cit.*, p. 89.

Chapter 3

MOTIVATION: THE INDIVIDUAL ASPECT

As POINTED out in the preceding chapter, there appear to be no human instincts in the usual sense of the term. Observation of human infants shortly after birth shows no great amount of organization of behavior. Such organization as is visible consists of a limited number of such reactions as crying, sucking, swallowing, coughing, sneezing, grasping, and others similar to these. Most of these, though not all, have clearly recognizable functions, and most can readily be set into action by a definite type of stimulation. These are conventionally termed reflexes. They are simpler than the hypothetical instincts, but are similar in their innate character.

The reflexes, interesting as they are, do not form the basis of later organized behavior. Some may weaken or disappear, as does the grasping reflex in the first few months of life, and others may put in their first appearance some time after birth. By the process of conditioning, all may be attached arbitrarily to stimuli which did not in the first place call them into action. But to "condition" the salivation reflex to come into play at the sound of a bell does not materially alter the reflex. Similarly, after all the conditioning that goes on in the experiences of life as well as by intention in the laboratory, coughing remains coughing, sneezing remains sneezing, the knee jerk is unaltered, and other reflexes remain as they always were. The advanced forms of behavior—walking, throwing, writing, speaking, playing a piano—are not known to be based in any way on the reflexes that are observed in early life.[1]

The above statement, however, is not intended to carry the thought that the biological individual makes no contribution to the kind of behavior performed by the whole person. In the first place, it must always be borne in mind that it is this organism that acts—no other organism but the human is capable of human behavior. The individual physiology must have the kind of complexity and versatility which allows such behavior to develop.

[1] See Chapter 5 for a fuller discussion of the role of conditioning.

While the biological nature of the organism apparently does not contain any adequate mechanisms for the motivation of complex activity, this is not to claim that physiology is irrelevant to motivation. Activity which must be learned before it can be performed—for example, food getting, sex activity—may be rewarded by pleasant physiological consequences and so established firmly in the repertoire of behavior. Physiological penalties—pain, nausea, dizziness, and the like—can also operate to weaken or destroy motivation of a type of action, or contribute to the motivation of its active avoidance.

In addition to the above, there appear to be certain more direct contributions of the physiological nature of the organism to motivation. These are discussed in the present chapter, and include: a kind of restlessness or general tendency to function, which is a part of the motivation of a considerable part of behavior; a tendency to carry through coordinated acts to completion, once they are under way, apart from the consideration of whether or not the presumed goal is obtained; a tendency for habitude to make certain wishes more specific and narrow than they originally are; and a special importance of novelty, complexity, and progress in activity. The nature of these tendencies—certainly an incomplete list—is not fully known, but they appear to be of some importance in determining certain aspects of human behavior.

The General Tendency of Living Things to Function

Apart from all patterned action, there is observable in the infant during almost every waking moment, as well as much of the sleeping time, from birth onward, a considerable amount of unorganized or slightly organized general muscular activity. This involves muscles in all parts of the body—the facial muscles move, the neck bends, trunk muscles pull back and forth, and arms and legs bend and thrust, sometimes together, sometimes alternately, sometimes separately. In the waking period of a healthy infant this activity seldom stops.[2]

It is this random activity, not the organized reflexes or any other

[2] Parents may become aware of this constant movement if they attempt to take an indoor snapshot of their infant. There is a long wait to get the baby quiet enough for a one-second time exposure.

fixed organization, that forms the basis of the complex skills which develop later. The organization, as is shown in the present and the following chapter, is a product of experience, for the most part of social experience. But this organization comes from outside the person—there is no indication of an innate disposition to become organized in any particular way. The contribution of the living organism to the system of habits and skills of an adult is principally that of an active mechanism with an almost constant disposition to move and to function, and a neuromuscular system which has a potentiality for organization far more complex than can be achieved by any animal other than man.

The implication of the stimulus-response approach to the explanation of behavior, and perhaps also of the concepts of homeostasis and least effort, is that the organism normally seeks a state of rest or minimum effort. There are aspects of human behavior that appear to conform to these notions—the body has mechanisms for maintaining stability of internal temperature, of hydrogen ion concentration, and other physiological conditions, and it has a disposition to reduce activity when weary. Moreover, people frequently resist work that is not of their own choosing, or that is uncongenial for any reason, and perform it if at all with least effort. But this is not a universal or dominant tendency of the human organism, which is in fact an active thing, needing exercise as much as it needs repose. A small boy, sent outdoors to rake leaves, may adequately illustrate a least-effort conception, but the same boy on a mountain trail may prefer challenging scrambles over logs and rocks to the smooth and easy path. The tendency to seek strenuous activity is perhaps most marked in childhood and youth, but even adults normally engage in much tension-seeking activity. The most basic and general human motive is probably the general impulse to be active.

The activity needs, probably traceable to tensions both in the nervous system and in the striped and unstriped muscles acting jointly, dominate a large share of the small child's waking hours. Infants may kick when hungry, thirsty, or cold, but they also do a good deal of kicking and rolling, a good deal of wriggling and smiling, when not in any manifest state of visceral need. The little child keeps himself active, knowing nothing worse than to have to keep still, just as the adult begins to feel below par when activity is allowed to fall to too low a level. If there is a need to eat, there is in exactly the same sense a need to use all of one's physical machinery.[3]

[3] Gardner Murphy, *Personality: A Biosocial Approach to Origins and Structure* (New York: Harper & Bros., 1947), p. 110.

THE PHYSIOLOGICAL BASES OF GENERAL ACTIVITY

Since there is little evidence of innate organization in the general bodily activity that forms the foundation for later skills, there is only a problem of explaining the sources of this power or necessity. To point out that man, with so complete a lack of natural defenses, could hardly have survived in the long struggle for existence if he always waited for external circumstances to prod him into activity, is still insufficient to locate the cause of his restlessness.

While the explanation cannot at the present time be complete, there is material to suggest that various parts of the organism, including muscles, the brain, endocrine glands, and other visceral mechanisms have tendencies to contribute to this active nature. Possibly it is correct to say that the organism as a whole is one that is efficiently planned to be restless. It has been shown by recent research, for example, that it is in the nature of muscles to move. Muscles, in relaxation, are actually in a charged state, in wait for a trigger to set them off. After they are discharged or put into action, they are recharged at once. They do not wait for external stimulation to get them ready. Rather, in the rested and relaxed muscles there is a constant readiness to act.

A biologist has recently given a description of certain aspects of this mechanism.[4] The energy for the muscular action is supplied by adenosine triphosphate, which is present in the muscle units when they are ready for action. A nervous impulse causes the units of the muscle, small actin globules, to spend the potential energy. The experimenter states: "The energy transmitted by adenosine triphosphate is then required to bring them back to the high-energy loaded or extended state. . . . The living structure is kept ready to fire and is loaded after firing, instead of the other way around."

The interaction of muscles constitutes another aspect of their part in the motivation of general activity. As Murphy comments: "Tension of a muscle group lowers thresholds for another contraction (as in the familiar reinforcement of knee jerks by gripping the hands). Muscle tone is constantly changing and causing new activity."[5]

The contribution of adrenalin to general activity is well stated by Boring:

[4] A. Szent-Gyorgyi, "Muscle Research," *Scientific American*, June, 1949, pp. 22-25.

[5] Murphy, *op. cit.*, p. 107.

The pattern of sympathetic excitation just described results in energizing the organism. The person experiencing emotion is ready for action; he is "rarin' to go." This fact has been shown in experiments where the visceral pattern of emotion has been artificially produced by the injection of adrenalin, whose action, as we have just learned, duplicates that of sympathetic stimulation. Few subjects report feeling a genuine emotion under these circumstances, but most of them report feeling tense, excited, and moved to action.[6]

Some of the ways in which adrenalin produces its effects are explained:

An increase in the amount of adrenalin in the blood has the following effects upon physiological activity: (1) it increases the tremor in striped (voluntary) muscles; (2) it causes relaxation of smooth (involuntary) muscle; (3) it counteracts fatigue in striped muscle, by facilitating the transmission between the adjustor and the muscle effector; (4) it alters distribution of the blood in the body, sending more blood to the voluntary muscles, less to the digestive tract; (5) it increases blood pressure; (6) it hastens clotting of blood; (7) it relaxes the bronchioles in the lungs; (8) it causes the liver to release sugar into the blood stream; and (9) it causes the spleen to secrete or release red corpuscles into the blood stream. All these physiological changes brought about by adrenalin may be considered emergency reactions which prepare an organism to meet situations calling for quick and probably prolonged discharge of energy.[7]

Recent knowledge of brain function shows that the brain is not an inert switchboard, waiting for outside influences to make it function. It is constantly in rhythmic action, and imposes its own patterns to some extent on any influences that reach it.[8] Damage to the brain not only affects the style and complexity of action, but influences the strength of motivation itself. One of the common observations concerning persons whose frontal areas have been damaged by accident or impaired by surgery is that they have a tendency to lose initiative. Apparently much of normal motivation requires more than muscular energy, glandular activity, and other visceral support. The formulated plans, the consciously organized goals which require complex brain activity, are a part of motivation itself.

In addition to the above contributors to general motivation of activity, Murphy lists a number of visceral drives which are relevant to human restlessness: hunger, thirst, excretory tensions, oxygen deprivation, vasomotor adjustment needs arising in response to

[6] Reprinted by permission from *Foundations of Psychology* by E. G. Boring, H. S. Langfeld, and H. P. Weld (eds.), published by John Wiley & Sons, Inc., 1948, p. 96.

[7] *Ibid.*, pp. 23-24.

[8] See Chapters 5 and 12 for further material on brain functioning.

temperature extremes, sexual tension deriving initially from gonad and other endocrine tensions; maternal tensions due in some degree to endocrine and lactation tensions.[9]

Not only is the whole mechanism of man essentially activity-seeking, but the restlessness of one part tends to spread about, and to build up to a general level of tension which requires action. As Murphy states:

Activity needs show summation as clearly as do visceral needs, many different centers of tension combining to throw us into overt activity. A given tension level results from the summation of many factors, but there is a center of maximal activity, as in the golfer's arms as he drives, the rest of the muscular system playing an abundant supporting part. In turn, activity drives may facilitate visceral drives, or vice versa. The energies of the happy, excited child—happy whether it be birthday ice cream or the expectation of a prize at school—tend to "spill over" into visceral or into striped-muscle expression. As far as is known, any stimulus whatever tends to raise the tension level; and Jacobson's data suggest that tension anywhere spreads to some extent to other regions.[10]

Some recent studies indicate that some animals may not need a specific drive in order to perform a certain type of activity. While it has been widely supposed that animals do not learn without some relation of their activity to a recognized drive, such as the hunger drive, it has been found by extensive studies at the Wisconsin Primate Laboratory that the giving or withholding of food is a variable of no importance in determining the learning performance of the monkey. D. Meyer has shown that this learning is equally efficient one hour, twenty-three hours, and forty-seven hours after eating.[11] H. F. Harlow, in commenting on these results, remarks, "It is possible, of course, that monkeys are not familiar with modern motivational theory." [12]

Harlow, perhaps by professional habit, applies the term "manipulatory *drive*" to general investigative activity of animals, but

[9] Murphy, *op. cit.*, p. 105.

[10] *Ibid.*, p. 111. The reference in the last sentence is to E. Jacobson, *Progressive Relaxation* (2d. ed.; Chicago: University of Chicago Press, 1938). Jacobson found that there is no imagery that does not also involve muscle tension. Complete relaxation of muscles is difficult to achieve, but it results in disappearance of thought and in falling asleep. The thinking process is related to action, and therefore to muscular tension, and does not operate separately from muscular activity.

[11] D. Meyer, "Food Deprivation and Discrimination Reversal Learning by Monkeys," *Journal of Experimental Psychology*, XLI (1951), 10-16.

[12] Harry F. Harlow, "Levels of Integration," chap. v in *Social Psychology at the Crossroads*, J. H. Rohrer and M. Sherif (eds.) (New York: Harper & Bros., 1951), p. 136.

makes it clear that this is not the same narrow kind of impulse as the hunger or sex drives.

We have found that monkeys can learn to solve mechanical problems which have never been associated with extrinsic incentive, and we have formally described their behavior as motivated by a manipulation drive. Some monkeys, at least, apparently solve problems as efficiently under this condition as the most skillful monkeys solve these puzzles for a food reward. There are, of course, many observations of chimpanzees' and children's solving mechanical puzzles where the only obvious motivation has been curiosity or manipulation. . . .

We once observed . . . an adult orangutan playing with two blocks of wood, one containing a cylindrical hole and the other a square hole, and two plungers, one with a circular and the other with a square face. He tried repeatedly to fit the square plug into the round hole. It is not the intellectual error which is of interest, however, but the fact that he would frequently work for many minutes on a task which was not reinforced by thirst, hunger, elimination, or sex. . . .

We do not believe that monkeys, apes, and men are the only deviant mammals with respect to current motivational theory. We are convinced that cats can learn on the basis of a manipulatory drive which is not derived from primary physiological needs; we strongly suspect that an affectional drive can be demonstrated in dogs under conditions which would preclude secondary conditioning to hunger . . .

We are convinced that social motivation is, in large if not predominant part, learned. . . .[13]

Thus we see an indication that the drive theory may also be inadequate as an account of the behavior of some of the lower animals, and that some of the principles of the present chapter may apply in this field also. The investigations are incomplete, however, and in controversy, and some time will pass before this field of knowledge achieves a settled condition.

The Completion Tendency

Human activity is not merely escape from disturbing influences, but tends to reach farther than the immediate situation and to become organized about distant goals. It is also characteristic that when one activity toward a goal has begun, there is usually some tendency in the person to impel him to complete it, even if the circumstances change to make the action no longer functional. A man who starts to tell a joke only to discover that his listeners have all heard it usually senses an impulse to finish it anyway. Some

[13] *Ibid.*, pp. 137-38.

persons actually do continue, others may abbreviate it, but even those who stop at once can generally, at least, feel the inner push to complete the story. A student in a statistics class was asked by the lecturer to perform a calculation for him, in order that the lecture might proceed. A few moments later, while the student was only part way through the task, the lecturer informed him that it was unnecessary—he already had the answer in his notes. Nevertheless, the student, never one to work voluntarily on arithmetic calculations, went on to complete the process.[14]

Illustrations of the principle are abundant in daily life, and are commonly recognized in the "drop the other shoe" jokes.[15] When a listener deserts a speaker in the middle of a sentence the speaker finds it irritating to have to stop speaking at once, and many persons tend to finish anyway, without a listener. If there is a general conversational gathering, the speaker may quickly turn to a new listener and finish the sentence on him.

A common cause of temper outbursts in small children is that parents do not recognize the goals that the children pursue in their simple activities. A child, playing on the floor with blocks, may be abruptly called to dinner, or to bed, while a definitely coordinated project is in process. The tendency to completion is often strong enough in small children to make interruption intolerable. The difficulty is easily avoided if the parent first ascertains what particular goal is in sight, and either gives permission to finish that before going to the meal, or promises that it can be completed immediately afterward.

Completion may occur after a considerable amount of delay, furnishing relief from a nagging tension that remains from the interruption. It is a common experience to accumulate a considerable amount of such tension during an evening of lively conversation with a roomful of people, particularly if the interchange consists of debate rather than small talk. In two or three hours of this activity, each person repeatedly tries and fails to get the floor for

[14] Experience of the author. This experience illustrates the completion tendency perfectly, but it should be understood that not all persons would act the same way—most students in fact would be able to drop the project with relief.

[15] The essence of the story is as follows: a hotel guest lies in bed, hearing someone in the room above getting ready for bed. He hears a shoe drop. Not hearing the second one fall, because it has been carefully placed on the floor by the man above, he is unable to sleep. Finally he shouts impatiently to "let the other shoe drop." A related story involves a person who knew that a musician lived in the apartment above, and who played loudly on his piano an unresolved chord. The musician tossed restlessly a while, then finally arose, went to his own piano, and finished the musical pattern so that he could get to sleep.

his arguments, experiences abrupt interruptions, and prepares responses which he cannot deliver. The tension then persists for some time after the party is over, and may delay sleep even if the person is weary. Often the content of dreams indicates that some of the incomplete activity is being brought to a more satisfactory conclusion even in sleep.

This persistence of an unfinished task is reflected in the tendency to remember unfinished business. There is no need to remember actions which are entirely completed—if we were to do this all the time our memory would be intolerably cluttered with history. Memory is needed to serve action, and it functions to hold for future completion those matters of business which are unfinished. The tendency to remember unfinished tasks is sometimes called the "Zeigarnik effect" in honor of an early experiment in which it was shown that simple manual tasks such as constructing cardboard boxes, making clay figures, and the like, were remembered approximately twice as well if they were interrupted.[16]

It may be asked why the results were not more spectacular. For one thing, it is possible that for some persons, some of the apparently completed tasks aroused certain associations that had the effect of making these tasks a part of some larger coordination which itself had incomplete aspects. For example, the making of a cardboard box may remind a person of a dollhouse he wants to make for his child and may suggest ways of construction that may be used for the dollhouse. Thus to the experimenter the task of making a cardboard box may appear to be a completed task, but to the person making it it is a part of an unfinished dollhouse project and perhaps an important part to keep in memory. It is likely that a considerable amount of such association takes place in even such simple activity as the experimental tasks, and that therefore a number of the tasks classified as having been completed actually took part in a mental coordination which had an incomplete aspect.

It is also possible that some of the incompleted tasks were forgotten because they were not fully accepted as tasks; that is, the persons did not embrace an intention to perform them and were as happy to abandon the tasks when interrupted as a disgruntled workman is happy to drop his tools at the sound of the factory whistle. This result is sometimes accounted for by reference to differential "ego-involvement," meaning that pride or self-regard becomes attached to the task. A study has shown that items

[16] B. Zeigarnik, "Uber das Behalten von Erledigten und Unerledigten Handlungen," *Psychol. Forsch.*, IX (1927), 1-86.

learned under conditions of "ego-involvement" are more readily
remembered than items that have merely "task-involvement," in
which the action is regarded impersonally and is done only to
satisfy the experimenter.[17]   Since it appears probable that involve-
ments other than self-regard are also effective, it may be more
accurate to conceive of the remembered tasks as those in which
the subject organizes himself to accomplish the task.   In the case
of actions performed merely to satisfy the experimenter there would
be no tendency to finish in the absence of the experimenter's request, and no function in remembering it.   Thus it may be that in
the Zeigarnik experiment some of the forgetting of unfinished tasks,
as well as some of the memory of finished tasks, may have occurred
because of the impossibility of arranging for a perfect separation
of types of task.   It is conceivable that if such a perfect separation
could be achieved, all the unfinished tasks and none of the finished
tasks would be remembered.[18]

The basis for the completion tendency is not known.   It is
difficult to conceive that it lies in some simple process.   Many of
the goals are too complex and indefinite to be describable as
muscle sets—we do not know what the goal will be like when we
reach it; we only know that we will recognize it when we get there.
It may be that the task is defined mentally, that is, that it is an organization of imagery, and therefore that the completion is defined
by the mental organization rather than by fulfillment of a muscle
set or other simple mechanism.   The satisfactory formulation of
the nature of the completion tendency thus awaits future research,
but there seems little doubt that this principle is an important aspect
of human motivation and that the recognition of it is of practical
importance in the matter of dealing skilfully with people.

EMERGENCE OF SPECIFIC WISHES:
THE PROCESS OF CANALIZATION

The general tendency of the human organism to be active has no
direction.   It produces a general random movement of muscles all
over the body and accomplishes nothing but exercise.   Even this
is satisfying in a sense—at least it is better than being inert.   There
is some relief involved in merely working the muscles in a rested
and healthy body.

[17] T. G. Alper, "Task-orientations vs. Ego-orientation in Learning and Retention," American Journal of Psychology, LIX (1946), 236-48.

[18] See Chapters 6 and 8 for further material on the factors that account for
differences in memory.

Direction is acquired in experience. The random activity necessarily has an exploratory character, and discoveries inevitably result. Certain activities turn out to be more interesting or in some way rewarding to the groping infant. Starched cloth turns sweet when sucked, and a piece of iron has a cool sour taste. A rattle makes an engaging sound when agitated, and beads are entertaining when they are clicked together. In the process of investigation and discovery, the generalized motive becomes narrowed down and is made specific. The infant now has a wish for something. Having this, he is somewhat less satisfied with mere general exercise.

This process of directing general motivation toward specific objects is called canalization. The term implies that both the experience and the original tendency of a general character are involved in every specific wish. There have been proposals that any action which is performed repeatedly may become a drive. Murphy, however, argues:

> . . . suppose that during a busy week a man reaches every day for a needed reference book on the top shelf and absent-mindedly puts it back in the old spot when finished with it. Does the reaching, as such, become a drive? Automobilists all learn the art of gear shifting as part of the process of driving a car; but do drivers go ceaselessly through gear-shifting motions through sheer love of the process, as they sit waiting in a parked car? As soon as the weather grows warm enough for a child to go barefooted, his shoelaces are powerless to start the shoe-lace-tying drive. Mechanisms do not seem to become drives at all. . . . It is essential to the definition that the canalized motives be still regarded as *motives*, each act reflecting some of the original diffuse quality of the original motive. The hunger for ripe olives is still hunger; the craving for the old familiar faces is still the craving for faces. It is therefore improbable that the present conception can be effectively stretched so as to assimilate to itself any of the theories of general organismic plasticity which posit that practiced activity has an intrinsic tendency to become a drive.[19]

In support of this contention, Murphy cites an experiment in the canalization of food preferences.[20] The experimenter presented to a number of subjects unfamiliar foods in small quantities. Familiar foods were given as controls. Some tendency was found for the new foods to become more acceptable as the subjects had time to became used to them, but the amount of change was not large. In a further trial, however, three subjects were deprived of food for

[19] Murphy, *op. cit.*, pp. 176-77.
[20] M. Lukomnik, "An Experiment to Test the Canalization Hypothesis" (Master's essay, Columbia University, 1940).

24 hours before the experiment, and the preference for the new foods made a more marked gain. The interpretation is that the generalized hunger became canalized, and without the hunger as basic motive the new experience has little or no tendency to become a wish.

Further research is needed before this contention can be regarded as established. While it seems clear that not all actions imposed upon persons become performed for their own sakes, there is nevertheless an impressive amount of evidence for the versatility and for the arbitrary character of the tastes of man. Many an instrumental act has become satisfying in itself, and many an incidental feature of enjoyable activity has come to be appreciated for itself. A young man was once heard to state in all sincerity that to him the most beautiful of all sounds was the multiple roar of the motors of the racing cars as they sped along the bricks of the Indianapolis speedway. There is hardly an unpleasant sound that has not been used in modern music, hardly a jarring combination of colors and shapes that is not appreciated in modern art, and few harsh physical sensations that are not offered for pleasure at amusement parks.

Nevertheless, Murphy's argument shows that a legitimate issue remains:

> We may well suspect that all sorts of people adjust to all sorts of cultural situations, but we need not draw the conclusion that they do so "equally easily." The fact that groups of people satisfy their needs in all sorts of different ways is no evidence that the means are really equally satisfying. They may be canalized, but less so than they would be with a more satisfying stimulus. The critical test is the readiness of young individuals to make shifts in one direction or another. When "cultural relativism" is construed to mean that people living under different cultural arrangements are equally satisfied with them, or that the arrangements are in some broad sense equally good, equally satisfying, we must contest the point, for the reasons just given.[21]

It is suggested that canalizations may be destroyed only by interference from competing canalizations. This, however, would

[21] Murphy, *op. cit.*, pp. 174-75. Conclusive experimental investigation of this point appears to be not impossible, but technically difficult. There is no satisfactory method of measuring the degree of satisfaction of an activity. The most promising approach would appear to be the study of order of preferences of a list of activities, but persons with different experiences have different orders of preference. The equalization of experience among subjects appears to be impossible to achieve. The readiness of young individuals to make shifts in one direction or another may appear to be promising, but the difficulty with young individuals appears to be that they have a readiness to make shifts in one direction and back again almost without limit.

not occur frequently, because of the apparent human capacity for
a great range of wishes. "The love of Bach does not destroy the
love of Shakespeare, nor does the love of raspberry sherbet destroy
the love of baseball. . . . One may develop many acquired wants
within one modality; he may learn to like many kinds of food, many
kinds of music." [22]

The Appeal of Novelty, Complexity, Progress

In the process of canalization, we learn to like whatever we can
do, providing that it somehow satisfies. There are obvious indications of a sequence of preferences, however. In general, satia-
tion and boredom are achieved early with very simple activities.
A somewhat more complicated form of the same or similar activity,
however, may satisfy. In time this may be insufficient but a further
elaboration re-engages the interest. This principle is well illustrated in the case of games. Young children may be contented to
bounce a ball by themselves for a time, but the more complicated
activity of bouncing it back and forth with others is generally preferred if a choice is available. Boys will toss a baseball and catch
it themselves, but will prefer throwing it back and forth with others,
and over that will prefer, if they know how to do it, a throwing
and batting exercise, and better yet an organized baseball game.
Simple versions of baseball are played with as few as three players,
but observations of boys on the playing field indicate that the more
complex forms are nearly always preferred, with the ideal being a
full game between two teams of nine players each.

The progress of individuals through sedentary games such as
card games, checkers and chess, dominoes, and the like, illustrates
the appeal of the higher levels of complexity. The simpler card
games played by children in time lose their appeal in favor of
more advanced types. The games themselves sometimes evolve
toward complexity—in the present century, for example, the popular card game of whist became more widely played after becoming
auction bridge, and gained again in popular interest as contract
bridge.

There is a similar progress in musical tastes, in the experience of
many persons. A small child may find pleasure in a single sweet
musical note, such as the sound of a bell or the tinkling ring of a
triangle. A sequence of notes making the pattern of a tune, however, soon becomes more appealing. In time there develops an

[22] *Ibid.*, pp. 167-69.

appreciation of tunes enriched by harmony, and perhaps later by counterpoint. There is something of a sequence of this sort for persons who progress to the appreciation of symphonic music. Tchaikovsky is among those composers whose appeal is easy to understand, and tends to be among the first whose music is acceptable. Brahms is appreciated somewhat later, and the most complex modern music even later, if at all. Not all persons pursue such a subject as music from the simple to the advanced and complex levels, but remain loyal to simple tunes as long as they live. These persons may go through a progressive experience in other lines of interest, however. Few adults can be long satisfied with the very simple activities which can hold the interest of small children.

It is shown in Chapter 5 that consciousness itself depends on the aspects of novelty in behavior. To remain conscious of anything and to retain interest in any activity appear to require that there be some fresh characteristic in it. This diversity is all but inevitable in life, since no two experiences can be duplicated exactly.

It appears likely that it is a human characteristic not only to be active in general, but to be active in such a fashion as to be conscious, to have problems continuously, and thereby to exercise the most elaborate mechanisms for efficient action. To see, to know, to think, is activity just as is muscular writhing, and employs the same muscles but in coordinated patterns. The outstanding characteristic of human nature is not to lie inert until external stimulation appears, nor even to remain occupied in routine activity. Man seeks activity which has progress, novelty, and enough complexity to hold his interest. Canalization, therefore, can never completely stop. Wishes wear out if they do not evolve. Throughout life new wishes emerge, or old wishes develop new aspects. There is no stability in the conscious life of man.[23]

[23] To persons who suffer almost continuous discomfort or pain, happiness may appear to be the lack of discomfort. Persons whose lives are excessively insecure tend to define happiness in terms of security. Similarly those with any strong unfulfilled wishes may see happiness as the achievement of the particular wishes. The satisfaction on being rid of pain, achieving security or fulfilling any particular wish, however, is short-lived. Restlessness sets in quickly if no new absorbing activities are found. Happiness is not simply the experience which follows the reaching of a goal. It appears rather to be a by-product of successful on-going activity in the pursuit of goals. It is not found in any instant or isolated sensation, but is a sort of generalization emerging from interesting, organized, and progressing activity. It probably requires a certain amount of foresight and retrospection to transform the concentrated attention to work into the general feeling of happiness.

SUMMARY

The basic motivating power of complex human actions does not lie in any such organized elements as instincts, reflexes, or separate drives, but in a general tendency to be active which is apparently a fundamental characteristic of the living organism. This tendency is found to be embedded in the whole system; muscles, glands and the nervous mechanism are designed for continuous activity rather than inert inactivity awaiting disturbance.

This general activity necessarily has an exploratory character, and individual discoveries are made of satisfying objects of action. Through experience, the general motive tends to become increasingly specific by means of the process of canalization.

There is apparently a tendency, not completely understood, for any coordination, however arbitrary, to develop some motivation of its own, and for the person to have an urge to complete the coordination once it has begun. There is also much indication of an instability in wishes which requires that man always seek a certain amount of novelty. Attention apparently cannot remain active if there is no change in an experience.

Thus to all appearances it is the nature of man to be active, restless, exploring, pursuing, and progressing. The life of happiness for him is a life of activity, not of idleness and peace. This is the basic motive of almost all human activity and it is the principal contribution of the individual physiological organism to the motivation of complex activity. It is generalized power, which gets its direction only in experience. A part of the experience that organizes this power and gives it direction is individual interaction with physical surroundings, but the larger and more important part is the experience that takes place in interaction with other persons. It is the social process which does the most to organize the general motivating power and to transform the individual into an efficient creature and a responsible member of a team.

SELECTED REFERENCES

MURPHY, GARDNER. *Personality: A Biosocial Approach to Origins and Structure.* New York: Harper & Bros., 1947. See chaps. v, vi, and viii.

YOUNG, KIMBALL. *Personality and Problems of Adjustment.* New York: Appleton-Century-Crofts, Inc., 1940. See chap. iv, "Drives, Cycles of Activity, and Emotions."

Chapter 4

MOTIVATION: SOCIAL SOURCES

SINCE IT appears to be clear that, in the human, the processes of physiology do not supply an adequate or detailed system of motivation, the next step in the inquiry is to find out what does. The answer appears to be that the major part of motivation is acquired in experience, and that by far the most important part of this is experience in organized social relations. Man acquires his effective motivation from social sources.

In such experience, certain vague and general cravings become narrow and specific, and other specific preferences become broadly generalized. Perhaps most important of all, wishes or desires are made to fit together into some kind of organized pattern, itself derived from the fact that social relations are always highly organized. One of the most important reasons for the rigidity and persistence of some motives comes from this fact of organization.

Because society and social groups of various kinds provide the instrument by means of which so many important wishes are gratified, an interest in sociability—in being a member of groups, of conforming to group expectations so that a welcome in organized life is always assured—tends to become one of the most dominant motives of the normal person. In the phenomena of esprit de corps and morale, the social motive becomes paramount over others, and the conquest of physiological dispositions by social motives becomes complete. The most powerful principle of social control of the individual may be that which operates by forming the person to the extent that he does not experience this control as an external pressure, but feels it as if it were his own nature.

THE ROLE OF CULTURE IN CANALIZATION

The generalized wish for food becomes specific as a result of the particular foods used to satisfy the hunger. Thus preferences are narrowed down, so that a person wants bread rather than oatmeal, and asks for a particular kind of bread, such as rye. It is of course the offerings of cultures that are most influential in determining these specific tastes, although within a culture there is individual variation that is a product of unique experiences of each person.

The world-wide variation in cultural preferences for food is impressive. Few peoples make use of all edible materials available to them—they avoid as well as select. Some African peoples eat grasshoppers and monkey meat, the French eat snails, Tibetans put butter in their tea, and Eskimos consider the contents of a deer's stomach an acceptable salad. Our culture has made us able to eat raw clams and moldy cheeses.

This power of culture to canalize general tendencies is not a distorting or frustrating influence standing in the way of normal natural tendencies of the individual. Throughout these chapters it is shown that culture is not merely an artificial system imposed on man, but that man and society are inextricable, and that neither is complete without the other. As Murphy writes:

. . . we must contest the point that some satisfiers are "natural" and others "artificial." The distinction between "natural" and "artificial" satisfiers can make a great deal of trouble if we think of the state of nature as giving man what satisfies him most completely, i.e., if we consistently disdain the work of culture in developing new satisfiers. If we think of social arrangements as satisfying the drives less adequately than the natural arrangements do, we shall be puzzled to find men everywhere cooking their food rather than eating it raw, complicating their music rather than making the most of the sounds of sea, wind, and running water. It is the rule, in fact, that wants are satisfied *less than optimally* when nature, unadorned, is the satisfier.[1]

There are, of course, limits to what culture can accomplish in creating desires. Man cannot be made to like everything. But the impressive fact is the variety of things that man can be influenced to desire. Civilization creates a vast number of desires for things which primitive people could never imagine, and in extreme circumstances the power of culture is impressive. As Ellsworth Faris writes:

Given an uncontradicted cultural medium we can see that the powerful drives of hunger, sex, and even the will to live are as nothing if they run counter to the mores. Confirmation of this is familiar to us all. Voluntary fasting, voluntary celibacy, voluntary mutilation and torture, voluntary suicide—examples abound to show the irresistibility of the cultural model. One can no more organize his personality independently than he can be born without a mother.[2]

[1] Gardner Murphy, *Personality: A Biosocial Approach to Origins and Structure* (New York: Harper & Bros., 1947), p. 175.

[2] By permission from *The Nature of Human Nature* by Ellsworth Faris. Copyright 1937 by McGraw-Hill Book Co., Inc. P. 279.

GENERALIZATION OF MOTIVES:
CURRENCY AND STORAGE ASPECTS

In addition to the processes of canalization, in which general appetites are narrowed down into specific wishes, there appears to be a process of generalization of separate values into broad motives. This is conveniently illustrated by reference to the interest in money. Small children value coins no more than they do beads or blocks, and they care even less for paper money or checks. It has been shown experimentally, however, that children, or even rats, can readily be trained to work hard to earn a token such as money if this is exchangeable for some such desired goal as candy, and that the closer to the goal the token is received the more effective it is in motivating behavior.[3] As children gain experience with money and the variety of gratifications that it brings, a general appreciation of money in time develops, so that it appears to be a value in itself. Before adulthood is reached, most persons have so generalized this sense of what money can do that money in any form—coin, bills, checks, or bonds—has strong aesthetic appeal. In the extreme case, the pathological miser may spend much time fondling and gazing on his tokens of exchange.

It is obvious that the wish for money is to most persons such a generalization of the various uses which money has. We do not have to list the number of satisfactions a ten-dollar bill could give us to enjoy an agreeable sense of its potentialities. Stage money does not have this power, and even foreign bills usually seem less appealing, for we have no association of benefits with their appearance. Money not only is translatable into many different kinds of satisfaction, but it can also be held for later enjoyment, and thus it performs a storage function. The larger bill is more pleasing partly because we sense that it takes care of the week after next.

Early instinct lists included an innate human tendency toward sociability or gregariousness. Such information as is available, however, indicates that we do not start life with any preference for persons, and we fail to develop any sociability at all in isolation. The mass of evidence indicates that sociability may be a generalization of the same sort as money. The young infant soon learns that nearly all his gratifications come through the agency of other persons, and as he grows older he becomes increasingly aware that activity with persons tends to be more complex, absorbing, and in-

[3] Unpublished studies by Richard L. Solomon.

teresting. Thus there is an early generalization of the variety of satisfactions that depend upon human cooperation into an interest in people as such. To join a group, to be with others, has various possibilities of furnishing interest and satisfaction, as does the possession of money, and it also shares with money the storage aspect. To be a member of a group pays in the future as well as in the present. Avoidance of the possibility of loneliness in times ahead makes us appreciate the value of our associations now. In the ultimate generalization, however, the attention is not on the benefits, but on the value of sociability itself. The basis for the generalization normally is forgotten, if it is ever realized at all, and the sociability motive appears to be so natural that it is easy to be persuaded that it is instinctive. Once this is so, there is a possibility of sociable or altruistic behavior which has no possibility of returning a reward.[4]

Similarly, the desire for prestige, recognition, or status, which has appeared on various lists of fundamental instincts or drives, appears to be a motive acquired by the same generalization process. All societies and nearly all groups within any society make distinctions of status. These are functional—they specify the kind of behavior that is to be expected of each person and thus aid in the coordination of behavior. Status distinctions are to some extent necessary to smooth performance of any kind of teamwork or cooperation.[5]

The higher levels of status are believed to be, and usually are, the more pleasant to occupy. They involve more power and influence, and thus a wider range of choices. In some organizations

[4] In times of conflict and disorganization it is easy to become persuaded that selfishness is more powerful than sociability. The relative influence of individualistic and cooperative tendencies, however, depends on various circumstances. There are incontrovertible proofs that purely altruistic actions are not only possible but common when conditions do not interfere. An example is furnished by the following trial: Postcards and stamped, addressed envelopes were dropped on sidewalks in a number of cities, to see how many would be picked up and mailed by thoughtful persons who could have no expectation of reward. Of the ordinary messages without enclosures, 85 per cent were picked up and mailed. Of the letters containing slugs the size of a half-dollar, 59 per cent were mailed. While this would not happen in all times and places, the fact that it can ever happen is powerful testimony to the breadth of the generalization of the sociability motive. See C. B. Merritt and R. G. Fowler, "The Pecuniary Honesty of the Public at Large," *Journal of Abnormal and Social Psychology*, XLIII (1948), 90-93.

[5] There is such a thing as apparently functionless differentiation of status, arising where patterns are transferred from one kind of organization to another. Many a purely social club which requires one official at most has, nevertheless, formally elected a president, vice-president, secretary, treasurer, and sergeant at arms. This appears to be a rather harmless formalism which has become established in United States culture.

they bring higher financial returns. The higher levels also give wider entrée into attractive associations—friendships with talented and popular persons, membership in exclusive clubs and circles, higher bargaining power in the marriage market, and other rewards. Here again the analogy with money is appropriate—high status can buy many types of satisfaction and can be stored for later use, and because of its various benefits comes to be valued for its own sake.[6]

An illustration of the kind of reward that follows a rise in general social status is shown in the following description of the experience of gaining entrée into the Main Line of the Philadelphia upper crust.

Not that ancestry means everything; even a newcomer can earn a share in the amenities of Main Line life. Let's suppose that you are the newcomer. You make, say, $18,000 a year. You are personable, your wife is attractive, your two daughters charming.

You visit G. Forde Hansell, the Ardmore real-estate man who looks like an ambassador, and he tells you that he has a few estates at, say, $200,000. Since you don't have $200,000, you agree upon a modern home for $38,000.

You enroll your daughters in one of the great Main Line schools, perhaps Agnes Irwin, most of whose graduates are presented to Philadelphia society. You note with pride that gradually your girls are accepted by the daughters of really important families. At table you may even hear them mention names like Cassatt or Biddle.

In the meantime your wife has joined half-a-dozen committees which concern themselves with hospitals, the Red Cross, sewing for refugees, and other good works, and slowly you and your wife become known as "substantial, dependable people." One day your wife casually remarks, "Young Mrs. Cadwalader says that Lois thinks our Jean is such a dear. We're having tea on Friday."

Slowly, over a couple of years, you begin to break the ice, not because you have a fair income but because your family is a pretty good sort. You join the Merion Cricket Club, the Philadelphia Skating Club and Humane Society, and ultimately the Radnor Hunt Club.

Still you aren't invited to the best parties, although your daughters are. Then you hear your name has been submitted for inclusion in the Philadelphia

[6] In some cases its value is impressively high. Men commonly work themselves to exhaustion, endangering health, for status rewards, and fight in desperation, sometimes to death, to avoid severe reduction in status. Small matters often become large when status is involved. It is reported that paratroopers of the Second World War, all men who had volunteered for highly dangerous tasks, were disgruntled when ordinary infantrymen's boots were substituted for their high-laced jump boots which had constituted one of their marks of distinction. Ninety-five per cent of the men said the jump boots meant a great deal to them as symbols. See Samuel A. Stouffer *et al., The American Soldier: Adjustment During Army Life* ("Studies in Social Psychology in World War II," Vol. I [Princeton, Princeton University Press, 1949]), p. 329.

Social Register. When the issue with your name appears, your wife ignores it with an airy, "It's really nothing but a telephone book." Because she knows that being in the Social Register doesn't mean much. You're there, but it's who calls you that counts.

When your daughters want to give a party for their friends, you hurry in to Philadelphia and visit Mrs. Edward J. MacMullan, who arranges such things for the better families. She's a tall handsome woman who used to run the big festivities for Mrs. Stotesbury. You find Mrs. MacMullan delightful. Your snide friends say, "Of course, you should have gone to Mrs. Wirt Thompson, of Haverford." But you disregard them. After all, Mrs. Mac-Mullan handled arrangements for one of the country's plushiest weddings—the duPont-Roosevelt nuptials—though on the Main Line you wouldn't stress the Roosevelt end of that gala affair.

Mrs. Mac checks up on your daughters and thinks she may be able to persuade a representative group to attend. You go down to Bailey, Banks and Biddle, still harboring some misgivings, and place your name and the date of your party in their official events book. Even being allowed to do this is an accolade, because this famous book dates back considerably in Philadelphia's social history. It was kept originally by Dreka, the stationer, and when B. B. and B. took it over they also acquired the services of Mr. George Rhefuss, who made the entries for Dreka.

Your daughter's party is a real success. Some of the best families are represented. And before long you are unexpectedly invited to the home of a social leader, and that night the host proposes to submit your name for membership in the Rabbit Club, which meets in ultra-exclusiveness in Fairmount Park. That same year your wife serves on the committee of the Devon Horse Show, and you have become an established family.

Of course, you are not so arrogant as to imagine that you could possibly be invited to the Assembly next December. This is Philadelphia's haughtiest dance, as exclusive as any held in America. Only the descendants of fifty-nine 18th Century Philadelphia families can gain admission, along with their wives and guests, and over the years since 1748, when the affair first became an institution, the exceptions have been too few to matter. You know of many families much richer and more famous than yours that have vainly tried to crash it. Nor does it matter that your daughter is being formally presented to Philadelphia society. Only fifteen out of 100 debs are eligible for the Assembly.

Then your eldest daughter becomes engaged to the son of an Assembly family, and you get a real thrill when you are able to say, in an offhand manner, "Jean won't join us tonight. She's attending the Assembly." [7]

There are, of course, many methods by which status is gained, many types of status, and many uses of it. Its rewards, however, are in general like those described above. They lie in the wider

[7] James A. Michener, "The Main Line," *Holiday*, April, 1950, pp. 40-41. Quoted by permission.

range of choices and the ability to enjoy a variety of satisfactions because of the high status.

There are other acquired motives which appear to be based on the same kind of generalizing from various specific benefits as in the case of money, sociability, and status. The interpretation would seem to apply to the common, though not universal, interest in self-development—the acquisition of general ability and skills. The desire for power of any kind appears to be a similar generalization, and has the currency and storage aspects. Perhaps the interest in security belongs in the same category, as well as a number of other wishes once believed to be unitary biological drives.

Institutional Integration of Motives

Institutional Roles.—Any interpretation of human motivation must necessarily recognize that many actions take place which are hard to trace to any individualistic or biological source. A common business instrument is a lease that is in effect for 99 years. The persons first agreeing to the lease assume that persons yet unborn will carry out the agreement being signed. In general their assumptions are fulfilled. It is therefore an important problem in motivation to account for a common tendency of living persons to act on the basis of commitments made by persons long dead.

The explanation appears to lie in the institutionalization of behavior. Organized systems grow up about purposes which are not purely individual in character. Persons are brought into the organization and given a role which is an expression not of their personal tendencies or of their biological drives, but of the requirements of the institution itself. The motivation for the role of the person within an institution does not come entirely from within the person, but is supplied by the organization. Persons with different individual inclinations, and the same person with varying dispositions, may nevertheless be impelled to maintain a predictable course of action within an institutional role.

There are, of course, variations in the degree in which institutional motivation penetrates the persons who work within the organization. It is possible, and perhaps not rare, for a person to affect an institutional role solely for the purpose of some individualistic reward. But it is characteristic of social organizations to imbue their members with the common purpose so that at least a part of their motivation comes from their dedication to the cause. One may teach in an academy with the sole motivation of drawing the

pay involved, but in such circumstances the performance is unlikely to have the quality that is desirable, and the institutions
generally have mechanisms which reject persons of this type. It
is more common even for the persons who begin with purely individualistic motives, to absorb from the organization an interest
in its purposes and eventually to perform work of a quality that is
not ordinarily produced by utter selfishness.

The indoctrination is a slow and somewhat complex process.
The job in an organization is not merely a specification of what work
is to be done; it has aspects of a social role. Organized expectations
of other persons are brought to bear on the person to direct his
manner of behavior, and departures of importance are punished
by the various means of informal social control—gestures of disapproval, partial ostracism, and general circulation of critical gos-
sip. Correct behavior is rewarded by opposite reactions, so that
it becomes a pleasant experience to be known as an exemplary performer in the role—a good foreman, a good chairman, a good
secretary.

To obtain these rewards, it is necessary to keep a part of one's
attention on the expectations of the organization and to become
sensitive to the reactions of approval or disapproval. Insincerity is
awkward to maintain for indefinite periods, and the easier course
is to yield to the social pressures and come to prefer the style of
action involved in the assigned role as well as the rewards that are
given for good performance. At this point, habitude appears in the
guise of nature, and the person tends to believe that the institutional motives are his natural inclinations.

The social systems into which we are born even more easily and
thoroughly form our personal preferences, so that here again a set
of wishes derived from a social source is readily confused with
innate drives. To us who live in a monogamous family system, in
which the dominant male chooses his wife in a courtship process,
it is tempting to base the institutional form of the family upon a
set of instincts. Persons in other cultures, however, adapt to quite
different forms of marriage as smoothly, for all we know, as we
adapt to our own.[8]

The necessities which call for institutionalization of activity are
those functions which require much organization, and which have

---

[8] A Hindu sociologist has described his experience in a marriage system not only
different from our own, but opposed to his original preferences. Though he had
taken a modern viewpoint, his parents insisted on his following the traditional ways
in marriage. His bride was chosen for him and the family life was governed by
seemingly oppressive institutional rules and restrictions. Nevertheless, the Hindu

a long-run or perpetual character. Generally they are neither drives nor are they necessarily needs or wishes of individual persons, but needs of the group or society. An example of a group need that is not an individual need is the provision for its own perpetuation. The purely individualistic interests of the members of an institution at any one time would not always require that it be preserved beyond their own periods of use of it. But all institutions that endure do so because of organized mechanisms that have the function of perpetuating themselves. These mechanisms require that certain officers be instilled with an interest in the institution and devotion to the cause, which must overrule any personal wishes they may have which might come in conflict with the group interest. This is successfully done in countless situations of everyday life. Members readily subordinate their personal concerns to the demands of a church, a college, a political party, a family, a nation, or any of countless other contemporary institutions.

The motivation a person may directly incorporate within himself from an institution is of great power in many cases. The person who is dominated in his actions by the fact that he holds office in an institution is expected to subordinate successfully not only his personal wishes, but also the powerful pressures that may come from primary group influences in conflict with the institutional interest. Ellsworth Faris insists on the importance of keeping the informal and the formal agencies of social control distinct, without designating either as superior to the other:

. . . the primary group is [not] a value concept and therefore superior to other types of groups. Human institutions are erected to meet human needs, and these needs may sometimes be better satisfied by institutions than by primary group relations. Indeed, primary group relations may intrude in a disorganizing manner, as when a police officer refuses to arrest a man because he is a friend. Here belong much of the corruption, bribery, nepotism, and "graft" of our modern life. Formal and institutional groups cannot perform their function unless the distinction between them and the primary group be kept with scrupulous clarity.[9]

The institutional office itself is a mechanism of social control, and in a sense an organized package of motives available for use by any incumbent. In the institution ". . . the person is no longer acting

reports that the marriage worked to his satisfaction and that of his wife, and that they loved each other intensely during a long and happy life together. See the pair of articles by D. N. Mitra, "A Hindu Marriage in Bengal" and "A Hindu Wife," *American Journal of Sociology*, LII, No. 3 (1946), 255-62.

[9] By permission from *The Nature of Human Nature* by Ellsworth Faris. Copyright 1937 by McGraw-Hill Book Co., Inc. P. 41.

freely but is acting in an office, performing a definite institutional function. When an institution operates in its typical character, the functionary manifests a minimum of personal relations. An institution might almost be defined as a social device to make emotion unnecessary." [10]

Everett Hughes has pointed out certain characteristics of the institutional office, including some aspects which derive from the fact that the office itself has a history.

An office is a standardized group of duties and privileges devolving upon a person in certain defined situations. . . . The person who fills . . . a great office is judged not as the common run of mankind but with reference to his predecessors in office and to the popular conception of what the office should be. He is exposed to special demands. He is also protected, in so far as the office sets the limits of his responsibility, from both the bludgeons of critics and the sharp thrusts of his own conscience. . . . He wards . . . off [critics] by declaring that whoever criticizes him attacks the sacred office.[11]

In the case of persons holding offices of high prestige, the most informative clue to the character of their official behavior may, in fact, be supplied by noting their conceptions of their place in history. A president of a nation in his first term of office may be motivated by a desire to be re-elected, but in his final term may be disposed to be governed in part by his expectations of the judgments to be made by future historians. This interest, of course, serves a useful function in providing a strong motive for taking a long range view of the institutional or national interest and discouraging the submission to temporary influences of any kind.[12]

Elaboration of Biological Elements.—Institutional aspects of life affect motivation in another manner by arranging elaborate complexes that entangle biological needs and sensations with arbitrary social arrangements into interwoven unities. Love between the

[10] *Ibid.*, p. 45.

[11] Everett C. Hughes, "Institutional Office and the Person," *American Journal of Sociology*, XLIII, No. 3 (1937), 404-6.

[12] Further down in the institutional structure, although the penalties for deviation may differ in character, the pressures are successful in producing a type of person devoted to the prescribed ways of his particular office. The irritating thing about a bureaucrat is that he does not appear to be a person, but a mechanical thing. Away from his work he may be a recognizable human being but in his office he is not free to act as himself. As an experienced bureaucrat explains: "The typical bureaucrat is a nervous individual. . . . The handling of all delicate situations requires a special technique. . . . Mastery of these techniques is of basic importance . . . neglect of the customary sacraments and rituals can prove troublesome in the extreme and sometimes results in hasty resignations or, in heinous cases, in the total extinction of parts of agencies or of whole units." From T. Swann Harding, "Uncle Sam Unwhiskered," *American Journal of Sociology*, L, No. 4 (1945), 307.

sexes has a biological aspect, though no sex instinct or drive is adequate as a motive to produce the observed behavior of courtship and mating in the human. Our romantic courtship patterns bind together in the complex such elements as an interest in poetry, sunsets, moonlight, ukuleles, flowers, music, dancing, and various other factors. It includes an elaborate set of loosely related beliefs and sentiments. One investigator has listed forty elements of the romantic complex, including such items as chivalry, emotional surges, disregard for convention, attraction of opposites, sense of destiny, belief in a single true love, and the like.[13] Not all couples involved in courtship make use of the whole complex, but few couples achieve marriage without any influence from the institutionally embedded romantic tradition.

A further contribution to our knowledge of the nature of courtship motivation has been made by Winch through the use of a factor analysis of the process among college students.[14] The data were gathered in 1941 from midwestern educational institutions but it is not unlikely that the finding can be somewhat generalized over a wider area and some years of time. For each of 435 male students, thirty-one variables were obtained and their intercorrelations computed. The process of factor analysis yielded one indeterminate and seven identifiable factors in the courtship complex. The principal finding can be stated about as follows: the amount of courtship behavior which these college men engage in is determined by several separate factors, the principal ones probably being (1) social adjustment, (2) socioeconomic status, or perhaps continuity tradition in the parental family, (3) family harmony, and (4) social maturity, plus two other factors relating to the influence of parents.[15] The analysis of courtship in college women produced somewhat different results. Apparently courtship in women is a different sort of activity in some respects. The factors

[13] Llewellyn Gross, "A Belief Pattern Scale for Measuring Attitudes Toward Romanticism," *American Sociological Review,* IX, No. 5 (1944), 463-72.

[14] Robert F. Winch, "Primary Factors in a Study of Courtship," *American Sociological Review,* XII, No. 6 (1947), 658-65. Also by the same author, "Courtship in College Women," *American Journal of Sociology,* LV, No. 3 (1949), 269-78. Factor analysis is a statistical method, based on correlation techniques, by which distinct factors may be inductively separated from one another and compared with reference to their mingled influence in a complex interrelation.

[15] The factor analysis process discovers the number of separate factors, but does not indicate their nature, except for showing how much each general factor is related to each variable. The naming of the factors is a matter of judgment, and involves the possibility of error. The important aspect of this particular study, for the purpose of the present inquiry, is that courtship is not based upon a single drive, but on a number of factors, most of which appear to be aspects of social relations rather than physiological drive.

involved here are (1) appearance, (2) the wish to be married, (3) the absence of determination to have a career, and (4) favorable circumstances in the early dating situation. These findings are in harmony with the tradition of male dominance, and suggest that the variables that account for courtship among college women are in part the absence of any reason not to accept dates. In a sense there is no "motivation" problem of an internal sort. It is the male who takes the initiative, and has to be motivated.

Not only courtship, but marriage, mating, and procreation are institutionally motivated. In the earlier rural pattern of the family farm, a wife was necessary to a man, and children were an economic advantage as soon as they were old enough to work. The unmarried woman had little place in this system, nor, for that matter, in the urban cultures of the past. The opening of a wide range of economic opportunities for women has reduced the penalty of being single, but there still remains a considerable amount of advantage to the woman who is married. In general, the earning power of a single woman is not equal to that of a man of equivalent ability. Furthermore, a large part of adult social life is organized for couples—dances, card parties, dinner parties, and the like. The spinster is called in now and then to fill a gap, but she understands her outside position.

Motivation to bear children is abundantly furnished by society. A psychologist, writing in the early years of the century, listed some of these pressures as they operated at that time.[16] Among these were: (1) the ideal of the "womanly woman," which pictured the normal woman as motherly and as finding her life with her children, in contrast with the masculine type of woman seen as abnormal and unattractive; (2) pressures of opinion, such as editorials and articles lauding maternity and deploring the falling birth rate, and such public gestures as that of the German Kaiser who offered to be godfather to the seventh, eighth, and ninth son in any family; (3) legal pressures, such as obstacles to the spreading of birth-control information, the use of sterility as grounds for divorce, and restrictions on the rights of possession and control of property by women; (4) religious influence, such as the advice to "multiply and replenish the earth," and the sentiment that family limitation constitutes a sin; (5) educational influences, such as the provision of home economics courses and finishing schools, together with artificial barriers against many types of vocational education;

---

[16] Leta Hollingworth, "Social Devices Impelling Women to Bear and Rear Children," American Journal of Sociology, XXII, No. 1 (1916), 19-29.

(6) artistic influences, such as madonna paintings, poetry of motherhood, songs to mothers; (7) illusions maintained by society, minimizing the risks and discomforts of childbearing, supporting the idea that child-bearing keeps a woman healthy, and that the only child is handicapped.

Some of the above influences have diminished, but in general the same forms of motivation operate today.[17] Certain informal, but effective, sources of motivation may be added. In many communities, a considerable amount of attention is given to women on the occasion of their first pregnancy, including flattering gestures, gift showers, and various minor privileges. In any circle of young wives who form a primary group, each member gets this sort of attention in turn until the last few become eager for pregnancy on this account alone. Also, just as the spinster is left out of many social occasions, the childless wife in a group of mothers is often helplessly left out of much of the conversation. A rich amount of organized activity among mothers forms about the matters of nursery schools, parent-teachers organizations, school activities, and other concerns with children. There is enough of such activity to give many childless women the sense that they are missing something.

Among the most powerful motives for bearing children must be listed the love of children. This has enough power in many persons to cause it to appear as instinctive. The analogy of parental love in the human with the behavior of lower mammals in their relations to their offspring may seem very close. But not all persons like children, not even all those who produce them. Full analysis is not possible, but it is conceivable that the richness of a parent's affection for his child may come from a mixture of sentiments such

---

[17] A recent study indicates the relation of birth control and the birth rate as affected by religious attitudes. A sample of 136 southern urban Negro mothers was interviewed on the matter of birth control and about half—sixty-seven—had unfavorable attitudes. The most common objection was given on religious grounds, both by mothers without stated religious affiliations and by those who belonged to churches. Women spoke of the practice of birth control as being no less sinful than infanticide. A woman with nine children called birth control ". . . the most ungodly thing I ever heard of," and considered the bearing of children a "womanly duty" whether or not they were born in wedlock. The attitude is shown to be related to actual number of children born: about twice as many women with one-child families had favorable attitudes toward birth control as had unfavorable attitudes, and about twice as many women with four or more children had unfavorable attitudes as had favorable attitudes toward the practice. It must be recognized that various factors are involved here besides a direct relation of religious attitudes and the birth rate, but it appears likely that these attitudes are an important part of the result. See Preston Valien and Alberta Price Fitzgerald, "Attitudes of the Negro Mother toward Birth Control," *American Journal of Sociology*, LV, No. 3 (1949), 279-83.

as the marveling at the completeness of the tiny body, amusement at the fumbling and groping of the developing person, pride concerning the feat of having created a human being, a sense of flattery at the physical resemblance, a moving sense of responsibility for the future welfare of the infant, and an engaging set of plans for future activities during the years to come. Whatever the nature of this motive, it appears to be both complex and acquired, and to many persons appears first in importance.

Preliterate peoples rely on innate drives to insure a supply of children no more than do civilized societies. In general, marriage systems are more tightly organized in simple societies than in our system, and childbearing is highly valued and encouraged by explicit sanctions. Among some of the Bantu peoples of Africa, for example, negotiations for a wife frequently begin at the time of the birth of a boy, and partial payments are made over a period of years. Fertility is valued above chastity. If a wife does not produce children, she may be divorced and the payments claimed. If the husband is impotent, another male may be called upon to impregnate his wife, or if it is the wife who is sterile, she may provide an equivalent to bear children for him. A wife owes children not merely to her husband, but to his family, and if he dies without children his widow may later give to his family a child born from a later union.[18] There is no assumption, implicit or explicit, that a mating instinct alone insures a supply of children to the society.

The powerful, and, it seems, culturally universal aversion to incest is easy to conceive as instinctive in nature and has been popularly interpreted as such. In a chapter on "The Incest Tabu," however, Thomas reviews the literature and arrives at agreement with Tylor's explanation that exogamy as a system is the result of a social policy.[19] Marriage outside the immediate family means the gaining of a set of relatives, and these are valuable. They bring a welcome extension of primary group relations, and along with this enrichment and security, many social pleasures. In simple cultures, a set of brothers-in-law means new allies, friends, companions in hunting, fishing, and gardening. It means villages where one is welcome to visit. All these advantages would be missed by a man who marries his sister.[20]

18 William I. Thomas, *Primitive Behavior* (New York: McGraw-Hill Book Co., Inc., 1937), p. 114.

19 *Ibid.*, pp. 178-97.

20 Some theorists would consider this an inadequate explanation, holding that while many tabus are explicable by social policy, the powerful emotional aversion to incest is not accounted for on these grounds. But it must be borne in mind that this

The Rigidity of Institutional Motivation.—Some theorists have adopted a policy of classifying actions as instinctive if they are extremely difficult to change on the grounds that acquired behavior should readily be abandoned. Some learned activity is in fact cheerfully discontinued when it is no longer useful, but there is rigidity in acquired activity when it becomes entangled in a complex system. According to any principle of "least effort," if such a principle were dominant in human activity, there should be no difficulty in adopting simplified spelling for the English language. Yet in spite of repeated organized efforts, little progress has been made toward simplification. Even the prestige of Theodore Roosevelt, who gave enthusiastic support to the reform during his occupancy of the White House, did not weigh sufficiently to break down the institutional resistance of the organized language.

A similar example is furnished by the attempt in Sweden to get rid of a cumbersome linguistic usage.[21] This concerned the use of the plural personal pronoun *ni* (you) which is used both as a distinguished form of respect and also, in the case of a person of high status addressing one of lower status, as an appellation of intolerable disrespect. In ordinary intercourse it is virtually tabu. Therefore, except for persons who are intimate enough to use *du* with one another, no word is available for "you," and awkward circumlocutions are made necessary. One may not ask, "Do you remember where you put your bag when you left?" but must put it in some such manner as "Does the young lady remember where the young lady put the young lady's bag when the young lady left?" According to Thomas, organizations have worked for years to persuade the Swedish people to use *ni*. Parliament once subsidized a pamphlet to help out, and a proposal was made that persons willing to do so wear a button reading, "*Ni* is used here." Such a projected reform, however, met the same kind of barrier as does simplified spelling.

Similar efforts have been made from time to time to abolish the custom of tipping. At the beginning of the Boy Scout movement,

emotional aversion is not present in all persons, and, in spite of the strong prohibition against the practice, incest does occur. Furthermore, behavior which threatens in a general way any social system often does invoke passionate opposition by those persons who sense the significance of the threat to their way of life, as any author or public speaker can learn if he attacks our family system, governmental system, or fundamental economic ways. There is in any society a general, if somewhat vague, sense of the importance of the social organization to all the satisfactions of life, and any words or actions which appear to have the potentiality of destroying the system can create a panicky reaction.

[21] *Ibid.,* p. 95.

scouts were forbidden to accept tips. Nontipping hotels and restaurants have tried from time to time to break the practice. A determined effort was made during the late 1940's by the Chesapeake and Ohio Railroad, which increased the wages of dining car waiters and forbade them to accept tips. Nevertheless, customers continued to offer tips and waiters continued to accept them, and in late spring of 1950 the railroad company abandoned the experiment. A somewhat similar experience has been noted among luggage handlers for those railroads which tried to substitute a fixed fee for their redcaps and abolish the tip. Similarly, at airports where signs indicate that a tip for the men who issue suitcases from the luggage room is not necessary, many passengers may be seen offering tips, which are never refused.

A standard, institutionalized practice in society resists change or abolition because it is supported by an organized set of sentiments and attitudes. In order to avoid awkwardness on the occasion of the change, sudden alterations of various kinds of practices and attitudes would be necessary. No large proportion of persons is willing to depart from standards to the extent that they suffer embarrassment and experience confusion. Institutional motivation is complex and it is organized; to go along with it means smoothness and harmony with other persons, to depart from it involves an assortment of penalties. At its strongest, as in the case of our complex of marriage and family practices, institutional motivation achieves an impressive likeness to the kind of innate motivation that is apparently observed in the behavior of simpler animals.

Life Organization.—In the normal progress of life in an organized society, each person tends to achieve some unity in his own patterns of activity and attitudes. This reconciliation of the various aspects of life also extends to future expectations, so that plans and goals are brought into a kind of system, which Thomas has referred to as "life organization."

To illustrate: A young man in college may conceive of his future in terms of a career as an attorney, member of a prominent firm, and well-known and highly respected person in his community. He may imagine owning a good home in the best residential neighborhood, having an attractive and popular wife and a son and daughter. He sees himself as a member of one of the best country clubs, with a respectable golf game. He conceives that before his own retirement his children will be well established in their adult callings, and supplied with healthy and attractive children of their own. Such expectations themselves operate as sources of motivation, continuing over the years of life. In college, the choice of courses of study is made with reference to the plan for a career. To some extent, friendships are guided by the vision of the future occupation and place in the community. Courtship behavior in college, as we have already seen, is influenced by the wish to be married and to found a family. Distractions and temptations are avoided in favor of study and decorous behavior, again because of their relation to the life plan.

This then is a distinctly human tendency in motivation. Far from being at the mercy of a limited set of instincts or similar drives, or from any physiological needs, man is motivated to a great extent by images, created by himself out of material provided in his society. These motives are organized, systematic, and powerful; not merely a fragile layer over the inflexible brute nature; not a thin veneer of civilization covering the basic savagery beneath. In the hierarchy of motivating elements of the normal person, those impulses deriving from the life organization belong at the top.[22]

The manner in which the life organization is acquired varies from person to person, but it is always actively organized by him, and always contains elements supplied by other persons. In some cases a young man absorbs most of the conception within his own family life. A physician's son may never remember making a decision of his own to follow his father's occupation and to pattern his life after that of his father; his absorption of the way of life at home is ordinarily a slow and inconspicuous process. In other cases, the suggestions may come from friends or acquaintances outside the family, or even through the inspiration of reading. Often it is the combination of all these and other sources, together with a certain amount of invention. It is always a constructed thing, however, existing in imagination, subject to revision, but with the possibility of being the most dominant and rigid motivating force in the whole experience of the person. It gains further strength and rigidity

[22] There are, of course, variations in the tightness and degree of unity achieved by various persons in their life organizations. In general, a person with a highly unified life organization is more completely dominated by it, while persons with very little fixed conception of a future may be dominated much more by segmental motives such as hunger, thirst, boredom, sex impulses, and the like. In the latter case the person is susceptible to the appeal of the vices. See R. E. L. Faris, chap. vii, *Social Disorganization* (The Ronald Press Co., New York: 1948).

Collapse of the life organization, in cases where it has been dominant over the behavior, may be a major catastrophe, and appears to be involved in many cases of suicide and in general personality disorganizations. See Chapter 12 for a discussion of this form of abnormal behavior.

by becoming integrated into the organized expectations and wishes of other members of the family, of friends and even the general public, so that it loses its character as a private affair and gains motivational force from the integrated influences of a social organization.

MORALE AS SOCIAL DOMINANCE OF MOTIVATION

As stated earlier, man derives his experiences and his satisfactions in processes, not in states, and, by virtue of his acquired social nature, he normally prefers experiences in organized social activity. The person who really wants to be free from social influence is exceptional and, if he achieves his wish, comes to be abnormal. Man knows the experience of morale—the willing, enthusiastic subordination to social organization.

Not all organizations for cooperation achieve high morale. The conditions for it are generally lacking when prisoners are given a task in which they have no interest, or in the case of military units composed of men who do not believe in their task or who believe it to be hopeless. Low morale is observable in some factories and work crews where hostility toward management is common. Low morale may develop in organizations which formerly had high morale, when conditions governing morale change.

A convenient illustration of high morale is offered by the example of a highly integrated and efficient athletic team. Among the members of a college football team, there are certain variable and important classes of mental characteristics which are functionally related to the maintenance of the pattern of integration and to effective cooperative action in the face of emergencies. The members of the team all accept the general purpose of the team activity—that of winning games and bringing honor or prestige to their team and to their college. Each member also knows how his own role contributes to that purpose. If morale is really high, each is willing to suppress those of his individual interests which are not in harmony with the aim of the team—a backfield man thus will pass the ball to a teammate who has a better chance of scoring, rather than make an effort to carry the ball himself in the hope of obtaining personal credit for a score. It is to the advantage of the team, furthermore, if each member has general confidence in the ability and the determination of all the other members to carry out their roles effectively—for example, the back who is assigned to make a long forward pass may better concentrate on his own skill and timing if he has a generalized confidence that the other members of his team will perform their roles in accordance with the pattern of the play.[23]

In general, all individualistic concerns, even the sensations of fatigue and pain, diminish or disappear among the members of a group in which morale is high. The experience of each member is typically a sense of high enthusiasm for the activity and a feeling that he shares in the group achievement, no matter what the nature of his particular role may be. It is probably in an active group with high morale that individualistic motivation is at its minimum and the person is most thoroughly dominated and guided by a collectivity.[24]

The teams of armed forces at war are closely analogous to athletic teams in this respect. Indoctrination is an essential; the soldiers must in some way believe in the necessity of fighting and in the rightness of their cause, although it probably is not necessary for each one to have a detailed conception of war aims. For many it may be enough to be able to say, "This is my country, and it is in a fight. Therefore, this is my fight too." It is desirable that a soldier know his role and how it fits into the whole pattern; without this there may be a sense that his activity is not worth while and therefore a loss of confidence in the enterprise. The requirement of the suppression of individualistic interests is more severe than in mere athletic contests, for the teamwork in a military organization may involve exposure to great danger or even, at times, a requirement of direct sacrifice of life. Where morale is high, achievement of such sacrifice is not unusual, but it will not com-

---

[23] Confidence in the teamwork is to be distinguished from complacency concerning success. It is possible for a team to be losing the game without becoming disorganized and without the disintegration of the equilibrium of confidence, just as a well-trained army may retire in good order in the face of superior force. Overconfidence is generally recognized to be a danger to an athletic team or a military organization.

[24] One may contend that the drives are still individual, even biological, in character, but under these circumstances the biological drives are satisfied in this particular manner. There is no method available, however, to trace a connection between any specified biological drives and such organized behavior, and it is frequently observed that a group with high morale can motivate its members more powerfully than any obvious physiological need such as hunger, avoidance of discomfort, or even the need to survive. The original motivation here would appear to be that general tendency to function presented in Chapter 3, but so canalized and transformed by social experience that it no longer is useful in explaining the details of behavior.

Social activity is not detached from physiology; it works through physiology. Morale may achieve part of its effect on the indifference to discomfort by means of endocrine secretions, but it is the social process that starts the secretions, not the other way around.

monly occur in armies disintegrating in panic. The equilibrium of confidence enables each section of a battle line to hold or to advance according to plan, the soldiers realizing that the inter-related parts of the army will carry out their tasks in the general pattern. Failure of one element to achieve its task does not nec-essarily shatter the organization, but ruptures in the general struc-ture of the team itself, for any reason, may start the process of panic.

The nature of morale and the methods of building it are widely misunderstood by the general public. Many persons conceive of morale in terms of minor comforts and pleasures, and a consider-able amount of "morale activity" during wartime consists of the provision of dances, shows, and various pleasures for soldiers. To many, "civilian morale" meant plenty of nylon hosiery, sugar and coffee, gasoline, and horse-racing. To a professional soldier, how-ever, the matter is seen very differently:

It is a serious misuse of the term and misunderstanding of the facts to say that morale is high when the table is bounteous and the warm overcoat fits well and there are clean sheets on the comfortable bed. Physically com-fortable conditions are pleasant, and they are conducive to health and well-being; there is no virtue per se in asceticism or in hardship. Nevertheless, physically comfortable surroundings have only this connection with a sol-dier's morale: he learns with experience and observation about what degree of ease and good living is compatible with military performance and how much it is reasonable to expect and under what training conditions. . . .

Within the limits of good sense, having in mind the avoidance of damage by excessive fatigue, men learn by maneuvers in the field what it is like to be red-eyed with weariness and still to carry on with planning and doing. It makes veterans of them, as nearly as may be short of battle with live ammunition. Parade-ground exercises will not teach men how to move a mechanized outfit rapidly through the black night, without lights, to points co-ordinated with the movements of other members of the intricately or-ganized team. Actually to have done it, even once, is a morale-builder of indispensable value.[25]

The above concept of morale has been the basis of much of military training policy, and has often produced the desired result. An illustration is furnished by the Marine Corps training program which turns ordinary recruits into leathernecks who are proud of their branch of service and noted for fighting qualities, courage, and high morale. The method of training in the ten weeks of "boot camp" was described in a recent article by a Marine veteran

[25] From Brigadier General James A. Ulio, U.S.A., "Military Morale," *American Journal of Sociology*, XLVII, No. 3 (1941), 324, 328.

of two Pacific assault landings and wearer of the Bronze Star with the Combat "V." [26] The first step in the process involves the stripping of all existing status from the new recruits so that they start from the lowest possible position, without pride and without the recognized possession of relevant knowledge and skills. On arrival at the training camp, they are roughly taken in hand by a corporal who defines them by his manner and by explicit verbiage as incompetent beginners. The principle is that "every recruit must land on Parris Island [the training station] in utter, crushing defeat." They are made to strip, given a close haircut while naked before mirrors, rudely deloused by spray guns, and issued rough clothing. As soon as they can get dressed, the drilling begins. The discipline is harsh and small deviations from rule are quickly crushed by sharp reprimands from the noncommissioned officers.

In the first indoctrination lecture they are again told directly that they are stupid, unimpressive persons, and that they will have to *earn* their right to be called Marines. They are required to adopt Navy language, and they are set at menial tasks, including the scrubbing of toilet bowls. All tasks, from saluting to bedmaking, must be done to perfection; the effort is exhausting.

The first night of sleep is from 10 P.M. until 4:30 A.M. A quick breakfast is followed by a taxing physical exercise drill—falling and rising, squatting and doing the duckwaddle forward and backward, various bends, push-ups, and sprints. By the end of the first session of this activity, according to the Marine who describes the process, resentment begins to smolder in most of the recruits. This resentment, however, eventually changes to pride when they have survived weeks of such ordeals.

The regime continues to be severe, and the punishments harsh. A man who drops his rifle may have to sleep on eight rifles that night. A man who leaves an activity to get a drink of water may be ordered to carry a full bucket of water for the next two days. The recruits thus learn to keep going in hot weather and cold, through rain and mud, disregarding the bites of insects and other annoyances and discomforts—all the time learning and growing stronger and more self-confident.

Along with the physical and military skills are taught the history and traditions of the Marine Corps, using motion pictures of some of the recent actions at places like Peleliu and Tarawa. The recruits learn that Marines do not break under fire, and that they

[26] James Finan, "The Making of a Leatherneck," *The Reader's Digest,* April, 1951, pp. 1-5.

can trust one another not to panic. They see how organization is maintained in the face of casualties so disastrous that a sergeant has to perform the functions of a general. At the completion of boot training, they are Marines, and though more training is to follow, with even greater hardships and danger, they will not again be treated as boots. The same sergeant who treated them with contempt ten weeks earlier now tells them that he would be proud to have any of them on his fire team.

At a few points there is objective research confirmation of the conception of morale stated here. A considerable amount of attention was paid to the problem of morale by the staff of the Research Branch, Information and Education Division of the Army during the Second World War.[27] The factor of indoctrination was clearly shown to be related to effective performance. It was further shown, by a series of statistical trials, that those soldiers who said they never had doubts that the war was worth fighting differed from other soldiers in registering higher percentages of: good spirits and feelings, of having a pretty good time in the Army; lack of worry or agitation; desire for combat; sense of their jobs being worth while; satisfaction with their work in the Army; belief that ability would probably be rewarded with promotion, and similar states of mind.[28] It is presumed that this complex of statements reflects to some extent the level of morale.

The importance of each person's having some conception of how his role fits into the whole is shown by the observation that soldiers, especially newly drafted soldiers, dislike being ordered to do something without knowing just what they are supposed to accomplish and why. Failure to understand this is associated with low morale.[29]

The role of general confidence in the organization is at least hinted at by a study of morale in relation to confidence in officers.[30] Two naval air squadrons in the Pacific area were studied, one having many indications of high morale, the other apparently having low morale. The men in each squadron were asked to choose those whom they would prefer to fly with. The results indicated a

---

[27] Fully reported in the four volumes, Samuel A. Stouffer *et al., Studies in Social Psychology During World War II* (Princeton: Princeton University Press, 1949).

[28] *Ibid.,* I, 460.

[29] *Ibid.,* p. 70 f.

[30] J. G. Jenkins, "The Nominating Technique, Its Uses and Limitations," paper delivered at the Eastern Psychological Association Annual Meeting, Atlantic City, April, 1947. Reported in David Krech and R. S. Crutchfield, *Theory and Problems of Social Psychology* (New York: McGraw-Hill Book Co., Inc., 1948), pp. 405-7.

marked contrast between the two squadrons. The high-morale squadron members, in general, preferred their fellows, including their officers. The commanding officer was chosen by eight of the men, and the executive officer by six. No choices were made outside the squadron, and no subcliques appeared within the squadron in the pattern of choices. In the low-morale squadron, no members chose their commanding officer or their executive officer, and nine votes rejected the latter. Four choices were made outside the squadron, and there were two subcliques of four men each. The important difference between the two groups appears to have been that in one group the members had confidence in one another and in the other group they did not.

The conception that the level of morale is actually related to motivation and makes a real difference in the quality of action is supported by several observations. Companies of soldiers in training were asked such questions as, "How well do you think you would fight?" and "Do you worry about injury in combat?" Three months later, after actual trial in battle, these soldiers were classified according to their grade of combat performance; above average, average, or below average. The expressed attitudes turned out to be related to combat performance, with men possessing better levels of performance having previously shown the attitudes more favorable to combat. In this experiment, the factors of age, marital status, education, AGCT and mechanical aptitude scores were all held constant by matching.[31]

Further evidence of this relation is provided by observations of the frequencies of nonbattle casualty rates consisting of neuropsychiatric cases, presumed to be reflection of low morale. The index used was the number of nonbattle casualties, divided by the average number of men available per day. High rates were observed in army groups in which unwillingness for combat as well as low confidence in the stamina and skill of the unit were common. A comparison of the best three, the medium three and the worst three companies in a unit showed consistent differences in the incidence of nonbattle casualties. When the three companies were graded into best, medium, and worst on the basis of scores achieved on the test of willingness for combat, the nonbattle casualty rates were, respectively, 17.3, 25.1, and 28.2. When the companies were graded on the basis of the results obtained in the test of confidence in combat stamina, the nonbattle casualty indices were 19.0, 23.8, and 26.8. A similar correspondence of results was obtained when

[31] Stouffer et al., op. cit., Vol. I, pp. 30 ff.

the companies were classified according to their attitudes toward their own combat skill. In those companies in which a low level of morale was shown by the scores obtained on the tests of willingness for combat, and confidence in battle stamina or skill, the element of fear seems to have had a greater chance to dominate, producing, in extreme cases, the abnormal reaction that is considered as a nonbattle casualty. An attempt to correlate nonbattle casualties with the attitudes of army groups toward battle and their own capabilities was attempted with army groups that had seen action in the Normandy offensive. Much the same results were obtained.[32]

The above comparisons and correlations thus show that those soldiers who tended to develop the characteristic neurotic symptoms to the extent of becoming nonbattle casualties were those who were exceptionally self-centered. Their fear made them less willing to participate in combat and more prepared to escape combat on impulse. They differed from other soldiers not in having fear, for practically all soldiers experience fear when danger is present, but in the extent to which they took their own fear seriously and let it dominate them. They were also set apart from the normal soldiers in having less than average confidence in their own combat skill as individuals, and in not being sufficiently good members of the team as a whole to derive support and confidence from the spirit of the group. Their personal dispositions were paramount over collective interests. Their behavior constituted a departure from normal sense of responsibility to the group—a condition which appears to reflect a partial isolation from ordinary social sources of motivation.

Social organization may be viewed as having various degrees of effectiveness and domination over individuals. At the one extreme is the closely knit, harmonious, enthusiastic, and dedicated group in which each member willingly and eagerly subordinates his every interest to the general aims of the groups, and derives his satisfactions from the realization that the teamwork is effective and that the group is making progress toward success. Such a group has high morale.[33] Its members care little for individualistic pleasures and are capable of disregarding fatigue, pain, and danger if it is necessary to do so in the course of the group activity.

[32] *Ibid.*, Vol. II, pp. 6-13.

[33] The concept of "individual morale" is used by some writers in reference to the characteristics of persons who are involved in groups in which morale is high. Confusion is avoided, however, if "morale" is reserved for the condition of a group and if the reflections of it in the members are described by other words.

On the other extreme is the condition of disorganization, in which most of or all the characteristics of effective teamwork are lacking. The domination of the behavior of persons by the general interest of the group becomes weak or disappears entirely. Unless these persons are absorbed in other groups their most individualistic traits become dominant. An illustration is afforded by the phenomenon of the panic or rout, in which the theme is "every man for himself."

In most of our social relations we are somewhere between the two conditions described above. Morale is often high in a militant religious sect, particularly during the early stages of its expansion. There is a common condition of moderately high morale among the students, administration, and faculties of most colleges and universities. Some business firms show evidence of having satisfactory morale. Many others do not, however, and a large body of research literature is being developed on the problems of low industrial morale. Morale is a variable characteristic of family life, and perhaps also of community life. Low morale in these aspects of social organization may be a part of the cause of rebellious and destructive behavior of teen-age youth. National morale in wartime may be estimated by the frequency of individualistic behavior which is contrary to the general interest—hoarding, violation of rationing rules, evasion of wartime restrictions, and the like, and is likely to be at a low point at the time of decisive national defeat. Perhaps the extreme degree of lack of morale has occurred among persons held in concentration camps during the Second World War. In some cases extreme demoralization apparently became general. The prisoners were not assimilated into the social organization of their conquerors, and were given little opportunity to rebuild an organization among themselves. Individualistic behavior toward one another was, in fact, encouraged by their conquerors by rewards for betrayal of violators of rules and similar measures. Some descriptions by survivors indicate that many persons lost virtually all their sense of loyalty to comrades and conducted themselves with only their own survival in mind. In such an atmosphere, there is no possibility of social organization and morale is nonexistent.

SUMMARY

The search for the elements of human motivation in internal processes of physiology failed to give any satisfactory key to the explanation of complex social behavior.[34] Therefore it becomes necessary to look for other principles of motivation. Social sources may be shown to canalize the original generalized need to function into specific preferences, and, in this sense, culture may be said to create motives. Culture does not produce the necessity for nutrition, but it always produces a specific set of food preferences. In the same way, it creates preferences in clothing styles, architecture, music, manners, and a great variety of the other aspects of life. It fuses these preferences into complexes which are, physiologically, entirely arbitrary. At its most powerful, social motivation apparently is capable of overruling any individualistic motive, even that of self-preservation.

Devices which, like money, have little intrinsic appeal to the human, may nevertheless in time become powerful incentives by virtue of their currency and storage functions—that is, their capacity to be translated into many different kinds of satisfactions immediately or at any future time. These storage and exchange functions appear to be part of the general and strong appeal of sociability, interest in prestige or status, desire for self-development, and perhaps other interests formerly considered fundamental motives rooted in biology.

Social motivation acquires an additional force if it is maintained by institutional forces. Behavior which is standardized, and about which a variety of organized relations are built, is difficult to resist, even when large numbers of persons are determined to do so. Perhaps a majority of a population could be persuaded to oppose the custom of tipping or to favor the simplification of spelling, but the fact that the practices are deeply rooted in an institutional complex has so far frustrated attempts at reform. Ordinarily, however, institutional arrangements are not opposed, but rather tend to be accepted as desirable, or even natural. Persons who wilfully or accidentally behave counter to institutional demands are brought into line by a variety of pressures from different sources so that they normally learn that conformity is the most satisfactory course of behavior. We thus are governed in a variety of ways without necessarily feeling governed or sensing any desire to resist.

[34] The conviction is not abandoned by all investigators, however. In the *Scientific American*, March, 1950, p. 39, J. H. Masserman states as one of four simple dogmatic principles of biodynamics applicable to both animal and human behavior: "All behavior is actuated by the current physical needs of the organism in the processes of survival, growth, and procreation." His illustrations in this article, however, are drawn from the behavior of cats. He does not attempt the far more difficult matter of erecting a bridge between the above hypothesis and the behavior of, say, an old man who plants an orchard without hope of living to enjoy its fruit.

The institutional system inculcates upon its members as they participate in it, a system of preferences which constitutes the individual aspect of the social process—internal motivation derived from external sources.

Institutional systems become intertwined with biological needs, not only providing means of efficient gratification, but adding a variety of elements of a totally social nature. Mating behavior is directed by the great complex of marriage and family systems, courtship customs, and the romantic complex of attitudes and practices. Childbearing is not left to nature, but is institutionally instigated by all human societies: even the function of eating becomes involved in institutional complexes with mealtime rituals and special banquets, feast celebrations, and picnics.

When organization reaches its greatest efficiency, a condition known as high morale is observable. Here the harmony of the members with the whole group is at its maximum and the members want nothing better than the progress of the group toward its objectives. The dominance of the collective over the individual is virtually complete, and involves on the part of its members a disregard of individualistic interests and feelings and an enthusiastic dedication to their roles.

When there is no opposition between the person and his social organizations, he not only has no sense of being dominated but even feels a power and experiences a freedom which are highly satisfying. It will be obvious to any reader, however, that this condition is not the lot of most persons any large part of the time. All civilized societies, and perhaps most societies of any kind, are in a perpetual condition of change and partial disorganization so that persons experience conflicts and frustrations, divided loyalties, and failures of various kinds along with their good times in life. Individuals become differentiated from one another in various ways, as is shown in later chapters, and do not go through life in smooth, colorless conformity. Rather, they undergo, for the most part, a rich variety of emotional experiences in their various encounters with the complexities of their separate careers.

SELECTED REFERENCES

American Journal of Sociology, Issue on "National Morale," XLVII, No. 3 (1941). Contains a number of papers on morale by representatives of various fields of knowledge.

BLUMER, HERBERT. "Morale," in *American Society in Wartime* (edited by W. F. Ogburn). Chicago: University of Chicago Press, 1943. A clear sociological statement on morale.

MURPHY, GARDNER. *Personality: A Biosocial Approach to Origins and Structure.* New York: Harper & Bros., 1947. See chap. viii.

STOUFFER, SAMUEL, *et al. Studies in Social Psychology in World War II.* Princeton: Princeton University Press, 1949. Vols. I and II, *The American Soldier.* Contains original research dealing with social motivation and morale.

THOMAS, WILLIAM I. *Primitive Behavior.* New York: McGraw-Hill Book Co., 1937. Contains a rich store of descriptive material on the variation of behavior in different cultures.

Chapter 5

THE EMERGENCE OF CONSCIOUSNESS

THE STUDY of human behavior has gone through several phases in the treatment of the subject of consciousness. For a period of its history, psychology was conceived mainly as the study of consciousness, but this viewpoint receded in the face of strong criticism. In this nineteenth century phase, the concept of consciousness was not clearly defined and not at all well understood. With some justification, critics found it to be somewhat vague and even mystical, and in time undertook a direct challenge of the utility of the concept.

In some theories, consciousness was conceded an existence, but as a completely nonfunctioning faculty of the mind that looked on without playing even a causal role in behavior.

On the other hand, some theorists, including John B. Watson and other extreme behaviorists of the early period of this school of thought, flatly disposed of the concept, and preferred to deal in psychology only with observable activity, virtually denying the existence of anything else. Their hope and intention was to construct a rigid scientific psychology on the basis of connections through a reflex arc between observable and measurable stimuli which originate or cause activity, and observable and measurable responses which result. The connections between stimuli and responses were assumed to be stable, so prediction and control of behavior were apparently possible when stimuli could be known. Changes could be made through the process of conditioning in these connections, thus allowing for learning and adaptation of various kinds. Thus there flourished for two or three decades a theory of human psychology that had no place for consciousness.

For reasons developed in the present chapter, however, this approach did not succeed. Stimuli do not start the process of activity, but are selected and are interpreted in the course of action. The knowledge of objective stimuli does not afford predictability of response in the human because of alterations performed on the stimuli in conscious activity. It became apparent that consciousness could not be disregarded; its function in behavior had to be recognized. It has become possible now to provide a plausible analysis of the nature and operation of consciousness, and, as the chapter title indicates, to offer an explanation of how it comes into being during the course of activity.

INADEQUACY OF THE CONCEPT OF CONDITIONING

There is no intention here of denying that such a process as the conditioning of responses exists or that it accounts for certain details of human behavior. There is a rich body of experimental material revealing the operation of the process on human beings as well as on animals from snails to monkeys. In order to comprehend the reason for the salivation in one of Pavlov's laboratory dogs, at a particular time, it may be essential to know that the salivation response had been conditioned to the sound of a bell and that the bell had sounded immediately before the salivation took place. Thus a minor detail of canine behavior is in part explained by reference to the mechanism of the conditioned response.

Laboratory experiment has provided abundant information on conditioning of responses in human subjects also. Both reflexes and acquired actions can be called out by conditioned stimuli, and among the responses studied in this manner are winking, opening of the mouth, contraction of the pupil of the eye, the knee jerk, and lifting the finger among others. There is little doubt that in the course of daily life most persons undergo accidental conditioning. The student who walks to lunch daily, passing the chimes tower with internal sensations of hunger, may in time experience hunger pangs on the occasion of the chiming of the bells alone. It is probable that many persons are startled on cues which have been linked by conditioning, and it is possible that certain details of breathing changes, galvanic skin reflex, vasomotor constriction, vasodilation, and other reactions take place by virtue of accidental conditioning.

The inadequacy of the concept of conditioning lies in its failure to aid in the explanation of complex activity, of learning of new patterns of actions, and of consciousness. Attempts have been made, and are made still, to have the concept serve one or more of these purposes, but careful inspection appears to reveal that the attempts have not been, and probably cannot be, successful.

A great many investigators have neglected to observe one of the most fundamental difficulties of the conditioning process as an explanation of the acquisition of new behavior. The difficulty

is this: *no new response is acquired in the process of conditioning.*
There is no learning in the ordinary sense of the word at all. The
change of the type produced by conditioning occurs when a response that was present before the process is produced by a stimulus which formerly did not evoke it. All the novelty is in the
stimulus—a dog with twelve reflexes could be conditioned for an
indefinite time in innumerable ways without learning any new
behavior. At the end of the process he would still be a dog with
twelve reflexes. To be influenced to salivate at the sound of the
bell instead of at exposure to food is not to acquire new behavior.
For a human to experience the knee jerk on the occasion of a flash
of light provides for no gain in skill. The conditioned response is
the same old response, evoked by a new signal.

In the effort to make the conditioning process serve as an explanation of the learning of new behavior, many theorists have begun
with a careful and exact statement of the original Pavlov salivation
experiment with dogs, showing the process at the start to be a linkage of S_1, the presentation of food, with R_1, and at the end to be a
linkage of S_2, the sounding of a bell with R_1. This statement is
accurate enough, but does not produce an R_2 or any other new
response. In order to get some novelty of action in the response,
it is necessary to alter the meanings of one or more of the three
terms—stimulus, conditioning, and response. This is often done
unwittingly, but sometimes intentionally and accompanied by jus-
tifying arguments.[1] One investigator says, for example, "After a
sufficient number of trials, i.e., pairings of the conditioned stimulus
with the unconditioned S-R combination, the conditioned stimulus
by itself, without the aid of the unconditioned stimulus, will call
forth *a new response,* the CR, with which it has never previously
been associated."[2] In this proposition, however, it is apparently
entirely overlooked that all the novelty is in the stimulus. To refer
to the new CR is to neglect the fact that only the stimulus is new.

An attempt is made by the same investigator to find novelty in a
mixture of two responses by virtue of the association of the two
stimuli that were attached to them.

---

[1] Support for this statement is so abundant in the vast literature on conditioning
and learning that it is impossible to present all the examples in a moderate space.
An unprejudiced reader, having once become aware of the verbal shifts, cannot fail
to find this error which is almost embarrassingly obvious in many a notable text in
psychology.

[2] By permission from W. N. Kellogg, "Conditioning and Motor Learning," chap.
ii in *Methods of Psychology* edited by T. G. Andrews; published by John Wiley &
Sons, Inc., 1948, p. 46. Italics by the present author.

In the conditioning of the eyewink, for example, three separate winks may occur on any given trial, each one of which is distinct from the others. The original or unconditional stimulus (S_1)—a puff of air blown upon the cornea of the eye—will produce a full-sized unconditioned blink (R_1). The conditioned stimulus (S_2), which is a beam of light directed into the pupil, will cause a smaller wink (R_2). If S_2 is presented slightly before S_1 for a sufficient number of trials, still a third wink, the CR, will appear. There are then three responses occurring in order on any given trial: R_2, the CR, and R_1. *The CR is the new and original element of the three and is an outgrowth of the conditioning situation alone. It is the learned feature of the entire sequence.*[3]

The terminology employed in the above statement, involving the use of R_2, the CR, and R_1, somewhat obscures the fact that each of these three is a wink of the eye, differing only in intensity. There is no evidence that anything whatever is learned, and it is extremely unlikely that the subjects even learned any degree of winking in the course of the experiment—they undoubtedly possessed all degrees of winking before they encountered the laboratory. The statement that the CR is new and original is clearly inaccurate. No mechanism of learning in the sense of acquiring new behavior is in any way provided.[4]

A recent review of the matter has produced the following judgment on the standards of clarity in the use of the concept of conditioning:

About one third of those who define the terms strictly as a substitute stimulus process, commit notable violations of their definition. . . . Of those not defining terms, about two thirds use the term more broadly than a strict

[3] *Ibid.*, p. 47. Italics by the present author. The research referred to is by E. R. Hilgard, "The Nature of the Conditioned Response: I. The Case for and Against Stimulus-Substitution," *Psychological Review,* XLIII (1936), 366-85.

[4] There is no intention of singling out this particular investigator for adhering to an effort in which so many competent persons have had hopes. In justice to him, and perhaps to others, it should be pointed out that the concluding statement of the chapter seems to reveal an emerging recognition of the difficulty which arises with the standard formulation of the concept of conditioning advanced a few pages before. "From the point of view of experimental psychology, conditioning is *not so much a kind of learning* as it is a basic laboratory technique for the study of the learning process. It is a *method* which specializes in the analysis of small, definable units, like specific movements to specific stimuli, rather than in gross or generalized behavior." *Ibid.*, pp. 58-59. The present chapter will show, however, that it may be a serious error to hope that all complex human behavior is explainable on the same basis of these small, definable units like specific movements coupled to specific stimuli. It is entirely proper to cultivate the values of the scientific experiment, and an understandable temptation to choose to investigate those problems which are most conveniently accessible to laboratory techniques. There is less justification, however, for the claim that the processes and principles revealed in the simplified situation account for all the complex events which are not at present subject to experimentation.

substitute stimulus definition would permit. . . . The present state of contradictory, inconsistent, and inexact usage, [which although recognizing cause and effect merely substitutes other terms for learning, contributes] no particular understanding of the psychological processes by which the cause produces the "effect" with the result that conditioning and related terms have "little communicative value." [5]

Murphy has pointed to another difficulty involved in the use of the conditioning process as an explanation of learning. Canalization, he shows, involves a consummatory element which is not necessary to conditioning. Canalization is not merely a process of conditioning.

Whatever object or form of stimulation satisfies a need becomes more and more adequate as a *satisfier*. The very form of the gastric contractions, in animal and man, depends on the food present in the stomach. The puppy eats the unaccustomed food, and the stomach cannot behave in its habitual normal way; thus the *form* of the consummatory response is altered. This is definitely something which he has learned. But it is not the same thing as to say that he is conditioned to one or the other food as he is conditioned to a bell or to a call to his kennel. The conditioning experiment involves a contingent, an adventitious connection not leading to a consummatory response. We noted that the tuning fork activates a preparatory response; indeed, a hungry dog may lick the light bulb that symbolizes food. But this does not put an end to the hunger contractions, he does not develop an acquired taste for light bulbs as a preferred means of satisfying hunger. In canalization we are dealing not merely with a signal that prepares for eating, but with a modification of consummatory behavior, as shown both in the intensity of the visceral manifestations and in the sheer discrimination between familiar and unfamiliar modes of satisfaction.[6]

Murphy further points out that conditioning is subject to extinction, while canalization is apparently not. Explorers may converse and daydream about the comforts of home and prisoners may imagine their activities if at liberty with no tendency for their cravings to become extinguished because of failure of satisfaction.[7]

Summarizing the distinction between canalization, which is one form of learning, and conditioning, Murphy states:

If the term canalization marked off no specific kind of event but were purely an alternative for such terms as conditioning, positive adaptation, or

[5] Donald O. Cowgill, "Variant Meanings of the Terms Conditioning and Conditioned Response," *Journal of Social Psychology*, XXVIII (1948), 247-55. The above judgment was based on an examination of the definitions and usage of terms in seventy-one texts and reference books.

[6] Gardner Murphy, *Personality: A Biosocial Approach to Origins and Structure* (New York: Harper & Bros., 1947), pp. 165-66.

[7] *Ibid.*, p. 166.

redintegration, there would be no justification in using it; we have enough terms already. In summary, however, there appears to be (1) a general tendency for motives to move toward greater specificity; (2) evidence that the consummatory responses, not the preparatory alone, are involved; (3) a hint that such responses are not merely connected with new signals but are intrinsically modified; and (4) a strong indication that they are not subject to extinction—the trend is unidirectional.[8]

Not only is the conditioning process unable to account for learning,[9] it also fails to account for complex behavior, particularly behavior of the sort that involves consciousness. More than that, conditioning of the simple laboratory model is apparently subject, in the human, to interference by these more complex processes. In a frequently cited experiment, Razran showed how recognition and attitude dominate the conditioned response.[10] Human subjects were conditioned to salivate, much in the manner of Pavlov's dogs, to such stimuli as the beat of a metronome. The results, however, were not as uniform as in the case of the simpler animals. Three patterns of responses resulted: successful conditioning of salivation to metronome; no change in salivation; and a diminished salivation. The factor which determined type of response was attitude of the subject. If the subject recognized what the point of the experiment was he would react—by increased salivation, if his attitude was essentially sympathetic to the experimenter, and by reduced salivation if it was not. Experimenting along this line with 37 adult subjects for two years and using various types of stimuli, the investigator concluded that, unlike conditioning in animals, the operation of the process in the human is primarily determined by the attitudes of the subjects. To a certain extent, we apparently select what conditionings we are to experience.

The "stimulus-response" conception of behavior in general fails to give an account of the complexities of human mechanisms. The system is not an inert thing, waiting for an outside source of power—a stimulus—to set it into momentary action—a reflex or response—after which it returns to repose. As shown in Chapter 3, the human is an active animal, ready and eager to function and disposed to search for activity when healthy and rested without waiting for a

[8] *Ibid.*, p. 172.

[9] It has not been the intention to deal with processes of learning here, except to show that they cannot successfully be explained by the conditioned response. Further material on the learning of new behavior and perfection of skills is presented in Chapter 8.

[10] G. H. S. Razran, "Attitudinal Control of Human Conditioning," *Journal of Psychology*, II (1936), 327-37.

stimulus or actively looking for the kind of stimuli appropriate to the actions preferred at the time.

This view is supported by modern knowledge of the central nervous system. According to Hebb,

Electrophysiology of the central nervous system indicates in brief that the brain is continuously active, in all its parts, and an afferent excitation must be superimposed on already existent excitation. It is therefore impossible that the consequence of a sensory event should often be uninfluenced by the pre-existing activity.[11]

It would appear that this on-going brain activity would determine whether any sound or light or other condition would act as a stimulus at all, and what kind of a stimulus it would be. A stimulus has little chance of getting to the central nervous system unaffected.

Herrick has stated that no simple sensory impulse can reach the cerebral cortex uninfluenced by subcortical association centers at which they pick up organized responses. These are alternatives from which the choice can be made. This is necessary for the meeting of emergencies; when there is no emergency, the matter is taken care of in the subcortical centers—that is, unconsciously.

[The] afferent impulse in its passage through the spinal cord and brain stem may, before reaching the cortex, discharge collateral impulses into the lower centers of reflex coordination, from which incipient (or even actually consummated) motor responses are discharged previous to the cortical reaction. These motor discharges may, through the "back stroke" action, in turn exert an influence upon the slower cortical reaction. Thus the lower reflex response may in a literal physiological sense act *into* the cortical stimulus complex and become an integral part of it.[12]

Consciousness and attention are not, therefore, at the mercy of whatever stimulus comes along or whatever conditionings have been established, intentionally or otherwise. Consciousness is selective, and it affects not only the responses which fit in with the direction of activity, but also, by selection and interpretation, the stimuli which are to be effective. The kind of automatic response illustrated by the conditioned knee-jerk reflex is only slightly affected by the central process, and not requiring attention or consciousness for operation, is close to illustrating the pure conditioned response in man. But for the activity which requires that attention

[11] Reprinted by permission from D. O. Hebb, *The Organization of Behavior: A Neuropsychological Theory* published by John Wiley & Sons, Inc., 1949, p. 7.

[12] C. Judson Herrick, "Some Reflections on the Origin and Significance of the Cerebral Cortex," *Journal of Animal Behavior*, III (1913), 228-33.

be given to problems of conscious choices, all stimuli and responses are tentative to begin with, and evolve as the action progresses. Bode has well described this tentative character of activity:

. . . let us . . . suppose that the subject is to make one of two alternative responses, according to the nature of the stimulus. His state of expectancy is accompanied by a certain bodily "set" or preparedness for the coming event, although the precise nature of the event is a matter of uncertainty. His nervous system is in readiness to respond this way or that, or rather, it has already started to act in both of the alternate ways. If the subject is to respond with the right hand to one stimulus and with the left hand to the other, both hands are in a state of activity before the stimulus appears. The organization of the temporary reflex through the agency of the cerebral cortex could not be achieved were it not for the fact that all the movements entering into the organization are nascently aroused before the spring is touched which permits the act to unroll itself in orderly sequence.[13]

The distinction between the automatic reflex, such as swallowing, and the more complex activity which requires consciousness, is amplified by Bode as follows:

The various successive movements, then, which make up our temporary reflex achieve their relationship to one another from the fact that they are started simultaneously, and this peculiarity constitutes a distinctive feature. Apparently this feature is absent from true reflexes. An act of swallowing, performed unconsciously, may start the complicated processes of digestion, but it is merely the first act of a series. . . . There is no evidence that the movements of the stomach and of the other organs concerned in digestion must be presupposed before the act of swallowing can take place. The swallowing may start the other processes, but we cannot say that these other processes react back upon the first act and make it one of swallowing rather than something else. Yet this "back stroke" is precisely what is necessary in our reaction experiment, for it is by virtue of this fact that the organization of the temporary reflex becomes a possibility. The first response cannot take place until the last is provided for. Thus the immediate act of looking has embodied in it the activity which is to follow later. The looking is not simply with the eye, but with the hands that are to complete the response. The optical response . . . prefigures or sketches out the act of a later moment. The nervous system is enabled to act as a unit, because the movements that are to occur at a later time are represented in the first stage of the complete act. . . .[14]

In a reflex act we may suppose that the stimulus which evokes the first stage in the response is like the first in a row of upstanding bricks, which in falling knocks down another. That is, the reflex arc is built up by agencies

[13] Boyd Bode, "Consciousness and Psychology," in John Dewey *et al.*, *Creative Intelligence* (copyright 1917 by Henry Holt & Co., copyright 1944 by John Dewey). All quotations from this work by permission of the publishers. P. 233.
[14] *Ibid.*, pp. 233-34.

that are quite independent of the subsequent act. The arc is all set up and ready for use by the time the reflex act appears upon the scene. In the case of conscious activity, on the other hand, we find a very different state of affairs. The arc is not first constructed and then used, but is constructed as the act proceeds; and this progressive organization is, in the end, what is meant by conscious behavior. If the course of a reflex act may be compared with traveling in a railroad train, the progress of a conscious act is more like that of a band of explorers, who hew their path and build their bridges as they go along. The direction of the act is not determined from without but from within; the end is internal to the process.[15]

Bold efforts have been made to force the concept of conditioning to account for the complex tentative behavior that is necessarily involved in the making of conscious choices. But in order to do this, it is necessary to go far beyond known observations, and to assume that conditionings are established far more quickly and in more complex chains than can be done by experiment. The efforts to stretch the conditioning concept this far, as has already been pointed out, generally involve unrecognized alterations in the meaning of the term "conditioning." It is clear that the whole effort is based on a faith motivated, perhaps, by a desire to connect the massive body of experimental research on conditioning in animals and human subjects with practical issues of human behavior.[16]

The Nature and Function of Consciousness

In the viewpoint of certain behaviorists, consciousness has been denied. Others, however, have conceded its existence, but have considered it inaccessible to objective research. In some theories consciousness has been considered existent but epiphenomenal; that is, not involved in the process of causation of behavior, but merely a kind of spectator. In this view, it is not necessary to take consciousness into account in explaining behavior. In the present discussion, however, evidence is organized to show the purposive nature of consciousness. The process is not epiphenomenal, automatic, or constant. Consciousness occurs only when it serves to guide action, to permit efficient choices, or to overcome obstacles that interrupt or threaten to interrupt on-going pursuit of goals.

[15] *Ibid.*, pp. 238 ff.

[16] The motivated faith is well illustrated by a statement of John Dollard, made in correspondence with W. F. Ogburn and M. F. Nimkoff, and printed on page 140 of their *Sociology* (Boston: Houghton Mifflin Co., 1946). Dollard confesses, "No one knows in detail how conditioning helps build a personality, though it 'must' be so." A balanced review of the evidence, however, not only fails to show that it must be so, but makes it clear that it is almost impossible to conceive of these complex processes being based on conditioned responses.

The Automatic Character of Habit.—Consciousness is not needed for activity which has no problem, novelty, or crisis aspect to it. Actions which are performed repeatedly, in familiar situations, do not require attention and are carried on automatically. Habits are those organized acquired actions which can be performed without the aid of conscious direction. This does not mean that they are repressed into a subconscious mind, and thus unavailable to intentional recall, but merely that they do not require the valuable and complex processes of consciousness.

An infant learning to walk must put all his attention on each step, and if his attention is called to something else, he may fall. The novel or problem character of walking at this stage requires virtually all the consciousness he has. In time, as experience with walking accumulates, the infant so learns the coordinated patterns that attention is no longer required. Attention will return to the process when walking encounters an obstacle, or some new condition, but not being needed otherwise, the walking will be entirely automatic. In time the person may be able to walk in his sleep, or to walk without knowing what he is doing, or without remembering later that he had walked.

A large part of each person's daily life consists of such routines which have been reduced by practice to automatic habit requiring no consciousness for effective performance. A man may arise in the morning, wash, dress, eat, and walk to his place of business so automatically that no detail will be subject to recall later. The automatic character of routine actions is illustrated by an experience common to many persons. A man, preoccupied with other thoughts and trusting to his habits, goes to his bedroom to change his shirt before going on an errand outdoors. He removes his coat, tie, and shirt automatically, and, since this routine is a part of a general habit of undressing kept fresh by daily practice, then finds himself in night clothes and approaching his bed before he realizes his error.

Such absent-minded behavior would happen much more frequently were it not that we often find a somewhat novel or problem aspect to some of our routines, or at least have them integrated to a larger project which demands attention. A person may dress automatically some days, but give his attention to the selection of harmonious attire at other times if he is to make a public speech, apply for a position, or attend a wedding. If he is to be photographed, he may be far less automatic than usual in the details of shaving, combing the hair, and tying the necktie.

The demands made upon the facilities of consciousness have some effect on how much can be spared for such routines as dressing, walking, or casual conversation. If future contingencies of great importance press for solution, routines may have to be carried out almost entirely without the help of attention, with the possibilities of being imperfectly performed. The preoccupied man may leave his home with an ear full of shaving soap, or button his vest wrongly, or fail to notice that he is walking through mud puddles instead of around them. In conversation he may respond with inappropriate clichés, and agree automatically with absurd statements, because his attention is elsewhere.[17]

The tendency to achieve the ability to perform routine and familiar actions automatically is, of course, a great source of efficiency in human behavior. It sets free the processes of consciousness to engage in the solution of other problems. If this were not so, we would never be able to get beyond the infantile stage of walking, and even as adults, would have so to concentrate on the muscular pattern of taking the steps that we could not talk, or plan ahead while this activity was in progress.

By reducing each newly acquired activity to routines as soon as possible and setting the processes of consciousness free to solve the next problem or to organize the next higher level of complexity, we have the potentiality of an indefinite progress in skill. This is illustrated by the course of progress in such an activity as that of learning to play a piano. The infant puts his concentrated attention on pressing a single key to obtain a sound from a piano. The beginning student has to put effort into the matter of pressing keys into a definite sequence in order to make the sounds fit into the pattern of a tune. When familiarity with simple movements of fingers on the keys is achieved, attention may be spared for reading the musical notes on the score. After much practice, both reading and playing may become largely automatic, so that attention may be spared for musical expression and perhaps after that for playing in coordination with other performers. The highest levels of fine musical expression are possible only after all matters of technique are so mastered as to be automatic, and the musical compositions so thoroughly memorized that no attention is required for reading. It is the ability to reduce routines to the auto-

---

[17] It is not at all difficult to trap persons into such automatic responses. In a reception line, the smiling remark, "My grandmother just died" may actually bring the response, "How very nice!" Many persons also can be shown to say "No!" entirely automatically to almost any request—perhaps others say "Yes!" just as quickly.

matic type of performance which makes possible all high skills of this sort, which means virtually all complex human skills of any kind.

This automatic character of habit is not to be confused with popular concepts of an "unconscious mind," which is a hypothetical organization of impulses and thoughts of such repulsive character that they are repressed and inaccessible to consciousness.[18] There is no kind of censor or other barrier to prevent automatic habits from inspection by consciousness; in fact they readily do become conscious whenever they are blocked or inappropriate to the on-going activity. They are automatic for the sake of efficiency—attention is a complex process and cannot be divided many ways. The limited amount of consciousness must be reserved for those services for which there is the most urgent need and cannot be wasted on routine which can be performed without it.

Consciousness as Adaptation to Crises.—As long as everything goes smoothly, without interruption or novelty, automatic habits carry on the routine activities without the aid of consciousness. This does not mean that the person is unconscious or asleep, but that his attention is engaged with other problems, future or hypothetical, rather than with the action at hand. Consciousness only turns to the ongoing activity when there is a change. As Boring writes:

. . . perception is always a response to some change or difference in the environment. If the world were perfectly homogeneous and we were in equilibrium with it, we should experience nothing. Let some condition change suddenly, or one receptor be stimulated and another not, and we sense the fact at once.[19]

For illustration he offers the simple experiment of holding a finger in water; after a few moments of adaptation neither the pressure from water or from air is felt, but the ring where the pressures meet is felt.

The principle is illustrated by occurrences of everyday life. An audience may occupy a room for any length of time without being aware of the low hum of ventilating machinery, only to become fully conscious of a change when the motor is shut off and the sound stops. Neither of the stable conditions of sound or silence ordi-

[18] The concept of "unconscious mind" is examined at length in Chap. 6, and judged to be of doubtful utility.

[19] Reprinted by permission from *Foundations of Psychology* by E. G. Boring, H. S. Langfeld, and H. P. Weld (eds.), published by John Wiley & Sons, Inc., 1948, p. 217.

narily enters into consciousness, but the change tends to be intrusive. Similarly a motorist who is thoroughly familiar with his car may drive along without awareness of the motor noise, but have his attention quickly involved if there is a change to an unusual quality in the sound—even if the change is too small to be detected by a passenger who is unfamiliar with the particular vehicle. Also, motion which is steady is no more perceived than lack of motion, but change in rate—acceleration or deceleration—may claim attention. Where acceleration or deceleration is almost continuous, as in automobile movements in city traffic, even these are not perceived unless there is an unexpected character to them. For example, a car with an automatic clutch, which disengages when the car slows below fifteen miles an hour, may approach a stop sign in gear, decelerating until the fifteen-mile-an-hour speed is reached and the clutch disengages. At this point there is an abrupt change to a slower speed produced by friction. The sudden change in rate of deceleration often claims the attention of the driver when the fact of regular deceleration did not.

Only changes, then, appear to be able to engage the processes of consciousness.[20] A specific class or type of change, however, appears to have a priority on the facilities of consciousness. This is a change in the conditions that affect any on-going action, particularly a change which threatens to interrupt or frustrate it. A commonplace illustration is furnished by the activity of walking along a sidewalk on the way to school or office. As long as conditions are perfectly familiar, the walking is automatic.[21] But some new condition that threatens to change the process, to block the walking, readily intrudes on the attention. A broken sidewalk with a mud puddle, for example, constitutes such a crisis for the

[20] This statement may appear to some to be too extreme. One may claim that he is able to stare at an object endlessly, holding it in his consciousness. As long as we keep consciousness fastened on it, however, we are probably continuing to find novelty in the object—in its shape, texture, color, and perhaps history, function, and other aspects. When all possibility of such novelty is worn out, it may be found impossible to keep the mind from wandering to other concerns, even if the eye remains fixed on the object. Persons undoubtedly differ in the capacity to find novelty in a commonplace object, but to some extent the act of concentrating appears to force a sense of novelty even where it is unexpected. To hold attention on such a familiar short word as "eat" will soon make this word appear so strange as to make some persons have a sense of never having seen it before.

[21] Many persons have had the experience of treading a familiar path so often that at times they proceed along it so automatically that they are unable, at the end of the walk, to remember any part of it. The result is sometimes a sense of partial disorientation, possibly resulting from the total break with surroundings during the automatic walking. For a moment everything appears strange, even though the person knows he is in familiar surroundings.

on-going activity. Now consciousness is required in order to get
the person beyond the barrier to the point at which the resumption
of routine walking is possible. Consciousness has the function of
discovering the proper adaptation and selecting the activity which
will make this possible.

This crisis could not be handled by a conditioned response,
which occurs only by means of repeated associations of stimuli.
The novel character of the situation is what makes it a crisis. If
mud puddles occurred commonly in the same path, the person
would have a routine method of getting past them, and they would
not constitute a crisis. Because the situation is in some respects
unprecedented, with no routine automatically suitable, the sur-
mounting of it requires some invention. It is the function of consciousness, an exploratory process, to accomplish this.

This general function of checking up on activity as it is going on
and guiding it accordingly has recently been given a name by
Norbert Wiener. The neologism is *cybernetics*—the title of his
book on the subject, published in New York in 1948—derived from
the Greek *kybernetes,* meaning steersman. Wiener illustrates his
concept by the following statement:

Suppose that I pick up a pencil. To do this I have to move certain
muscles. Only an expert anatomist knows what all these muscles are, and
even an anatomist could hardly perform the act by a conscious exertion of
the will to contract each muscle concerned in succession. Actually what we
will is not to move individual muscles but to pick up the pencil. Once we
have determined on this, the motion of the arm and hand proceeds in such
a way that we may say that the amount by which the pencil is not yet picked
up is decreased at each stage. This part of the action is not in full consciousness.

To perform an action in such a manner, there must be a report to the
nervous system, conscious or unconscious, of the amount by which we have
failed to pick up the pencil at each instant. The report may be visual, at
least in part, but it is more generally kinesthetic, or to use a term now in
vogue, proprioceptive. If the proprioceptive sensations are wanting, and
we do not replace them by a visual or other substitute, we are unable to perform the act of picking up the pencil, and find ourselves in a state known as
ataxia. On the other hand, an excessive feedback is likely to be just as serious a handicap. In the latter case the muscles overshoot the mark and go
into an uncontrollable oscillation. This condition, often associated with
injury to the cerebellum, is known as purpose tremor.

Here, then, is a significant parallel between the workings of the nervous
system and of certain machines. The feedback principle introduces an important new idea in nerve physiology. The central nervous system no longer
appears to be a self-contained organ receiving signals from the senses and

discharging into the muscles. On the contrary, some of its most characteristic activities are explainable only as circular processes, traveling from the
nervous system into the muscles and re-entering the nervous system through
the sense organs.   This finding seems to mark a step forward in the study of
the nervous system as an integrated whole.[22]

This idea, without the term "cybernetics," may correctly be
called "a step forward," but the step was made not in 1948 by
Wiener, but at least as far back as 1896 by John Dewey in his celebrated paper on "The Reflex Arc Concept in Psychology." Wiener
has, however, extended the concept to fields other than psychology
and biology, applying it to all kinds of mechanical "feedback"
devices such as governors on steam engines, and regulators of electrical devices, calculating machines, and the like.

The essence of the process of consciousness is thus a trial-and-
error probing of a crisis. Various actions are imagined, along with
their consequences. For example, in the mud puddle crisis, the
person may first consider stepping across—i.e., he imagines himself
taking a long step. This imagined step, however, carries him a
foot or so short of the dry area and gets his shoe wet, again in his
imagination. There is thus no temptation to permit the imagined
step to be carried into overt action. Another possibility is conceived, that of walking around. But on one side there is a high
stone wall, and toward the street there is the thick mud of an
excavation; moreover, the street itself is filled with swift cars which
splash dirty water on persons passing close by. A third possibility
is to jump across, but the approach is wet and the spot required
for the takeoff has slippery mud and the image of skidding into a
bath of muddy water is vivid and repelling. A solution that offers
more promise is to move a nearby plank to form a bridge; the plank
seems long enough and the imagined crossing appears to be so successful that the idea is put into actual performance. The crisis is
then passed, and routine walking again takes over. Consciousness
is no longer required for this activity and is set free to take up whatever other problem, present or future, real or hypothetical, is then
most pressing for attention.[23]

[22] From the *Scientific American*, November 1948, p. 14.

[23] In this example, trial and error is carried on in imagination until a successful
solution is pictured. This is, of course, a quicker method than overt trial and error,
and less wasteful. The consequences of actual trial of each of the solutions would
mean wet shoes, then splashed clothing, then a bath in dirty water. Nevertheless
there are times when overt trials are used, particularly when it is difficult to imagine
the consequences. Simpler animals employ overt trial and error for many of the
problems which humans can work out in imagination. Children require actual trial
more often than adults. In daily life we often use a combination of both methods,

It would not be accurate to apply the conditioned response formula to this situation by referring to the puddle as a stimulus, and the moving of the plank as a response. At the beginning of the crisis there is neither a stimulus nor a response; activity is blocked. During the process of trial-and-error in imagination, there are tentative and unfolding stimuli and responses, incomplete and not carried into overt activity. The stimulus is not complete and sufficient to initiate behavior until the response has been tried out and found adequate. The two evolve together. As Bode points out, in the early stages of a crisis the stimulus is problematical; is it a puddle that can be jumped, or a puddle that will be a trap?

And similarly the response has neither the predetermined organization of the reflex nor the aimless character of a response that issues in a set of random movements. It is, so to speak, of a generalized character. . . . In uttering a sentence, for example, we know in advance what we are going to say, yet the sentence shapes itself into definite form only as we proceed; or perhaps we get "stuck" and by hemming and hawing bear witness that a struggle for a certain kind of organization is going on.[24]

Conscious behavior thus is seen to differ from the mechanical character of the reflex by virtue of its experimental character. The response is not fixed, but uncertain, and consciousness is a process which has as its purpose the clearing up of the uncertainty.

It seems clear, then, that conscious behavior involves a certain *process of organization* which constitutes a differential. The units entering into this process are "definitely organized systems of neural discharge," the antecedent organization of these several systems being due either to the inherited or to the acquired structure of the nervous system. Given a certain amount of plasticity, the nervous system builds up specific forms of response for certain objects or situations, and these forms of response subsequently become the material from which new organizations or new modes of response are constructed.[25]

Dewey criticized the conventional reflex arc concept as early as 1896, pointing out that the stimulus does not start the action, but becomes defined and takes its form during the action. The unit of behavior is not the arc of stimulus, central activity, and response, but on-going behavior, crisis, and reconstruction, during which both stimulus and response are in process of being evolved.

but the advance of skill involves the use of intelligence and consciousness as much as possible, and the human has a great ability for making many of his trials in imagination and saving time and trouble.

[24] Bode, *op. cit.*, p. 249.
[25] *Ibid.*, p. 237.

If one is reading a book, if one is hunting, if one is watching in a dark place on a lonely night, if one is performing a chemical experiment, in each case, . . . noise has a very different mental value; it is a different experience. In any case, what precedes the stimulus is a whole act, a sensori-motor co-ordination. What is more to the point, the "stimulus" emerges out of this coordination; it is born from it as its matrix; it represents as it were an escape from it.[26]

Bode has given a penetrating analysis of the nature of the trial-and-error process by which blocked behavior is reorganized.

This process of organization and purposive direction is exemplified in every act of attention. Is that noise, for example, a horse in the street, or is it the rain on the roof? What we find in such a situation is not a paralysis of activity, but a redirection. The incompatibility of responses is purely relative. There is indeed a mutual inhibition of the responses for hoofbeats and rain respectively, in the sense that neither has undisputed possession of the field; but this very inhibition sets free the process of attention, in which the various responses participate and cooperate. There is no static balancing of forces, but rather a process in which the conflict is simply a condition for an activity of a different kind. If I am near a window facing the street, my eye turns thither for a clue; if the appeal to wisdom be eliminated, the eye becomes unseeing and cooperates with the ear by excluding all that is irrelevant to the matter in hand. In this process the nervous system functions as a unit, with reference to the task of determining the source and character of the sound. This task or problem dominates the situation. A voice in an adjoining room may break in, but only as something to be ignored and shut out; whereas a voice in the street may become all-absorbing as possibly indicating the driver of the hypothetical horse. That is, the reason why the conflict of responses does not end in a deadlock, but in a redirection, is that a certain selectiveness of response comes into play. Out of the mass of more or less inchoate activities a certain response is selected as a rallying-point for the rest, and this selection is of a purposive character. The selection is determined by reference to the task in hand, which is to restore a certain harmony of response. Accordingly, that response is selected which gives promise of forwarding the business of the moment. By virtue of this selective character, one of the constituents of the total activity becomes exalted among its fellows and is entrusted with the function of determining further behavior.[27]

The simultaneous uncertainty of both stimulus and response is further shown in an illustration by Dewey.

But now take a child who, upon reaching for bright light . . . has sometimes had a delightful exercise, sometimes found something good to eat, and sometimes burned himself. *Now the response is not only uncertain, but the*

[26] John Dewey, *Philosophy and Civilization* (New York: G. P. Putnam's Sons, 1931), p. 238.
[27] Bode, *op. cit.*, p. 239.

stimulus is equally uncertain; one is uncertain only in so far as the other is.
The real problem may be equally well stated as either to discover the right
stimulus, to constitute the stimulus, or to discover, to constitute, the response.
The question of whether to reach or to abstain from reaching is the question, "What sort of bright light have we here? Is it the one which means
playing with one's hands, eating milk, or burning one's fingers?" The stimulus
must be constituted for the response to occur.[28]

According to Dewey, this uncertainty, expressed by tentative
or anticipatory movements, is the essence of consciousness itself.

The conscious sensation of a stimulus is not a thing or existence by itself;
it is that phase of a coordination requiring attention because, by reason of
the conflict within the coordination, it is uncertain how to complete it. Uncertainty as to the next act, whether to reach or not, gives the motive to
examining the act. The end to follow is, in this sense, the stimulus. It furnishes the motivation to attend to what has just taken place; to define it
more carefully. From this point of view the discovery of the stimulus is the
"response" to possible movement as "stimulus." We must have an anticipatory sensation, an image, of the movements that may occur, together with
their respective values, before attention will go to the seeing to break it up
as a sensation of light, and of light of this particular kind. It is the initiated
activities of reaching, which, inhibited by the conflict in the coordination,
turn around, as it were, upon the seeing, and hold it from passing over into
further act until its quality is determined. Just here the act as objective
stimulus becomes transformed into sensation as possible, or conscious, stimulus. Just here also, motion as conscious response emerges.[29]

Consciousness solves problems by looking ahead, trying out the
future first as a set of possibilities before committing overt activity.
As Bode puts it,

Future results or consequences must be converted into present stimuli; and
the accomplishment of this conversion is the miracle of consciousness. To be
conscious is to have a future possible result of present behavior embodied as
a present existence functioning as a stimulus to further behavior. Thus the
qualities of a perceptual experience may be interpreted, without exception,
as anticipations of the results of activities which are as yet in an embryonic
stage.[30]

The person never enters a crisis entirely bare of potential responses. There is a repertory of previous habits or solutions which
can be tried out, and perhaps adapted by a certain amount of inventiveness. The choices made, during the crisis or blocking of

[28] Dewey, *op. cit.,* pp. 244-45.
[29] *Ibid.,* p. 245.
[30] Bode, *op. cit.,* p. 240.

activity, are selections from this store of organized action, already in tension or partial movement but inhibited because alternate ones are competing for dominance. The successful one, to be chosen, must fit the interpreted situation somewhat as a key fits a lock. The trigger to the resumption of full overt activity is not just the final element that provides the solution, it is the organized pre-figured response fitting into the interpreted situation.

The Muscular Aspect of Consciousness.—As previously stated, the imagined responses involved in the trial-and-error process of consciousness are actual muscular behavior. Muscular tensions, usually imperceptible without the aid of instruments, actually sketch out the activity conceived of as a possible solution, as well as the reaction to the imagined consequences. Laboratory results suggest that it is impossible to think at all without some pat-terned muscular movement. A person who is told to be ready to press a reaction key at a given signal can be shown, by use of an instrument which shows pressure, to have made actual anticipatory downward pressure on the key before the signal is given and the full movement carried out.[31] In some instances, the person may even carry out the movement before the signal because of an over-intensified set, in the same manner as a football player goes offside before the play starts. This observation supports the conception that images are actions which are held in check, but which never-theless are subject to the completion tendency discussed in Chap-ter 3. An image is itself a tendency toward action, and the more vivid the image the more the tendency for it to break into full overt action.

Other experimental measurements have been made of such muscular aspects of imagery. Tongue movements have been dem-onstrated in subjects who were instructed to think of certain words. Recording instruments have shown that a person who is instructed to keep his head still, but to think of turning his head to the right, actually does make a slight movement to the right. The subject, however, generally does not realize that he has made an actual movement.[32]

It might be thought that some imagery, at least visual perception of objects in sight, might exist without the involvement of muscles,

---

[31] Boring, Langfeld and Weld, *op. cit.*, p. 49.

[32] *Ibid.*, p. 48. A considerable amount of evidence of this connection between thought and muscle tensions is provided in the researches of Jacobson. See Edmund Jacobson, *Progressive Relaxation* (2d ed.; Chicago: University of Chicago Press, 1938).

but this is apparently not so. According to Hebb, "Activation of the *motor system*, overt or implicit . . . contributes essentially to the development of visual integration without being sufficient to it." In support, Hebb mentions that

> Kennard found a one-sided loss of vision by monkeys on extirpation of the opposite frontal eyefield, a cortical motor area for head-and-eye movement. Clark and Lashley have demonstrated this phenomenon convincingly, with an adequate method of testing. The most significant and striking observation was startle by the monkey when an object was passed from the blind side into the seeing side, at the moment of passing the midline. One might have argued that the animal could "see" an object in his apparently hemianopic field but was not able to move his eyes toward it. The observation referred to rules that interpretation out, and other observations showed that the hemianopia is a genuine failure to see . . .[33]

Here again is powerful research testimony against the conception that action begins with a sensory stimulus. In this case, without motor activity, no stimulus can occur. The two studies cited by Hebb are: K. M. S. Kennard, "Alterations in Response to Visual Stimuli Following Lesions of Frontal Lobe in Monkeys," *Archives of Neurology and Psychiatry*, XLI (1939), 1153-65, and G. Clark and K. Lashley, "Visual Disturbances Following Frontal Ablations in the Monkey," *Anatomical Record*, XCVII (1947), 326.

Conscious Behavior and the Operation of Processes Which Insure Orientation.—An appropriate question to raise concerning the operation of consciousness in carrying action past crises is how the person knows that there is a crisis. Sometimes, of course, there is no anticipation; the mud puddle announces itself by engulfing the shoes of the absent-minded walker. It is more common, however, to be aware in time that the present course cannot continue without trouble. On-going activity, even of the fairly mechanical sort, involves a considerable amount of looking ahead. Automatic walking is not merely a simple chain of leg responses. The whole perceptive system constantly feels out the way that lies ahead, and steps are not taken confidently unless this process continues to show that the way is open. When the perceptive system is unable to insure that the way is open, as in the case of a puddle too wide to cross by the kind of routine walking that is going on, the steps are *automatically inhibited,* the situation claims the person's attention, and the conflicting possibilities are mediated by conscious activity. Even in routine and automatic activity, to act with confidence

[33] Hebb, *op. cit.*, pp. 34-35. Reprinted by permission of John Wiley & Sons.

requires that all the supporting evidence confirm the probable success of the on-going action. An ever-changing but adequate orientation, operating somewhat in advance of overt activity, is a requirement for routine action.[34]

All complex human activity takes place within an orientation. The same object is treated differently in different situations, and the same person may require different treatment in the various settings in which we find him. We deal with a brother in one fashion at home, in another at a formal reception, and perhaps a third way in a committee meeting. If all three situations are familiar, and we are well oriented in each place, there is no necessary crisis, and routine action may take care of most of the business we have to do. All behavior is thus in a context, and a part of the most routine behavior consists in keeping the orientation efficiently reconstructed so that the action may remain confident and avoid crises as far as possible.

Complex and Hypothetical Crises.—The mud puddle example serves to illustrate the fundamental character of the relation of consciousness to activity. So far as we know, the same principles apply to all kinds of activity and to all consciousness.

When walking is automatic and makes no claim on consciousness, the person doing the walking does not then fall asleep. There are enough problems whose solutions have been postponed, or enough which can be anticipated, to engage the problem-solving process of consciousness. One may look ahead a short way and prepare solutions for probable crises—"Will there be many mud

[34] A simple illustration is found in the behavior of some typists whose skill is imperfect. When typing at full speed a finger may sometimes be incorrectly aimed and instead of hitting the proper key squarely, straddle two keys. Often in this case the blow is light. The full activity of the finger falters when orientation changes.

A recent spectacular investigation of this principle has been made by Grant Fairbanks of the University of Illinois. Fairbanks arranged for mechanical interference with the normal cybernetic process in which a person who is speaking checks back on his own vocal activity by means of hearing what he is saying. The experiment indicates that it is difficult for speech to continue without this constant report of the result. In the demonstration, the subject speaks into a microphone which transmits the sound pattern to a tape recorder which plays it back after a slight delay, so amplified that it overpowers the sound of the words the person is speaking at the instant. The speaker thus hears not what he is currently saying, but what he has said a moment before, and his speech sounds are not synchronized with the activity of his vocal organs as in the case of ordinary talking. When the delay between his speaking and the amplified playback is approximately one twenty-fifth of a second the following results are observed: "The speaker is slowly driven toward the gibbering stage. His words won't come; he stammers, repeats, screams in agonized frustration. His face turns red; he sweats and trembles, showing many of the symptoms of emotional disorder. After the test is over, the victim quickly recovers." *Time*, January 8, 1951.

puddles today after the heavy rains? Should I stop in a store and buy some rubbers, or should I take a bus to the office?" Or one may take up a matter left over from the day before—a sister, having been the object of mild banter, suddenly burst into tears and left the room. Here was a blocking of on-going activity; familiar, friendly joking was suddenly frustrated. What action was then appropriate? Was she ill or had there been a quarrel with her fiancee? Had the joking touched on a subject concerning which she had some private reason to be sensitive? By terminating the interchange, the sister left the problem unsolved, and the brother may find such an unfinished issue making strong claims on his attention the next day, or for many days, until some apparently workable relation is re-established.

The most pressing problems are, in fact, likely to be those of personal relations, for social interaction has many complexities and difficulties. Effectiveness of interaction with others requires that problems be anticipated and solutions be ready in advance. A man who knows that on the following day he will be introduced to someone who may be of importance to his career is likely to give the interview a considerable amount of advance thought. Essentially this takes the form of the study of ways to meet possible crises in the interaction. "What if the man should ask about my experience? Should I tell of the occasions on which I did not perform well? If I conceal them, might he have heard of them anyway and form an unfavorable judgment of my lack of candor? Could I get away with making an airy acknowledgment of some slips from excellence, hoping he will not regard them as serious?" Such thoughts, often carried into details of hypothetical conversations with reactions of slight blushes, shudders, or tingling pride, according to how the results are imagined, are of the same kind as are the imagined solutions to the simpler problems of the mud puddle.

When no immediate problems are intrusive it is not uncommon for persons to reach out for problems of a highly hypothetical nature. Persons waiting for a train at a railroad station may speculate on what would be the best course of action for one who is caught in a railroad tunnel wide enough for only one track. Would it be better to press against the wall, or to lie so flat between the rails that the train would clear the body? Would it be better to turn the head on the side, or face downward? Even though the possibility of being in such a situation is remote, the imagination of clinging to the ties may produce a clenching of fists, and a withering shudder as the train is pictured as roaring a fraction of an inch above the scalp.

Wishes, Dreads, Dreams, and Daydreams as Trial Solutions to Hypothetical or Imaginary Crises.—If it is conceived that all consciousness is function and that it plays the role of getting past a crisis to allow the resumption of on-going activity, it is necessary to show how fantasy thinking can be so interpreted.[35] To all surface appearance, wishes, dreads, dreams, and daydreams may appear to have no connection with practical action. In view of the tendency, however, for the active human to look ahead and to work on future problems when none are pressing in his present activity, and to prepare himself for very remote contingencies by working on hypothetical problems, it is possible to conceive of much of fantasy thinking as having a remote and hypothetical function.

One essential activity is that of building, reconstructing, and preserving orientation. This involves the interpretive activity of perception.[36] Like any other action, an incomplete perception calls forth the completion tendency discussed in Chapter 3. This does not mean that any sight or sound which has an indefinite character arouses the completion tendency, but rather that any sensation or combination of sensations which relate to on-going action, present or hypothetical, presents a problem to be solved, or an incomplete picture to be filled out.[37] Fantasy thinking answers questions which have some relation to incomplete perceptions. It is well-known that persons who are deprived of something they desire tend to experience wishful daydreams in which the missing

[35] Kimball Young, among others, holds that there are two kinds of thinking—objective and fantasy thinking. The former is the instrumental process that has just been discussed, and the latter is considered to be of a different character and nonfunctional. See his *Personality and Problems of Adjustment* (New York: Appleton-Century-Crofts, Inc., 1947), pp. 201 ff.

[36] Further materials on the nature of perception are presented in Chapter 8. Perception is problem-solving activity in the same sense that the mud puddle example is problem-solving activity. It requires an organizing process which involves the neuro-muscular system, and it serves to find the way past crises and allow resumption of overt automatic activity.

[37] Abundant observations have been made of the tendency of perception to make a complete perception out of indefinite material. Artists and caricaturists have long made use of the principle, presenting incomplete line drawings which the viewers see as satisfying complete images. The large experimental literature on perception and on thematic apperception reveals not only this tendency to complete a perception, but also shows the close relation between the particular manner in which any person organizes the indefinite material and his own mental organization—that is, his purposes and habitual actions. The connection is not always obvious or easy to discover, but the bulk of the impressive mass of evidence suggests that none of the fantasy thinking is unconnected with the organized activity system of the person.

satisfaction is supplied.[38] Travelers or exiles often daydream of life at home, starving people have rich fantasies of food, separated lovers cherish images of each other. The problem-solving aspect of this imagery may in some cases be essentially the answer to this question, "What will it be like when I get it?" Or, to conceive of it in terms of action, "What will I do about it, and what will the consequences be?" Soldiers, living in danger and discomfort far from home sometimes engage in lengthy conversations which are in the form of planning sessions for the good times they intend to have when they return—the feasts they will consume, the celebrations they will hold, the return to familiar and well-loved activities such as fishing from a favorite spot or playing poker with old friends.

There is an additional function in certain of these fantasy wishes to return to old friends and places. The person often has a fear that he may partially forget what his old life was like, or how his friends look. Separated lovers also sometimes fear that they will partly forget the appearance and personality of one another, and so may make intentional efforts to preserve memories. It is also likely that a fantasy has the function of preserving an orientation which will, the person hopes, have future application and so is not only a fantasy of past memories, but also of future plans.

Daydreaming has some times been considered to be wish fulfilment. There is no evidence, however, that it in any way fulfils or satisfies. It appears to be more plausible to consider it as preparation for hypothetical activity rather than as consummation. It is an attempted solution of a problem which is expected to or which could conceivably occur in the future experience of the person. In building up the orientation for a hypothetical event—essentially answering the question, "What will it be like and how will I act?"— there is no internal guarantee that the answer will be favorable, as would be expected if the process were governed by a tendency to wish fulfilment. Dreads, fears and worries, as well as happy anticipations are involved in fantasies in both daydreams and night dreams.[39] They report that the outlook is unfavorable and warn

---

[38] See M. Sherif, *An Outline of Social Psychology* (New York: Harper & Bros., 1948), chap. iv, "Deprivation at the Human Level." Sherif reviews the research evidence concerning increased motivation to overcome the deprivation, and the tendency to dream and daydream of the missing satisfactions.

[39] It is possible to preserve the theory of wish fulfilment in the face of this contradictory evidence by a process of circular reasoning. Some psychoanalysts have held that the dreads and fears are actually, though unconsciously, desired because of a wish for self-punishment, or a death wish.

the person to be prepared for unpleasant or dangerous consequences.

Night dreams would appear to be more difficult to interpret as functional because of their incoherent character and apparent irrelevancies. Nevertheless, there is a good deal of evidence that some dreams are related to organized activity and constitute attempts to solve problems. Some dreams are obvious and direct attempts and are not uncommon among scientists or inventors blocked by a specific difficulty. Cases are known in which solutions are dreamed night after night, producing a sense of triumph and happiness during the dream, but generally being recognized as shallow and absurd after the dreamer wakes.[40]

Dreams often have obvious relation to unfinished business which is completed in the fantasy of the dreamer. Persons who have been frequently interrupted during a busy day may find that some of the interrupted tasks provide theme material for dreams. A lively evening of discussion and debate frequently leaves a person with unfinished intentions which can be carried to apparent fulfilment in the dream.

An example of the direct problem-solving dream follows:

Some days before I was due to leave for New York City I made a reservation at a recommended hotel. Not knowing its location in the city I looked for a map, but failed to find it. I asked my wife, but she knew of no map of New York City in the house. I gave up the search and said I would ask my friend who lived in New York the next time I wrote.

That night I dreamed that I was in New York City. Apparently I had just arrived there, for I had a suitcase in each hand. I was walking north on Broadway, thinking that I might encounter my friend on his way home from his work. I did meet him, and after we greeted each other I asked him for the location of the hotel. He said, "Come along this way," and I turned around and accompanied him, presumably toward the hotel. I awakened before we reached the hotel, however.[41]

[40] It is not entirely impossible that a correct solution to a problem may be achieved in a dream, but if the problem is complex and requires any high degree of efficiency this would be an extremely rare occurrence. Because of the low efficiency of thought and the poor orientation during sleep, the dreamer is no capable judge of the quality of his dreamed achievements. Often after waking he remembers only that he had conceived a wonderfully new and important idea, or that he delivered a remarkably fluent speech, but unfortunately cannot remember the idea or the words of the speech. In the examples in which the dreamer did remember the content, the pride in the dream achievement is almost never justified. A dreamer who woke up from anesthetization remembering that he had conceived such an idea of world importance, held on to the magnificent thought long enough to record it, and wrote "The stench is terrible."

[41] From the author's collection of dreams, recorded by students, friends, and by himself.

Important projects which require preparatory activity generate tensions of incompletion, some of which may furnish the content of dreams. A planned ocean voyage requires the purchase of clothing and equipment, the arrangements for passage, the disposition of home responsibilities, the planning of travel to the port of departure, and other matters of importance. On occasions, the prospective voyager may think of something which must be done but which he cannot attend to at the moment because of other business. Incompletion of this sort may later be completed in the dream, or completion may be attempted without success, or some consequences of neglecting the necessary task may be anticipated. Here again the popular conception of the dream as wish fulfilment is not justified. Illustrations are abundant of dreams of missing the boat or the train, or of being late for an important meeting. A study of the dreams of schoolteachers shows that certain kinds of dreams occur commonly, and in the case of some teachers the same kind of dream may occur repeatedly.[42] An example is the dreaded event of a classroom out of control, with noisy and unruly pupils, and of the unexpected appearance of the superintendent. College teachers sometimes dream of the unpleasant experience of facing a class with nothing to say, and perhaps with an important visitor present. Some have also reported a dream, usually occurring late in the summer vacation, of having forgotten to return on time and returning to classes too late, weeks after the opening date. This last dream may reflect their uncompleted intentions to prepare for the return, and may constitute a report on the consequences of not finishing the preparations.

Orientation is, of course, poor in dreams. The dreamer virtually never knows that he is in bed or dreaming and so has not only an incorrect orientation, but one which is generally highly unstable—at one moment he dreams that he is in one set of surroundings, then, without any transition or any sense of surprise, he finds himself in a different setting. His orientation is built in part from the materials related to the problem which he is working on, but there appears also to be a certain amount of dream activity incorporating current sounds and sensations into the orientation of the dream. The following is a characteristic example:

Last night I boarded a Pullman car to take the night train home. I went to bed and was asleep before the train left the station. I dreamed that a clock on a nearby table began to shake, and was annoyed at the defective-

42 Willard Waller, *The Sociology of Teaching* (New York: John Wiley & Sons, Inc., 1932).

ness of the clock. The shaking became more violent and gradually the ground commenced to shake with it. That irritated me further and I would have liked to have ordered it to stop shaking. The vibrations kept up and became more and more vigorous. Then I realized that it must be an earthquake, and was at once relieved because the annoyance did not result from the defectiveness of the clock. But when the movement showed no signs of abating, I became alarmed. As I awoke, I found the train in motion, and the movements of the earthquake merged into the movements of the car.[43]

In the dream orientation, the motion of the Pullman car is not correctly identified. The disguised form in which sensations are interpreted in the dream has been interpreted by Freud and others as a reflection of the inability of the conscious mind to face revolting meanings. It is a kind of repression by a censoring mechanism of the mind. This interpretation is not necessary in the present illustration, or, for that matter, in a great many other instances of misinterpretation of sensations in dreams. The train motion would be in no way difficult to face consciously, if the information necessary to its full recognition were present. The sensation is not disguised, it is misunderstood; and misunderstood because of insufficient material for correct orientation and inefficiency of mental processes during sleep. The dream is, in a sense, a very poor hypothesis for the interpretation of an indefinite sensation. In similar cases, a hissing radiator may be misinterpreted as a fire engine, a passing freight train as a hurricane, a rumbling garage door as thunder, and coolness of the body as being unclothed in public. Research has shown that dreams of falling can be induced by removing support from the head, and evidence has been found to account for some levitation dreams in terms of vasomotor reactions to definable external stimuli occurring during sleep.[44]

Dreams, then, may be understood as essentially the same process of consciousness that functions in one who is awake, but with far less coherence, efficiency, and effectiveness because of the low physiological efficiency and poor orientation to the actual surroundings during sleep. The psychoanalytic view that dreams are the disguised expressions of impulses, sexual or otherwise, that

[43] From the author's collection of dreams.

[44] See the following: Robert R. Sears, *Survey of Objective Studies of Psychoanalytic Concepts,* Social Science Research Council, Bulletin No. 51, New York, 1943; D. B. Klein, "The Experimental Production of Dreams During Hypnosis," *University of Texas Bulletin,* No. 3009, 1930; A. T. Jersild, F. V. Markey, and C. L. Jersild, "Children's Fears, Dreams, Wishes, Daydreams, Likes, Dislikes, Pleasant and Unpleasant Memories," *Child Development Monographs,* No. 12, 1933; L. H. Horton, "Levitation Dreams: Their Physiology," *Journal of Abnormal Psychology,* XIV (1919), 145-72.

are too unpleasant to face, is unnecessary in the above instances. Symbolic elements are sometimes theoretically identified as indications of repressed sexual impulses, but these elements may sometimes be found in dreams along with a considerable amount of frank sexual content.

It has been contended that something like the psychoanalytic theory is necessary to account for the particular direction of the erroneous perceptions and interpretations in some dreams. The direction, however, is not as fantastic or as sexual as one might conclude from a casual familiarity with psychoanalytic literature. A recent psychological survey of over ten thousand dreams of normal persons indicates that there is no problem of the pattern of distortion because the content of most dreams, apart from its general inefficiency and incoherence, apparently is not very much different from that of daily life.[45] The investigator found the settings in these dreams "overwhelmingly commonplace." The dreamer finds himself in a dwelling, a car, a place of recreation, or a street. "Seldom does he dream of a bizarre or exotic environment." Nor is the sex element predominant—men dream about males twice as often as about females. Moreover they do the most commonplace things in the majority of their dreams—going places, playing, and other ordinary activities for example. Only one fourth of the dreams are judged unpleasant by the dreamers, nearly half are pleasant, and the rest neutral or mixed. The investigator concludes, "Dreaming is thinking that occurs during sleep . . . in the form of images, usually visual images. . . . The dreamer thinks about himself: what kind of person he is and how well fitted he is to deal with his conflicts and anxieties."

The Relation of Emotion to Action.—Emotion has been popularly supposed to be a form of behavior which exists in amounts, like a quantity of fluid, and which is differentiated into clear types, such as rage, fear, and love.[46] It has also been popularly believed

---

[45] Calvin S. Hall, "What People Dream About," *Scientific American,* May 1951, pp. 60-63.

[46] The catharsis concept, still widely popular in psychology, clearly has both of these elements. Persons are believed to have, or to accumulate, quantities of rage, and these quantities are believed to be as indestructible as matter. The rage is either inside a person or outside. Overt conflict lets it out, and when it is out, there is none left inside until more is built up. The catharsis hypothesis does not grant that these emotions are interchangeable—one cannot let rage, for example, take the place of fear. As the present discussion shows, modern knowledge does not give strong support to either of these essential aspects of the catharsis concept. Nor does that conception of emotion fit in with the general organization of consciousness and behavior as formulated in the present volume.

that each of these emotions produces a characteristic and identifiable muscular pattern of response, particularly distinguishable in facial expressions, and that each emotion proceeds from separate internal mechanisms.

As Murphy points out, however, modern physiological and psychological research shows that "there is no sharp distinction between the different emotions; they overlap too much. Nor is there a sharp distinction between emotions and other motives . . ." [47]

Emotion may be understood as an aspect of the process which takes place in the blocking of routine activity. As long as routine takes care of the situation, action is automatic and neither consciousness nor emotion is involved. When activity is blocked, invention and effort are required to find a means of resumption. Here is an emergency, and the physiological system adapts to the potential requirement of more strenuous actions. Muscles become tense, respiration and heart action speed up, and various other internal changes take place. "Certainly the cerebral cortex is involved, and certainly the lower centers, especially in the thalamic region, are profoundly concerned. Certainly also there is abundant discharge both to striped and to unstriped muscles and to duct and ductless glands." [48] Physiologically this is a preparation for an emergency; some even prefer the term "emergency response" to "emotion."

The physiological emergency response may exist in varying degrees from slight irritation to overpowering reactions. In general, it aids activity which requires strenuous exertion and sustained effort—running, fist-fighting, lifting of heavy burdens, and the like. It makes possible speed, power, and endurance in degrees not available in the calmer physiological states. But it does not help in all kinds of emergency. Where high skill, fine judgments, or complex reorganization of activity is required, as in many team sports, a degree of excitement too intense may interfere with the capacity to make good decisions. Whether it helps or not, however, it is difficult to avoid, and persons facing such a crisis as an important interview or examination generally experience internal sensations which, however great help they might be in a desperate escape from danger, are only unwelcome in circumstances requiring calm efficiency.

The sensations experienced as a result of the physiological preparation for emergency require interpretation before they have

[47] Murphy, *op. cit.*, p. 119.
[48] *Ibid.*, p. 118.

meaning. The same sensation may be pleasant or unpleasant, depending on the context and implications. It is to a considerable
extent, if not entirely, the context that differentiates the sensations
into the separate identifiable and recognizable "emotions," and
it is only after this identification or interpretation is made that the
conventional facial expressions and muscular patterns communicate
to others the emotion experienced. There is a considerable amount
of flexibility in this interpretation of internal sensations—the same
feeling may be considered unpleasant on one occasion and pleasant
on another. For example, a girl student expecting a proposal of
marriage may enjoy the internal tingling which, apart from the
context, could not be distinguished from the tingling sensation,
generally considered highly unpleasant, that precedes a disciplinary conference with a dean.

Even the same sensation in the same context may be redefined
from unpleasant to pleasant, or from pleasant to unpleasant. The
visceral sensations that accompany a ride in a roller coaster are
purchased with good money, but in most cases surely constitute an
acquired taste. The first ride, particularly if no indoctrination has
been achieved in advance, may in fact be highly unpleasant. Persons similarly learn to appreciate the shudders produced by crime
fiction and horror motion pictures. One can detest quarrels, but in
time come to enjoy a "good fight." Within very wide limits, if
there are any limits at all, the meaning of an experience of internal
sensations of emergency response is the result of interpretation, the
most important sources of definition being the social groups to
which we belong. Individual experiences, however, play a part
in the processes of definition and produce much individual differentiation in the interpretation of sensations.

Emotion, then, is physiologically a preparation for more strenuous effort and endurance necessitated when on-going activity is
blocked. In the process of reorganization of activity, the trial-and-
error process of imagination and the tentative movements which
are a part of the imagination appear to generate the emergency
response and at the same time to give it its meaning of anger, fear,
pleasant excitement, and the like. Dembo has performed a simple
experiment which illustrates this relation of emotion to imagined
action during a crisis. Persons were told to stand inside of a marked
square and reach for a flower four feet away, without moving out
of the square. There were two possible ways of obtaining the
flower under the rules, but the subjects were told that there were
three ways, and were urged to discover the third. The experi-

menter's insistence produced imagined methods, such as having the room filled with water so that the flower would float to the subject, and resulted in much tension and anger.[49]

The internal sensations themselves may cause restlessness or discomfort, but are not recognized as emotion unless there is content in the imagination which gives them meaning. Fear, for example, occurs not only from internal sensations, but also from the recognition of danger, which then may arouse the internal stirrings and give them meaning. Fear requires imagination and imagination must have material to work on. Bravery may in some cases be attributable to nothing but ignorance. Soldiers who have never seen battle are more likely to be ostentatiously braver than those who have. A study made during the Second World War shows this clearly. A list of ten fear symptoms was shown to soldiers who had been in combat, and each was asked how many of these he had experienced. The soldiers from the companies with few casualties, who had not seen any close friends killed and who had never witnessed an enemy atrocity selected fewer symptoms. Those who had all the above experiences admitted to the most symptoms.[50]

MENTAL ORGANIZATION RESULTING FROM THE PROCESS OF INTERCOMMUNICATION

If we consider that mind refers to organization of behavior, it follows from abundant evidence that mind itself is acquired. Since the process by means of which the organization is achieved involves to an important extent interaction between persons, mind can be said to be acquired in the social process. As Mead has stated,

. . . if . . . you presuppose the existence of mind at the start, as explaining or making possible the social process of experience, then the origin of minds and the interaction among minds become mysteries. But if, on the other hand, you regard the social process of experience as prior . . . to the existence of mind and explain the origin of minds in terms of the interaction among individuals within that process, then not only the origin of minds, but also the interaction among minds . . . cease to seem mysterious or miraculous.

[49] T. Dembo, "Anger as a Dynamic Problem," *Psychol. Forsch*, XV, 1931. Cited in David Krech and R. S. Crutchfield, *Theory and Problems of Social Psychology* (New York: McGraw-Hill Book Co., Inc., 1948), pp. 114-15.

[50] Samuel Stouffer, *et al.*, *The American Soldier: Combat and Aftermath* ("Studies in Social Psychology in World War II," Vol. II [Princeton: Princeton University Press, 1949]), p. 81.

Mind arises through communication by a conversation of gestures in a social process or context of experience—not communication through mind.[51]

Mead drew a distinction between a conversation of gestures, such as can be observed in a fight between two dogs, and the interaction based on significent gestures which appears to be distinctly human. One dog may advance growling toward another, causing the second dog to retreat; the second dog may then turn and bark, causing the first dog to stop. The growling of the first dog may be thought of as a gesture which causes a response in the other dog, and the bark of the second dog is in turn a gesture which elicits a response from the first. The gesture is the beginning of an act, and it calls forth a response which may also be a gesture.

In this case we have a situation in which certain parts of the act become a stimulus to the other form [dog] to adjust itself to those responses; and that adjustment in turn becomes a stimulus to the first form to change his own act and start on a different one. There are a series of attitudes, movements, on the part of these forms which belong to the beginnings of acts that are the stimuli for the responses that take place. The beginning of a response becomes the stimulus to the first form to change his attitude, to adopt a different act. The term "gesture" may be identified with these beginnings of social acts which are stimuli for the response of other forms.[52]

In the case of the growling dog, the attitude means attack, since it calls out the kind of response that attack calls out. But it is not assumed that the dog intends it to mean attack—he is merely behaving according to his relatively automatic canine ways. In human interaction, however, there may occur gestures which Mead calls significant. A significant gesture is made with the intention to convey a particular meaning to the other.

. . . if somebody shakes his fist in your face you assume that he has not only a hostile attitude but that he has some idea behind it. You assume that it means not only a possible attack, but that the individual has an idea in his experience. When, now, that gesture means this idea behind it and it arouses that idea in the other individual, then we have a significant symbol . . . which answers to a meaning in the experience of the first individual and which also calls out that meaning in the second individual. Where the gesture reaches that situation it has become what we call "language." It is now a significant symbol and it signifies a certain meaning.[53]

[51] George H. Mead, *Mind, Self, and Society* (Chicago: University of Chicago Press, 1934), p. 50.
[52] *Ibid.*, p. 43.
[53] *Ibid.*, pp. 45-46.

The psychological process by means of which gestures become significant is that of responding to one's own gestures as others tend to respond to them, and redirecting one's own behavior so that one finds the gesture which arouses in oneself the response one wishes to arouse in the other. This is in effect an internalization of a social process. Instead of waiting for the response of the other, as in the example of the dog fight, to provide the stimulus for the next step in activity, the person performs in imagination the response of the other, based on his familiarity with characteristic responses he has seen in social interaction.

The function of the gesture is to make adjustment possible among the individuals implicated in any given social act with reference to the object or objects with which that act is concerned; and the significant gesture or significant symbol affords far greater facilities for such adjustment and readjustment than does the non-significant gesture, because it calls out in the individual making it the same attitude toward it (or toward its meaning) that it calls out in the other individuals participating with him in the given social act, and thus makes him conscious of their attitude toward it [as a component of his behavior] and enables him to adjust his subsequent behavior to theirs in the light of that attitude. In short, the conscious or significant conversation of gestures is a much more adequate and effective mechanism of mutual adjustment within the social act—involving, as it does, the taking, by each of the individuals carrying it on, of the attitudes of the others toward himself— than is the unconscious or non-significant conversation of gestures.[54]

This is the nature of the thought process on a higher level of complexity than is involved in a simple blocking of behavior by such an obstacle as a mud puddle. In the mud puddle problem, the objective factors in the situation remain relatively constant, so that a single solution is all that is needed. In the perpetual problem that is involved in all social interaction the situation is never stable. An intelligent conversation requires the kind of internalization of the conversation of gestures as described above. Mead states:

Only in terms of gestures as significant symbols is the existence of mind or intelligence possible; for only in terms of gestures which are significant symbols can thinking—which is simply an internalized or implicit conversation of the individual with himself by means of such gestures—take place.[55]

Mind, then, is an acquisition. It is an internal organization of experience, built up through participation in social processes. It is essentially an incorporation of social organization into the internal

[54] *Ibid.*, p. 46.
[55] *Ibid.*, p. 47.

psychological organization of a person; each person achieving a unique organization because of his particular experiences within the social organization—experiences which can never be identical with those of any other person. In summary,

Mind arises in the social process only when that process as a whole enters into, or is present in, the experience of any one of the given individuals involved in that process. . . . It is by means of reflexiveness—the turning-back of the experience of the individual upon himself—that the whole social process is thus brought into the experience of the individuals involved in it; it is by such means, which enable the individual to take the attitude of the other toward himself, that the individual is able consciously to adjust himself to that process, and to modify the resultant of that process in any given social act in terms of his adjustment to it. Reflexiveness, then, is the essential condition, within the social process, for the development of mind.[56]

While it does not appear valuable to divide the mind into two clearly separated portions—the conscious and the unconscious—it is worth recalling that consciousness is not required for most activity. As soon as the problem aspect of any on-going activity is solved, routine mechanisms take over and consciousness is free to work on some other aspect of behavior. Each solution of a problem leaves a residue of habit so that a cumulative structure of automatic organization grows as we think our way through the problematic aspects of life. In a sense, the mind may be thought of as an unstable structure of habits, and consciousness as the process by which this structure is revised to meet new situations. Since we live and work with other persons, we derive most of the organization of the structure from the social process, and find a large proportion of our problems within that process. Any part of this organization may fail to function, lose its automatic character and be subject to revision by the processes of consciousness. Whether it is conscious or unconscious at any one time depends upon how smoothly the course of activity progresses.[57]

Summary

Consciousness has often been considered too complex to be explained and thus forever mysterious, or else denied as either nonexistent or unimportant in the causal processes of human activity. The latter approach was stimulated in the early part of the present century by the interest in the conditioned response, which to some

[56] *Ibid.*, p. 134.

[57] The concept of the unconscious mind is critically examined in great detail in Chapter 6.

investigators appeared to offer a process which could account for both consciousness and learning.

There is no reason to doubt that such a process as conditioning exists. A mass of laboratory experiments on a wide range of animals as well as on man has succeeded in establishing a number of clear principles of conditioning. A wide range of responses may be attached to a new stimulus by means of repeated associations with an old adequate stimulus which elicited the response previously. But there is no indication in the careful experimental research findings that a really new response is acquired by the process of conditioning. Nor does the conditioning process account for the meeting of emergency situations by the solution of problems. In the human, in fact, the conditioned response is apparently subject to some interference or interpretation according to the set or attitude of the persons at the time of the conditioning—in short, he is not dominated by the process.

It is shown that the "stimulus-response" conception of human behavior, which implies that activity begins with stimulation of sense organs from an external source, does not fit present knowledge of neuromuscular activity. Activity, in the rested and healthy human, is constant and does not wait for a stimulus to start it. The muscular system and the central nervous system are continuously active in all their parts; far from being started by external stimulation, they determine what external stimuli are to be allowed to exert an influence on the course of action.

Consciousness is a complex process but its function is not difficult to understand. It is not merely an epiphenomenal aspect of psychological functioning, standing by to look on without affecting behavior. It has an important function in keeping behavior efficient and is employed only for its peculiar use and not wasted in unnecessary exercise. The larger part of man's daily activity is performed by routine habit which does not require consciousness as long as the activity proceeds smoothly. Most persons, in fact, can and do perform complex sequences of habitual activity without being aware of it, and sometimes without even remembering having done it.

Consciousness functions when routine activity no longer is able to proceed smoothly. When some sort of crisis or blocking occurs to interrupt the routine, the person finds himself geared for action but temporarily unable to act. The process of consciousness that now comes into play to get the person past the crisis is a trial-and-error process that operates in the imagination. He imagines various activities which might seem to solve the problem, and imagines their consequences. The process of imagination appears to involve actual patterns of muscular tension—tentative and inhibited actions. It is a kind of internalization of the same trial-and-error process that is done overtly by animals and by young children, as well as by some adults who do not have the mental equipment to solve a given problem. When the imagined act has imagined consequences which appear to be satisfactory, the inhibited pattern is then allowed to have overt expression and the action goes on. If the imagination is efficient the problem is solved and routine processes can carry it on from there.

If stimulus is used to designate whatever cue releases the overt activity that solves the problem, it can be argued that this stimulus does not start the process of finding a solution, but has to be discovered during the process. Both stimulus and response evolve together during the progress of conscious activity—one does not precede or cause the other.

As routine activity resumes and no longer requires consciousness, the process does not necessarily discontinue and leave the formerly conscious person in a coma. Ordinarily, each person has a number of problems, some imminent, some visibly looming, some involving an indefinite future, and some hypothetical. Normally one turns to one of these when consciousness is not needed for the immediate operations. Dreams and daydreams may be understood as functional in the same sense as all consciousness, but operating with less efficiency and being concerned with relatively hypothetical problems rather than pressing practical issues.

Emotion appears during the crisis as a physiological preparation for an emergency response requiring more strenuous and enduring activity. It is given meaning by the context of experience, not by physiological differences in types of emotion. An emotion is pleasant or unpleasant according to our highly flexible capacity to define it, and the actual definition we adopt often is that which is standard in the social group to which we belong.

Mind is an acquired organization of behavior, actively built up during the processes of social interaction. In our relations with other persons we do not wait for the overt responses of other persons to inform us of the consequences of our own gestures, but we respond to our own gestures in the early stages of their expression and redirect them according to our judgment of their meaning and our intentions. This is an internalization of a social process, and provides the means for an internalization of a social organization.

This internal organization, in turn, always unique because of the varying experiences of each person, is mind. Its stable aspect is habit and attitude and its conscious aspect is the part that fails to function smoothly at any particular time.

Selected References

Bode, Boyd. "Consciousness and Psychology," in John Dewey *et al., Creative Intelligence.* New York: Henry Holt & Co., 1917. An important statement of the nature and function of consciousness.

Dewey, John. *Philosophy and Civilization.* New York: G. P. Putnam's Sons, 1931. Chapter on "The Unit of Behavior." This is a reprint of the famous 1896 paper which dealt with the function of consciousness, and which needs no revision today.

Mead, George Herbert. *Mind, Self and Society.* Chicago: University of Chicago Press, 1934. One of the most important works ever written on the origin of mind and self.

Chapter 6

THE CONCEPT OF UNCONSCIOUS MIND

MANY THEORISTS, influenced by Freud and his disciples, have considered it useful to regard the mind as being divided into two parts, the conscious and the unconscious. In further elaboration, there has also been a division into three parts: the Id, the Ego, and the Superego; referring respectively to basic unrecognized physiological impulses and instincts, to conscious activity, and to the organized conscience that is derived from social sources.

It is the function of this chapter to examine this formulation and to arrive at a judgment concerning its utility, and to see what value any kind of conception of unconscious mental process may have. Such an examination requires that the confusion of meanings concerning unconsciousness be cleared up, and that all theoretical material be measured against objective evidence. As this is done, it becomes apparent that there is a great deal of misuse of the concept in both popular and technical discourse, and that a considerable amount of revision of popular psychological theory is necessary if the subject of unconscious mental operations is to be made compatible with the knowledge presented in the other chapters of the present work.

It will appear obvious to the reader that there are difficulties in making a separation of the mind into two independently organized parts. Consciousness is not an organ, it is a process. It does not look constantly upon the entire scene and activity of the person, it is efficiently restricted to just those aspects of behavior which require its operation. It is not set sharply apart from automatic behavior, but emerges to act when automatic behavior is inadequate, and turns to other problems when the automatic habits can safely resume control.

The conscious process does not work independently of automatic habits as part of a separate mental organization, but operates through habits. In the crisis where conscious thought is used to solve a problem of action, the trial-and-error process is a method of choice among various available habits. Each new solution, when

114

tried and found successful, in turn becomes an automatic habit. Moreover, although automatic habits operate without requiring the continuous aid of consciousness, they are not to be regarded as inaccessible to consciousness in any way. Consciousness leaves habits to operate automatically, not because of any process of repression which forbids the habits to be consciously recognized, but only because consciousness is not needed. There are enough problems in a normal life to engage the problem-solving activity of consciousness without requiring that this complex and active process make continuous inspection of all the routine drudgery of life.

Consciousness is not an organization. The organization of mind lies in the solved situations—the work of habits and attitudes. Consciousness exists when and where there is insufficient organization, or organization that does not work. It covers the new, unforeseen, problematical, unorganized aspect of life, and guides the construction of new organization. Thus there are not two separate organizations, the conscious and the automatic, but only one—the automatic system of habits, which grows and is revised with the aid of the problem-solving activity of the process of consciousness.

In the psychoanalytic conceptions of an organized unconscious mind there is maintained the concept of the Id, composed, according to the theory, of instincts and unrecognized motives. The instinct theory has already been criticized in Chapter 2—there the conclusion was reached that there is apparently little value in employing the concept in human psychology. Physiological motivation, whether needs, drives, or general tension, does little more than produce restlessness until it is defined and attached to habit, and, similarly, it was shown in Chapter 3 that there is little evidence in the human of any physiological motivation that is more specific than a general tendency to function—a tension without any particular goal. Specific motivation is all acquired, largely from social sources (see Chapter 4).

The fact that persons do not always have complete insight into their own motivation is sometimes offered as evidence of the source of motivation in an unconscious mind. This notion, however, rests on a misconception of the role of consciousness. There is no organ of insight which has the capacity of explaining why we do things, and thus it is not necessary to invent another organ to explain why this nonexistent one does not succeed. The motivation for any act is, if completely described, the complex history of the person's actions in all similar situations and the social influences which have played a part in the formation of his habits and attitudes. Memory is no more automatic than is consciousness—it is selective and functional. There is no direct way of looking into oneself to gain this complex history, and it would be an inefficient method of operating for a mind to store every complex experience so that it would all be available at any time.

The conception, then, that there is a small and discrete list of motives, instinctive and repressed from consciousness, that dominate details of human behavior is a vestige of an obsolete formulation which is unsupported by modern evidence. Motivation is never fully understood by anyone, not because of repression of the motive into the unconsciousness, but because motivation, like any other kind of causation, is complex.

Popular and Technical Uses of the Concepts of Unconsciousness and Unconscious Mind

Efficient communication requires that the meanings of terms be clearly understood and that the meanings not be changed without warning. In the literature which deals with processes of unconsciousness these standards have not been adequately maintained. In confusion of the meanings of the words, unnecessary issues have arisen. J. G. Miller has examined the literature for variations in meaning of the concept of unconsciousness and has listed sixteen different meanings in current usage.[1] In many instances the intended meaning is explicitly given and the statement noncontroversial, but the term often appears without clear indication of intended meaning and thus fails to function efficiently in communication. It is instructive to consider briefly each of these current uses of the concept.

1. *Unconsciousness as the inanimate or subhuman.* In this sense a stone is unconscious, as presumably is a worm or a fly or a human corpse. The meaning here is essentially that the object is not the kind that is capable of consciousness.

2. *Unconsciousness as a lack of response to stimulation.* This covers absent-mindedness, daydreaming, as well as the condition of being anesthetized. It would appear that the coverage is too broad, as the absent-minded person is not unconscious in general, as is the anesthetized person, but is concentrating his consciousness on a private problem. Since all consciousness is concentrated in

---

[1] James Grier Miller, *Unconsciousness* (New York: John Wiley & Sons, Inc., 1942), pp. 21 ff.

some way, unconsciousness is not a useful term to describe this characteristic of consciousness.

3. *Unconsciousness as that which is not mental.* The growth of hair is a part of the life process in the human, but is not a mental matter. It adds little, however, to our understanding of anything to say that hair grows unconsciously.

4. *Unconsciousness as a lack of discrimination.* We may not notice colors of books we pick up because of the irrelevance of color. This is of course another recognition that consciousness does not survey the total surroundings, but only that aspect which may contribute to a solution of the problem of action. We pay no attention to the color of a book if the color makes no difference in our behavior, and there is ordinarily little misunderstanding when we say that we are unconscious of the color. The jump from this statement to the assertion that the color is known in an unconscious mind, however, is entirely unwarranted, and the cause of communication would be served better if "unconsciousness" were not used in this connection at all.

5. *Unconsciousness as conditioning.* The reasons for salivating, for jerking the knee, and similar automatic responses, may lie in a conditioning process and therefore may not be a matter involving consciousness. But in pronouncing these functions to be unconsciousness, there is a risk of being understood as saying that the person is not aware of what is going on, which is not necessarily true. Conditioning can be established without the operation of consciousness, but it can best be described as, simply, "conditioning," which is less likely to be misunderstood than "unconsciousness."

6. *Unconsciousness as an inability to sense.* When stimuli are inadequate, or do not reach the organism at all, or when the sensory tract is incapable of conveying the stimuli, the person naturally is unable to be conscious of it, just as he is unable to pick out the meaning of the radio waves that pass through his body, without a receiving apparatus. To say that one is not conscious of a stimulus, though, does not justify one in stating that one knows it unconsciously, or in an unconscious mind.

7. *Unconsciousness meaning "not noticing."* This is a meaning similar to the second in the list.

8. *Unconsciousness as insightlessness.* As shown in the introduction to the present Chapter, and as further developed in a later section, there is no inevitable or automatic insight at any time.

Insight is knowledge, and must be acquired. Insightlessness is mere ignorance, not unconscious knowledge.

9. *Unconsciousness as unremembering or unremembered.* This usage covers both simple forgetting and such processes as alterative forgetting, dissociation, suppression, and repression. This is the most common and most nearly justifiable use of the concept of unconsciousness, and, to the extent that such concepts as repression are useful, the most useful. This matter is fully discussed in a later section of the present chapter.

10. *Unconsciousness as instinctive, unlearned and inherited behavior.* This is clearly an inefficient usage. Sneezing is an unlearned, innate mechanism which is performed involuntarily, but it is not, in any sense, unconscious.

11. *Unconsciousness as unrecognizing or unrecognized.* This is similar to the second and seventh meanings listed and is subject to the same criticism.

12. *Unconsciousness as involuntariness.* Both reflexes and habits are involuntary unless interrupted or blocked, at which time we may become conscious of them. This sense of unconsciousness is about the same as the automatic character of any habit; it does not mean that there is repression to an unconscious mind, but merely that consciousness is not required where action proceeds smoothly.

13. *Unconsciousness as inability to communicate, or incommunicability.* Communication operates through symbols which are always imperfect. Nothing that is known is entirely incommunicable, and nothing is ever entirely communicable. The extent and efficiency of communication depends on the degrees of consensus and human skill; it is not a matter of the degrees of consciousness or unconsciousness.

14. *Unconsciousness as that which is ignored.* Ordinary ignoring implies consciousness but refusal to admit or communicate the matter. This is not efficiently designated as unconsciousness.

15. *Unconsciousness in the psychoanalytic meaning of "the unconscious."* This refers to an organized aspect of mind, dynamically repressed from consciousness, not under voluntary control, and available to consciousness only by the use of special techniques such as hypnosis and psychoanalysis. The following sections of the present Chapter examine at length the justification for this conception.

16. *Unconsciousness as unawareness of discrimination, or unavailability to awareness.* Discriminations, like all other percep-

tions, are not automatic, but occur when they are relevant to the problem-solving activity of consciousness in a crisis. Irrelevant discriminations do not come into consciousness, but this should not be understood to mean that they do exist in an unconscious part of the mind.

It is clear from the above list that loose and inconsistent usage of the concept of unconsciousness has made communication inefficient and analysis difficult. A number of the listed meanings appear to be logically objectionable. In other cases, however, it is possible to examine evidence to see whether or not there is objective support for the implied theory involved in the usage. In the following sections, certain of these topics are so examined.

INSIGHTLESS BEHAVIOR

The fact that we do things that we do not understand, or the motives for which we never fully realize, is often mentioned in support of a conception of an organized unconscious mind that motivates action but disguises the motive in such a manner as to prevent direct or even indirect recognition by consciousness. As previously stated, this view implies that there is some natural tendency to have insight and to understand motives, a tendency which is frustrated by a separate agency. There is, however, no evidence for, or reason to assume, such a natural insight—the conception is in fact contrary to our knowledge that consciousness is restricted to aspects of behavior relevant to a crisis. We become conscious of motivation only when it appears to be useful for us to do so in the solving of a problem, and we are aware of it then not by direct insight, but by looking for evidence and evaluating it, in the same manner that we attain any other kind of knowledge.

In any on-going behavior we never have continuous and complete insight into what we are doing—this would be an intolerable burden on the mental processes. We efficiently pay attention only to those aspects of our behavior which are in some way problematical. But again, *not knowing* should not be taken to mean *knowing unconsciously*. Lack of insight, as previously stated, is simply lack of knowledge. We do not know why our hearts beat, unless we learn it as we learn anything else. There is no reason to say that the unconscious mind knows why the heart beats—there is no evidence of an internal encyclopedia of science. Nor do we necessarily know why we yawn, or why we are restless, or that we need more salt in our diets, unless we acquire this kind of knowledge through ordinary learning processes. We lack automatic insight into anything until we learn. Insightlessness is ignorance, not unconsciousness.

Freud conceived of the sex drive as fully organized and specific in direction even though not conscious. The desire of a male child for his mother, in his conception, is dynamically repressed from consciousness because of the social rule against its expression. But as the evidence shown in Chapter 2 indicates, there is no reason to suspect that there exists such a fully organized instinct, particularly at early ages. Sex impulses are only vague tensions, inadequate to lead to copulation unless there is learning or some canalization through experience.

It may be that sex tensions enter into some of the mother-child interaction such as fondling and expressions of affection. The behavior itself, however, is fully approved and is not repressed into unconsciousness. The theory of repression is not that the behavior is repressed, but that the sexual element in the motivation is not allowed into consciousness. The refutation of this thesis, however, rests on the same basis as the argument concerning insight into the reason for the beating of the heart. We do not know either the reason for the heart beat or the sexual element unless we learn it. Some persons do, to be sure, refuse to accept a sexual interpretation of motivation, but their intentional rejection of this motive does not mean that they have repressed it and does not argue for the existence of the mechanism of repression.[2]

A clear example of insightless behavior in which there is no suspicion of repression is furnished by the behavior of certain blind persons, who have a degree of ability to perceive certain obstacles in their pathway. They sense that they are near a wall or other object, and, to some extent, are even able to judge its solidity—that is, whether it is a brick wall or a picket fence. There is no natural insight into the nature of this ability of some of the blind—some think of it as a cutaneous sensation of face or forehead. Research has shown, however, that if the ears are stopped the faculty is almost entirely lost, but that if the face is covered with heavy felt with openings for the ears, they do not lose the ability to judge. It is clear, then, that the sense of hearing informs them of the object,

---

[2] Evidence is presented later in the Chapter to show that some persons who deny an interpretation of their own behavior, or who claim ignorance of certain aspects of it, nevertheless know what it is that they deny. There are social reasons for wanting to appear ignorant of some aspects of our behavior, and denials can be made with such stubbornness and appearance of sincerity that they are readily, though mistakenly, interpreted as evidence of true repression.

but it is also clear that these persons do not necessarily know this. It is not a matter of knowledge which is repressed into unconsciousness, but only another case of a lack of insight resulting from not having learned what is somewhat subtle and difficult to perceive.

Boring, in reference to this matter, states:

The auditory clues must be very subtle indeed, since very few blind men are aware that it is hearing which warns them of obstacles. Yet that should not surprise us. A clue to be effective in perception does not have to be conscious in the sense that the organism which uses the clue knows that he has the clue or that he uses it. Unawareness of clues is rather the rule in well-established perceptions like the perceptions of spatial relations. Most proprioceptive clues are unconscious. We do not directly perceive excitation from the nonauditory labyrinth, although we perceive the effects in the perception of rotation, dizziness, and the visual "swimming" of nystagmus.[3]

Studies of opiate addiction give additional evidence for the lack of automatic insight into motivation. Lindesmith found that habituation to opiates (organic adaptation) may occur without addiction (conscious desire for the drug and a habit of using it). A subject may experience all the symptoms of withdrawal distress without any tendency to desire the drug as long as he is ignorant of the connection between his discomfort and the discontinuation of the drug. Addiction takes place when the person learns, usually by being told, of this relationship, and then proves it to himself by trying the opiate.[4] Until he is told, however, he completely lacks insight into the meaning of his restlessness, not because of repression—there is no knowledge of the relation in an unconscious mind —but because of simple ignorance.

One may also be unaware of his motivation simply because the whole act is habitual. It has been observed that some persons when hungry or thirsty obtain food or drink without noticing that they do it. Both the motive and the action are unnoticed, but not repressed into an unconscious mind. They remain outside of consciousness because there is no necessity for consciousness in these instances. Should a necessity occur, both the motivating condition of hunger or thirst and the action required to answer it would readily be examined by the processes of consciousness.[5]

[3] Reprinted by permission from *Foundations of Psychology* by E. G. Boring, H. S. Langfeld, and H. P. Weld (eds.), published by John Wiley & Sons, Inc., 1948, p. 386.

[4] Alfred R. Lindesmith, *Opiate Addiction* (Bloomington: The Principia Press, Inc., Indiana), 1947, pp. 45 ff.

[5] See E. G. Boring, "Processes Referred to the Alimentary and Urinary Tracts," *Psychological Review*, XXII (1915), 307-10. Also E. G. Boring and A. Luce, "The Psychological Basis of Appetite," *American Journal of Psychology*, XXVIII (1917), 443-53.

Guilt feelings, even of a mild character, are presumed by some theorists to be repressed on occasion with the result that there exists no conscious sense of having done wrong, but only certain betraying symptoms to indicate that the guilt is preserved in an unconscious part of the mind. Posner attempted to demonstrate this in an experiment with eight-year-old children.[6]   Each child was given two toys to play with, one highly preferred, the other not. He was asked to give one of the toys to a friend, and was then asked which toy he thought the friend would have given him. Those who gave away the less desirable of the two toys are reported to be inclined to defend themselves by saying that their friend would have given them the same toy. There is no conclusive evidence, however, that the child actually lacks understanding of his motives. He undoubtedly knows that there is no way to check on his sincerity, and is perhaps making a surface, bluffing denial of selfishness, knowing he can get away with it. In the nature of the case he could be expected to adhere to his point in the face of a challenge. The experiment could be performed better if, on another occasion and in an indirect way which the child would not link with this experience, the child could be asked to guess which of the same two toys any particular friend would give him.

Lack of insight, the inability to recognize an aspect of motivation, or the inability to remember what was done or why, does not in any way require the concept of repression. Memory is an active process, and can only occur for those materials which have been actively bound into a mental organization by a process of relating.[7] Memories are not retained automatically for unlimited periods, but survive by virtue of being employed and freshly related to new experiences, and by being replaced in contemporary contexts. If this is not done, they become more and more difficult to recover and sometimes may present the superficial appearance of being repressed. A person's name which has not been thoroughly learned or recently used may resist recall as if there were some barrier in an unconscious process. Often, however, a check on the difficulty, made after the actual name has been found, will show that the barrier is a conscious matter—often the trouble is that the person trying to remember the name confines his search to names beginning with the letter "L" when the name in question actually

---

[6] B. A. Posner, "Selfishness, Guilt Feelings, and Social Distance" (Master's thesis, University of Iowa, 1940).

[7] See Chapter 8 for a full presentation of the processes of remembering.

starts with "B." The blocking occurs because of an error in association or context, and in no way requires a hypothesis of unconscious mind or repression.

When habits take over routines, the conscious knowledge that may have been required for the acquisition of the habit may, in time, fade away, and deliberate efforts to remember it fail. This knowledge is lost because its function has been replaced. An illustration familiar to many musicians is furnished by the experience of attempting to remember the fingering of a piano composition which has been thoroughly memorized. At certain stages of the attempt, no amount of effort will succeed in obtaining a direct recall of the fingering, but it may be recovered by sitting down at the piano, looking away from the keyboard, making a start and letting the habits find their own way. The memory, in a common figure of speech, is "in the fingers," and can be recovered more easily if the attention is removed from the fingers as they go through the established patterns.

A similar experience, common in daily life, occurs when a preoccupied person reaches in routine fashion for a familiar object in a familiar setting, for example, an envelope in his own desk drawer. Before his hand gets to the drawer there is an interruption—perhaps a sound outside of the door—which momentarily claims his attention. He may then try to return to his former action but not be able to remember just what it was that he had been about to do. He may be aware that there was some kind of impulse in the direction of the drawer and may even extend his hand toward it but still be unable to remember which of several drawers is involved, or what object he wanted from it. Here again there is no mechanism of repression present. Because it was routine, the action was assigned to an automatic habit which was disorganized by the interruption and so was unable to resume without a fresh assignment.

The whole issue of the relation of insightless behavior to the theory of repression and unconscious mind is thus confused by the assumption that insight ordinarily is automatic. But perception, knowledge, and memory occur only by virtue of complex mental activity, and failure to notice, ignorance, and forgetting are largely a result of the lack of, or the interference with the patterns of the activity. Insightless behavior can be adequately explained without requiring the conceptions of repression and unconscious mind.

REPRESSION, SUPPRESSION, SUBLIMATION

The concept of repression, said by Freud to be the pillar on which rests the psychoanalytic edifice, involves an active agency in an unconscious mind which causes material of which persons were once conscious to become inaccessible to ordinary recall, however strenuous are the efforts to remember. Miller summarized Freud's position on repressive forgetting as follows:

The actions which satisfy any instinct are inherently pleasant and are performed because of the pleasure principle, that is, the tendency to do what is pleasant and avoid what is unpleasant. However, the super-ego, which is the internationalization of parental discipline, acts to thwart the expression of most instincts which well up from the id. Super-ego anxiety is aroused because of unpleasant experiences which occurred at other times when the instinct was satisfied. In infancy and early childhood this anxiety concerns only the danger of repetition of punishment, but later conscience develops. Thereafter the instinctive desires may not be allowed to rise to consciousness, because the individual can suffer much pain simply from realizing that he has the instincts. The satisfaction of instincts, which was innately pleasant, is now accompanied by painful anxiety, and the pleasure principle serves to cause repression of even the very fact that the instincts exist. . . .

The goal of every sort of repression is to eliminate instincts entirely from having effect in action. This goal is rarely achieved, and the instincts frequently influence behavior, ideation, or emotion, although less than they would influence it if they were not repressed. Some of these modes of influence which psychoanalysis has stressed are dreams, slips of the tongue and pen, erroneous acts, symbolic behavior, neurotic symptoms, and forgetting. Repression is like law enforcement; if the guardianship of propriety is even momentarily relaxed, the antisocial instincts find some way to break and enter into consciousness or overt behavior.[8]

Miller further states that the result of the efforts of experimental psychology to put this theory to the test has been to verify the "essentials of the clinical description of the mechanism of unconsciousness."[9] His own summary of the evidence, however, does not fully support the theory as he summarized it in the foregoing paragraphs. The experiments cited are not crucial, and in some cases are subject to alternative and equally plausible interpretations. It has been shown in Chapter 5 of the present volume that the fantastic distortion that occurs in dreams does not require

[8] By permission from Miller, *op. cit.*, pp. 234-35.
[9] *Ibid.*, p. 235.

such a theory of repression and symbolization. More work needs to be done regarding common errors such as slips of the tongue or pen, but it has not been demonstrated that all these errors, or any of them, must be interpreted as the result of the mechanism described by Freud. Selective remembering and forgetting can also be explained on a more adequate basis than is provided by this theory.[10]

Sears, on the basis of an examination of available research, arrives at a conclusion concerning amnesia with regard to experiences of childhood and infancy directly opposite that of Freud who held that the reason we do not remember early experiences is that they are repressed. Adult memories of childhood go back to the period from the third to fifth year for most persons. There is no apparent tendency to remember only pleasant aspects of childhood—sexual memories, accompanied by a realization of the forbidden character of the experience, are not uncommon. Anger, fear, awe, shame, and jealousy are among the qualities of early memories, and one count of two hundred early memories found that approximately 40 per cent of them involved fear.[11] Sears further finds:

> The evidence that factors other than repression are responsible for the relatively scanty recall from infancy has been well summarized by Brooks. In order for an apparent decrement or deficiency of recall to be called an amnesia (loss of memory), there must be adequate evidence that the response was originally learned; the explanation of infantile amnesia, of course, assumes this. To Freud, impressed by the evident vividness of children's experiences, it seemed a truism that early emotional experiences were as well learned as the later ones of adults. This naive assumption has long since been blasted. The fact is that no matter how the process of memorizing during infancy is measured, there is clear proof that it is far below the efficiency of that of the older child or adult.[12]

Suppression, a concept sometimes assumed to be related to repression, is actually a voluntary turning away from a thought or subject, and a refusal to talk about it or recognize it. This is actually not repression at all, but a diversion of consciousness to other topics. The shunned material is not put away in an inaccessible unconscious mind, but has the character of any stored memory. The person who wishes to avoid having such material come into

[10] See Chapter 8.

[11] Robert R. Sears, *Survey of Objective Studies of Psychoanalytic Concepts,* Social Science Research Council, Bulletin No. 51, 1943, pp. 106 ff.

[12] *Ibid.,* pp. 107 f. The reference in the first sentence is to F. D. Brooks, cited by L. F. Shaffer in *Child Psychology* (Boston: Houghton Mifflin Co., 1937).

consciousness can intentionally avoid preoccupation with any subject matter which might be linked with it, and thus avoid the unpleasantness of the thought. Many persons have experienced one or more excruciatingly embarrassing experiences the recall of which is accompanied by shuddering discomfort, but have been able to take up another subject which directs attention away from the unwelcome memory. This is simply an application of the principles of consciousness and attention, and not in any way an operation of a mechanism of repression, or any illustration of a conception of an unconscious mind.

Sublimation, also offered as a concept related to repression, implies that the activity stimulated by some unacceptable motive is translated into some related but more approved kind of activity which can be carried on without discomfort of conscience and without awareness of the nature of the motivation. An illustration is offered by Blanchard, who describes the case of a boy known to have strong and definite sexual interests, who took an interest in animal breeding, and also in a male Sunday School teacher.[13] Before such a case can furnish conclusive evidence of actual sublimation, however, it would have to be established that the boy did not have or desire any direct sexual activity, and also that he did not have any awareness of a connection between a sexual interest and the sublimated interests. Furthermore, a mere denial on his part could not be accepted as sufficient evidence of ignorance since various social pressures may operate to make young persons withhold their more private thoughts.

Such an investigation was apparently not made in the above case, but an investigation by Taylor which took these factors into account gives no support to the theory of sublimation.[14] Sears agrees with his conclusion in the following statement.

The empirical evidence is sharply against the theory. Taylor investigated the sources of sexual gratification of 40 brilliant, healthy, aesthetically refined young men and discovered that, although all were unmarried, all habitually obtained direct genital gratification by means of either autoerotic or illicit heterosexual activity. The men's characters and their achievements were of an order to make them clear cases of sublimation, *but no such agenitality existed.*[15]

[13] Phyllis Blanchard, "Adolescent Experience in Relation to Personality and Behavior," chap. xxii, in J. McV. Hunt, *Personality and the Behavior Disorders* (New York: The Ronald Press Co., 1944), pp. 705 f.

[14] W. S. Taylor, "A Critique of Sublimation in Males: A Study of Forty Superior Single Men," *Genetic Psychology Monograph*, Vol. 13, No. 1 (1933).

[15] Robert R. Sears, "Experimental Analysis of Psychoanalytic Phenomena," chap. ix, in Hunt, *op. cit.*, p. 320.

DIFFERENTIAL MEMORY AND UNPLEASANTNESS

Many attempts have been made to test the theory of repression and an unconscious mind by means of examining the relation of memory to pleasantness and unpleasantness. According to the theory of repression, highly unpleasant thoughts are pushed into the unconscious part of the mind and not allowed to emerge in recognizable form. Thus it has been hoped that a study of the tendency to remember pleasant things more than unpleasant would show the operation of the repressing mechanism.

A number of such studies have been made, and in general the finding is that there is somewhat better recall of subject matter which is pleasant. A few examples may be mentioned. An early study involved the presentation to subjects of both sexes of statements about women—some statements favorable and others unfavorable. A week later the women were shown to have remembered more of the favorable statements and the men more of the unfavorable ones.[16] More recently, college students were presented with statements concerning the Soviet Union and it was found that the pro-Russian students learned the favorable material faster and remembered it better than did the anti-Russian students.[17] These studies, however, do not furnish crucial proof of any operation of repression. An efficient repressing mechanism should work better—in this experiment, not all unpleasant material was forgotten; there was simply a richer recall of the pleasant. The results could be explained just as well by the assumption, not of a process that caused the forgetting of unpleasant material, but of one that aids the retention of the pleasant. It is not difficult to conceive of such a process in terms of ordinary efficiency of thought. Women may be expected to get into an occasional dispute concerning the battle of the sexes, and students certainly become involved in political discussions about Russia. When statements are presented on the side favored by the subject, they have for him a possible utility in a future argument, and may be seized upon and remembered because of that function. There is naturally less interest in dwelling on the materials which, because they are contrary to one's belief or preference, are not likely to be of future use in a controversy.

[16] M. Zillig, "Einstellung und Aussage," *Zeitschrift für Psychologie*, CVI (1928), 58-106.

[17] J. M. Levine and G. Murphy, "The Learning and Forgetting of Controversial Material," *Journal of Abnormal and Social Psychology*, XXXVIII (1943), 507-17.

Koch found some selective remembering of class grades by students who were inclined more often to remember their high grades than their low ones.[18] In a course in educational psychology, the students were given a percentage grade on each of ten quizzes. As each grade was reported to the student, he was asked to mark on the paper whether the grade caused him to be discouraged, mildly discouraged, indifferent, mildly happy, or very happy. Several weeks afterward, each student's memory of his grades was tested. Since more of the pleasant than the unpleasant grades were recalled, some have accepted the experiment as support of the repression hypothesis. But here again there is no evidence of instinct being denied by a Superego, nor is there any certainty that the difference could not have been produced by a differentiating tendency by which high grades were kept in the memory by rehearsal, by telling friends, and by relating them to welcome consequences. Furthermore, the poorest recall was not of the lowest grades, but of those to which the student felt indifferent —those which he had no reason to remember for any later action.

Miller cites a study by Sharp which is presumed to support the Freudian doctrine of repression.

Sharp used three groups of subjects. One learned fifteen *acceptable* phrases; the second fifteen *unacceptable,* and the third, fifteen *neutral* [i.e., acceptable or otherwise, emotionally, to 130 patients of a psychiatric clinic as interpreted from case histories]. . . . Then recall was tested two, nine, and sixteen days later. After the last recall relearning was carried out. The unacceptable phrases were more poorly recalled and more difficult to relearn than the neutral. The acceptable were forgotten to a degree at the time of the first memory test, but showed an enhanced recall [an actual increase in the number of items remembered] thereafter. In the long run, therefore, the acceptable phases were better retained than the neutral.[19]

Once more, however, the differential recall is as consistent with the hypothesis of the preservation of pleasant memories because of their potential utility in future action as with the concept of repression of unpleasantness. The enhanced recall after the first memory test suggests, in fact, the operation of the rehearsal and organizing activity of the acceptable memories. In any case, the experiment cannot be considered as furnishing crucial or even substantial support to the repression hypothesis. In addition to the

[18] H. L. Koch, "The Influence of Some Affective Factors upon Recall," *Journal of Genetic Psychology,* IV (1930), 171-90.

[19] Miller, *op. cit.,* p. 255. The study is: A. A. Sharp, "An Experimental Test of Freud's Doctrine of the Relation of Hedonic Tone to Memory Revival," *Journal of Experimental Psychology,* XXII (1938), 395-418.

methodological inadequacies mentioned, there is also the failure of a repetition of the experiment to obtain the same results. Heathers and Sears followed the Sharp technique closely, and reported:

> Neither with this group [normal subjects similar in scholastic and general background to Sharp's group of normals], however, nor with college students, were differences in recall between the two lists obtained. A number of variations in procedure were introduced but none influenced the negative findings. Whatever may have been the source of the differences between the two sets of data, it seems probable that this method is too uncertain and unreliable for extensive investigation.[20]

The same conclusion may fairly be made on all the experimental research which is cited in support of the repression hypothesis. None of it gives crucial support to the hypothesis; in fact, nearly all of it gives as much or more support to the functional interpretation of memory—the conception presented at length in this volume that memory has nothing automatic about it, but occurs as the result of the active organization of experience with reference to present, future, and hypothetical action. All the differential memory research shows that some unpleasant material is remembered, though not always as well as pleasant material. Ordinarily, there would not be as much use for unfavorable material in planning for future activity, although certain unpleasant items may be remembered as warnings of things to avoid. Certain materials, moreover, may be dropped from memory because of alterations in their interpretations. When presented with factual material in opposition to a fixed belief, most persons prevent the new and opposed argument from destroying their organized belief not by means of repression, but by a rationalizing activity which puts a different interpretation on the factual findings.[21]

MEMORY AND CONTEXT [22]

Certain memories which are not readily subject to recall, and which therefore may appear to be repressed, elude consciousness

---

[20] Sears, *Survey of Objective Studies of Psychoanalytic Concepts,* p. 115.

[21] A. L. Edwards, "Rationalization in Recognition as a Result of a Political Frame of Reference," *Journal of Abnormal and Social Psychology,* XXXVI (1941), 224-35.

[22] The principal section dealing with memory is in Chapter 8, but since differential memory is so important a part of the evidence used to support the doctrines of repression and an unconscious mind, it seems desirable to explain, in the present Chapter, certain of the factors of context and rehearsal which produce the effects attributed by some theorists to repression.

because the context in which they would normally appear is missing. For example, after prolonged absence from a city of former residence, it is common to find that we are unable to remember certain of the once-familiar telephone numbers and names of streets and buildings. But, on returning to the former house and neighborhood, we find that some of these names and numbers are again readily available to memory even though we have not looked them up or been told of them. Rather, the return to familiar surroundings restores the supporting context without requiring special study or effort to remember.

The inability to remember accurately the details of sudden and exciting events is sometimes attributed to the repression of highly emotional material associated with shock and fear. Numerous demonstrations have shown that a staged incident which shocks and surprises an audience—sudden gunplay and entrance and exits of shouting masked men, police, and doctors—is badly jumbled in the memories of the persons who are present. It is possible, however, that the inaccuracies of recall are the result of the fact that the new events happen so suddenly and so devoid of accompanying contexts that they are over before most persons are able to construct a mental organization in which the new event will fit logically. The experiences then have an imperfect context and, like dream material, insufficient structure in which remembered data can be stored.

As Boring points out, forgetting is not closely correlated with the passing of time.[23] It is what goes on during the time that determined how fast material is forgotten. Research has shown that there is much less loss of remembered material during the time spent in sleep than during the same number of waking hours. Old material fades out because of interference by new material, and because contexts become transformed with experience so that not all items which formerly did fit in are now harmonious with the structure. An example is given in the study by Jenkins and Dallenbach in which subjects were given nonsense syllables to memorize, and tested one, two, four, and eight hours later. In some cases, the subjects slept during these periods and in others they remained awake. On the average, more than twice as many syllables were remembered after intervals of sleep than after waking periods. Interfering experiences and the formation of new associations in which the nonsense syllables had no part occurred during the active life of the waking period. There is, of course, no suspicion in the

---

[23] Boring, Langfeld, and Weld, *op. cit.*, pp. 172-73.

case of results of this type that such a process as the repression of unacceptable instincts could produce the results described.[24]

As has been frequently stated in the present volume, mental organization is constructed with reference to action—to carry ongoing activity past a block or crisis, and to avoid crises in future activity. Any mental structure tends to remain alive according to the expectancy that it will be useful in some action. Memories which are tied to such structures are thus retained, possibly through the rehearsal which occurs in the trial-and-error process going on in imagination as problem-solving activity is carried out. There is interconnected evidence which supports this interpretation.

Boring reports a finding of differential memory for pleasant experiences which appears to be of this type.[25] The investigator, on the first day of classes after the Christmas vacation, asked his students to write down their experiences during the vacation period and to classify them as pleasant or unpleasant. Six weeks later, when the students were again asked to describe their experiences, they recalled 53 per cent of the pleasant experiences, and less than 40 per cent of those classified as unpleasant. Boring interprets this result not in terms of the concept of an unconscious mind, but mainly as a consequence of the "greater tendency to rehearse our pleasurable experiences." [26]

A recent study has caused its author to conclude that while memory is affected by rehearsal, rehearsal alone is not a sufficient condition to assure recall. The rehearsal which binds material into memory is that kind of integrating activity which forms new relationships between established contexts and the new material.[27] The same process appears to be sufficient to account for the results of the Rosenzweig study in which the superiority of memory for unfinished tasks over finished tasks was shown to occur mainly when pride and self-esteem are involved in the tasks.[28] This latter con-

[24] J. G. Jenkins and K. M. Dallenbach, "Oblivescence During Sleep and Waking," *American Journal of Psychology*, XXXV (1924), 605-12.

[25] Boring, Langfeld, and Weld, *op. cit.*, p. 170.

[26] This difference in the remembering of pleasant and unpleasant experiences, about thirteen percentage points, is not as large as that produced by other factors. Far more important is the difference between memory of meaningful and nonsense material. Ebbinghaus' curve shows that nonsense syllables were less than 35 per cent recalled after an interval of only *one day*, while the retention curve for meaningful material (objects observed briefly) shows that 90 per cent are retained after 30 days. This is an enormous contrast—far greater than any reported between pleasant and unpleasant materials of any kind in the literature of careful experiments on this topic.

[27] Thelma G. Alper, "Task-orientation and Ego-orientation as Factors in Reminiscence," *Journal of Experimental Psychology*, XXXVIII (1948), 224-38.

[28] S. Rosenzweig, "The Experimental Study of Repression," in H. A. Murray, *Explorations in Personality* (New York: Oxford University Press, 1938), pp. 472-90.

dition requires the integration of one's activity with considerations of the self and one's ability to do tasks, and therefore puts the memory into a supporting context of some importance.

General judgments on the body of knowledge of experiments bearing on the relation of differential memory to the repression hypothesis have been expressed by the authors of the two thorough reviews of the literature. Miller concludes: "Evidence for the hypothesis of repression derived from these researches is slim, but what there is is favorable. The hypothesis is complex, and will require much more carefully worked out investigations than any yet performed to confirm or disprove it." [29] Sears' conclusion is less favorable to the repression hypothesis; referring to the psychoanalytic concepts which make Freud's writings distinctive, he states that "it is these very concepts that remain hidden in the objective data. Nothing supports them; nothing refutes them." [30] A fair conclusion in the light of present research knowledge would seem to be that the experiments on memory make no contribution to the hypothesis of repression; in fact, they have the effect of placing a heavy burden of proof on those theorists who employ it. The amount of variation in learning and forgetting traced to measured factors is so large, and the amount related to unpleasantness is so slight and so plausibly explained by the connections between pleasantness and other known factors, that it cannot at present be regarded as proved that unpleasantness by itself has any repressive effects on memory.

FURTHER METHODOLOGICAL DIFFICULTIES IN THE CONCEPT OF UNCONSCIOUS MIND

Alternative Interpretations of Reports of Subjects.—When persons report lack of memory or ignorance of certain material, it is by no means safe research procedure to accept their statements at face value, even if the subjects give every surface appearance of sincerity and adhere to their declaration in the face of challenge. An experiment has found a difference in the remembering of nonsense syllables with and without sexual connotations—a result presumed to give support to the repression hypothesis.[31] It is entirely possible, however, that instead of repressing those syllables with

[29] Miller, *op. cit.*, p. 237.
[30] Sears, *op. cit.*, p. 75.
[31] D. Flanagan, "The Influence of Emotional Inhibition on Learning and Recall" (Unpublished dissertation, University of Chicago, 1930).

thinly disguised sexual connotations, the subjects deliberately avoided betraying the fact that they recognized the connotations— a fact which would indicate that they possessed a somewhat forbidden vocabulary. The desire to avoid embarrassment could cause the subjects to take the extra effort to avoid the natural context in which the syllables could be readily remembered, and to search for a nonsexual context—a process which could cause delay and inferior memory. ·While there are persons who would not need to do this, it is certain that many would not only go through this process, but would deny to an experimenter that any sexual connection entered their minds.

The present author has observed in the behavior of a schizophrenic patient a disposition to make claims and insist on them so firmly that most observers assumed he meant them literally. One such claim was that he had no memory of events before a recent date. Any direct challenge or suspicious questioning would result in vehement insistence on his part, but highly indirect conversational and sympathetic questioning could lead him to discuss happenings in his lifetime of various periods before the date of his claimed amnesia.[32]

Cameron, discussing hysteria and malingering, states:

. . . while there are many cases which are either one or the other, there are many others in which pretense and self-deception are so intermingled as to make clear distinction impossible. It is frequently said, for instance, that in malingering the patient resents being examined and that his symptomatology is apt to be unstable, inconsistent, and subject to bizzare modifications induced by deliberate suggestions on the examiner's part. But all of these characteristics of malingering can also be found in the patient, who is indubitably hysterical, but feels unjustly suspected and overplays his hand in defense of his own conviction. Indeed, a distinction can sometimes be made only by watching the course and outcome of therapy.[33]

It could be added that even the outcome of therapy does not necessarily furnish a crucial test of the difference—sincerity exists in degrees and is extremely difficult to measure. No research which avoids this problem can make a sound contribution toward the

[32] A summary of the case is published in "Reflections of Social Disorganization in the Behavior of a Schizophrenic Patient," *American Journal of Sociology,* L, No. 2 (1944), 134-41.

[33] Norman Cameron, *The Psychology of Behavior Disorders* (Boston: Houghton Mifflin Co., 1947), p. 384. Cameron cites a study of amnesia which produces the same conclusion—that the difference between hysterical amnesia and malingering is only one of degree. See D. Parfitt and C. Gall, "Psychogenic Amnesia: the Refusal to Remember," *Journal of Mental Science,* XC (1944), 511-31.

hypothesis of repression. Where satisfactory indirect methods are used to check the subject's report, it is sometimes found that repression is not actually present—that what the subject says he does not know, he actually does know, what he says he does not remember he does remember, and what he claims he cannot see, he actually does see. An instance is reported in which a person with "hysterical blindness" claimed that he could not see, but was nevertheless successfully conditioned to blink at a light, after associating the light with a puff of air, showing that at least his nervous system was entirely capable of response to light.[34] Luriĩa has also found evidence that what is to all appearances hypnotic amnesia is actually no more than suppression, or refusal to communicate or to admit the forbidden knowledge.[35] In the experiment, a hypnotized subject showed emotional responses on a test to material which, because of the hypnotic command, he was not supposed to be able to remember.

Hypnosis as Evidence for the Repression Hypothesis.—Unlike the almost negligible evidence afforded by experiments on differential memory, the demonstrations of hypnotic repression are generally taken to be an absolute matter—what is ordered to be ignored or forgotten under hypnosis is believed by many theorists to be actually unknown or completely forgotten. To the extent that hypnosis has been carried on as demonstrations rather than as definitive experiments, this point of view has appeared to be upheld. For many years, in fact, the bulk of work with hypnosis has apparently not been undertaken with any skeptical inquiry into the mechanism.[36]

[34] L. H. Cohen, E. R. Hilgard, and G. R. Wendt, "Sensitivity to Light in a Case of Hysterical Blindness Studied by Reinforcement, Inhibition and Conditioning Methods," *Yale Journal of Biological Medicine*, VI (1933), 61-67.

[35] A. R. Luriĩa, *The Nature of Human Conflicts* (New York: Liveright Publishing Corp., 1932), pp. 128-49.

[36] The distinction between demonstration and experiment is well illustrated by the display of exceptional strength and resistance to fatigue of the person in the hypnotic trance who is informed that he is powerful. In the shows conventionally put on for college classes and popular audiences, the subject admits that he is powerful, and volunteers from the audience are invited to press down on an extended arm and discover what appears to be great strength. When *measurement* by instruments of either strength or fatigue is employed, however, no such abnormal strength appears (see Boring, Langfeld, and Weld, *op. cit.*, p. 56). The present writer has made such measurements on subjects under hypnosis and found an actual decline of strength of grip when the subject was in the trance. In this case, the experimenter doing the hypnotizing was working with his favorite subject with whom he had had years of experience. The subject had shortly before "demonstrated"—without measurement—his normal strength and the hypnotist had predicted confidently that the grip would be far more powerful when the subject was put in a trance. He had been making

To a considerable extent, the belief that hypnosis demonstrates an absolute process of repression rests on exhibitions of post-hypnotic suggestion. The subject, having been ordered during the trance state to perform a specified action later on a given signal, and to be ignorant of the fact that he had been so ordered, often does carry out the action and, on being questioned concerning why he did it, replies that he does not know, or gives some contrived answer. He is presumed actually to have repressed the knowledge or memory of the command, and not to know why he performs the action. The typical demonstration stops at this point, having convinced the experimenter and the audience that a successful demonstration of hypnotic repression has been made. This acceptance at face value of the subject's statement is a serious methodological error, in view of the well-known tendency of many subjects to report what they are told to report even when they actually know otherwise. It is never safe to accept the report of the subject, even if he gives every appearance of sincerity, without an extensive and indirect investigation of what he actually sees, remembers, or knows.

The writer has collaborated with an experienced investigator of hypnosis in the following experiment. The hypnotist put the subject in a trance and ordered him to obey all instructions by the writer. All further orders by the writer were repeated by the hypnotist, to make sure that the subject would understand what he was supposed to do. The subject was then informed that he would be shown a white card, with no markings on it, and ordered to see no markings of any kind. He was shown a card with a large star outlined in ink, inside of which was a small, solid black crescent. As he looked at the card, he was again told that there were no markings there, and ordered to see no markings. The card was then removed and for a short time unrelated matters were taken up. Then the writer asked the subject if he remembered looking at a white card, and the latter reported that he did. He was asked if there was any kind of mark or design on it, and he answered that there was not. After a question or two on other matters he was told that not long before he had seen, somewhere, an outline

such demonstrations for years, before students and faculty of a psychology department and a prominent medical university, and it apparently had never occurred to him that comparative measurements were necessary to establish what he had been assuming to be true. Although there has, of course, been careful experimentation in the field of hypnosis, the spirit of demonstration has for many years been far more popular, and has been responsible for the perpetuation of a large amount of misconception about what hypnosis accomplishes.

drawing of a star, and was ordered to remember it. He admitted that he did remember it. He was then asked if he could remember any design inside of star. For some moments he appeared to struggle internally, after which he stated that there was a small, dark object within the star, and after further urging stated that he had seen a crescent. He thus was shown actually to have seen and to have remembered what he had been ordered not to see, in spite of the firm belief expressed by the hypnotist before the experiment that the subject, when ordered not to see something, actually does not see it and has no more experience of the object before him than if no such object had ever been there.

Essentially the same finding is made by the use of an ingenious device to deceive the subject. A box with an opening for each eye is shown to the subject. Opposite these openings the subject observes that there are disks of colored glass, red opposite the left opening and green opposite the right opening. The subject does not know that inside the box are prisms which make each line of vision cross to the other side. Then, when he is hypnotized and after he is told that he is blind in his left eye, the subject is given the box, told to look in with both eyes, and tell what color he sees. He reports that he sees green, not knowing that that color is actually visible only with the left eye. In short, he reports not his actual visual experience, but what he thinks he ought to report on the basis of the command given him.[37]

Pattie has successfully shown the same effect with reference not only to alleged hypnotic blindness of one eye, but to anesthesia of one hand, and deafness in one ear as well.[38] The technique in the deafness experiment consisted of first hypnotizing the subjects and telling them that they were deaf in one specified ear. Telephone receivers, muffled in sponge rubber to avoid bone conduction, were put on the subjects. The two sides of the receivers produced tones of slightly different frequencies, so that if both were heard at once the subject would be aware of a single, fluctuating tone. The subjects were then asked, by means of a written question, whether the tone they heard, presumably in the good ear since one was supposed to be deaf, was steady or fluctuating. All four of the subjects reported hearing the fluctuating tone, and some indicated by hand movements the periods of fluctuations with great accuracy.

---

[37] See Boring, Langfeld, and Weld, *op. cit.*, pp. 56-57. Boring remarks, "Experiments of this sort make hypnosis resemble faking, but it is a very insistent and enthusiastic kind of faking."

[38] Frank A. Pattie, "The Genuineness of Unilateral Deafness Produced by Hypnosis," *American Journal of Psychology*, LXIII (1950), 84-86.

Two subjects after a while began to report a steady tone, but the investigator reasons that a report of this kind "would be called malingering if it had occurred in non-hypnotized subjects."

Miller reports that subjects under hypnosis have electrocardiograms and breathing records more like persons who are awake than like those who are asleep. He claims, moreover, that although the subject is thought not to perceive if ordered not to do so, there are three reasons why it is certain that this is not always true. He has found that (a) many subjects admit later that they were playacting, and that, although their attention appeared deflected from something, they nevertheless were aware of it; (b) in some cases, subjects refused to obey certain orders, showing that they knew what was involved; and (c) one subject, told that he was in a rotating chair, agreed that he was, but did not show the eye movements that normally accompany such rotation. "Dorcus concluded," Miller continues, "that the true facts of behavior under hypnosis are unconscious, not in the sense of unavailable to awareness, but *merely in the sense of being incommunicable.*" [39]

It has sometimes been supposed that persons under hypnosis may be made to regress to an earlier stage of development, and by the use of a demonstration without definitive experiment this may appear to be so. Careful technique, however, makes it appear that the supposed regression of the subject is actually not different from a simulated performance. One experimenter hypnotized nine college freshmen, ordered them to be three years old, and then administered a Binet test. Their average mental age in this condition was five years and eleven months, with a range from four years, seven months to six years, nine months. As a control, seven subjects who were not hypnotized were asked to simulate such a performance. The results were virtually the same—their average mental age was five years, five months and the range about the same as that of the experimental group.[40]

In a similar study a seventeen-year-old girl was hypnotized and told to be a schoolgirl of thirteen. On the Stanford Binet test she scored significantly lower than her age level on the reasoning and abstract tests, but only slightly lower on memory tests, and no lower at all on verbal tests such as those measuring vocabulary.

[39] Miller, *op. cit.*, pp. 118-19. The reference in the last statement is to R. M. Dorcus, "Modification by Suggestion of Some Vestibular and Visual Responses," *American Journal of Psychology*, XC (1937), 82-87.

[40] P. C. Young, "Hypnotic Regression—Fact or Artifact?" *Journal of Abnormal and Social Psychology*, XXXV (1940), 273-78.

This result has the pattern that would be expected of a simulated performance.[41]

It may be possible, through more critical experimentation, to formulate the precise nature of the somewhat spectacular obedience of the hypnotized subject to the orders of the experimenter, manifested in the subject's refusal to communicate what he apparently knows and remembers but has been ordered to forget. It is conceivable that such exceptional obedience may be a result of the authority and prestige of the scientist, and of the impressive and almost supernatural air of the experience which might convince the subject of the authenticity of the phenomenon at the start and prepare him to go along with any orders in the belief that any departure from what is expected is his own fault and need not be admitted. Boring states:

> The hypnotized person behaves as if he were enthusiastically acting out a big lie in order to please the hypnotist, acting it out and believing it as he acts. Sometimes he has to perceive something in order to know that it is something he is supposed not to perceive. . . . This desire to please the hypnotist has to take its chances along with all the other desires that fight for dominance. Will a subject under hypnosis stab a man with a dagger? He will stab a friend with a cardboard dagger if he knows the dagger is cardboard. A habitual stabber might be persuaded to stab an enemy with a real dagger. A college student was once induced under hypnosis to throw what he knew certainly to be strong nitric acid at the face of a very good friend. The acid never reached its goal because invisible glass was interposed, but the student did not know about the glass. Still he did know that he was in a psychological laboratory where strange things may happen without permanent harm to anyone, and he may have been trusting the hypnotist to protect him from the apparent consequences of his act.[42]

This type of willingness to obey a seemingly outrageous order is not a phenomenon of hypnosis only. Initiation ceremonies of lodges and fraternities sometimes involve such commands as to fall forward toward the fixed point of a sword, or to jump barefooted from a platform into a scattering of tacks. The initiate may not see how he can be protected from the danger or pain, but has acquired, as a part of his orientation, the knowledge that all the present members of the order survived the same ceremony, and the realization that he was chosen for membership because he was desired as a comrade. Every adult knows that there are tricks which are difficult to fathom at a glance, and so depends, per-

[41] G. Keir, "An Experiment in Mental Testing Under Hypnosis," *Journal of Mental Science*, XCI (1945), 346-52.

[42] Boring, Langfeld, and Weld, *op. cit.*, p. 57. By permission of John Wiley & Sons.

haps, on this realization in submitting to what appear to be the dangers in such staged affairs as initiations and hypnosis. It requires no hypothesis of unconsciousness or of abnormal loss of autonomy to account for the willingness of some subjects to go along with the command of the hypnotist, especially if we remember that by no means all subjects obey the unreasonable, embarrassing, and dangerous commands.

Regression and Unconsciousness.—According to some formulations, it is supposed that in experiencing certain frustrations the person unconsciously tends to regress to an earlier stage of his psychological development by assuming the mental characteristics of a youth, child, infant, or even fetus. Thus an adult woman, in reaction to a certain type of shock, may put ribbons in her hair and play with dolls, return to childlike speech and habits of thought. In even more severe cases, such as the curled-up bed posture observed in some catatonic schizophrenics, it is assumed that the person is unconsciously assuming the fetal posture and reflecting the desire to return to the conditions of intrauterine life.

Certain aspects of the behavior of a child following the birth of a younger sibling have also been interpreted as regression. The older child is sometimes observed to return to certain earlier habits such as sucking the thumb, preferring to drink milk from a bottle with a nipple, and attempting to crawl into the infant's crib. Some theorists, in fact, advise that it is best to permit such behavior on the ground that it is natural and that harmful consequences might follow its frustration.[43] It is unsafe methodologically, however, to make such an interpretation of child behavior without careful controls in the experiment. Children without younger siblings and with no obvious reason to regress can also be observed to take an interest in such activity; this tendency is even more marked when all adult attention is on an infant who is so occupied.

The resumption by an adult of youthful or childlike interests is also often explicable on grounds simpler than regression theory. Old activities may be abandoned for many years because there is no use for them, only to reappear on occasions when some use for them arises. As Murphy has pointed out:

[43] In such a case we have an illustration of a not uncommon methodological circularity in which a policy, based on a hypothesis, can produce results which easily appear to support the hypothesis itself. Some persons, under the influence of psychoanalytic conceptions, expect their older child to "regress" in this fashion after the arrival of a new baby, and make provisions for it—such as keeping a bottle with a nipple on it to be used at will by the older child. The latter thus is encouraged to support the theory of regression, and usually is willing to comply.

The adolescent has not merely lost his interest in playing marbles or pinning the tail on the donkey which so delighted him five years earlier; his *picture of himself,* his need to see himself as an almost-grownup is sufficient to block the expression of the more childish tastes. The adolescent or adult may, however, dream childishly; he may, though not "frustrated," nevertheless "regress" to the old canalizations which are still physiologically there but need a field situation (such as a college or an American Legion reunion) to permit their fresh expression. The canalizations are not lost, they are overlaid by new activities; let the crust be removed, free expression granted, and they reappear without the need of new cultivation. The young father has not played with an electric train for twenty years; but when he buys one for Junior's Christmas, there he is on the floor, utterly engrossed in it.[44]

The interpretation of certain aspects of schizophrenic behavior as regression has encountered formidable barriers in the results of objective studies. Research by Cameron, for example, has shown that the style of reasoning displayed by the schizophrenic is not readily explained by a hypothesis of regression. In their use of types of explanation, children and schizophrenics were found to be quite unlike; in fact, the schizophrenics actually found it more difficult to indulge in childish types of thought than in adult types.[45]

The example of use of the fetal posture of the schizophrenic used to support the regression theory is also inadequate without comparable observations on the sleeping postures of nonschizophrenics. Such a study has been made, and it gives no support to the theory of regression in this illness.[46] Among the schizophrenics observed, only 9 per cent of the total number of postures and 6 per cent of the total sleeping time represented fetal position. This did not differ materially from the sleeping postures frequently observed in the one normal man available as a control.

Automatic Writing as Operation of Unconscious Mind.—It has been thought that a sort of free association technique known as automatic writing could directly bring out material from unconscious portions of the mind. Some investigators have tried to put themselves into a condition in which the hand could proceed with continuous writing without any guidance from consciousness. It is difficult, however, to make an objective check on a person's claim

[44] Gardner Murphy, *Personality: A Biosocial Approach to Origins and Structure* (New York: Harper & Bros., 1947), p. 188.

[45] Cameron, "Reasoning, Regression and Communication in Schizophrenics." *Psychological Monographs,* L, No. 1, 1938. And "A Study of Thinking in Senile Deterioration and Schizophrenic Disorganization," *American Journal of Psychology,* LI (1938), 650-64.

[46] P. H. DuBois and T. W. Forbes, "Studies of Catatonia, III. Bodily Postures Assumed While Sleeping," *Psychiatric Quarterly,* VIII (1934), 546-52.

that he did not know at the time what he was writing, and it is possible and even likely that a large part of what is purported to be automatic writing is actually done by ordinary means and is no more mysterious than the Ouija board, which works best when the operators are entirely conscious of the message the board is to report.

One famous poem, sometimes thought to be a clear example of automatic writing, offers, upon analysis, a convenient illustration of what the process probably is.   In 1816, Samuel Taylor Coleridge published an imaginative poem entitled "Kubla Khan" which he offered as "rather a psychological curiosity than on the ground of any supposed *poetic* merits."   He explained that some years before —in fact in early summer in 1798—he had been feeling ill and had taken a prescribed dose of laudanum (opium). The drug took effect and put him to sleep in his chair as he was reading a passage in *Purchas His Pilgrimage.* He slept for about three hours, during which he experienced a vivid dream, the content of which he attempted to put into a poem on the instant of awakening.

The resulting poem, "Kubla Khan," has been widely appreciated for its captivating imagery and has also been of strong psychological interest as a representation of unconscious workings of the mind as released by opium. More than one attempt has been made to devise a psychoanalytic interpretation of the poem. Robert Graves, for one, built up, on the basis of superficial evidence and unnecessary theory, a rich interpretation in terms of Coleridge's difficulties with his wife and a supposed unconscious tendency to retreat from life as illustrated by the imagery of caves with underground oceans.[47]

Because of the unusually rich record of the activities, thoughts, and reading available on Coleridge, however, it has been possible to locate more sources of the ideas and images of the poem. This was done by John Livingston Lowes, whose book, *The Road to Xanadu,* contains what must be one of the most thorough feats of detective work ever performed in tracing the sources of a poem. The triumph appears to be complete. The entire content of the poem is adequately accounted for and is shown to be unmistakably related to Coleridge's life and interests. The sudden shifts to what appear to be unrelated themes in the poem are shown to have intelligible connections in the light of Coleridge's mental content.

[47] Robert Graves, *The Meaning of Dreams,* London 1924, pp. 145-58; cited in John Livingston Lowes, *The Road to Xanadu* (Boston, Houghton Mifflin Co., 1927), p. 593.

In general it seems fair to say that no assumptions of abnormality of any kind are required to account for the nature of the poem, and there is no necessity to refer to repressed material or any other aspects of unconscious mentality. Possibly the effect of opium may have been to make Coleridge unable to put himself in the role of a reader, as he composed the piece in such a manner that the themes were not made self-explanatory. In general, however, the material of the poem had been consciously sought for and selected by Coleridge, and in the poem was organized as logically as works of art ordinarily demand, and expressed in a manner no different from many another consciously invented piece of literature.

The words Coleridge was reading at the time he passed into the opium sleep were:

In Xamdu did Cublai Can build a stately Palace, encompassing sixteene miles of plaine ground with a wall, wherein are fertile Meddowes, pleasant springs, delightfull Streames, and all sorts of beasts of chase and game, and in the middest thereof a sumptuous house of pleasure, . . .

The relation of these lines to the beginning of the poem is obvious:

In Xanadu did Kubla Khan
A stately pleasure-dome decree:
Where Alph, the sacred river, ran
Through caverns measureless to man
    Down to a sunless sea.
So twice five miles of fertile ground
With walls and towers were girdled round:
And there were gardens bright with sinuous rills,
Where blossomed many an incense-bearing tree;
And here were forests ancient as the hills,
Enfolding sunny spots of greenery.

Not content with showing the general relation of these two images—from Purchas and from Coleridge's poem—Lowes successfully pursued each of the details. Why, for example, was Xamdu altered to Xanadu? Coleridge invented the latter name, but he did not have to exert himself to do it—he was familiar with variations on the name, such as Xaindu and Xandu. A veteran poet, however, and author of such a rhythmical work as the *Rime of the Ancient Mariner,* he had no hesitation in adding the right syllable where rhythm demands it.

The account by Purchas said nothing about a dome in connection with the Palace and the houses of pleasure. But Coleridge had read various accounts of legends of such retreats of distant monarchs, and he left evidence in his notebooks that they fascinated him and that he sought for more legends of the same kind. Some of these accounts, notably in descriptions of the pleasure-houses of Cashmere kings, did speak of domes, perhaps similar to the marble dome of the Taj Mahal.

Alph, the sacred river which traveled through caverns down to a sunless sea, is a sort of composite of legends of sacred rivers, including the Nile, which are supposed in some stories to have such a subterranean course. The name appears to have come from Alpheus, one such legendary river about which Coleridge had read. Thomas Taylor, an author whose writings Coleridge had referred to as "darling studies," had translated a statement from Pausanias that the Alpheus runs a violent part of its course underground, and that a fable ascribed a similar course to the Nile. Strabo, whose writings were also known to Coleridge, had also linked the two rivers in the same way. Seneca, another writer whose works were known to Coleridge, wrote in his Sixth Book that " . . . there are underground rivers and a hidden sea . . . the Alpheus . . . sink(s) in Achaia and, having crossed beneath the sea, pour(s) forth in Sicily . . . the Nile in summer . . . bursts forth from the ground." Even the character of "the lifeless ocean" and "the sunless sea" of the poem appear in Seneca:

. . . the depths of earth contain a vast sea with winding shores. I see nothing to prevent or oppose the existence of a beach down there in the obscurity, or a sea finding its way through the hidden entrances to its appointed place. There, too, . . . the hidden regions being desert without inhabitant give freer scope to the waves of the nether ocean.

The sacred rivers ran (the fourth line) "Through caverns measureless to man." Numerous writings concerning the fountains of the Nile, caverns in the earth out of which this sacred river issues, referred to futile attempts to find a bottom. Herodotus, for one, pronounced them "impossible to fathom," explaining that Psammetichus " . . . had caused a rope to be made, many thousand fathoms in length, and had sounded the fountain with it, but could find no bottom."

Some of the imagery comes from legends of Abyssinia. The image of "Ancestral voices prophesying war" in the poem came partly from legendary hermits and holy men of Abyssinia who loudly foretold war. "His flashing eyes, his floating hair" in a later part of the poem were characteristics of an Abyssinian king, whose eyes had been described as the only features visible because of "long hair floating all around his face." The poem mentions an Abyssinian maid who played on a dulcimer "Singing of Mount Abora." Abora appears to be a dream creation formed from names of the rivers Abola and Astoboras, and was applied by Coleridge to Mount Amara, an Abyssinian mountain where kings kept their sons under safeguard. And in such fashion Lowes lays bare the sources of the ideas, images, and figures of speech of the poem in ninety pages of text and extensive added notes.

All this comes from material in which Coleridge had a live and conscious interest. He read extensively, and with full intentions of writing. Whatever the operations of his mind may have been in creating a poem of this sort, there is no indication that any concealed symbolism or any mysterious aspects of a hidden unconscious mind are involved. The inventions and distortions are no different in character from those made by any poet in the interest of euphony and rhythm, and freshness and vividness of figure.

Summary

In the modern view, consciousness is not an organ but a process. It is an interaction of images produced by tentative actions; occurring at the time of a blocking of hitherto on-going activity, it serves to find a means of resumption. When the solution is found and the routine re-established, the operation of consciousness is no longer required for this problem and turns to other problems. As long as activity proceeds smoothly, the aid of the process of consciousness is not required; habits normally work automatically. Any habit may, if some problem arises in connection with its operation, immediately become the subject of inspection by consciousness.

There is thus no automatic consciousness of our activity, surroundings, motivation, or anything else, except as it enters into the problems arising from blocked activity. We require no concept of repression into an unconscious mind to account for the ignorance of certain aspects of our surroundings, or ignorance of the reasons why we perform certain actions. Material which has never been studied as relevant to a problem does not have to be repressed, for it never has made any impression on the nervous system. It is neither in the unconscious nor the conscious mind; it is not present at all.

To a considerable extent, the inquiry into the nature of unconsciousness is obstructed by confusion in the use of the term, as illustrated by Miller's list of sixteen different meanings of "unconsciousness" in current usage. In certain of these usages, communication is obviously served by using some other term—as in the case of unconsciousness as "unawareness," or unconsciousness as "not knowing."

The psychoanalytic conception of consciousness, however, is popular and influential enough to justify examination. This theory maintains the existence of instincts which, since their expression would meet with severe disapproval, cannot be faced consciously and are thus repressed into an unconscious part of the mind. While the research is not as definitive as could be desired, enough objective material is available to make possible a tentative assessment of the theory. The result of such assessment is that the theory is supported by little other than uncontrolled "clinical" and common-sense observation. To the extent that research approaches the rigor of the controlled experiment, the theory appears to be less and less necessary to account for behavior.

The fact that persons often perform actions for reasons they do not sufficiently understand—without insight regarding their own motivation—is sometimes cited as evidence of the repression of the instincts which cause these actions. But an examination of evidence shows that there is never any automatic insight. No mechanisms exist to give us a complete account of our own motivation, and what knowledge we have, we gain by the same method used to obtain knowledge of any kind. Ignorance of one's own motivation is of the same nature as ignorance of anything and requires no theory of repression to account for it.

Much of the objective evidence offered in favor of the repression hypothesis consists of the reported tendency to remember pleasant material better than unpleasant. Careful inspection of the evidence does not, however, give firm support to this generalization. The notion that early memories of childhood and infancy are lacking because of repression of the unpleasant character of early experience has, as Sears states, " ... long since been blasted." The lack of early memories is the result of the undeveloped ability to remember. Between the ages of three and five most children acquire lasting memories, with no measurable excess of pleasant over unpleasant types. Although experiments on the relation of memory to pleasantness have sometimes shown an apparent disposition to remember somewhat better the material which is presumed to be of a pleasant character, in all these studies a considerable amount of unpleasant material was also remembered—the mechanism of repression, if there was any, operating at low efficiency in such cases. The results of such researches, however, are not uniform. In one prominent example, a repetition of the experiment by other investigators failed to discover the differential memory. In general, the studies which found some differences in favor of the memory of pleasant items failed to control the possibility that these may have had more meaning and function in terms of future activity, and therefore were remembered by the same processes that anything is remembered. There is no conclusive evidence, nor in fact any strong support in the research, for the conception that unpleasant material is actively repressed.

A methodological difficulty, too often overlooked in the investigation of processes of unconsciousness, is the problem of knowing how much of the subject's report of his own experience can be accepted at face value. It is clear from research experience that some persons, for various reasons, fail to state accurately what they see, feel, know, and remember. Some subjects claiming inability to see can be shown to react to light. Some who claim to have no memory of a certain event, or of any events before a certain date, can be shown by indirect means to be incorrectly describing their states of mind. It is possible, and in fact highly probable, that a considerable amount of systematic error in the investigation of hysteria, hypnosis, and behavior of psychotic and neurotic persons results from inadequate consideration of this difficulty.

Hypnotic phenomena have been considered by many to furnish crucial support of the hypothesis of repression and of the concept of an unconscious mind. Taken at face value, the demonstrations appear spectacular, but careful experimental technique places many of the conventional notions of the process in a doubtful status. Generations of students have witnessed demonstrations of the abnormal strength and resistance to fatigue of a subject under hypnosis, but measurement by instruments always fails to support this illusion. Similarly, audiences have been impressed by the phenomenon of posthypnotic suggestion, a demonstration in which it appears that the subject remembers and obeys a command contained only in his unconscious mind without knowing consciously why he is performing the specified act. In view of the evidence concerning the unreliability of a subject's own report, however, it is unsafe to accept the testimony of the subject concerning his inability to remember the command to perform the action. Elaborate and indirect methods, in fact, can be employed to trap him into a betrayal of a memory which he is determined not to admit.

There is impressive evidence to suggest that the demonstrations of the hypnotized subjects represent a kind of "enthusiastic faking" in compliance with an authoritative expectation by the hypnotist, whose authority is supported by the general atmosphere of a laboratory, the prestige of psychology, and to a considerable extent the prestige of all science. In order to simulate an experience, however, the subject must know how to do so. Experiments reveal that the subjects simulate only what they believe to be the experience they are asked to have, and in cases of imperfect knowledge they fall considerably short of achieving the expected phenomenon. When ordered to regress to an early age, they enact what they believe to be the characteristic behavior of that age, often missing the true pattern by a large margin.

Further support for the theory of an unconscious mind is sometimes supposed to be indicated by the phenomena of regression. Here again, however, the observations are subject to criticism on the grounds of inadequate controls. A resumption of early interests may result from normal processes and so requires no notion of unconsciousness—children may find certain of the activities of a new infant engaging enough to imitate without any motive of jealousy, and adults may engage in children's play in appropriate contexts. Even the schizophrenic may deliberately adopt an infantile role for conscious reasons which fit in with his private mental organization. As Cameron's research has shown, the schizophrenics do not actually duplicate the mental characteristics of children.

Citation of a curled-up sleeping posture by some schizophrenic patients as evidence of a wish to regress to intrauterine life is unjustified inasmuch as there is lack of evidence that this phenomenon occurs with high frequency in schizophrenics, or that it occurs with greater frequency among schizophrenics than among normal persons. There are various reasons for curling up in bed—to keep warm when covers are inadequate, to fit into a sagging bed, to rest stretched muscles and so forth. Posture cannot firmly be linked to a theory of unconsciousness without an inquiry considerably more sophisticated than psychological intuition or "clinical method."

In general, there appears to be little actual necessity in social psychology for a concept of unconscious mind. There are, of course, many automatic processes—most of our behavior is, in fact, automatic. These can, however, be described in other terms and do not have to be characterized as mental. The heartbeat does not require consciousness, nor is there any need for insight into the motivation for the heart to beat; it is entirely unnecessary as well to characterize as part of an unconscious mind the mechanism that keeps this organ going. Nor, finally, is this mythology useful to describe the automatic character of habit, the functioning of memory and forgetting, or the behavior of psychotics and hypnotized subjects.

SELECTED REFERENCES

MILLER, JAMES GRIER. *Unconsciousness.* New York: John Wiley & Sons, Inc., 1942. A critical survey of the literature dealing with the concept of unconsciousness.

SEARS, ROBERT R. *Survey of Objective Studies of Psychoanalytic Concepts.* New York: Social Science Research Council, Bulletin No. 51, 1943. An integrated review of objective research bearing on various aspects of Freudian doctrine. Contains an extensive bibliography.

Chapter 7

THE EMERGENCE OF SELF-CONSCIOUSNESS
IN SOCIAL INTERACTION

THE GENESIS OF THE SELF

MAN IS not born with a self, or with consciousness of self. Each person becomes an object to himself by virtue of an active process of discovery. The material for building a conception of self is acquired in the process of interaction with other persons. The self is defined in the reactions of others.

Those theorists who have been most influenced by the instinctivist point of view have been disposed to conceive of the self as an organization present before birth, equipped in the intrauterine life with desires, resentments, jealousies, and other complex sentiments. This conception, however, does not have the support of direct observation or objective research. As Cameron has pointed out,

> We have no objective evidence whatever to support the hypothesis that a fetus can react in terms of complex interpersonal relationships, or that retention and recall of the circumstances of intrauterine life are biologically possible. The many studies made of infant behavior during early postnatal life yield no sign of these abilities. The burden of proof, therefore, rests heavily upon those who claim that a relatively undeveloped fetus, confined in the amniotic bag of waters, can react to its surroundings in ways that are far beyond its postnatal abilities weeks or months later, and under environmental conditions that are infinitely more favorable.[1]

There is of course no single organ which can be called the self, nor any uniform part of the body believed by all persons to contain the self. An investigation of the testimony of persons of various ages asked to give the spatial location of the self within them showed that while many were able to report a feeling of spatial location there was a great variety of such places named. Some felt the self to be in the head, others in the face, brain, heart, genitals,

---

[1] Norman Cameron, *The Psychology of Behavior Disorders* (Boston: Houghton Mifflin Co., 1947), p. 20.

chest, and elsewhere.[2] Some persons, of course, conceive of no particular location of self within the body, but think of the self as occupying most of or all the body, if they think of the matter at all. As is shown below, the body is only one aspect of self and is built more on the basis of organized ways of acting than on the character of the physiological organism.

Over half a century ago, Baldwin began the development of the investigation of the self as an actively organized concept.[3] He observed that the child originally has no conception of self, but develops one along with the development of conceptions of other persons. He believed that the earliest forms of the conception of self were merged with other persons; that is, the self of a very small child includes his mother, brothers and sisters, and other persons close to him. Only with experience does he learn to differentiate himself from his first primary group. Others have seen the process in similar terms and have contributed details concerning the characteristic order of discoveries regarding the self.[4]

The conception that others are discovered before the self receives some support in the observation made by several students of infant behavior that infants learn the pronouns referring to others before they learn their own; that is, the pronoun "I" is the last one to be learned.[5] The child may commonly be observed to call himself by the name "baby" or his given name before learning to use either "I" or "me." In part, however, this may be attributable to the greater complexity of the pronouns, the referents or antecedents of which vary with the person who is speaking. "Tom," for example, always refers to the same person no matter who says it, and should therefore be easier to learn than "you," which may mean anyone, depending on who is speaking and to whom the words are addressed. Nevertheless, the use of "I" may serve as an indication that the core of a self-concept has developed.

INTERNALIZATION OF THE SOCIAL PROCESS

George H. Mead has shown in a detailed and impressive statement how the discovery or the organization of a sense of self may

[2] E. L. Horowitz, "Spatial Localization of the Self," *Journal of Social Psychology,* VI (1935), 379-87.

[3] J. M. Baldwin, *Mental Development in the Child and the Race* (New York: The Macmillan Co., 1895).

[4] See M. Sherif and H. Cantril, *The Psychology of Ego-Involvements* (New York: John Wiley & Sons, Inc., 1947), chap. vii, "The Genetic Formation of the Ego," pp. 156-98. The chapter contains a 64-item bibliography on the process of organizing the self.

[5] *Ibid.,* p. 177.

take place within a process of social interaction.[6] Without such a social process there would be no way for a person to discover himself.

How can an individual get outside himself (experientially) in such a way as to become an object to himself? This is the essential psychological problem of selfhood or of self-consciousness; and its solution is to be found by referring to the process of social conduct or activity in which the given person or individual is implicated. The individual experiences himself as such, not directly, but only indirectly, from the particular standpoints of other individual members of the same social group, or from the generalized standpoint of the social group as a whole to which he belongs . . . he becomes an object to himself only by taking the attitudes of other individuals toward himself within a social environment or context of experience and behavior in which both he and they are involved.[7]

The essence of this ability, sometimes referred to as "social intelligence," consists of taking the role of another person, or putting oneself in the place of another. We do this, as has been pointed out, by responding to our own gestures as others respond to them.

We must be constantly responding to the gesture we make if we are to carry on successful vocal conversation. The meaning of what we are saying is the tendency to respond to it. You ask somebody to bring a visitor a chair. You arouse the tendency to get the chair in the other, but if he is slow to act you get the chair yourself. The response to the vocal gesture is the doing of a certain thing and you arouse that same tendency in yourself. You are always replying to yourself, just as other people reply.[8]

The tendency to respond to one's own gestures is, of course, a faint, inhibited muscular tendency in normal situations, measurable by instruments but not otherwise noticed. In certain circumstances, such as high excitement, the muscular tendency becomes visible. Spectators at a prize fight may be heard to shout, "Hit him!" and respond to their own command by a fistic assault on the atmosphere, and football watchers may assume a tackling gesture as they implore the players to stop an opposing runner. This is a simple instance of the internalization of a social process involving a gesture and a response, while acting in the role of another.

[6] George Herbert Mead, *Mind, Self, and Society* (Chicago: University of Chicago Press, 1934). Mead's statement was put together by students after his death, from notes of his classroom lectures, and thus may not contain all the qualifications and details it might have if he had personally written and revised his work. His formulation, however, has been highly influential and is believed by many to furnish the best key to the relations between mind, self, and society without relying on mysticism or the use of dubious biological assumptions.

[7] *Ibid.*, p. 138.

[8] *Ibid.*, p. 67.

In a more complex process, the human engages in a long inter-change between his own gestures and those representing an imagi-nary other person. Small children do this commonly in play. One child may take the role of a baby and another of a parent, but a solitary child often takes both roles, or the two simultaneous roles of himself and an imaginary companion. In this case, though the two roles are clearly separate, they are both played by the same person as simultaneous organizations of gestures. Since the ges-tures on both sides are overt, this kind of play may be considered to be intermediate between the automatic conversation of gestures, such as seen in the previous illustration of a dog fight, and the full internalization of simultaneous roles as found in self-conscious behavior.

A somewhat more complex situation occurs in an organized game, when it is required that a player be ready to take not one, but several roles, into consideration. In baseball, the player must know what to expect from each of the other persons in any con-ceivable playing situation. Mead writes,

What he does is controlled by his being everyone else on that team, at least in so far as those attitudes affect his own particular response. We get then an "other" which is an organization of the attitudes of those involved in the same process.[9]

Such a game is a type of social organization, and furnishes or-ganization of a self when the interrelations of persons in the game become a set of interrelated attitudes in the person.

The game has a logic, so that such an organization of the self is rendered possible: there is a definite end to be obtained; the actions of the different individuals are all related to each other with reference to that end so that they do not conflict; one is not in conflict with himself in the attitude of another man on the team. If one has the attitude of the person throwing the ball he can also have the response of catching the ball. The two are related so that they further the purpose of the game itself. They are interrelated in a uni-tary, organic fashion.[10]

The organized set of possible actions of all the other persons in such a game as baseball become a set of tendencies held simul-taneously in the internal organization of a person. Mead desig-nates the organization as a whole the "generalized other," since the player who is familiar with the game tends to apprehend the organization as a whole and to generalize on the game. He re-

[9] *Ibid.*, p. 154.
[10] *Ibid.*, pp. 158-59.

sponds not merely to other persons as individuals, but if he knows the baseball game well, he is able to have organized responses to this "generalized other."

The set of responses which a person gets from his participation in organized social relations also become generalized into a self, which has unity corresponding to the organization in the social groups. "The organized community or social group which gives to the individual his unity of self [is] the generalized other." [11] Common responses, internalized from the same social organization, give the possibility of communication between persons. Mead states that ". . . only through the taking by individuals of the attitude or attitudes of the generalized other toward themselves is the existence of a universe of discourse, as that system of common or social meanings which thinking presupposes as its context, rendered possible." [12] Thus:

> What goes to make up the organized self is the organization of the attitudes which are common to the group. A person is a personality because he belongs to a community, because he takes over the institutions of that community into his own conduct. He takes its language as a medium by which he gets his personality, and then through a process of taking the different roles that all the others furnish he comes to get the attitudes of the members of the community. Such, in a certain sense, is the structure of a man's personality.[13]

The vagueness of the distinction in the infant between his own self and that of other persons, as noted by Baldwin, is reduced in later experience. But, according to Mead, the connection never disappears, because the origin of the self is in other selves.

> Selves can only exist in definite relation to other selves. No hard-and-fast line can be drawn between our own selves and the selves of others, since our own selves exist and enter as such into our experience only in so far as the selves of others exist and enter as such into our experience also. The individual possesses a self only in relation to the selves of the other members of his social group; and the structure of his self expresses or reflects the general pattern of this social group to which he belongs, just as does the structure of the self of every other individual belonging to this social group.[14]

Social organization, however, is not a simple unity. We belong to a society which has suborganizations, themselves divided into groups, each with its own degree of separation from the large or-

[11] *Ibid.*, p. 154.
[12] *Ibid.*, p. 154.
[13] *Ibid.*, p. 162.
[14] *Ibid.*, p. 164.

ganization of all our relations. Normally the self derives organization from each of the organized groups in which the person participates. The result is a versatile person, made up of multiple selves, which are somewhat distinct from one another without being entirely dissociated.

We divide ourselves up in all sorts of different selves with reference to our acquaintances. We discuss politics with one and religion with another. There are all sorts of different selves answering to all sorts of different social reactions. It is the social process itself that is responsible for the appearance of the self; it is not there as a self apart from this type of experience.[15]

A multiple personality is in a certain sense normal . . . within the sort of community as a whole to which we belong, there is a unified self. . . . The unity and structure of the complete self reflects the unity and structure of the social process as a whole; and each of the elementary selves of which it is composed reflects the unity and structure of one of the various aspects of that process in which the individual is implicated. In other words, the various elementary selves which constitute, or are organized into, a complete self are the various aspects of the structure of that complete self answering to the various aspects of the structure of the social process as a whole; the structure of the complete self is thus a reflection of the complete social process.[16]

The complete dissociation of the separate selves within the same person is a rare abnormality, if it ever does occur.[17] As stated

[15] *Ibid.*, p. 142.

[16] *Ibid.*, pp. 143 ff.

[17] It is generally accepted that complete dissociation is possible, but the evidence is built on a small number of cases, most of which occurred in the period in which social psychology was based on unsophisticated method. Gardner Murphy concludes his careful discussion of the phenomenon [see his *Personality: A Biosocial Approach to Origins and Structure* (New York: Harper & Bros., 1947), p. 450] with the declaration, "We shall have to admit that two or more egos, two or more self-aware autonomous individualities, each not only historically but fundamentally hostile to the other, may in certain rare cases exist within the same living organism, either in alternation or concurrently." But his evidence for this statement is based on such instances as the ancient case of Ansel Bourne, the early observations by Morton Prince, the early work of Janet and Binet in France, and the like. No such clear-cut case is reported within the last twenty years or so, in spite of the far greater popularity of psychology and the larger number of psychologists. Furthermore, careful examination of some of the famous cases may convince one that inadequate methodology was employed by the observer who usually displayed an unsophisticated credulity. It is known that many subjects, for various reasons, maintain fictions which may appear to be completely sincere but may be shown by indirect tricks to be intentional distortions all the same.

It is not maintained here, however, that there is no such thing as complete dissociation, but rather that the wiser policy is to suspend a judgment until new cases can be found and put to the same careful tests which have shown, in other cases, and to the surprise of many psychologists, that persons with hysterical blindness actually do see, even when they insist that they do not. The fact that the accounts fit in with what is to be expeced in view of general theory is not sufficient grounds for

above, the various selves we normally have in different groups and situations are only partly dissociated. One self may participate in another, in varying degrees. Where one is dominant, others may be somewhat involved. For example, a man playing for the moment the lover may leave his bank-president personality out of the interaction, but his expression of love may be more interesting because of the implication understood by both persons involved that it comes from an important person. If he is kittenish, the charm or effect is greater because of the implied contrast. A president is funnier when clowning, because he is a president.

Ordinarily, however, the degree of integration between the various selves in a person is a fair reflection of the degree of integration in the various social organizations to which he belongs. A student finds that his role among his dormitory or fraternity comrades is different from his role in the classroom, and in more ways different from his role in his family. The personality he has for each of the groups to which he belongs may have unity, but the difference is usually easy to perceive. On occasions when two somewhat separate social groups exert their influence simultaneously, the opposition of roles may produce an uncomfortable internal conflict. Many a college student has felt a sense of awkwardness on the occasion of a visit by his family to his fraternity house or dormitory. Both the role of family member and collegiate madcap may be called out at the same time and each be incapable of full expression because of the duality of influences. A compromise may be made by adopting behavior somewhat in between the two sets of expectations, but this is not always satisfactory—the student senses the simultaneous disapproval of his family and the amusement of his fellow students.

THE SOCIAL FUNCTION OF SELF-CONSCIOUSNESS

The most important way in which any social organization controls its members is by means of the influences it exerts upon the social self. The self is constructed, as has been shown, out of social materials in the first place, and therefore most of the dispositions of each person are normally in harmony with the expectations of the groups to which he belongs. But no self is a mere carbon copy of a social code. There are always inconsistencies in a social or-

accepting these accounts at face value. The same mistake of overanxious credulity was made in the instance of the "Wolf Children" of India, who were cited for years as authentic cases of feral development.

ganization, and each person is subjected to different combinations of social influences and therefore achieves a unique organization of personality. Here is an important source of individuality and of conflict between persons and the groups in which they participate.

All groups but the most simple and homogeneous require a mechanism of social control to keep the behavior of their members in harmony with group demands. Formal control, through established penalties, is widely used, but far more important is the informal control based on gestures of disapproval. Every normal person directs his behavior to some extent with reference to his conception of himself. "This is the kind of person I am and so must I behave." If he can conceive of himself as attractive, popular, influential, his behavior will reflect this conception by being confident and dominant, and he may enjoy the feeling of effectiveness that accompanies his interaction with others.

Informal social control operates by forcing a revision of the concept of self when the person offends against the expectations of the group. By various means—statements of disapproval, frowns and other gestures, coolness of manner, avoidance, behind-the-back talk which reaches the ears of the transgressor, and others of varying degrees of subtlety—the group shows the offender that his status is less than he may have conceived and that he is less attractive and privileged than he has been assuming. According to the strength of this influence, the person experiences various degrees of embarrassment or humiliation which are, normally, unpleasant enough to force him to alter his behavior.[18]

The conception of self, then, is a key element in the process by which a group controls a person. One can scarcely act toward another person without guiding his actions by reference to his conception of himself. For social behavior to be smooth and confi-

[18] In extreme instances the consequences can be crushing. An illustration is furnished by an incident which occurred many years ago at a large university. A freshman let it be known at the beginning of the first term that he had high ambitions, among them to join the "best" fraternity. He did not know at the time which fraternity was the best, but he planned to find out and to offer himself as a member. As a prank, a number of older students informed him that the best fraternity was Alpha Sigma Sigma, a society they invented for the occasion, and invited him to membership. On his acceptance they arranged a banquet in honor of his pledge to join. Toasts and speeches were made in his honor which he accepted in innocence of the jest. After the banquet, either someone told him or he discovered the joke for himself, for he left town and was not further heard from on that campus. The elaborate prank presumably forced a crushing revision of his conception of self—from that of a popular and promising character to that of an exceptional fool. He correctly judged that he could never succeed in rebuilding a satisfactory reputation at that university.

dent, there must be harmony between actions and conception of self. One cannot command a group of soldiers unless one can conceive of oneself in the role of officer. One cannot make love unless he can find something attractive in his conception of himself as a lover. One cannot beg if he can conceive of himself only as dominant and powerful. Furthermore, a person cannot have these necessary conceptions of self without corroborative defining responses from others. Alone, one has no way of knowing whether he is dominant, popular, appealing, or persuasive. The group must let each one know what his possible roles are, and what kind of conception of himself he can entertain, before the person can know how to act.

In a sense there is a dramatic aspect to all social behavior. We assume roles for our various groups and revise the roles in the light of experience. When a person is inadequate or awkward in his social behavior, it is sometimes possible to produce a sudden improvement merely by suggesting a different role. A timid person can sometimes be given confidence if he can be convinced that he is attractive and entertaining to everyone, and unwelcome intrusiveness can sometimes be cured by convincing the overconfident person that his status is less than he has been assuming. The head of an organization can be freed of uncertainty about his manner of behavior by the reminder that he is the president.

In many instances, such as the above examples, persons given explicit definitions of their roles readily achieve a corresponding conception of self. There are many social occasions, however, which provide for no such convenient help in reaching a definition of self. In these cases each person has the task of figuring out for himself, on the basis of whatever clues are available, just what sort of person he is. There is no exact source of information to draw on. The social mirror in which we must try to discover ourselves is difficult to read, for it consists of other persons' responses often distorted by tact, unwillingness to make issues, and inarticulateness.

To discover from the social mirror a reasonably accurate working conception of self requires a rich skill in interpretation of the meaning of the behavior of others. Even such a simple matter as a girl's attempting to discover whether or not her new hat looks suitable requires a good deal of interpretive activity. It is not enough to ask directly of an acquaintance if the effect is good. Few persons, even good friends, can be trusted to be completely frank; most will in fact pay a gushing tribute to the new hat no matter how it actually makes the wearer appear. An unsolicited remark is worth more, but even that cannot be trusted, since there is an etiquette which requires that friends pay compliments to such a new possession. Overheard remarks which could not be presumed to be meant for the ears of the eavesdropper are worth more. Requests to have the name of the store, or to borrow the hat, are moderately convincing. No single clue is certain, however, and the final judgment is based on the weighing of the sincerity and the taste of the various persons who have in some way reacted to the hat.

Similarly, the man who would like to assume that he is smart, urbane, witty, and popular, and hopes to enjoy acceptance in circles of like persons, needs to put his conception of himself to a test to insure that it will work. If an invitation is to be examined as evidence, he must know whether or not the person who extended it felt under any kind of obligation to do so. The meaning of the invitation also depends on the kind of persons who form the rest of the company; if other guests are of low status it suggests that the honor of being present is not great. A last-minute invitation implies that the guest is needed as an emergency replacement. On the other hand, if the circle is small and consists of a choice group, there is some justification in inferring satisfactory status. Frequent invitations of a similar kind provide strong confirmation. Thus are evaluations made; in many cases, however, the subtleties and inconsistencies of the various meaningful clues make the task difficult and incapable of complete solution.

There is no possibility of complete accuracy in the discovery of a conception of oneself. Clues available for possible interpretation are too numerous and too indefinite to trace down completely. Furthermore, there is no exact model to which one could correspond—there is no objective conception of self which can be said to exist in the consensus of other persons. Different persons disagree on what one is, and even the same person takes a different view at various times. Beyond a certain point, there is no value in trying to be exact. Normal behavior requires only a reasonable harmony between one's conception of himself and the conceptions others have of him. People are tolerant of minor deviations from expectations; the penalties come into play when the disparity is of some importance and shows a tendency to become chronic.

Normally each person has a fairly well organized conception of himself for each of the major social groups in which he participates, and can, on most occasions, guide his behavior in harmony with these conceptions. To the extent that the agreement between his conception of himself and the conception others have of him is adequate, he can behave with such confidence that he need not be actively self-conscious. The self is involved in the activity, but automatically, through the habits that are established in the particular type of social situation. Active self-consciousness arises, as does all consciousness, when there is some problem aspect to the relation of the self to social interaction. A conception of self that loses its compatibility with the social interaction must now be examined and revised in the face of the unexpected reactions. In some cases, this may be accomplished quickly, but in others there may be weeks of study given to the matter, with accompanying uncertainty of action until the revision is complete.

For illustration we may consider the hypothetical example of a man who conceives of himself as popular and influential in his neighborhood. An issue arises which requires community decision, and at a meeting he proposes an action which, in the light of his professional knowledge, appears to him to be a satisfactory solution. But no one speaks up to second his motion, and after an embarrassing silence, the assembly proceeds with its business. This experience arouses a lively train of thought which is an attempt to interpret the experience. "What is the matter? I thought everyone here respected my judgment. Am I less influential than I had thought? The least I might expect would be that someone second the motion out of friendship, to spare me the acute embarrassment of being utterly alone in my stand. How do my friends and neighbors really think of me now?" To answer such questions involves such speculations as whether someone has been furtively plotting against him, whether some unpleasant rumor has been spread with reference to an improper interest he is thought to have in the community action, or whether there is some item of knowledge affecting the issue known to everyone but himself. If the last is the case, if his proposed action is known by all but himself to be extremely damaging to someone liked by all members of the community, his eventual discovery of the fact provides the solution and obviates the necessity of a drastic revision of his conception of himself. He may still wonder, however, why he was the only person in the whole group who was unaware of the consequences of his motion. If this fact cannot be explained by a recent absence or other condition, it means that he may not be in the confidence of his neighbors to the degree he had thought. If he revises his conception of self to fit this observation, he will no longer conceive of himself as nearly absolute in influence and authority in his community, but will thenceforth consider it wise to sound out his neighbors on a proposed course of action before he commits himself to it by offering it in a formal motion.

As is true of any other habitual activity, then, the self enters smoothly and automatically into the process of interaction and requires consciousness only when there is some kind of failure which calls for its revision. The solution, like that for other kinds of problems, is provided by means of a trial-and-error process in the imagination. When the solution is reached, consciousness is set free for other matters and the self resumes its automatic functioning.

Because of the impossibility of achieving exactness of fit between one's conception of self and that entertained by others, and because of the shifting conditions of social interaction which preserve novelty in the social process, persons normally must undertake a certain amount of this revision from time to time during their entire lives. This is an important means by which we continue to adapt to changing conditions and avoid the handicap of obsolescence that proceeds from fixed habits or certainty regarding the nature of oneself. A veteran college teacher has stated:

It's a daunting business being a professor. . . . You will have, if you join this curious trade, to walk in public an endless slack wire over incredible abysses. It's a quivering wire, which seems to be constantly and maliciously shaken, but you will have to walk it right through to the day (which won't be very cheerful when it comes) when you are retired Emeritus. All your lives, you will be teetering on that wire. You will never be quite sure whether you are uttering words of inspired . . . aptness, or whether you are being completely inept. Often you will find yourself incompetent enough to be fired at once if anybody was intelligent enough to see you as you are. You will find yourself, during your lectures, in your private conferences, quite constantly starting sentences without the faintest idea of where they are going to end. . . . "Am I, or am I not, a fraud?" That is a question which is going to mean more and more to you year by year. At first it seems to be agonizing; after that, it becomes familiar and habitual.[19]

There is thus a powerful motive to know the answer to the question, "What am I?" and to control our own behavior so that the answer will not be distressing. The social self is the meeting place of the forces of informal social control and the self-governing activity of the person. The function of the self is to keep harmony be-

---

[19] I. A. Richards, in Bernice B. Cronkhite, *Handbook for College Teachers* (Cambridge: Harvard University Press, 1950), p. 7.

tween the activities of the person and the demands of the social organizations in which he participates.

UNCERTAINTY AND FLUCTUATIONS IN THE SELF-CONCEPT

Normality of social behavior requires that there be reasonable harmony between one's conception of himself and that conception of him held by other persons. As stated above, perfect agreement is impossible, and it is also unnecessary, since there is general tolerance by the group of a certain amount of deviation from expectations.

Individuals differ considerably in their skill in interpreting the reactions of other persons in their effort to achieve this working relation of self to other. One basis of this difference is clearly physiological. The activity of self-consciousness is one of the most complex of mental operations and is readily impaired by a defectiveness of the nervous system. It is quick to reveal the effects of alcohol for one thing—the suppression of self-consciousness is, in fact, one of the principal bases of the appeal of alcoholic beverages. Fatigue and diseases can have similar effects. Contemporary knowledge of brain processes indicates that the frontal lobes function importantly in this type of thinking, and that injuries in this area, though not necessarily rendering a person helpless or even essentially abnormal, do cripple the status-perceiving ability of self-consciousness.[20]

But an efficient nervous mechanism is not all that is required. There must also be a massive amount of information and knowledge, generalized in the course of rich experience over a long period of time in social situations. We learn from an extensive array of our own mistakes, and perhaps even more from the mistakes made by others, for in the latter it is often easier to learn the full consequences of the errors. We are also enriched by our discoveries of successful ways to earn the approval of others, and, again, make these discoveries most often by inspecting others' examples.

It is difficult to convey the vastness of the task of acquisition of this type of skill. For illustration we may consider just the one question of personal policy regarding generosity. We are aware of a social pressure to avoid conspicuous selfishness; at an early age we are even admonished to share our toys in play with other children. But indiscriminate giving may also involve a social penalty

[20] See Chapter 14 for an elaboration of this statement.

by incurring suspicion of our motives and even a kind of contempt. Each person has the problem of finding for himself the most satisfactory course between being a tightwad and a sucker. There may be no course which is completely immune to criticism from every quarter, but the more skilful course will produce a reasonably good conformity to the expectations of others.

The material for discovering the proper course comes in part from formal teaching, but even more from the interpretation of a number of relevant personal experiences. For example, a small boy, with the conventional tendency of children to keep his possessions to himself, sees his father perform a minor act of generosity. The father is having a final conversation with a young soldier who is about to depart for active duty, and when the soldier expresses admiration of a device, say a cigarette lighter, owned by the father, the latter immediately presses it upon him as a gift. Some time later the boy finds himself in a similar situation at school, when another boy offers to buy a small pocket tool from him. Inspired by his father's definition of the situation, the boy immediately presents the object to his schoolmate as a gift. When later he finds that he desires a similar object from his schoolmate and is only given the chance to purchase it, he revises his policy toward generosity with the realization that direct giving furnishes him little credit among small boys. By these and a number of similar experiences, interpreted in relation to his conception of self, the boy arrives at a policy that is suitably in agreement with prevailing convention.

Any condition that deprives a person of rich experience in primary relations with other persons affects his ability to find a suitable interpretation of himself. Unfamiliarity with a culture, as experienced by a migrant, leaves a person weak in this regard— the tourist abroad, for example, frequently gives offense without being aware of the consequences of his awkwardness, and the permanent immigrant to this land commits errors of the same order but usually with a consequence of more severe penalties. The immigrant to this country who carries with him expectations of the same hospitality folkways of his former country may surprise Americans in the fashion of the man who came to dinner and stayed a month. Others may err in America by expecting deference to title and occupation as is usual in some European societies. Even within this country, a Northerner may easily and without intention blunder into unpopularity on a brief visit to the South, as may a westerner who visits the conservative sections of New England.

Skill in evaluating the effects of one's own behavior has the inescapable requirement of a profound knowledge of the folkways of the other persons involved in the interaction.

A personal factor in the lack of status-perceiving skill may result from a degree of isolation which cripples the skill by failing to provide adequate experience and knowledge of the ways of others. The point is well illustrated by a not uncommon type of person who may be an outstanding success in his career but a failure in personal relations. Such a person may have the respect of all who hold a status above his own, but is greatly disliked by all who are on his level or below. His formal courtesy may leave little to be desired—he may shake hands with an engaging bow and smile and always be last of any group to pass through a door, but in his competitive relations with others he will characteristically, and undoubtedly without intention or realization, leave a wide wake of fury behind. In some cases this type of person has a history of a childhood and school life spent alone or with adults, with adequate exposure to formal adult ways but with little opportunity of learning the more subtle informal reactions of human beings.

There is some reason to conclude that the crucial period for acquisition of the required knowledge and skill concerning these more subtle reactions of others is about the same as the school years —from the age of about five through the teen ages. A child who is isolated from his agemates during this period misses an experience that is all but impossible to acquire later. The frank brutality of juvenile comments on appearance and behavior is apparently an important part of the educational process in status-perceiving and evaluation of the self. An adult who offends others by odor may not be told about it even by his best friends, but children give this type of information in such uninhibited declarations as "You stink!" By exposure to direct and caustic expressions, a child learns that one who does not use a toothbrush will hear comments on his "green teeth," that one whose hair is not clean may be a "lousecage," and that other irregularities of manner make one a "drip." The figures of speech change with the times, but the frank character of the comments does not, and these provide for each generation a relatively undistorted mirror in which children and youth may find an immediate reflection of their characteristics, particularly those that are repulsive to others. Some fifteen years of such educational experience may be an actual requirement for the building of the kind of skill an adult needs for winning friends and influencing people, and for reasonably accurate evaluations of himself. It is almost inconceivable that a serious deficiency in this training could be made up for by a brief course in formal instruction, or by study of a book on self-improvement.

An unpublished study by Donald G. McKinley at the University of Washington in 1951 furnishes some objective support for the contention that accurate judgment of one's own personality characteristics is a condition favoring successful relations with other persons. By the use of a set of questions of his own devising, McKinley obtained, in a sample of high-school students, a measure of the amount of agreement between each subject's rating of himself in a number of traits, and the rating on the same traits given to him by his schoolmates. Those subjects whose self-ratings agreed most closely with the rating given by others were assumed to be skilful and realistic in their conceptions of self, and a low but significant relation was established between this kind of agreement and generally high status in the eyes of schoolmates.

A similar unpublished study at the University of Washington in 1951 by Ely Chertok gives some indication that different aspects of personality may be derived from different primary groups, or from different persons within primary groups. The subjects, mainly college students, scored themselves on the Bernreuter Personality Inventory, and each was also scored separately on the same inventory by his or her mother, father, and closest friend of each sex. Thus there were provided his estimate of himself, and an estimate of him by each of these other persons. For the section of the inventory revealing self-sufficiency the self-estimates were not nearly in agreement with the estimates provided by female friends; a relation measured by a Pearsonian correlation of .35. Since most of the subjects were females, these were mainly like-sex friends. The relation of the self-estimates of these same characteristics to the estimates by the subjects' mothers was an insignificant .05. The dominance-submission self-estimates also agreed most closely with the etimates provided by female friends with a correlation of .66. The correlations of these same self-estimates with the estimates by mothers and fathers were, again, considerably lower, .44 and .26 respectively. On the trait of confidence in self, however, the self-estimates bore the closest resemblance to the estimates by the fathers, with a correlation of .63, and only a low correlation of .27 to the estimates by the female friends. Although these studies need further development, they suggest that separate aspects of personality may be generated in some definite mechanisms of primary interaction rather than in a generalized primary group experience only, and that different aspects of the conception of self have different sources within the primary groups.

All information available supports the conception that the primary group relations are of critical importance in building the conception of self. In cases of extreme isolation from agemates during the years of childhood and youth, serious abnormalities may develop.[21] In many cases involving a paranoid complex of ideas of grandeur and persecution, there is a history of close attachment during childhood to admiring parents, much reading and study, a record of high grades in school, and a partial separation from children of their own ages. As a result, such persons are presented with some objective evidence of mental, and perhaps moral, superiority, but not with the balancing knowledge that would have come from sharing the experiences of other children. In their informal interaction, children and young persons normally learn that there are kinds of ability other than those reflected by school grades, that status is not a certain reward for inherent superiority but must continually be earned, and that progress and success and even justice are not dependably automatic at any time—that some persons obviously have better breaks in life than others.

Without such knowledge, unreasonable expectations may be formed by inference from inflated parental hopes, or even from fictional literature. If these expectations appear more real than the expectations that ordinarily come from the consensus of other normal persons, failures in career and in social life cannot but appear to be unjust, and in the characteristic rationalization of the paranoid personality, the result of a vicious and subtle personal plot against him.

Another consequence of this type of isolation occurs in cases in which there is a lack of judgment regarding the amount of guilt that normally should accompany minor transgressions of mores and laws. In childhood we are exposed to two points of view regarding sin, one being formal and partly theological, the other informal and realistic. The informal type serves to correct distortions in the other, and to offer protection to a minor transgressor against an unreasonable amount of guilt. In spite of solemn adult warnings of the magnitude of the sin of lying, most children normally learn that even good people occasionally transgress in this manner in order to get out of difficult situations. Children learn that there are persons who break rules and get away with it, and that there are persons who although caught in infractions are

[21] See Chapter 14 for a full discussion of abnormalities associated with isolation.

forgiven in time. They learn that sins painted black in formal teaching have in reality many shades of tolerable gray, and that there are lies that are even considered to be white. They learn of the varying attitudes and practices regarding alcoholic beverages, the variations in degrees and kinds of sex practices, and the many shadings of honesty and extenuated dishonesty which are spoken of as white-collar criminality.

But a person who, through partial isolation, is deprived of the comfort of this rich knowledge of the inner and private lives of ordinary men may, through an unbalanced and literal acceptance of the formal and theological conceptions, act on the basis of a dangerously unreal view of human behavior. Such a person may be shocked into suicide on the discovery of a transgression by someone hitherto honored and trusted. Or, on the occasion of some moral slip of his own, he may become so convinced that his guilt is visible to others and that their condemnation of him is violent that he will consider his status to be hopelessly destroyed.

Consistent Underestimation of Status.—Underestimation of one's own status yields a less picturesque system of reactions than that of the paranoid personality, but it tends to produce an unattractive character which may be punished through resentment and avoidance by others. Jennings has described a good example of this kind of personality in the case of Amelia, a girl who is designated a near-isolate.[22] Amelia, a resident of a disciplinary training school for girls, made no attempt to be attractive in appearance but tried to win affection by being agreeable and doing favors for everyone. Her associates, however, considered her "almost painfully unassuming" and expressed disgust at her gullibility. They spoke of her as "pitiful" and stated that she is "always being somebody's maid," and "she can't say no," and that she had "no character at all." Some said that they avoided her because to talk with her would be too much like a conversation with oneself, and that one would not get anything out of being associated with her.

Cases of this type indicate that any social group tends to exert pressure on its members to make their conceptions of status come into tolerable agreement with the group consensus, and that deviations in either direction—whether by too high or too low a conception of own status—are resented and bring some kind of penalty.

[22] Helen H. Jennings, *Leadership and Isolation* (New York: Longmans, Green & Co., 1943), pp. 166-69.

Unstable Conceptions of Status.—Not only may one err by entertaining too high or too low a conception of his own status, but he may also encounter social difficulties if he is too quick to revise his conception of himself. Reactions of others fluctuate according to moods which have no relation to oneself, and so it is unrealistic to revise an organized self after every compliment or rebuff. Normally there is enough stability in each organized self to protect it from minor inconsistent reactions. But there are persons who never achieve a stable and confident organization of self and who are so responsive to others that they are excessively elated at a kindly remark by a friend, or unconventionally depressed by a minor social failure. This tendency appears to be related to the general trait of indecision. Not being able to decide on the meaning of the reactions of others and to build the interpretations into a firm organization, this type of person is suggestible and sensitive—thin-skinned in the give-and-take of social interaction.

Such a tendency appears to other persons as inexplicable shifting of mood. The person with an unstable self-conception may have spells of days in which a depressed mood is noticeable, and other times when he displays an elation which has no obvious foundation. The persistence of such moods appears in some cases to be the result of slowness and difficulty in re-achieving a satisfactory conception of self after a rebuff of some sort, or of a continued delight in some upward revision of the conception of self and the pleasant consequences to be expected from it. Both the acute consciousness of self and the pleasure or distress that is experienced in connection with revision of status occur mainly during the active process of revision and tend to disappear after a reasonably stable conception has been developed. The reason for the duration of the mood, then, is to be found in the inefficiency and indecisiveness of the person who takes longer than usual to work out a revision and spreads the experience over several days rather than to make a quick readjustment.

The unstable concept of self, resulting from inadequate ability to achieve a firmly organized self-concept, appears to be related to a high degree of sociability, suggestibility, and eagerness to go along with a group and be pleasing to everyone. The firm organization of a conception of self requires some resistance to certain social influences if there is to be any consistency of character. No one can, in an inconsistent social world, be both completely consistent and completely sociable at the same time; and to be either completely is to be abnormal. The paranoid schizophrenic is an

example of an approach to utter consistency in self-conception—
he has little or no suggestibility and is relatively immune to influences that in normal persons cause revision of the conception of self.
A certain amount of isolation is necessary for the development of
such consistency, and in the completely sociable and suggestible
person there is no isolation or mental privacy, and thus no opportunity to select and organize material for a consistent and independent self. In the extreme case there is virtually no independent
self—the person is without character and will follow the lead of
whatever social influence is exerted.

Such a tendency may develop in members of a large and harmonious family, particularly among the younger females who desire above everything else to keep harmony among other members.
Some such persons will go along with any proposal rather than
allow a dispute or an issue to arise, and in extreme cases will never
even express a personal preference. If the question comes up
concerning what to do, their attitude is that anything the others
desire is suitable to them—it is sometimes impossible to force this
type of person to express a personal preference if there is any
chance that it could be opposed to the preference of another. In
being agreeable to everyone, they fail to achieve any stable character of their own, and therefore no stable conception of self.
They do not know what they are because they are not anything
definitely. With little in themselves that is stable, and with little
practice in deciding and organizing, it is not surprising that such
self-conception as they develop is fragile and subject to unusual
fluctuation in the face of experiences of minor importance.

In interaction with others, the excessively sociable person may
fall into an inconspicuous role. Persons with definite character
are more interesting because of their differences from others. The
person who never asserts or disputes, but is completely agreeable
to everything, has nothing to contribute to a conversation, and is
likely to be overlooked, taken for granted, or even exploited. The
fact that other persons react to this type somewhat automatically
makes it even harder for the unstable personality to obtain any
meaningful reactions that can be interpreted and thereby help to
produce a satisfactory conception of self.[23]

---

[23] Sometimes sudden outbreaks of activity of a new and conspicuous character
may occur in persons of this type. They appear in some cases to constitute a kind
of rebellion against the selfless status. A modest, frugal, inconspicuous housewife
may break into an extravagant shopping spree and indulge in showy costumes in a
quick and desperate attempt to be somebody. If the behavior does not succeed in
producing a satisfactory revision of the self, there may be a period of contrition and

SUMMARY

The self is not a phenomenon of immediate experience, nor is it present at or before birth. Rather it is an organization actively created out of material gained by experience in social interaction. The infant begins life with no objects at all in his experience, and must learn to separate things from the general unorganized sensations of his experience. It is well known that he makes an early differentiation of persons from other objects, and soon comes to know different persons—in most cases it is the mother who is first recognized as different from other things and other persons.

Only after having developed organized conceptions of other persons, apparently, is it possible to achieve a conception of self. Each person sees himself reflected in the reactions of other persons toward him, and by taking the attitude of others toward himself, and by organizing them into some kind of consistent image of himself, he builds up his own self-concept.

The process cannot be as simple as the mere incorporation of a pattern that is presented to the person. The social mirror in which we discover ourselves is a distorted kind of glass. There are inconsistencies in the reactions of each person toward us, and differences in the reactions of various persons. Frank reactions are uncommon, and a great deal of distortion arises from the common habit of tactfulness and from the unwillingness of others to become involved in the complexities of disputes and hurt feelings.

Active evaluation of the significant reactions of other persons is thus required in the process of building the conception of self. The evaluated reactions must then be generalized, and, to a certain extent, this generalization is derived from the organized responses in the social interaction. In the figure of speech used by Mead, the "organized community or social group which gives to the individual his unity of self is the generalized other."

We live, however, not in a single and consistent social organization, but in a society which is composed of many subgroups. For each of the groups to which we belong, we normally have something of a separate role, and thus a separate self, or personality. These separate personalities are not completely distinct from one another, but can have large characteristic differences. Though

depression afterward. To other persons, even close friends and members of the family, such outbreaks generally appear to be utterly unintelligible and are often interpreted as a kind of "nervous breakdown."

complete dissociation occurs rarely, if it at all, it is normal to have multiple personalities.

The conception of self which each person must organize out of the social material which is available to him for interpretation is not a mere onlooker, but has a function in the direction of behavior and in the control of the person by the social organizations in which he participates. Most of our behavior is conduct of a whole person —we direct our behavior with reference to our notion of what kind of person we are and would like others think we are. The judgments of others constitute the guiding pressures on the social self, and thus operate as powerful influences on behavior.

Normally each person evolves a reasonably stable conception of self which adequately agrees with the views of him held by other persons. Though his social conduct is performed with reference to this self-concept, no acute self-consciousness is required as long as interaction proceeds smoothly. When the reactions of others are as we would expect them, it can usually be assumed that the self-concept is reasonably harmonious with the judgment of others. Active self-consciousness arises, as does consciousness of anything, when the routine fails to operate successfully. When reactions are not as expected, the conception of self no longer fits the social situation. The same kind of imaginative trial-and-error process that was illustrated in the problem of crossing the mud puddle now is used to revise the conception of self so that social interaction may be resumed and again proceed smoothly.

If the process of revision requires a reorganization to a higher status or more favorable conception of self, the process itself is pleasant and welcome implications and consequences come into imagination. If the reorganization is to a lower status, the experience is unpleasant and depressing. The process has within it its own rewards and punishments, which can be very powerful.

Persons who are in some way handicapped in the matter of perceiving and evaluating the reactions of others encounter difficulties in achieving a satisfactory conception of self, and thus in engaging in harmonious interaction with other persons. This deficiency can occur from physiological causes—brain defect, drugs, disease, fatigue, for example—which limit the capacity for complex thought and organization. But it can also occur because of abnormalities of social relations. Isolation, or partial isolation, may deprive a person of the rich knowledge of human nature and social relations which is essential for one who is to make accurate interpretations of the meanings of the reactions of others. Unfamiliarity with a culture may also produce crippling social ignorance. On the other hand, insufficient privacy or lack of any opportunity to withdraw from the immediate pressures of sociability may limit the possibility of achieving any stability in the conception of self, so that the person remains suggestible to any social influence and never develops a consistent character of his own.

Selected References

Cooley, Charles H. *Human Nature and the Social Order.* New York: Chas. Scribner's Sons, 1902.

Cottrell, Leonard S., Jr. "Some Neglected Problems in Social Psychology," *American Sociological Review,* XV, No. 6 (1950), 705-12. A discussion of empathic responses and the self.

Cottrell, Leonard S., Jr., and Dymond, Rosalind F. "The Empathic Responses," *Psychiatry,* XII (November, 1949), 355-59.

Mead, George H. *Mind, Self, and Society.* Chicago: University of Chicago Press, 1934.

Sherif, Muzafer, and Cantril, Hadley. *The Psychology of Ego-Involvements.* New York: John Wiley & Sons, Inc., 1947.

Chapter 8

SOCIAL DETERMINATION OF LEARNING, PERCEPTION, AND MEMORY

IN PREVIOUS CHAPTERS it has been shown that it is possible to relate all conscious experience to activity, and that consciousness functions to carry activity past interruptions. An important problem concerns the appearance of new patterns of activity, on what occasions they arise, and how it is possible for them to develop.

There is nothing obvious in the physiological mechanism which appears to make necessary the emergence of new patterns in behavior. Not only the routine physiological processes, but also many complex habits seem to remain stable. Lacking some interfering condition, they continue to function indefinitely in the same fashion.

Circumstances of life, however, do not permit persons to live undisturbed in a simple rut. Conditions change, and crises occur which break up established relations between fixed habits and the physical and social surroundings. The necessity for adopting new ways comes from outside, and it is a constant and insistent force. Somehow the person must acquire new organizations of activity which meet the recurrent crises; learning of new behavior is a requirement of life.[1]

THE ACQUISITION OF NEW BEHAVIOR

Individual Problem Solving.—One hypothesis of how individuals solve problems is that of insight—a sudden emergence of an adequate conceptualization of the problem. This concept furnishes

[1] The subject of learning is of course an important field in general psychology and one covered by a vast literature. For the most part this literature deals with physiological processes and details which do not concern us in the present discussion. Except where stated, however, no opposition is implied between the present statements and the accumulated knowledge contained in the experimental literature. To the extent that the literature on this question contains varying meanings of the term "learning" and embraces a number of rival theories, however, some conflict is inevitable.

a name, but no analysis, and so fails to solve the problem. Furthermore, careful modern observations have failed to give any evidence of abrupt solutions to problems.[2] Both human and animal subjects appear to require a lengthy background of trial-and-error learning before sudden solutions to problems can be achieved.

Harlow has formulated a hypothesis of learning which requires no assumptions of mystical insight, and which does not make use of strenuous extension of the concept of the conditioned response. The key concept in this hypothesis is the "learning set." The essentials are stated as follows:

> Suppose we picture mental activity as a continuous structure built up, step by step, by the solution of increasingly difficult problems, from the simplest problem in learning to the most complex one in thinking. At each level the individual tries out various responses to solve each given task. At the lowest level he selects from unlearned responses or previously learned habits. As his experience increases, habits that do not help in the solution drop out and useful habits become established. After solving many problems of a certain kind, he develops organized patterns of responses that meet the demands of this type of situation. These patterns, or learning sets, can also be applied to the solution of still more complex problems. Eventually the individual may organize simple learning sets into more complex patterns of learning sets, which in turn are available for transfer as units to new situations.[3]

It may be added that the principles underlying each learning set need not be explicitly formulated by the person who is learning, and their application to analogous situations can be made by him automatically, or at least without awareness of the history behind his acquisition of the principles.

The learning set is a type of attitude toward a problem—a definition of the general form of the solution in terms of previously successful trial-and-error experience with problems of a similar character. The acquisition of each learning set enables the person to deal with different problems of the same general type, and a rich equipment of learning sets becomes, as Harlow puts it, ". . . the raw material for human thinking." [4]

[2] Harry F. Harlow and Margaret K. Harlow, "Learning to Think," *Scientific American*, August, 1949, pp. 36-39. The investigators point out that Koehler, who held this conception of insight learning, had based his observations on chimpanzees which had been captured in the jungle, and was therefore unable to know their backgrounds of learning experience. Chimpanzees born in captivity, observed by Herbert Birch, were given problems similar to those solved by Koehler's animals, and showed no indication of sudden solution of problems by insight. At first they did not even show signs of any ability to use sticks as tools. Other observations on both apes and children failed to find insight without a long preceding trial-and-error period.

[3] *Ibid.*, p. 38.

[4] *Ibid.*, p. 36.

Evidence that insight follows the acquisition of learning sets, rather than constitutes the process of learning itself, is supplied by research at the University of Wisconsin using both children and monkeys as subjects. When learning sets for a class of problems had been acquired, then the solutions for other problems in these same classes were sometimes reached by a sudden process which is obviously the kind of insight which Koehler mistakenly identified as the learning process itself. Harlow and his associates gave monkeys a discrimination test, requiring them to pick out the correct one of two objects differing in color, size, and shape. In Harlow's words,

When the monkeys first faced this test, they learned by the slow, laborious, fumble-and-find process. But as a monkey solved problem after problem of the same basic kind, its behavior changed in a most dramatic way. It learned each new problem with progressively greater efficiency, until eventually the monkey showed perfect insight when faced with this particular kind of situation—it solved the problem in one trial. If it chose the correct object on the first trial, it rarely made an error on subsequent trials. If it chose the incorrect object on the first trial, it immediately shifted to the correct object, and subsequently responded almost perfectly.[5]

The learning process in children is reported to be the same as that in monkeys. Harlow found that the children learned more rapidly than the monkeys, but made the same type of errors. There was some overlapping of ability in the two types of subjects—the fastest-learning monkeys surpassed the slowest children.

The experiments demonstrated the ability of monkeys to handle problems involving some abstraction and symbolization. According to Harlow:

Though monkeys do not talk, they can learn to identify symbols with appropriate learning sets. We have trained our monkeys to respond to signs in the form of differently colored trays on which the test objects appear. In one test the monkeys were presented with three different objects—a red U-shaped block, a green U-shaped block, and a red cross-shaped block. Thus two of the objects were alike in form and two alike in color. When the objects were shown on an orange tray, the monkeys had to choose the green block, that is, the object that was odd in color. When they were shown on a cream-colored tray, the animals had to choose the cross-shaped block, that is, the object odd in form. After the monkeys had formed these two learning sets, the color cue of the tray enabled them to make the proper choice, trial after trial, without error. In a sense, the animals responded to a simple sign language.[6]

[5] *Ibid.*, p. 36.
[6] *Ibid.*, pp. 38-39.

In a more difficult test, the monkeys showed impressive ability to choose the odd object from a group three. In this test:

> It is not the shape that is important, but its relation to the other two. . . . The problem is something like the one a child faces in trying to learn the words "I," "you," and "he" properly. The meaning of the words changes according to the speaker. . . . Monkeys and children were trained on a series of these oddity problems, 24 trials being allowed for the solution of each problem. At first they floundered, but they improved from problem to problem until they learned to respond to each new problem with perfect or nearly perfect scores. And on this complex type of problem the monkeys did better than most of the children.[7]

The most difficult test in the Harlow research involved the monkey's ability to recognize similarities and differences:

> Nine objects were placed on a tray and the monkey was handed one of them as a sample. The animal's problem was to pick out all identical objects, leaving all the rest on the tray. In the most complicated form of this test the monkey was given a sample which was not identical with the objects to be selected but was only a symbol for them. The animal was handed an unpainted triangle as a sign to pick out all red objects, and an unpainted circle as a sign to select all blue objects. One monkey learned to respond almost perfectly. Given a triangle, he would pick every object with any red on it; given a circle, he selected only the objects with blue on them.[8]

Harlow states that the learning acquired in this fashion is lasting. The monkeys retain their learning sets for long periods and can use them appropriately as the occasion demands. Even after a year of disuse, a relatively short period of practice, much less than the time originally required to build the learning set, is sufficient to restore top efficiency.

Such is possibly the basic process of learning, both in humans and in simpler animals. We begin by actively exploring and so learn the consequences of our interaction with surroundings. We generalize on these consequences, and employ the generalizations in later situations where they are appropriate, thus saving ourselves the effort and delay that would be involved if we always had to solve the same problems over again each time we encountered them.

In infancy we pick up much of the basic experience by exploring things actively with our muscles and sense organs. Sandpaper becomes known as something that scratches and makes a kind of noise that sets the nerves on edge. Chalk, we learn, will mark on

---

[7] *Ibid.*, p. 38.
[8] *Ibid.*, p. 39.

a blackboard or sidewalk and will break if dropped, and, when held a certain way and moved along the surface of a blackboard, will produce an excruciating squeak which, when familiar, can be anticipated with a general muscular shudder. To have this shudder in our equipment is to define the situation in advance, and to enable us to avoid the full experience by redirecting our actions in connection with the chalk and the blackboard.

Thus do the consequences of actions become experienced in advance as tentative, inhibited responses; that is to say, as images. Having the capacity to have such images, the human can respond to them, and can thus in time short-circuit the more laborious process of overt trial and error. He must first, however, have acquired in experience the equipment to do so. As shown in Chapter 5, the process of conscious thought is simply this trial-and-error process carried out in imagination, using previous habits, attitudes, solutions, or learning sets as the units from which some solution can be selected so that blocked activity can be successfully resumed.

"Expedient Learning" and "Proper Learning."—Gibson has proposed that the acquisition of that behavior which functions merely to satisfy individual considerations, including the reduction of "drives," be designated "expedient learning" in order to differentiate it from the acquisition of behavior which is directed to conforming to the expectations and demands of a social group.[9] Animals are presumably governed by expedient behavior, as are persons when they are isolated or in circumstances of extreme social disorganization. Persons behaving normally in groups, however, are not reducing drives or pursuing individual goals of any kind. As Gibson states:

Human adults do not, when hungry, appropriate and eat food when they see it; they go through roundabout and inexpedient acts such as purchase. Human adults do not often, when sexually excited, approach the nearest visible female or male; the approach tends to be highly roundabout and is usually stereotyped. . . . Moreover, people in groups do not go to sleep when they are sleepy, they do not take off their shoes when their feet are pinched, and they do not take off their clothes when they are hot.[10]

The tendency in experimental psychology has been to give most of the attention to expedient learning, and to generalize about all

[9] James J. Gibson, "The Implications of Learning Theory for Social Psychology," in J. G. Miller (ed.), *Experiments in Social Process* (New York: McGraw-Hill Book Co., Inc., 1950), pp. 147-67.

[10] *Ibid.*, pp. 154 f. By permission of McGraw-Hill Book Co., Inc.

kinds of learning on the basis of the findings. But, as Gibson
points out:

The difficulty is that the experimentally founded theories—Hull's, for
instance—do *not* fit the facts of social learning in one important respect. As
now formulated, they do not account for the astonishing prevalence of moral
behavior among human adults. Having a high regard for biological facts, as
these theories do, the relation of learning to need satisfaction tends to be
their central emphasis, and having animal behavior as a main source of experimental data, their orientation is toward animal learning.[11]

In a sense most of human learning is done collectively, that is,
each person draws on the accumulated fund of solutions preserved
in the culture of his groups and his society, rather than to take the
trouble to work out a solution by his own efforts. The problem
of how these solutions are obtained in the first place is the problem
of invention, which is treated in the sociological literature. The
problem of how each person obtains the solution from his group
is essentially the question of how social patterns become incorporated into the individual's repertoire.

Learning From Social Patterns; Unwitting Imitation.—There
has long been observed in human behavior a tendency to acquire
patterns of behavior directly from the example presented by other
persons without any visible individual process of trial and error or
any other problem-solving behavior. This phenomenon has been
called by several names: the German concept of "Einfühlung"
(literally in-feeling), the term "empathy," the phrase "taking the
role of the other," and the term "unwitting imitation." It is well
illustrated in the following statement:

[Imitation is] . . . typified by the widely observed and familiar phenomenon
of acquiring a dialect, speech habits, tricks of manner, and gestures, as well
as opinions, ideals, and beliefs. We have called this the slow, unwitting
type. The writer, after some weeks in France, discovered with surprise
that he was shrugging his shoulders like those he talked to. It was a new
gesture and had been acquired without intention or knowledge. An even
more striking experience was to have adopted, while living with an uncivilized
tribe where the practice was general, a rather inelegant gesture, which consisted of pointing with the lips instead of the hand. The lips were protruded
in an exaggerated fashion toward the object indicated. One could hardly
imagine oneself wishing to acquire this gesture, and when a friend one

[11] *Ibid.,* p. 152. By permission of McGraw-Hill Book Co., Inc.

day told me I was doing it, I denied the statement, but a little later, when caught in the act, had to confess.[12]

George H. Mead has noted the same phenomenon in the following statement:

We are more or less unconsciously seeing ourselves as others see us. We are unconsciously addressing ourselves as others address us; in the same way as the sparrow takes up the note of the canary we pick up the dialects about us. Of course, there must be these particular responses in our own mechanism. We are calling out in the other person something we are calling out in ourselves, so that unconsciously we take over these attitudes. We are unconsciously putting ourselves in the place of others and acting as others act.[13]

By stating that this takes place "more or less unconsciously" Mead presumably means unwittingly rather than in a completely repressed fashion. We are not *unconscious* when we respond to others, we are merely unaware of the extent to which our attention involves a pattern of muscular response which carries out the same action as that of the person or thing we are watching. It is, of course, possible to do this intentionally as an actor does, but to do it intentionally is a wastefully complicated matter, for it involves an extra process of looking back on ourselves. In the natural course of having our attention absorbed in another, we acquire his pattern efficiently because our attention is on *him* and *his* actions, not split between him and ourselves. Even when we try to be aware of our impersonation of another, we cannot completely or accurately do so—there is no mechanism of knowing directly and accurately what each of our muscles is doing.

In the passage quoted above, Mead stated that the responses must already be present in our makeup and thus by-passed the problem of how they came to be there in the first place. But the problem of how we learn by unwitting imitation cannot be solved by ignoring it. Perhaps the state of knowledge is insufficiently advanced to provide a solution, but it appears worth while to consider some possible ways in which such learning can take place.

As pointed out in Chapter 5, attention always involves muscular activity. In a sense, we perceive things by exploring them with our muscles, not overtly but by faint, inhibited movements which appear to be an essential aspect of consciousness. When we look attentively at, or listen to, someone, we are engaged in an action,

---

[12] By permission from *The Nature of Human Nature* by Ellsworth Faris. Copyright 1937 by McGraw-Hill Book Co., Inc., p. 78.

[13] *Mind, Self and Society* (Chicago: University of Chicago Press, 1934), pp. 68-69.

in a muscular process. This activity is required for an interpretation of what is seen and heard. When we are too weary to respond fully, we are aware only of lights, movements, and general noises, without knowing what the things about us are. Even in this stage the muscular response is not entirely absent, but rather is inadequate to play its part in enabling us to define the sensations. It is entirely absent only in a dreamless sleep.

Evidence in support of this muscular activity is provided by the Jacobson studies of relaxation.[14] There is additional evidence in commonplace experience. Everyone is familiar with the tendency one experiences when a slow talker hesitates—to finish his sentence for him, speaking aloud. There is also the readily observed tendency, when listening to music, to whistle it, hum it, beat time to it, or in some way conceive it by complex muscular tensions. When we watch athletes in action, we tend to follow their activity with varying degrees of tension. We punch while watching a prize-fighter and flinch when he is hit; we tackle with a football player and slide with a base runner. There is reason to suspect that it is impossible to perceive unless we perform such activity along with experiencing it by the sense organs. Even when we do not wish to permit our muscles to follow the pattern we are observing, it is difficult to avoid doing so. When we listen sympathetically to a stutterer, determined not to embarrass him by echoing his stuttering, our very intensity of concentration often betrays us and we stutter in spite of our resolution.

The process of learning socially by unwitting imitation, then, may be simply a by-product of the normal operation of consciousness. We learn to do as we perceive others in action. The intensity of concentration on the others may be related to the intensity of the muscular activity, and perhaps to the efficiency of the learning.

There is support for this conception of learning in the experience of persons who acquire new athletic skills by association with experienced athletes. It is of course possible to benefit by a certain amount of coaching in which one is instructed to hold his arms in a certain way, and move muscles in a described pattern, but it is doubtful that the bulk of athletic skills comes from this kind of teaching. Many of the finest golfers have been caddies who have watched first-class players so much that in the very process of observation they acquired the smooth rhythmical swing and other

<hr>

[14] E. Jacobson, *Progressive Relaxation* (2d ed.; Chicago: University of Chicago Press, 1938).

subtle knacks that are essential to the sport. An outstanding tennis player, swimmer, or runner may influence other youths to be superior athletes by the model he presents to them as they watch him. Unwittingly taking his role as they watch him perform, they learn his athletic style and practice it as long as they are either watching him or thinking about him in action.[15]

It is possible, of course, to perceive and to interact with other persons without acquiring any of their mannerisms. This is done by paying attention to certain aspects of their behavior and not their activity as whole persons. In certain kinds of interaction we may sometimes even regard other persons as if they were non-human, moving physical objects. For example, when we try to hurry along a sidewalk crowded with pedestrians, the person in our way may have to us a character more like a mobile obstacle than of a human being with a personality. He is an obstruction, like a moving fence post, to be pushed about, dodged, and manipulated, but not understood or communicated with. To the extent that we can achieve such detachment from a personal relation, we are probably immune from the process of absorption of his behavior mannerisms.

However, when we deal with other humans as whole persons, like ourselves, and feel that we understand them, we then are required to maintain a kind of sympathetic attention. We are influenced according to the degree that this kind of sympathy (also known as empathy, or identification) is involved in our attitude. It is possible to travel abroad seeing strange people and strange ways without being influenced when our attitude toward those foreigners resembles more our attitude toward animals than toward persons like ourselves. It is this variable of sympathy, among others, which is undoubtedly responsible for the fact that social control is most effective in primary groups, where mutual similarity and sympathy are greatest.[16]

[15] Some instructors of skilled activities base their methods on this principle, and thus do very little of verbal direction. They provide models, in their own performances or those of advanced persons, which the students may impersonate. This has been successfully done with golf, swimming, and other sports, and to a certain extent, the method is used in the teaching of some aspects of musical skills. It also probably enters in wherever there is instruction in any kind of skill, whether the instructors are aware of it or not.

[16] Little objective research on this matter is available at present. An attempt at scaling is available in an article by Rosalind Dymond, "A Scale for the Measurement of Empathetic Ability," *Journal of Consulting Psychology*, XIII (1949), 127-33. A more complete report is available in an unpublished Ph.D. thesis by the same author, "Empathic Ability: An Exploratory Study" (Cornell University, 1949). General discussion with research proposals appears in papers by Leonard S. Cottrell, Jr.,

Acquisition of Speech Through Role-Taking.—The acquisition of meaningful speech is among the most important learning achievements required of each child. It makes possible the system of significant communication on which virtually the entire structure of society rests. The process of speech-learning itself is social in character and apparently is similar to that of the unwitting acquisition of mannerisms discussed above.

Attempts have been made to account for the incorporation by the young child of the elaborate system of speech symbols by a kind of accidental conditioning process. In this theory, the child, in random babbling, happens to utter a syllable which has meaning in the language and then has it defined for him and fixed in his habits by the response of others toward it. For example, an infant will sometimes strike by accident on the syllable "ma," causing his mother to rush to him with a spectacular display of delight, thus presenting him with both a definition and a reward. He will thus continue saying it, knowing that it will bring this particular person and cause a happy experience.

It is quite likely that this process does happen occasionally in every infant's experience, and that it provides him with a few syllables which have a general meaning. This process, however, is much too slow to provide by itself the vocabulary and structure of a language. Once a child gains the ability to speak in sentences, the development of speaking ability ordinarily becomes fairly rapid, and new words and phrases are built up on the basis of a single hearing, with no random babbling to be defined by an associated response.

Possibly the discovery that utterances of sound have exciting consequences is the main discovery that comes by accidental babbling and response. After that, the meanings of words emerge in the rich interaction of the infant with elders long before these words are pronounced by the infant.[17] Thus not only does language function for the infant before he is able to speak, but he also possesses adequate motivation for paying close attention to the speech of others. In the process of fastening attention on the speech he hears, he necessarily builds up sublingual speech habits

"The Empathic Responses: A Neglected Field for Research," *Psychiatry*, XII (1949), 355-59. And "Some Neglected Problems in Social Psychology," *American Sociological Review*, XV, No. 6 (1950).

[17] This apparently occurs at least as early as the age of seven months, according to S. and M. G. Blanton, who stated that one of their subjects of that age gave "positive evidence" of knowing what the word "milk" meant, though she did not use it. Cited in K. Young, *Personality and Problems of Adjustment* (New York: Appleton-Century-Crofts, Inc., 1940), p. 151.

for himself. Observations of infant behavior indicate that new words and phrases emerge into use too abruptly to be accounted for by any process other than this slow learning before use.

Language acquisition is thus one form of role-taking, and the role aspect is apparently more important in the major part of speaking activity than is the function of precise transmission of ideas. Virtually everyone uses words which have no definite meaning for him as he utters the standard clichés for routine situations. Children are especially prone to employ words the meanings of which they do not know. What they do know is that in such a situation it is conventional to say such things, which is to say that they are taking the role of someone who has talked in this fashion.

THE SOCIAL FACTOR IN PERCEPTION

Perception as an Active Process.—It has for some time been recognized that perception is not a mere passive intake of meaningful sensations. To an inactive person, sensations are never meaningful. It requires an active operation to make an interpretation of any sensation so that it has meaning and can lead to appropriate activity.[18] The operation is not local, but involves a complex interaction of sense organs, central nervous system, and muscular system. Apparently the phenomenon of imagery, as pointed out previously, cannot even occur without organized muscular movements.

Hebb, referring to evidence that activity in the motor part of the brain is always involved in perception, concludes that muscles are thus necessarily a part of the process.

Now the question is what the motor cortex can have to do with visual perception—unless perception intimately involves a motor activity, liminal or subliminal. There is no reason to think that the frontal cortex has anything to do with the reception of visual sensation, and the alternative seems to be that it must have something to do with the *elaboration of sensation into visual perceptions.* In Chapter 5 will be found a treatment of perception which supposes that perception of even a simple object involves a "phase sequence." This is a chain of central cortical events with motor links. *Although the*

---

[18] A great deal of evidence for this statement is available in the literature of the *Gestalt* school in which it is shown experimentally that the perception of patterns is an action. Also important is the work by F. C. Bartlett, *Remembering* (Cambridge: Cambridge University Press, 1932). A convenient general treatment of the point may be found in M. Sherif and H. Cantril, *The Psychology of Ego-Involvements* (New York: John Wiley & Sons, Inc., 1947), chap. ii.

motor activations may be subliminal and do not always produce overt re-sponse, their role is essential in any perception.[19]

What this activity accomplishes in making an indefinite sensation meaningful is described by Allport and Postman:

Whenever a stimulus field is of potential importance to an individual, but at the same time unclear, or susceptible of divergent interpretations, a subjective structuring process is started. Although the process is complex (involving, as it does, leveling, sharpening, and assimilation), its essential nature can be characterized as an effort to reduce the stimulus to a simple and meaningful structure that has adaptive significance for the individual in terms of his own interests and experience. The process begins at the moment the ambiguous situation is perceived, but the effects are greatest if memory intervenes.[20]

The relation of these characterizations of the perception process to the analysis of consciousness in Chapter 5 is obvious. To perceive is to become conscious of meaning. We do not automatically perceive all our surrounding sights, sounds, pressures, and smells, but only those, as Allport and Postman point out, "of potential importance." They become of potential importance when they in some way interfere with on-going, routine activity and thus constitute a problem, block, obstacle, or crisis, which must be solved if efficient and confident activity is to be resumed.

Perception is thus relevant to our purposes and we select for interpretation, from the overabundant potential stimuli in our surroundings, those which have some kind of relevance. We look at and interpret those objects which are potential obstacles in our path, or potential instruments for the by-passing of the obstacles, and we listen only to sounds which threaten to obstruct or to aid in what we are already doing. In the course of action, we carry with us an orientation which provides for the exclusion of sensations which we judge in advance to have no possibility of being relevant—thus an athlete in action who knows that much irrelevant shouting is to be expected during his contest is able to shut out all perception of distracting noises, even noises of great intensity. A football player may have no trouble hearing the signals of a quarterback but at the same time never hear the louder roar of the crowd of spectators. The former sound is essential to define his course of action; the latter is irrelevant.

[19] By permission from D. O. Hebb, *The Organization of Behavior: A Neuropsychological Theory,* published by John Wiley & Sons, Inc., 1949, p. 35. Italics in the quotation by the present author.

[20] Gordon W. Allport and Leo J. Postman, "The Basic Psychology of Rumor," *Transactions of the New York Academy of Sciences,* VIII, Series II (1945), 61-81.

Since our common feeling about perception is that it is immediate and automatic, there is no natural realization of the complexity or of the function of the process. The ordinary illusion is that we see and hear everything about us, and that we see and hear them as they are, immediately and without any delay of interpretation. This notion is easy to dispel by simple experiments, however, such as the many familiar optical illusions which demonstrate how easily our interpretations may go wrong.

Perception as Learned Behavior.—It has been adequately demonstrated that the ability to interpret the meaningless visual, auditory and other sensations is not instinctive but must be acquired. The process of learning to perceive ordinarily takes place in infancy and is not preserved in the memory. Experimentally blinded animals, however, give definite evidence of inability to make useful perceptions, and persons who become able to see after having been blind from birth, always face a slow and difficult problem of learning to see. At first they apparently cannot make sense out of anything—the visual experience is nothing but utter confusion.

According to Hebb, the course of perceptual learning in man is a gradual process, proceeding from a dominance of color, through a period of separate attention to each part of a figure, to a gradually arrived at identification of the whole as a whole: an apparently simultaneous instead of a serial apprehension. He cites the experiment by which a patient, who had gained sight for the first time, was trained to discriminate squares from triangles, over a period of 13 days. The patient at the end of this time had learned so little

. . . that he could not report their form without counting corners one after another. . . . And yet it seems that the recognition process was beginning already to be automatic, so that some day the judgment "square" would be given with simple vision, which would then easily lead to the belief that form was always simultaneously given.[21]

Hebb further points out that, in this experiment, the shortest time in which a patient achieved normal perception, even when learning was confined to a small number of objects, seems to have been about a month.

To perceive such a simple form as a square or circle in the early stages of learning, actual eye movements and multiple visual fixations are required. There is no immediate recognition of the whole until this muscular exploration has been made many times. It is of

[21] M. N. Senden, cited in Hebb, *op. cit.*, pp. 32-33.

course not known precisely how this movement can produce an integrated and stable image, though some ingenious speculation has been made concerning this problem.[22] The fact that such conceptions must actively be achieved, however, seems to be securely established.[23]

Orientation and Perception.—Meaningful perception thus is possible only when there exists a mental organization which has been achieved through extensive experience. The existing organization forms a background which is essential to the interpretation of the raw material encountered by the acting neuromuscular system. This background merges previous experience with the new materials encountered, and it requires that there be an implicit recognition of the present relation of the person to his surroundings—that is, that he be oriented with regard to his position in time and space, as well as in his social relations.

On awakening after a period of sleep, a person normally is satisfactorily oriented because his last experience before going to sleep was oriented to the same place and because he has awakened there many times before. Thus, even before opening his eyes, he may correctly interpret the sounds about him as rain on the roof, cars on the street, footsteps in the hall, and the like. Without this orientation, however, each of these sounds could have other possible meanings, and there may be difficulty in finding the correct one.

Orientation may, of course, be the object of attention, as it is when we ask, "Where am I?," or "Do you see what I see, or am I crazy?" But ordinarily we do not need to pay attention, and so do not notice the function of orientation in the process of perceiving. We ordinarily act by keeping our orientation revised and up-to-the-minute so that we know where we stand and what is the sequence of recent experiences. We have such confidence that this knowledge is sound, however, that we do not feel the need to examine it. Not being aware of the general role this orientation plays in perception, we are easily fooled when it plays tricks on our perceptual operations. We look at snow in a shadow and call it white,

---

[22] See Hebb, *op. cit.*, pp. 80 ff for a carefully conceived hypothesis.

[23] News and magazine stories in mid-September, 1950, reported a trial by a graduate student of the University of Wichita, Fred Snyder, who wore for 30 days a set of inverting lenses which made his vision upside-down and backward. At first he was confused and awkward in his movements, but in time learned to see effectively, reorganizing his visual habits to meet the new conditions. When the lenses were removed at the end of the period he promptly fell down, and had to face the task of learning to see again without the lenses. See *Life*, September 18, 1950, pp. 87 ff.

when it actually sends a blue signal up the optic nerve, and we pronounce grass green, even though the bright sunlight makes it more nearly yellow.[24]

When there is a question, in the case of an inconsistent sense experience, concerning whether the defect is in the person or in his objective environment, a check of either may often quickly solve the problem. The check is made, however, by broadening the orientation—there is no immediate experience which guarantees correct information. If a defectively printed newspaper, doubly printed with the two impressions of the same type not quite superimposed, is quickly presented to a person, his first experience may be, not that he is seeing double printing, but that his vision is defective, causing him to "see double." The correct orientation is quickly gained, of course, by looking about. Since the newspaper is the only thing seen double, the defect is not in the viewer's own sense processes. If, however, one cared to take the trouble of constructing a room in which every object is ingeniously contrived to give a double profile, similar to that of the printed page, correct orientation would not be so quickly regained.[25]

Certain optical illusions deceive the viewer by presenting him with a false orientation. A familiar amusement park device gives persons a sense of a mysterious force which pulls them to one side of a room, and which makes balls appear to run uphill and ropes hang toward the side rather than down. The effect is achieved by first breaking up the orientation, destroying its continuity with previous orientation by having persons pass through a dark, twisting passage with various tilts to the floors and walls. As they enter the room where the "mysterious force" is to be experienced, they literally do not know which way is up, or rather, they think they do, but they are incorrect. The room is tilted uniformly; walls,

[24] By his training, the artist may learn to report more accurately on colors, but he may, on occasion, have to break up his orientation to achieve this—by looking at a scene upside down, or through a frame, or in a mirror.

[25] The present author once stepped outdoors in Rhode Island on a *cloudy* winter morning, looked down at the fresh snow on the ground and quickly experienced *sunlight* at dawn. Another upward look revealed grey clouds completely covering the sky. For a moment the matter was in confusion, then a more careful look at the snow showed that its sunlit appearance was the result of a thin orange-pink powder on the surface. News reports on the phenomenon carried the meteorologists' explanation that the deposit came from a far-travelling western dust storm. Doubtless in the areas where such dust was familiar persons would be so oriented to it that they would not have the experience of mistaking it for sunlight on a cloudy morning. The writer probably would not have seen it as sunlight either if the time had been noon—the early morning hour was a part of the time orientation necessary to that particular visual experience.

floors, objects which normally hang and appear to be hanging, and even the scenery outside the window are in reality fixed to a certain slant. All visual cues are consistent, so the expectation of gravity is that it operates parallel to the walls. Since it does not so operate here in actuality, the sideways pull is not identified, and is perceived as an extra and inexplicable force. The effect of course would not be experienced had not the continuity with previous orientation been destroyed by the passage through the confusing, dark route.

Adelbert Ames, Jr. has devised an optical illusion which deceives the perception of size. An open-sided room of three walls, floor, and ceiling is so constructed that from one particular spot on the open side everything appears to be normally rectangular, although actually one corner of the back wall is much farther away than the other corner. If a viewer can be brought to view the scene from this point without knowing of the distortion or without previously seeing it from any other position, he will perceive the room as one of conventional shape, since even the two chairs, bench, doors and windows are so distorted as to harmonize perfectly with the apparent orthogonality of the scene. When persons stand in the two back corners, however, one person appears much larger than the other since they are at unequal distances from the viewer. The experience is of almost fantastic distortion of sizes, however, because there is nothing in the orientation to favor the correct perception of distance. Of course any movement of the viewer to another perspective would immediately establish the fact of distortion of the room and provide him with the orientation which would allow him to see the persons in their familiar sizes.

Observations of this sort make it clear that orientation furnishes a part of the necessary material used in perceiving.[26] To be efficient in the process of perceiving requires a continuous revision of orientation to keep a consistent relation to surroundings. A slight disorientation may result from intense preoccupation while a change in surroundings is taking place—for example, while walking along a street—so that no attention is given to keeping in touch with cues of location. Many persons have on such occasions experienced the temporary sense of strangeness in their surroundings even while realizing that they are actually at a familiar place.

Certain types of interference with nervous processes also appar-

[26] See Adelbert Ames, Jr., *Sensations, Their Nature and Origin* (Hanover: Dartmouth Eye Institute, 1945). Hadley Cantril of Princeton University has also constructed certain of these demonstrations.

ently effect a temporary break in orientation. It is reported that after electro-shock treatment of the brain there is commonly such an experience.

The patient spends from three to ten minutes in a state of complete disorientation. About ten minutes after shock, however, when the patient is sufficiently reoriented to answer questions, he very often exhibits the phenomenon of *jamais vu*. Everything about him seems strange and new. He cannot remember ever having seen the examiner before nor the place he is in. He sometimes does not even remember his own name, and women will often give their maiden rather than married names. After a little while this *jamais vu* phenomenon seems to disappear, either of its own accord or through the patient's relearning by renewed contact with his environment.[27]

In our behavior as members of social organizations, orientation to the social situation is a factor in our interpretation of experience. Weeping on the occasion of a wedding is perceived differently from the same behavior on the occasion of a funeral. A sense of propriety depends as much on the ability to be correctly oriented to the meaning of a social occasion as on the repertoire of actions possessed by the person. In a new situation, we have to answer the question, before we can correctly respond to the expectations of others, "What kind of affair is this?" Orientation to social situations is usually more complex than other kinds of orientation, partly because of the great range of possibilities in these situations, and partly because of their instability.

Social Contexts of Perception.—Each person must create for himself, and keep in a state of revision, the unique aspects of his own orientation. No other person can share his history or his spatial relations to his surroundings, and so each person's orientation is necessarily different from that of all other persons. There are, however, many important aspects of life which we experience in common with other persons or in some organized cooperative way. We therefore have certain perspectives that we share, at least in part. For many aspects of life the social contexts are important and influential on perception.

Bruner and Goodman have obtained experimental results which indicate that the conventional meanings, the collective definitions of certain objects influence even the visual judgment concerning

[27] By permission from Joseph Zubin, "Objective Studies of Disordered Persons." Chap. xx in T. G. Andrews, *Methods of Psychology*, published by John Wiley & Sons, Inc., 1948, pp. 611-12.

size.[28] Ten-year-old children made size comparisons of various discs and coins. Some judged the coins to be larger than discs of the same size. The poorer children in particular judged the coins to be larger. In experiments on a similar point, R. L. Solomon found that children trained to receive a token which could later be exchanged for candy or other desirable objects would judge the token to be larger than it had been judged to be before the training experience. The size overestimation disappeared after the token was made no longer redeemable in terms of a reward.[29]

In judgments of matters less objective than physical size, convention has even better opportunities to affect perception. Zillig has reported an experiment linking the degree of social prejudice with judgments of mistakes in calisthenic exercises.[30] Two groups of children performed the exercises before an audience of their classmates. One group was composed of children who were generally liked, the other of disliked children. The children who were liked by their fellows were deliberately instructed and trained to make mistakes in their performance whereas the disliked children were trained to be perfect. The experimenter reports that the audience nevertheless judged that the disliked children made more mistakes. The social attitude prevailed over visual evidence.

Sherif reports a somewhat similar experience with students who were asked to rate literary passages according to their quality.[31] In general, the passages attributed to highly honored authors, whether actually written by such authors or not, were given the most favorable ratings. The implication is that, in making judgments on matters which are not easily evaluated objectively, there is a tendency to rely on what is believed to be the collective judgment of the society to which one belongs rather than to trust one's own uncertain impulses.

The selective tendency of perception does not necessarily always operate in the wishful direction, nor does it always distort reality. Studies at Harvard and Radcliffe have shown that persons with anti-Semitic prejudices are actually more accurate than are persons with no such prejudice in the matter of identifying Jews

[28] Jerome S. Bruner and C. C. Goodman, "Value and Need as Organizing Factors in Perception," *Journal of Abnormal and Social Psychology*, XLII (1947), 33-44.

[29] From studies at the Harvard Laboratory of Social Relations, presumably to be published.

[30] M. Zillig, cited in D. Krech and R. S. Crutchfield, *Theory and Problems of Social Psychology* (New York: McGraw-Hill Book Co., Inc., 1948), pp. 105-6.

[31] M. Sherif and H. Cantril, *op. cit.*, p. 72.

by their facial appearance.[32] Presumably, the functional aspect of the anti-Semitism is responsible for the careful attention to distinguishing features given by the prejudiced students.

THE STRUCTURE OF MEMORY

As pointed out in Chapter 6, there is no automatic process of memory which records, indiscriminately, all experience. A completely reduplicative memory would be not only unnecessary but an intolerable burden on the psychological equipment. Experiments show that the skilled perceiver does not take in all the detail and build it into a whole, but rather that he begins with a general impression and adds such detail as may seem appropriate. Some of the detail is added by construction and is seldom literally observed. In some cases, it may even be distorted or completely wrong. It appears there because it fits in with the general organization which precedes it.[33]

The Relation of Memory to Wish and Attitude.—Memory is inevitably selective because of the selective character of attention at the time of the remembered experience. We pay attention to those aspects of experience which relate to organized activity—the rest is unnoticed and so cannot be remembered. Wishes and attitudes are aspects of the mental organization for action, and their influence is easily observable in selective attention and memory. Lazarsfeld and his associates have illustrated the process in an unpublished study of the reaction of a heterogeneous audience to a war motion picture.[34] In general, the native white Americans saw and remembered the picture as a demonstration of American armed might and of the heroic character of General Mark Clark. Negroes, on the other hand, had a richer memory of the participation of Negro troops shown in the film, while Italo-Americans were most impressed by the scenes of devastation.[35]

A considerable number of studies have provided illustration of

[32] From studies of G. W. Allport, B. M. Kramer, and G. E. Lindzey, as reported in the *Report for the Five Years 1946–1951* of the Laboratory of Social Relations of Harvard University.

[33] See Bartlett, *op. cit.*, pp. 204 ff.

[34] Cited in Sherif and Cantril, *op. cit.*, pp. 59-60.

[35] While wishes play a part in this selectivity of attention and memory, it is not a matter merely of remembering what is wished for, or what is pleasant, and of repressing the unpleasant (see Chapter 6). The Italo-Americans did not wish the devastation they remembered, but their memory could possibly be related to an intention to defend and justify the future behavior of Italy and of themselves.

this principle. For example, white persons with unfavorable attitudes toward Negroes have been found to see and interpret photographs of Negroes differently from those persons with favorable
attitudes. In another study, students summarized an article on differences between Negroes and whites, showing the same kinds of
selectivity.[36]

Memory may also be directly influenced by wish when there is
a reason to wish to remember something. Boring states:

> The amount of material retained is influenced to a considerable extent by
> the method used in learning it initially. The set with which material is
> studied affects the degree to which it is remembered. Retention is greater
> when the material to be learned is studied with the intent to remember it over
> a long perod than when it is studied with the set to learn it only for imme-
> diate recall.[37]

A clear demonstration of this statement is available in a study by
Heyer and Kelly.[38] A group of seventy-nine students was given
twenty nonsense syllables to learn. Part of the group was given
a reason for wanting to remember; they were told that the test provided an index of how hard they were trying and that the memory
score would count for 10 per cent of their grade in the course. This
subgroup made significantly better memory performance on the
test a week after the learning than did the unmotivated subgroup,
although the two subgroups did not differ significantly in the original learning performance.

The Dependence of Memory on Relationships.—All memory is
embedded in a supporting matrix of relationships, the absence of
which can interfere with memory or completely obstruct it.[39]
Boring has provided useful illustrations of this principle of
memory:

> Forgetting will occur because some of the stimuli present during the origi-
> nal learning are missing during recall, or it will occur when new stimuli are
> present which evoke competing responses sufficiently strong to block the

[36] Sherif and Cantril, *op. cit.*, p. 64.

[37] Boring, Langfeld, and Weld, *op. cit.*, p. 171. This point is another reason why
differential memory cannot be considered to be necessarily an evidence of repression.
Pleasant experiences are more likely to be accompanied by such a resolution to
remember for a long time.

[38] A. W. Heyer, Jr., and L. I. Kelly, "Studies in Motivation and Retention: II.
Retention of Nonsense Syllables Learned under Different Degrees of Motivation,"
Journal of Psychology, XXVII (1949), 143-52.

[39] The development of this point is necessary here as it also was in Chapter 6.
A review of the section dealing with memory in contexts is of use when reading
the present action.

originally learned ones. These stimuli are both external (like the furniture in the room, the apparatus, the experimenter) and internal (like sensation resulting from posture, responses made during learning). Recall may be reduced merely because the learning has taken place in one classroom, whereas the testing of retention is conducted in a different room. Similarly, when words are learned with one color of background, recall is reduced when the color is changed. A language learned in one setting may be poorly retained in a different setting.[40]

Boring mentions the example of a person who lived in China and learned the Chinese language. After a two-year vacation in the United States, his Chinese virtually disappeared, but on his return to China he "was astonished to discover that he was again able to speak the language fluently."

But more important than this relation to background conditions is the relation of memory to that mental organization which is used in action—that is, to the meaningfulness of the material to be remembered. Referring to the factor that accounts for differences in ease of learning as well as remembering, Boring states:

Probably the most important factor is the meaningfulness of the material to be learned. It is possible to rank a large number of verbal materials from low to high with respect to their meaningfulness. On such a scale, nonsense syllables [artificial syllables like ROP, BAV, GEX] are placed well toward the lower end, single words are higher, poetry and prose are still higher. An almost perfect relationship is found between meaningfulness and ease of learning, so that it may be said that, over a wide range of materials, rate of learning is a direct function of the meaningfulness of the material, provided everything else remains constant.[41]

Mental organization, like any other kind of organization, may have structures within structures. An essay may have an organization as a whole, with paragraphs as suborganization, sentences as organizations of a lesser order, and words and even syllables as still lesser organizations. The place of material in such suborganizations is related to our memory of them. Thorndike used the concept of "belongingness" to account for the result in his experiment, here related by Boring:

[40] Boring, Langfeld, and Weld, op. cit., p. 174.

[41] Ibid., p. 155. In an experiment cited by Boring, the nonsense syllables required nine times as much time to learn as poetry. This difference is of an entirely different order of magnitude from the relatively unimportant differences in the memory of pleasant and unpleasant material. The result again points to the necessity of at least equating the meaningfulness in the materials before drawing any conclusions about the repression of unpleasantness.

He demonstrated this principle in an experiment in which he read a series of twenty-four unrelated sentences several times to a group of students. The students were then asked to name the word that had followed the word now read by the experimenter. In 42 per cent of the cases the students were able to give the second word of a sentence when the first was read, but in less than 1 per cent were they able to give the first word of the following sentence when the last word of the preceding sentence had been read. The difference was attributed to the fact that words in a sentence "belong" together in a way that the words in different sentences do not. . . . If we make up pairs like table-chair, green-grass, they will be learned much more rapidly than combinations like book-dog, candle-rose. . . . It seems probable that a certain amount of learning has already taken place.[42]

Boring further states that logical learning is easier than verbatim learning—the *ideas* in a statement are easier learned and remembered than are the exact *words,* and can be learned in about one third of the time required to learn the words. Furthermore, persons who can find meaning in nonsense can learn the material faster than those who cannot.[43]

Exceptional ability at memorizing meaningless material does not necessarily imply high general intelligence, and may occasionally occur in persons whose tested intelligence is in fact far below the general average. His performance depends rather on his tendency to find meaningful relations which can form a context to hold the memory of the material. As Boring states:

The exceptional memorizer is highly motivated to put into relation and recall the materials with which he works. He groups the items, uses them whenever possible and *utilizes many of the basic methods of learning and recalling.* With sufficient motivation almost anyone could do as well. In one experiment the feat of a memory expert was duplicated with relatively little practice by a group of college students. This expert could recall the order of a 52-card deck of shuffled cards after twenty minutes of study. The college students were able to duplicate this performance after an average of

---

[42] *Ibid.,* p. 155.

[43] *Ibid.,* p. 156. The memory of digits depends on the same principle. No matter how random a string of digits, some persons can find meanings and associations in a considerable number of digit combinations, and thus remember the combination easily as a unit. To illustrate, the present writer consults, at the moment of writing, a table of random digits and finds the first ten digits 2317142431. To remember these does not require ten separate memorizations, one for each digit. The first two immediately suggest "23 skidoo," the second three the number of a much discussed Initiative in the State of Washington, the next four constitute the author's age last year and this, leaving unity to end the series. Having made no memorization effort at all except to write this out, the author finds the entire series easy to remember. This can of course be done with any series of numbers, and something like this is done by persons who demonstrate remarkable memory of digits, as well as of other apparently meaningless material.

5.25 practice periods of twenty minutes each. Two students did it at the first sitting and twelve at the third.[44]

This memory principle, so well demonstrated in experimental research, almost surely is the principal vehicle of remembering things in everyday life. The experience of each person is organized about his activity, about his patterns of communication and co-operation with others, and about the general organization of his society. Perception and experience is interpreted through these matrices and is thus preserved in memory because of its organic character. Cameron has indicated the importance of language in this process:

Conflicts remain inaccessible if they have never been adequately formulated in language or in socially organized thinking. Language is a powerful instrument of recall, and thinking which has been organized in its terms shares it advantages in this respect also. For most persons the imagery of recall does not go far in recapturing past sequences unless they can fill in with talk. . . . One of the chief reasons for the scantiness and patchy character of genuine infantile and early childhood memories is that the infant and the young child lack an adequate sequential language system. This is probably also an important reason for the speed of fading in dreams and daydreams. It is not the Censor, not the Superego, but the paucity of language behavior in dream and fantasy that leaves imagery kaleidoscopic and makes recall in verbal currency meager and uncertain.[45]

In the organization of perceived matter for the purpose of understanding and remembering, there is, of course, some transformation of the experience. In the telling and retelling, as well as in successive recalls, this transformation may continue to operate, until the experience has been made quite harmonious with the mental organization of the persons who remember and tell. Bartlett has shown this effect in a familiar type of experiment.[46] Subjects were asked to read a short North American Indian folk tale twice, then to relate it twenty hours later, and again eight days later. In these retellings, the accounts became progressively integrated, coherent, and conventional according to the subject's culture, omitting the special Indian categories which have no counterparts in modern United States culture. The same kind of transformation has been shown to occur to rumors in the retelling.[47]

[44] *Ibid.*, p. 169.
[45] Norman Cameron, *The Psychology of Behavior Disorders: A Biosocial Interpretation* (Boston: Houghton Mifflin Co., 1947), p. 138.
[46] Bartlett, cited in Newcomb and Hartley, *op. cit.*, pp. 69-71.
[47] Gordon W. Allport and Leo Postman, *The Psychology of Rumor* (New York: Henry Holt & Co., Inc., 1947).

Bartlett also points out the organic relation of memory to matters integrated in culture, referring to reports of what might, at first impression, appear to be exceptional memory ability on the part of the herdsmen of the Swazi culture.[48]   It is stated that these people are able to remember year-old transactions regarding cattle with great accuracy of detail. Bartlett, however, found no indication of better than ordinary memory on other matters; a message, for example, given to a native boy, was remembered no better than an English boy would remember it.

Halbwachs has extensively discussed this relation between memory and the social frameworks which support it.[49] He points out that the most important part of mental organization is derived from social organization; that most of the contexts which carry human memory are social. Memory thus is mainly a collective process. He contends that even early childhood memories, which involve experiences in which the child was alone, are collective and exist only because the child's mind is organized by a social process and perceives and remembers within a social context.

SUMMARY

Learning, perception, and memory are actions of individual persons, but in actual life, these individual processes are subject to so much guidance by organized social life that they are, to a great extent, collective performances. The human, like simpler animals, apparently begins his learning by a process of overt trial and error. In the course of arriving at solutions he develops "learning sets" which have a certain degree of generality and can be applied as model solutions to situations which are analogous.

In time the developing human child acquires the ability to let a tentative muscular movement stand for the whole act; that is he is able to imagine the act and to imagine the solution. The trial-and-error process is thus made internal and therefore faster and more efficient. This kind of process is needed throughout life; one never learns enough to meet all situations by routine activity. Social life is forever complex, and one's participation in it is never the same as that of another person; individual problem-solving activity is never-ending and inescapable.

Fortunately, the individual does not have to work out every-

---

[48] *Ibid.*, p. 74.
[49] Maurice Halbwachs, *Les Cadres sociaux de la mémoire* (Paris: Alcan, 1925), and *Mémoire et société* (Paris: Alcan, 1949).

thing for himself, however.   He is guided by his society at all stages of learning by being protected in infancy from certain difficulties, by being provided with materials which make solutions possible, and by being shown in advance the errors in a trial-and-error process.   There is also, apparently, a process by which persons may acquire from others a new pattern of muscular activity without laborious trial-and-error drudgery.   This is the unwitting absorption or imitation, also called empathy and *Einfühlung,* by means of which we take over language, customs, skills, mannerisms, and other behavior directly from the model unintentionally presented by the activity of the persons who surround us.   Most of the repertory of actions with which each person is provided is probably acquired by this means, and the individual problem-solving activity is, to a considerable extent, the activity of choosing, among these possible actions, the one most appropriate to the situation.

This unwitting imitation or empathy may be merely a consequence of the attention which requires a muscular response of an exploratory character in order to comprehend the thing perceived. To the extent that we pay attention to a person, we are required to duplicate his role in inhibited form by our own muscular activity, and in so doing, learn his behavior.   For this influence to be effective, it is probably necessary for the person to be perceiving others *as persons,* rather than as impersonal physical objects.   It is possible that this distinction is a variable with possibilities of infinite degrees of modification; it may be that slight differences in the amount of sympathetic feelings may be related to differences in the rate of learning by unwitting imitation.

One of the most important feats of learning each child must perform is that of acquiring significant speech.   Random babbling begins early and appears to be no more difficult to acquire than other random muscular movements.   Attempts have been made to account for the origin of significant speech by supposing a systematic attachment of random meaningful syllables to meaningful material through a process of conditioning.   Although this may occur to some extent, it seems unlikely that such a process could account for the rapid absorption of the language which ordinarily occurs during the third year of life.   It appears much more likely that, after the relatively slow discovery that words have meanings of considerable interest to his activities and wishes, the child is motivated to pay special attention to the speech of the persons about him.   In the process of listening with intense absorption the child simultaneously acquires, by the unwitting imitation described above, both the patterns of speech behavior and the meanings attached to them.

It has already been shown in Chapter 5 that perception is an active, even partly muscular, exploratory process which functions to overcome obstacles to action. Although it appears to an adult that he sees and hears things "as they are" in a sort of immediate comprehension, it has been demonstrated that the testimony of eyes and ears is completely meaningless until the person has learned, by a slow and laborious process, to perform the active organizing process which discovers the meaning in sensations. Ordinarily this is learned so early in life that the learning of it is forgotten, but cases of persons who gain sight for the first time in adulthood show what a difficult and slow process is required in learning to perceive.

The basic process in learning to perceive is probably a kind of trial-and-error exploration, at first largely overt then more and more based on trial in imagination; that is, by the efficient use of consciousness. Organized backgrounds are built up to serve as orientations which, in a particular situation, reduce the possibilities from which a solution must be selected. Information from any sources may be used in building up this organized structure of knowledge, but social sources play a large part. We are furnished with an indispensable fund of ready-made definitions of objects and situations by the society in which we live. Furthermore, we are presented with a general conventional orientation for many of the standard social situations, such as a funeral or a celebration, so that we have at hand the background material to account for, say, the weeping of certain persons who are present at such occasions.

Memory also depends on organized structures. Just as organizing activity is required for perception to take place, so is there a necessity for a relating activity to hold aspects of any experience in memory. This activity may be intentionally performed, and is so done by memory demonstrators and by persons who know the tricks of remembering. Persons who do not know the tricks as such nevertheless perform the same relating activity when there is some reason to be interested in the material to be remembered, or when circumstances in some way aid them in finding a relationship which will preserve the memory.

Social influences may help build the structure of memory simply and directly by suggesting these relationships, as in the case of remembering the number 57 by reference to the varieties of food produced by Heinz. More fundamentally, however, the entire organization of society contributes to the processes of memory by furnishing an abundance of ready-made organization to which a new experience is easily related. The development in a person of the use of language itself is a part of this mass of organization, as the experiments in the "meaningfulness" and "belongingness" aspects of memory show.

It has also been shown that the general integration of a culture serves as a supporting structure for memories. Folk tales from other cultures, told and retold and remembered in our society, tend to lose those elements which have no meaning in our culture—there being nothing in the general structure to relate them to, they therefore are less readily remembered. Similarly, features of a culture which are emphasized and highly organized, as the cattle of the Swazi, are easily remembered by one who shares that culture, but not by outsiders.

In any society the greatest part of information about what has happened is carried as collective memory, that is, as history. We remember all history before our time only as it is carried in this collective process, which necessarily organizes and transforms the original experience, harmonizing it with the organized character of the culture. Even matters of our own experience, shared with others, become told and retold so that our memory of the experience is not individual, but largely the sharing of a legend which has evolved, been leveled, sharpened, and assimilated, to use Allport's terms, and become organized in the collective process of retelling. Thus, though we begin our mental interaction with the world almost alone, it may fairly be said that a dominant part of our interaction with our surroundings eventually becomes in large part a collective process. The individual aspect never disappears —persons never have identical experiences with one another—but it is, on the other hand, never adequate by itself to guide the person through his perpetual crises.

Selected References

Ames, Adelbert, Jr. *Sensations, Their Nature and Origin.* Hanover: Dartmouth Eye Institute, 1945. Experiments on perception making use of ingenious illusions.
Bartlett, F. C. *Remembering.* Cambridge: Cambridge University Press, 1932. A classic on the subject.
Gibson, James J. "The Implications of Learning Theory for Social Psychology," in Miller, James G., *Experiments in Social Process.* New York: McGraw-Hill Book

Co., Inc., 1950. A modern and valuable interpretation of what is known about learning.

HALBWACHS, MAURICE. *Les Cadres sociaux de la mémoire.* Paris: Alcan, 1925. An important contribution to our knowledge of the social determination of memory.

HEBB, DONALD O. *The Organization of Behavior: A Neuro-Psychological Theory.* New York: John Wiley & Sons, Inc., 1949. An original and closely reasoned theory of learning, perception, and consciousness, based partly on recent physiological research.

HILGARD, ERNEST R. *Theories of Learning.* New York: Appleton-Century-Crofts, Inc., 1948. Review of the learning theories of Thorndike, Guthrie, Hull, Skinner, *et al.,* and the author's own point of view on contemporary learning theories.

SPENCE, KENNETH W. "Theoretical Interpretations of Learning," in Moss, F. A. *Comparative Psychology.* New York: Prentice-Hall Book Co. Inc., 1942. Contains a bibliography of seventy-seven items on learning.

Chapter 9

SOCIAL DETERMINATION OF ATTITUDES AND BELIEFS

THE EMERGENCE of the concept of social attitudes has represented a minor revolution in social psychological theory. Previously, as pointed out in Chapter 2, it had been supposed that physiological processes, operating through instincts, needs, or drives, provided in some detail the direction of behavior. Contemporary knowledge, however, has failed to support that conception. It is now known that the detailed direction of human behavior does not come from physiology but from experience—mainly from social experience. We act in expression of attitudes which are not innate but constructed. They are also much more flexible than innate motives could be, and therefore account far better for human versatility and fickleness. Also, as the material in the present Chapter indicates, the concept of social attitudes is furnished abundant support in objective and methodical research.

THE CONCEPT OF SOCIAL ATTITUDES

Definition of Social Attitudes.—An attitude is an organized conceptualization of an object, person, or situation, which defines its potential relation to the activity of the person holding the attitude. It thus includes latent activity but not necessarily a specific habit. There are individual attitudes, worked out by the person in the pursuit of his solitary interests, but in the normal person these constitute a small fraction of the attitudinal equipment. The amount of organizing to be done in the course of living is so immense that it is highly inefficient to attempt to do it alone without the aid of the standard solutions provided by a social organization. Few persons actually make any attempt at independence from their culture, and those who do gain little independence and lose much efficiency in life.

The social attitude is a conceptualization of the same nature as specified above, which derives all or nearly all its organization in

200

a collective process, and thus is given to each individual ready-made. There are few examples of social attitudes which could be said to apply to our entire heterogeneous society with its undefined borders, but such a social attitude as that toward the national flag is general enough to serve as an illustration. The person who shares this attitude with probably the majority of citizens of the United States has a generally favorable aesthetic feeling toward the colors and the patterns, a sense of pride and perhaps power when reacting to the flag on display. If called upon to handle it in public, his actions are defined by organized custom so that they will imply a solemn respect. These and other reactions which are standard constitute the prevalent social attitude in the United States toward the flag. For subgroups within the nation—church members, baseball fans, coal mine workers, Daughters of the Confederacy—reasonably standard examples such as a statue of a saint, Babe Ruth's bat, a printed copy of whatever principal labor law is in force, and a portrait of Robert E. Lee are all appropriate for illustration.

In each case, the social attitude is clearly a matter that is not derived from the physical properties of the object. The hero, for example, is always transformed into a legendary form which may bear little resemblance to the actual human who is its subject. Lincoln the man is little known to the American public, and is hardly related to the legendary Emancipator. The actual George Washington is hardly recognizable to those who only know the standard legend. The same could essentially be true of contemporary leaders and popular figures of the sports and film world—the attitude is a creation which fits in with the general organized interests of the public, but does not necessarily conform to physical reality or factual history.

To communicate and to cooperate, it is required that we share conceptions and attitudes of those who live and work with us. In so doing, however, some individuality and freedom are inevitably lost. As Cameron writes,

Human beings pay for the gift of words by losses in the individuality of their attitudes and in privacy. Language begins by conventionalizing one's social behavior and then goes on to intrude upon one's private thought. To be able to communicate, of course, a person must speak as others speak, say the things they say, and arrive at conventional conclusions by conventional routes.[1]

[1] Norman Cameron, *The Psychology of Behavior Disorders* (Boston: Houghton-Mifflin Co., 1947), pp. 85-86.

The Defining Function of Social Attitudes.—Attitudes provide
definitions of objects, persons, and situations. These definitions are
in terms of standard ways of acting toward these objects and, since
perceptions, as previously shown, are incipient or tentative actions,
they dominate our perceptions of the objects.

We may, in our interaction with objects, manufacture our own
private definitions in terms of our individual and unconventional
actions toward these objects. A child may, for example, employ a
hammer as an object to suck and perceive it in terms of oral exploration of the sour coolness of the steel head. Since there is in the culture a social attitude, a standard definition, concerning hammers,
such individual attitudes are normally replaced by the social attitude. If our culture provides no definition of an object, as in the
case of a pair of chopsticks, the child is free to entertain his own as
long as he is inclined to do so.

The most common way in which objects are defined and attitudes toward them provided socially is through the example of
their standard uses by experienced persons. Small children see
other, older children pointing toy pistols and pretending to shoot
bandits and soon absorb the pattern, so that any gun becomes an
interesting object to be picked up in a certain way, pointed at the
nearest person, and fired. Sometimes an attitude may be transmitted by a single experience which provides the model of a defining response. A mother with a great terror of lightning and thunder may, by the example of her own terror reactions, define these
phenomena in the same way to her small child. A shift in attitudes
may be similarly produced; a skilled biologist may so impersonally
define a dead frog in his casual but sure approach to dissection that
hitherto queasy students may readily abandon their old attitudes
toward a dead animal and see it only as a fascinating subject for
dismantling and study. In so doing, they in effect take the role of
the demonstrator and assume the actions which constitute the definition.

Styles are governed by social attitudes, though the actions involved are more variable and difficult to specify. At various times
in recent American history the majority reaction has successfully
produced a prevalent favorable response to such feminine embellishments as bustles, ear buns, big shoulders, flapping galoshes, and
shingle bobs. In the field of art, such radicals as Renoir and Van
Gogh have in time become defined as masters, as have also but to
a smaller circle Cézanne and Picasso. In the field of music, atti-

tudes had to be revised before Beethoven and Wagner, and later Debussy and Hindemith, came to be widely accepted as competent.

In some cases it appears to be an important element in the definition of style or taste that authority, either of prominent persons or of an influential minority, pronounces the new element to be acceptable. The operation of this principle is abundantly illustrated in the research literature on suggestion; the following experiment will suffice for illustration.

The experimenters presented to several hundred subjects, mostly high school and college students, specimens of recorded music unfamiliar to most of the subjects. The presentation purported to be a sample of a masterpiece of great quality by an honored composer, and of a second sample considered by experts to be an inferior imitation of the former. The two samples of music, however, were in fact identical—a part of the Brahms Symphony No. 1, fourth movement. The subjects were then asked to give their reactions to the music "honestly as you really feel."

The statement which defined the record which was presented as an inferior piece of music was as follows: "Concerning the music of the new variation, we will, and may, express our opinion very briefly; it struck us throughout as an exaggerated imitation of a well known masterpiece, totally deficient in self-subsistence and beauty. From first to last we missed originality of invention and plastic power, nay, even natural sense for what is lovely; on the other hand, the variation exhibits an astonishing familiarity, or rather complete identification with all Master's modes of expression and means of effect. Even when there were no direct reminiscences, we always heard Master's voice. Such palpable imitation of a master has invariably a disagreeable effect: in the present case, that effect is actually painful."

Less than 5 per cent of the subjects recognized the two records as providing the same music; almost 96 per cent accepting the suggestion that they were different from each other. Approximately 59 per cent agreed with the presented judgment concerning which record contained the superior piece of music. It made no appreciable difference whether the first or the second record was represented as the inferior one.

Each subject was asked to state in words the kind of meaning each sample of music had to him. One stated that the preferred record "expresses my feeling at the time and . . . has more beauty" and that it sounded like "a happy person thinking of the sorrows and joys of life," while the second record sounded like a "call to arms." Another hearer saw in the preferred record "philosophical contemplation of life" and in the other a jerky composition which spoiled the mood. A third found a "higher artistic quality" in the first record, which had a "deeper feeling for religion" while the second was experienced as "tendency to mere pleasure." Another reported the preferred record to be "more harmonious and artistic," conveying "rest and peace" while the other record produced a "sensation of harshness [with] no particular meaning." [2]

Persons are given a collective definition in the standardization of interaction in primary groups where the status of each person tends to achieve stability. Types and categories of persons are always defined in a culture so that standard actions are specified toward them. A fool (the name varies but the general concept is fairly stable) is not to be taken seriously, not to be given responsibility, but to be handled tolerantly and, to some extent, enjoyed as entertainment. A hero is to be respected, followed, and emulated when possible. To small boys, girls are defined variously at different ages; they may be successively playmates, objects to avoid or tease, then finally objects of romantic interest—each definition being a social attitude of the age group.

Perceptions and actions are importantly dominated by these social attitudes. Race relations are to a considerable extent determined by these collective definitions of Negro, Jew, Oriental, and (to minority peoples) native white Americans. This type of attitude makes possible the killing that is necessary in warfare by the definition of the enemy as something less than human that can be killed like a beast. At the same time the process may make it difficult to slaughter a lamb which has been given a name and treated as a pet.

The definition of a type includes in certain cases a physical stereotype, a standard image to which the type is believed to correspond. Thus an enemy has a repulsive and somewhat cruel countenance, a religious fanatic a dedicated and exalted appearance, a leader is tall, rugged, and competent of aspect. To a certain extent the existence of the stereotype, by eliminating from the role a portion of the persons who deviate markedly from it, may support itself by being emulated. In a check on this point some years ago, an investigator wrote to a number of leaders in various categories, inquiring about height and weight. In general, the average dimensions of those who replied were well above the average size of males in the general population. Of the 100 railroad executives, for example, the 55 who replied had an average height of almost five feet, eleven inches and an average weight of 186 pounds. Of 76 university presidents, the 61 who replied averaged about the same height and about 181 pounds. Governors were

[2] P. A. Sorokin and J. W. Boldyreff, "An Experimental Study of the Influence of Suggestion on the Discrimination and Valuation of People," *American Journal of Sociology*, XXXVII, No. 5 (1932), 720-37.

slightly taller than these presidents, and about the same weight. Similar high averages of height and weight were found for many other catgories of leadership, including senators, presidents of labor organizations, bishops, mayors, and other categories of leadership. Musicians, however, had an average in this study of less than five and one half feet, and a weight of 162 pounds.[3]

Any culture also contains numerous powerful definitions of general situations and, in many cases, various alternative definitions of the same subject. Social attitudes are a part of the rewards and penalties of following the professions of judge, poet, junk dealer, undertaker, and others. School has acquired a collective definition in the tradition of children, and this somewhat unfavorable defini-tion constitutes one of the great barriers to learning by interfering with the necessary motivation for study. College life is defined one way by fiction and motion pictures—as four years of horseplay, sport, and fun—and another by the faculty and serious students. The general subject of sex is defined by avoidance and by reactions of embarrassment, shame, and harsh correction of the minor slips of children, as an evil and shocking kind of interest; for many persons the necessary redefinition to achieve harmonious marital satisfaction is a difficult transition to make.

Burgess and Locke present the following illustration of the de-fining power of an authoritative and perhaps emotional judgment by a respected adult. A woman relates the following incident:

When I was seven years old I spent the day with my uncle and aunt whose little granddaughter was visiting them. She and I were playing with our dolls on the porch when she said, "My dolls have nothing to wear so I will let them go naked." My uncle heard the remark and said that "nice little girls do not talk about being naked." I felt that we had been wicked and for years I had a guilty feeling when I heard the word.[4]

The Authority of Group and Culture.—By virtue of the fact that it can present us with definitions of objects, persons, and situations before we ever have direct experience with them, the culture is able to predetermine our perceptions. Thus we are often entirely un-aware of the influence of social attitudes upon our own judgments and activity; our subjective feeling is that we make up our own minds and freely choose our activity, even though detached obser-

[3] E. B. Gowin, *The Executive and His Control of Men* (New York: The Macmillan Co., 1915), pp. 22-29. Quoted in Kimball Young, *Source Book for Social Psychology* (New York: Appleton-Century-Crofts, Inc., 1927), pp. 553-55.

[4] E. W. Burgess and Harvey J. Locke, *The Family* (New York: American Book Co., 1945), p. 276.

vation shows that we are clearly dominated by collective definitions. Thus the culture owes much of its controlling power to the
invisibility of its influence on our perceptions.

It has been repeatedly shown that persons may have strong attitudes toward matters with which they have had little or no experience and concerning which they have little factual knowledge; a
point well illustrated by the example of political attitudes. Most
persons obtain their major political preference from the group to
which they belong, most frequently from the family and community.[5] This is true even of many who claim to be independent
voters. In a study of the point it was found that at least half of
those who represented themselves as independents actually voted
straight tickets at election time, and over half voted according to
their father's political affiliation.[6]

It is thus apparently not at all necessary to know about a subject
in order to have an attitude concerning it, and many persons in fact
do not. A study of attitudes concerning fascism revealed that persons claiming to be hostile to it not only have little knowledge of it,
but may actually accept some of the fascist doctrines.[7] Opinion
polls published in newspapers in 1947 revealed that the majority
of the random sample of adults in the United States expressed an
unfavorable attitude toward the Taft-Hartley labor act, apparently
without knowing its contents. When asked about the law's provisions separately, without identification with the law, these persons gave a majority vote in favor of each one. An intensive campaign against the law had apparently succeeded in giving the law
an unfavorable definition in the public mind.[8]

[5] See M. Sherif and H. Cantril, *The Psychology of Ego-Involvements* (New York:
John Wiley & Sons, Inc., 1947), pp. 76 ff. The present author witnessed a perfect
illustration of the process in a conversation between a seven-year-old boy and his
father. The son asked a series of questions about the meanings of "Democrat" and
"Republican," and when the contrasting faiths had been satisfactorily explained to
him, further asked, "And what do *we* believe?"

[6] A special examination of those who behaved like true independents showed that
even this group is not entirely free from control by social attitudes. Many had
status in groups with conflicting political attitudes, that is, they belonged to religious
groups, economic categories, and neighborhoods which were unlike, and were therefore subject to political "cross-pressure." These persons were found to take longer
to make up their minds in an election, but even then the question for some appeared
to be not, *"What are the issues?"* but rather *"Which group do I really belong to?"*
or *"To which do I owe first loyalty?"* See P. F. Lazarsfeld, B. Berelson, and H.
Gaudet, *The People's Choice* (New York: Duell, Sloan & Pearce, Inc., 1944).

[7] Sherif and Cantril, *op. cit.*, p. 76.

[8] Tone of voice alone can sometimes carry an unfavorable definition, in complete
absence of understanding of the matter. On a candid microphone program an
interviewer stood in front of a store and accosted a man who was about to enter,

The same principle applies to the social attitudes that dominate race relations. Attitudes of racial antagonism and definitions of members of disliked races are acquired by each person not by logical organization of experiences with persons of those races, but rather are taken over from the standard social attitudes of their own groups. Horowitz has shown that white children acquire anti-Negro attitudes this way, usually so early in life that the origin is not remembered.[9] Exposure to Negroes, even though it involves the presentation of evidence contrary to the collective definition, does not change the attitude. It was found, in fact, that to some extent Negroes may absorb the attitude themselves. A similar finding is made in connection with attitudes held by students at Princeton University. The students were asked to list the traits of ten specified ethnic groups, and the result showed stereotypes that could not have been based on actual contact with or direct knowledge of the groups.[10] Similarly, a study by Radke has shown that many children who had not had any personal experiences with either Jews or Negroes nevertheless held social attitudes of antagonistic prejudice.[11] Sherif and Cantril present findings of several studies which reveal that attitudes, both favorable and unfavorable, concerning occupations, depend mainly on collective judgment rather than on personal experience of those holding the attitudes.[12]

It should be obvious from such evidence that attempts to provide a general explanation of racial antagonisms in terms of individual mental abnormality are on unsafe grounds. It is normal for a member of a society to accept the prevailing social attitudes of his group, even though some of these attitudes may be undesirable from a broad moral point of view. The notion that race prejudice is an individual phenomenon of displacement, in which persons with unresolved aggressive tendencies seek out a scapegoat, is receding in the face of modern research. A recent elaborately controlled experiment which involved the participation of a prominent former supporter of the scapegoat theory of race prejudice has shown that persons who are highly prejudiced do not differ

asking in an earnest voice, "Sir, do you know that this store is retroactive?" The man had not realized it, and after being assured by the interviewer that it truly was a "retroactive" store, he turned away from it.

[9] E. L. Horowitz, "Development of Attitudes toward Negroes," *Archives of Psychology*, No. 194 (1936).

[10] T. M. Newcomb and E. L. Hartley (eds.), *Readings in Social Psychology* (New York: Henry Holt & Co., 1947), pp. 204-10.

[11] M. Radke, "Children's Attitudes toward Minority Groups," *Annals of the American Academy of Political and Social Science*, No. 244 (1946), 168 ff.

[12] Sherif and Cantril, *op. cit.*, pp. 68-69.

significantly from those with little prejudice in their tendency to employ the mechanism of displacement in this fashion.[13]

The influence exerted by standardized social attitudes on perception by individuals has been repeatedly shown. Rice demonstrated it some years ago in a study of stereotypes.[14] He presented to groups of college students nine portraits, each of a prominent person who also represented a standard social type. These included such persons as the then Premier of France, a prominent contemporary labor leader, a bootlegger, a senator, a manufacturer, the Soviet Ambassador, and others. The students were asked to look at the faces and to make estimates of intelligence and of craftiness. When the pictures were shown with the identities correctly labeled the men holding honored positions were rated high in intelligence and the others low. In the trials involving false labeling of the pictures it became evident that the students were judging more from the known status than from the physiognomy. When the Premier of France was identified falsely as the Soviet Ambassador, his intelligence was judged lower than it had been judged when his true identity was known, and the Russian scored higher when he was labeled a senator. The manufacturer and the senator were given lower ratings when identified as labor leader and bootlegger respectively, while the bootlegger was judged more intelligent when presented as a manufacturer.

A similar principle is revealed in a study of student attitudes toward professions.[15] Four groups of college students were asked to rank ten professions on the amount of intelligence required, on their social usefulness, and other respects. Some of the students were told that five hundred college students had ranked the profession of politics highest, others were told that it had been ranked lowest, one group was given no suggestion on this point, and one group was told that it had been ranked highest in intelligence and lowest in social usefulness. In general, the suggestions had influence. The group which was told that politics ranked high in both respects gave that profession average ranks of 8.1 and 8.2 (out of a possible 10—the high numbers reflecting high ratings) in intelligence and social usefulness, while the group given the contrary suggestion ranked it 4.1 highest on both traits. The fourth group

[13] From studies conducted by Gardner E. Lindzey and G. W. Allport, reported in *Report for the Five Years 1946–1951*, Harvard Laboratory of Social Relations.

[14] Reported in K. Young, *op. cit.*, pp. 443 ff.

[15] S. E. Asch, H. Block, and M. Hertzman, "Studies in the Principles of Judgments and Attitudes: II. Determination of Judgments by Group and by Ego Standards," *Journal of Social Psychology*, XII (1940), 433-65.

also followed the suggestion, ranking politics high (8.9), on intelligence; and low (4.9), on social usefulness.

In imposing its authority upon its members and presenting them with ready-made attitudes, the social organization operates through various types of influence. The primary group appears to be the most powerful agency of control of attitude as it is of other forms of social control, and the family—first among the primary groups—is particularly influential. There are important defining influences, however, coming from persons who are not in any way close to the persons affected. Authority may reside in a public person who is trusted and admired so that his words and actions may succeed in defining matters for many who have never seen him. In a crisis a popular political leader may, with favorable circumstances, create a public attitude with a single well-chosen phrase, as shown by various examples in the two world wars and particularly in the actions of Wilson, Churchill, and Roosevelt.

Institutions present to their members, and often attempt to impose on nonmembers, various social attitudes. Labor unions have had considerable success in defining a strike as a "right" and a picket line as too sacred to cross, even to causing a number of persons who have no connection with a union to assume the corresponding attitudes and behavior. Lodges and fraternities, colleges, religious organizations, and even commercial organizations—all contain a mass of attitudes which are collectively preserved.

There are also influences in the culture in general which are picked up through various sources and which present standardized definitions to individuals. An important part of the production of individual attitudes from social sources comes from the media of mass communication—radio, motion pictures, newspapers, magazines, and so forth. A study of reading by children has shown the defining influences of this behavior.[16] For the child, reading may sometimes have an organizing influence on personality, "defining his role and conception of himself and relating [it] to his personal problems." Among the illustrations Lind presents are the emotional effect of early Bible and folk stories, inspiration from historical and biographical works bearing on the reader's vocational aims, and attitudes toward animals from such stories as *Black Beauty*.

Social Influences in the Alteration of Attitudes.—A conspicuous instrument for changing attitudes is that activity popularly known

[16] Katherine N. Lind, "The Social Psychology of Children's Reading," *American Journal of Sociology*, XLI, No. 4 (1936), 461.

as propagandizing—the deliberate effort to redefine certain things by means of mass communication. In the public conception, propaganda is assumed to have powerful effects; and most persons fear hostile propaganda and are eager to use the same kind of effort on behalf of their own causes. The effects, however, are not always as much as they are believed to be, and in some cases propaganda appears to have little effect at all. In still other instances it appears to have important accidental effects, some of which may even be contrary to the intention of the propagandists.[17]

Experimental research has shown that many propaganda efforts which are generally assumed by the public to be effective actually produce no measurable changes in the persons subjected to their influence. During the Second World War, a series of films was produced for the purpose of indoctrinating soldiers to fight by defining the cause and so thereby producing the desired attitudes toward the nation and against the enemy. These "Why We Fight" films were shown to a sample of soldiers in an experimental test, with the conclusion that "the films had no effects on items prepared for the purpose of measuring effects on the men's motivations to serve as soldiers, which was considered the ultimate objective of the orientation program." [18]

An experimental effort to alter racial attitudes by means of exposure of the subjects to a series of cartoons also failed to show a result.[19] The prejudiced attitudes were lampooned by attributing them to a "Mr. Biggott" who held the attitudes and beliefs of the prejudiced subjects used in the study. Measurements indicated no alteration of prejudice. The subjects were found to have reinterpreted the cartoons, extricating themselves from identification with "Mr. Biggott."

---

[17] Among unintentional effects may be mentioned a rapid decline in hat sales among young men, following the showing of hatless leading men in motion pictures. Intentional propaganda by hat manufacturers apparently has done little to counteract this influence. It is also reported that a single picture, *It Happened One Night*, because it contained a scene showing Clark Gable getting ready for bed and revealed that he wore no undershirt, had a sudden and spectacular adverse influence on the sale of undershirts, reducing the sales of this item by 40 per cent within a year.

An effect contrary to intention has been mentioned in connection with a dentifrice campaign which warned against pyorrhea and "pink tooth brush" (bleeding of the gums). Drug stores were said to have reported a number of requests for pink tooth brushes.

[18] Samuel Stouffer *et al.*, *The American Soldier: Adjustment During Army Life* ("Studies in Social Psychology in World War II," Vol. I [Princeton: Princeton University Press, 1949]), pp. 461-62.

[19] E. Cooper and M. Jahoda, "The Evasion of Propaganda: How Prejudiced People Respond to Anti-Prejudice Propaganda," *Journal of Psychology*, XXIII (1947), 15-25.

Another failure to uproot a general social definition is reported by an experimenter who tried the lecture method.[20] Groups of psychology students were used as subjects and were presented a lecture concerning the lack of proof for the popular conceptions of intellectual inferiority of women. Four days after the lecture the subjects were given a quiz testing their beliefs on sixteen types of sex differences in ability. A majority of students, even including the women, continued to hold the popular notions which the lecture was presumed to oppose.

There are, of course, various possible explanations of these negative findings. For one thing, there is little reason to suppose that a single motion picture, article, or lecture could easily reverse the fixed beliefs on the opposite side no matter how fallacious the latter may be. If all his life the student has seen persons of both sexes act as if women were inferior to men, it could require more than a single lecture by a college instructor to counteract the accepted viewpoint. The possibly superior authority of the lecturer in the classroom may be offset by the contrary opinions of other professors in other fields of thought, and by the fact that few colleges and universities actually appear to carry out a concept of equality of the sexes in their appointment policies.

Furthermore, propaganda has probably been deprived of some of its possible effect by the fact that the subject is aware of it. From at least as far back as the First World War, the American public has been aware of the fact that various nations and interests have been bombarding the people with indoctrinating material and has acquired a great degree of distrust of anything which has the general appearance of propaganda. In fact, to many persons, propaganda means *false* propaganda, and for them to identify any material as propaganda automatically negates its influence. During the 1930's many persons drew lessons from the confessions and historical exposures showing the distortions of truth during the First World War and made use of these lessons in an attempt to maintain neutrality in the face of a developing international crisis. "Propaganda analysis," which amounted to little more than identification of material as propaganda and revealing its source, became popular in newspapers, magazines, and even college textbooks and courses. The result, possibly, has been a partial immunization of at least the reading population to the influence of the more obvious forms of propaganda.

[20] Samuel W. Fernberger, "Persistence of Stereotypes Concerning Sex Differences," *Journal of Abnormal and Social Psychology*, XLIII (1948), 97-110.

An even more important reason for the failure of propaganda to change attitudes may lie in the fact that it attempts to change a single belief or closely associated set of beliefs, the persistence of which lies to some extent in the fact that they are a part of an extensive organization of attitudes and policies. All knowledge and beliefs, in fact, tend to hang toegther in an organic way. It is normal and usual for a person to reject a piece of strong evidence if it is contrary to the organized mass of his beliefs; he does not know what is wrong with the new evidence but is unwilling to discard all he thinks he does know because one new element does not fit in. Even science works in this way—the majority of principles do not rest on a single unassailable discovery, but derive their strength from the fact that they fit in harmoniously with an organized body of knowledge. According to Lewin and Grabbe,

Methods and procedures which seek to change convictions item by item are of little avail in bringing about the desired change of heart. This is found to be one of the most important experiences for those engaged in the field of re-education. Arguments proceeding logically from one point to another may drive the individual into a corner. But as a rule he will find some way—if necessary a very illogical way—to retain his beliefs. [In order to succeed] the re-educative process has to fulfill a task which is essentially equivalent to a change in culture.[21]

Research at Harvard has provided a description of some of the common reactions of persons in the course of resistance to information which is contrary to their dispositions.[22] Among the common techniques of rejecting such material are the following: (a) accept the item of information at face value but dismiss it as atypical or partial truth; (b) transform the item by placing it in a broader context in which its meaning is changed; (c) reject the item by a failure to understand it, or by a denial of its truth, pointing to the "absurdity" of conclusions that could be drawn from it, or by citing "related" contradictory information.

Not all propaganda efforts fail, however. Krech and Crutchfield are able to cite a number of studies in which racial and national prejudices were shown to be altered by such measures as sociology courses in race relations, selected reading matter given to high school students, and conducted tours of Harlem—the Negro city within a city—for graduate students.[23] These were, of course, more

[21] Kurt Lewin and P. Grabbe, "Conduct, Knowledge and Acceptance of New Values," *Journal of Social Issues*, I, No. 3 (1945), 53-64.

[22] Studies by R. W. White, J. S. Bruner, and M. B. Smith, summarized in *Report for the Five Years 1946–1951*, Harvard Laboratory of Social Relations.

[23] Krech and Crutchfield, *op. cit.*, pp. 194-95.

complete efforts than the presentation of a single film or lecture. They do not show that every trial of a course of study, a reading list, or a tour has this effect—it is likely that the skill of the propagandist and the previous attitudes of the subjects are the deciding variables.[24]

An example of one of the apparently more successful attempts to decrease racial antagonisms is provided in a report by Bogardus.[25] In a controlled experiment at the University of Southern California, the influence of a six-week summer Intercultural Workshop on the reduction of "ethnic distance" (essentially, race prejudice) was measured. The experimental group consisted of thirty-two graduate students enrolled in the workshop, and were persons who had already shown "tangible evidence of their interest in ethnic and racial problems" and who had rather low ethnic distance scores at the beginning. An experienced director was in charge of the Workshop and a prominent and personally engaging Negro scholar and author was present as lecturer and discussant during the entire period. The program included lectures, reading, films, field trips, and discussion.

The effects of the program are shown in the comparison of the average Ethnic Distance Quotients found at the beginning and at the end of the program—the initial average being 1.65 and the final one being 1.44. Since the lowest possible score was 1, the reduction of .21 is clearly significant statistically. Nine months later a follow-up measure was made by mail, and the average score (with four members missing) remained essentially as it had been at the end of the workshop period, that is, 1.43. A control group of the same size, consisting of graduate students not in the workshop but in other education courses, was balanced but not individually

---

[24] It may be possible to obtain valuable results by methodical disentangling of attitudes and beliefs to show what influence various propaganda efforts have. Many practical workers have been attempting to improve race relations by attacking the concept of race itself on the grounds that to destroy the notion that a Jewish race exists is to undercut the reason for hostility to Jews. An analysis of this approach was made in a Ph.D. thesis (Department of Psychology, Syracuse University, 1947) by Nancy Morse. Using what appears to be an adequately representative sample of Syracuse adults (not merely college students), the study revealed that although there is a crude relation between the belief that there is a Jewish race or essence and an attitude of hostility toward Jews, this relation is largely the result of an associated belief that Jews have an internal loyalty to their own group greater than to the nation. When this latter belief is held constant through analysis of covariance, a technical statistical calculation which essentially removes it as a factor, the remaining relationship between belief in a Jewish race and hostility to Jews virtually disappears.

[25] Emory S. Bogardus, "Measuring Changes in Ethnic Reactions," *American Sociological Review*, XVI, No. 1 (1951), 48-51.

matched, on level of university education, type of occupation, years of occupational experience, income level, age, sex, race and ethnic backgrounds, urban and rural backgrounds, and religious back-grounds. This group had an initially higher score than did the experimental group (indicating somewhat more ethnic distance or prejudice) since the members were not selected, and during the same six-week period experienced virtually no change—the scores at the beginning and end being 1.731 and 1.727.

It thus seems clear that the workshop experience had some effect of making rather tolerant persons somewhat more tolerant toward other ethnic groups. The effect was not uniform, however, on all members, for four were virtually uninfluenced and two members showed a slight increase in their ethnic distance measures.

The state of knowledge concerning the influence of intentional propaganda efforts is on the whole, however, rather unsatisfactory. A few experimental efforts have shown that attitudes can be changed by campaigns and educational programs, but the emer-gence of contemporary research findings tends for the most part to reduce the popular belief in the responsiveness of the public to propaganda efforts. The most detailed experimental efforts and probably the most adequate technically—those performed on samples drawn from members of the armed forces during the Sec-ond World War—have principally succeeded in casting doubt upon this prevalent conception.[26] In general these experiments based on the use of films for orientation and indoctrination of soldiers found: (1) that attention to and interest in a film is not a reliable indication of its effectiveness; (2) that making people better in-formed does not necessarily lead them to develop sounder opinions or motivate them to act in accordance with these opinions; (3) that it is doubtful that the prevalent notion is correct that propaganda merely reinforces opinions already held—the relationship is not a simple and direct one; and (4) that although large, immediate gains in factual knowledge resulting from any communication diminish in time, opinion changes resulting from communication often actually increase in time, and sometimes lose their specific character and become changes in attitudes.

[26] Carl I. Hovland, A. A. Lumsdaine, and F. D. Sheffield, *Experiments on Mass Communication* ("Studies in Social Psychology in World War II," Vol. III [Prince-ton: Princeton University Press, 1949]), 448-50.

The Social Basis of Belief

Folk Knowledge.—Of the knowledge actually held by each person and used in his daily life, only a small proportion has been acquired by his own individual problem-solving activity or analytical perception. Each person derives the great mass of his knowledge and information from social sources, efficiently drawing on the achieved content which is already there and thereby saving the time and effort that would be required if he were to build up even a small part of it by himself.

The cultural content of knowledge contains a high proportion of the traditional folk knowledge which is passed from generation to generation informally. In a society so committed to literacy as is ours, much of this content is written down, but even so, most of the transmission from person to person is by word of mouth and by example rather than by means of books. Even where, among modern populations, science has made considerable penetration into the culture, the larger part of daily activity is governed by folk practices, folk speech, and folk knowledge and belief. Even the scientist or educator, who is required in the pursuit of his occupation to speak the technical language, normally falls back into folk speech among his family and friends. The occasional one who does not is conspicuous and is likely to have inadequate social relations.

Even individual discoveries of a technical nature, if diffused among the members of a population, tend to find a place in the integrated culture and become a part of folk knowledge. Such a transformation, for example, has virtually occurred for much of the technical knowledge of the gasoline engine. Among males, at least in America, knowledge of the basic principles of construction, repair, and operation of automobiles has for some time been part of their standard cultural equipment. Though technical literature is available, few have actually used it to obtain their knowledge, but rather have picked it up from informal sources in casual apprenticeship relations similar to those by which farm boys learn the basic operations of agriculture and girls learn domestic arts.[27]

[27] This heritage of folk knowledge of gas engines and machinery has turned out to be valuable in time of mechanized war. It is difficult to train quickly by formal instruction a large mass of soldiers who are to operate military machines. Without habits based on long usage and the memory of matters which are integrated with the total culture, easy skill with engines is lacking, and crucial items may be forgotten to the detriment of efficiency. It is reported that U.S. machines, put in the hands of troops from countries with lower standards of living and no general cultural

It is normal for most persons to have a great confidence in folk knowledge. This is the kind of knowledge which virtually everybody, it appears, accepts. It agrees with everything else we think we know, and, so far as we are aware, has always been accepted. Our habits and the habitual activity of the people we live with are based on belief in the implicit truth of this kind of knowledge. Although within recent decades a portion of the population of the most literate nations has learned to accept science as a superior authority, the majority of persons continue to place their greatest reliance on folk belief—knowledge which carries the authority of the society and of tradition which has no known origin.

Rumors—Transitory Beliefs.—Organized knowledge is not available for every matter on which there is need for information. There is a zone of novelty, uncertainty, and undefined conceptions in which the person who needs to know is receptive to rumors which have little or no support from traditional knowledge or from any organized evidence. As pointed out in Chapter 3, the completion tendency can operate with scanty material to work on—the mind can conceive many a complex and meaningful object out of a random inkblot or a pattern of twigs or clouds. It can also make a rumor, story, or legend out of the slightest shred of information with the same kind of organizing and completing activity. Where the uncertainty and the necessity for information are widespread, rumors and legends readily become contagious and, in fact, evolve into their final form in the process of transmission from person to person.

In times of war and adjacent periods, there is a recognition by the public that some events are concealed from their knowledge and that much false information is necessarily supplied to them. Ordinarily trusted sources of knowledge are no longer available, yet the need for knowledge of many kinds is even greater than before in order to avoid many of the inconveniences war brings. Rumors and scares and even panics are particularly prone to occur at these times. The type and degree of distrust of official statements of information is shown by the prevalence of rumors of governmental mismanagement and duplicity.[28] In May, 1943, a sam-

---

experience with gas engines and vehicles, were quickly ruined in action. Here there was no second-nature understanding of the importance of lubrication, the dangers of freezing, and the various ways in which motors can be abused and overstrained and vehicles driven to destruction.

[28] Floyd H. Allport and Milton Lepkin, "Wartime Rumors of Waste and Special Privilege: Why Some People Believe Them," *Journal of Abnormal and Social Psychology*, XL (1945), 3-36.

ple of 537 adults of Syracuse, New York, was questioned concerning wartime rumors they had heard and believed. The rumor that "gasoline storage tanks of the producing companies are so full of gasoline that ocean-going tankers are dumping their cargoes at sea" had been heard by 27 per cent of the sample and was believed by 14 per cent. The rumor that "there is plenty of coffee in the U.S.— the big companies have cornered the market and are holding out for higher prices" was familiar to 44 per cent of the sample, and believed by 34 per cent. A number of similar rumors were examined in this study, which showed a relation of rumor to an intense wish to know, a realization of inadequacy of information, and a distrust of the administration's candor.

A similar inference may be drawn from the example of the Orson Welles Hallowe'en scare of 1938. A fictional broadcast dramatized the fantasy of an invasion from Mars. Though labeled as fiction at the beginning and during interruption for commercial announcements in the middle of the program, many persons apparently did not hear this, and so accepted the broadcast as a description of an actual event taking place at the time. A study made the next day estimated that about a million persons in the country were disturbed by the story, and a considerable number fled in panic from their homes.[29] The event appeared to be related to the tension and uncertainty resulting from the imminence of war prevailing in this period. Some persons, in fact, interpreted the broadcast as an invasion from Germany by air.

Any disturbing and unexpected event has the possibility of jarring public confidence in the adequacy of information, thus permitting the rapid flight of rumors. It is reported that after the great earthquake and fire in San Francisco in 1906, a number of fantastic rumors circulated in the region of central California.[30] Among them were: that a tidal wave had engulfed New York at the same time as the earthquake; that Chicago had slid into Lake Michigan; that the quake had released zoo animals which were devouring refugees in Golden Gate Park; and that men were to be seen hanging from lamp posts, having been caught with women's jeweled fingers, obtained by a hasty robbing of bodies, in their pockets.

A classification of rumors circulating in the United States during the summer of 1942 reveals some meaningful variation by regions

---

[29] Hadley Cantril, Hazel Gaudet, and Herta Hertzog, *The Invasion from Mars* (Princeton: Princeton University Press, 1940).

[30] Gordon W. Allport and Leo Postman, *The Psychology of Rumor* (New York: Henry Holt & Co., Inc., 1947), p. 205.

of the country.[31] In general, among the thousand or so rumors listed, there was some association of anti-British and anti-Semitic rumors with the New England region, of antiadministration rumors with the Midwest; of anti-Negro, spy, sabotage, and fifth-column rumors with the South, and antilabor, antibusiness, and atrocity rumors with the Far West. These fit in with the well-known, conspicuous regional worries and antagonisms and take the pattern that is expected from a knowledge of the nature of rumor.[32]

Clear and authoritative information should be expected to reduce the frequency of rumors and to quell rumors already in circulation, if the above generalizations are correct. Allport and Postman mention a study in which this is found to be the case.[33] On February 20, 1942, 200 undergraduates were asked, "Do you believe our losses at Pearl Harbor were greater, much greater, the same, less, or much less than have been officially stated?" The responses were: "greater or much greater," 69 per cent; "the same or less," 31 per cent. Three days later President Roosevelt made a "fireside" radio talk which had a reassuring tone and content. On February 25th an equivalent group of 200 students was asked the same question. The results were tabulated separately for those who had heard the speech and for those who had not. The answers of the students who had not heard the speech were about the same as those of the prespeech trial. For those who had heard it, however, there was much less apprehension—46 per cent of this group now thought the damage was greater and 54 per cent thought it was the same or less.

Rumors, like folk knowledge and other cultural content, become adapted to the requirements of communication and to the general organization of the culture. A story which begins to circulate in one form may evolve to quite a different form in this process; there seems, moreover, to be some tendency in the rumor to reach a kind of classic perfection and thereafter undergo little further change. In this process, according to Allport and Postman, some of the same transformations occur that belong to the perception process itself. Rumors in traveling from person to person undergo *leveling*—the loss of detail (in one trial involving oral

[31] *Ibid.*, pp. 12-13.

[32] It would be an error to attempt to find wish-fulfilment in all rumors. The illustrations cited above, and the one in the following paragraph, show that rumors of things dreaded are also frequent. The wish element is the *wish to know*, and the human mind appears to imagine unpleasant possibilities as well as pleasant when knowledge is incomplete.

[33] *Ibid.*, p. 5.

transmission along a chain of six persons, a story lost 70 per cent of its original detail). They also undergo *sharpening*—selective perception, retention, and reporting of a limited number of details from a larger context.[34] There is also a type of change called *assimilation*—transformation of an account or image to make it harmonious with the existing mental organization. In looking at a picture of a street scene, women tend to notice clothing on some of the pedestrians, policemen are aware of the members of their profession if any are present in the scene, racially hostile persons tend to pick out elements reflecting racial issues, and so forth. The assimilation occurs not only with respect to individual dispositions and interests, but, in the case of rumors, also applies to the organized cultural traditions of the group in which they circulate.

Rumors, therefore, are a part of the process by which a group attempts collectively to obtain knowledge, and in their evolution are analogous to the individual process of constructing a perception on the basis of incomplete material. Where there is a meaningless or ambiguous situation and a need or desire to understand it in order to take appropriate action, both individuals and groups will supply the missing elements. The necessary acts of creation may produce a highly unreal and inefficient construct—there is no guarantee of accuracy in the process. But also there is a possibility of obtaining, checking, and organizing information in order to make knowledge and action efficient, and where conditions are favorable, both individuals and groups are, of course, capable of making efficient discoveries.

Summary

In the course of action, things, persons, and situations acquire consistent meanings; that is to say they become defined in terms of our potential actions concerning them. We may arrive at such definitions individually as a consequence of our unique experiences, and we may also take over from the cultural content of the groups to which we belong the collective definitions which are standard for those groups. In the experience of any person, the number of socially defined attitudes greatly exceeds those created in his individual interaction with things. Because of this, a great deal of time and energy are saved each member of a society. Cooperation, moreover, is greatly facilitated by the resulting consensus.

A social attitude toward a thing does not ever consist of an anal-

[34] *Ibid.*, pp. 75 ff.

ysis of its real and total nature. Attitudes, rather, are selective in terms of human purposes. The physical properties of woven cloth and a dyed pattern are irrelevant to the symbolic nature of a flag, and the true character of a national hero is irrelevant to the functioning of the national definition of the "Father of the Country," "The Great Emancipator," or "The Rough Rider."

Attitudes guide the behavior of persons toward the objects involved. The collective attitude toward mice, prevalent among some persons, provides a mechanism of near panic when a mouse is seen. A small kitten may, however, evoke spontaneous cuddling and fondling reactions because of a contrary prevailing definition. Convention so defines a judge that a certain respectful character of behavior toward him results. To define some behavior as sinful, silly, or otherwise socially disapproved is to provide motivation for its inhibition.

In providing such definitions for its members, the authority of a society may be powerful, particularly when there is no disagreement within the group. Individual experience which conflicts with this authoritative character of the society is generally disregarded or reinterpreted in such fashion that it cannot interfere. To most persons, the authority of the group is closer to reality than the testimony of his own senses and reasoning ability. Thus, as in the Sorokin and Boldyreff experiment, persons can believe, if told in convincing and authoritative fashion, that the same symphonic movement played twice in close succession is in fact two quite different pieces of music, greatly differing in artistic quality. Similarly, they can and do hold attitudes which define racial and corresponding character types in the absence of individual experience with members of such races, and even in conflict with the testimony of their senses. Race relations are to a considerable extent dominated by such collective attitudes, as are also the reactions of people toward members of other nations, other social classes, and other occupational categories.

Political processes, too, are illuminated by an understanding of the nature of social attitudes. Since the task of knowing enough about candidates and issues is too great for the ordinary voter, he turns to the authority of those in whom he has the most trust and takes from them a collective definition of the political situation. The definitions of Republican, Democrat, radical, reactionary, New Dealer, Dixiecrat, and so forth, provide the general character of political expression and action. There are, of course, generally two meanings for each of the above terms—one of favorable implication for those who belong in the same category, and another of contrasting character for those who oppose it.

A considerable influence in the processes of defining matters for a population is exerted by the media of mass communication—newspapers, magazines, radio, motion pictures, television. Methodical research in this field is still in its early stages, but certain examples have been cited to suggest an impressive power to influence definitions and to produce attitudes—particularly in situations which are hitherto undefined. It was also shown, however, that not all propaganda by such means succeeds, and that, in general, the secret of what is required to produce a deliberate change in public attitudes has so far largely eluded research.

The knowledge and belief possessed by persons is principally drawn from social sources—the proportion of independent discovery in each person's fund of knowledge is typically minute. Beliefs are embedded in an organized culture, and they partake of the organization in such fashion as to share the general solidity of the culture itself. As folk knowledge, then, certain beliefs have a strong resistance to contrary scientific evidence.

Even scientific knowledge, when it has become diffused among a population, tends to be worked into the general organic body of belief in such a way that it gains essentially the nature of folk knowledge. The understanding of the gas engine and automotive machinery, for example, have become a part of the folk knowledge of young American men.

Rumors arise and spread on matters for which there is no satisfactory authoritative social definition or information, and concerning which there is a desire for knowledge. They reflect an unorganized or disorganized state of public information. The rumors represent a kind of emergency effort to repair the defect and are readily displaced when a more solid type of knowledge is supplied.

SELECTED REFERENCES

ALLPORT, GORDON W., and POSTMAN, LEO. *The Psychology of Rumor.* New York: Henry Holt & Co., Inc., 1947. An organization of recent research on rumor with a bibliography.

HOVLAND, CARL I., LUMSDAINE, ARTHUR A., and SHEFFIELD, FRED D. *Experiments on Mass Communication.* Princeton: Princeton University Press, 1949. Contains valuable experimental material on the changing of attitudes by the use of propaganda devices.

KRECH, DAVID, and CRUTCHFIELD, RICHARD S. *Theory and Problems of Social Psychology.* New York: McGraw-Hill Book Co., Inc., 1948.

NEWCOMB, THEODORE M., *Personality and Social Change*. New York: Dryden Press, 1943. An experimental study showing the importance of primary relations in the formation of attitudes.

YOUNG, KIMBALL (ed.). *Social Attitudes*. New York: Henry Holt & Co., Inc., 1931. Fifteen contributions by different authors.

Chapter 10

THE SOCIAL FACTOR IN ABILITY

In a competitive society an important basis of individual difference is the amount of mental ability possessed by each member. This has always been emphasized in social psychology, but until recent years the prevailing conception of this factor has been in terms of fixed innate levels of mental capacity. Without denying the existence of innate differences which operate both directly and very indirectly and affect mental efficiency, it can be said on the basis of contemporary knowledge that a much more important source of the variation of mental ability in the population is the quality of the experiences which influence ability. As the present chapter indicates, the social organization to a certain extent differentiates its members into various levels of mental performance. Moreover, certain accidental circumstances which influence the type of mental organization a person builds may also contribute to the level of ability.

It is difficult to disentangle the various factors which enter into the totality of a person's mental ability, for not only do the various social factors intertwine with each other, but there is also mutual influencing of these with such physiological characteristics as size, strength, and quickness of reaction. It will suffice here to indicate some of the kinds of processes which reveal the significance of social experience.

THE NATURE OF INTELLIGENCE

The variations of definitions in the literature on this subject indicate the difficulty of defining mental efficiency in terms of a stable component of ability in each person—a component unaffected by differing opportunities, interests, and methods of thought or attack on a problem. Stoddard has avoided the difficulty in the following definition:

Intelligence is the ability to undertake activities that are characterized by (1) difficulty, (2) complexity, (3) abstractness, (4) economy, (5) adap-

223

tiveness to a goal, (6) social value, and (7) the emergence of originals, and to maintain such activities under conditions that demand a concentration of energy and a resistance to emotional forces.[1]

Not only is the social value mentioned in the above definition relative to arbitrary social standards, but so also are most of the other elements in some respects. Stoddard is aware of this, in fact, and does not consider it possible to devise a concept of intelligence which is independent of human standards. Not all investigators have abandoned the search for an innate physiological level of ability, however, but the outlook for early success in this inquiry is not hopeful.

The difficulty of devising a test of intelligence which is "culture-free," that is, one so independent of culture that it is an equally fair test for members of any culture, appears insurmountable. If, as some have proposed, the more important element in human intellectual differentiation is cultural, such a search is of little practical importance in accounting for such differences as exist among persons. A test involving multiplication may appear to be fair for children who have been trained by the same methods in our schools, but it would not be an equal task for one child using our methods and another who knew only the Roman numeral system. The addition of the symbol for zero and the Arabic method of computing, a purely cultural matter, has produced gains in efficiency far larger than the normal variation among school children. For persons who have no writing and no written number system at all, the problem is still different. An example of a preliterate native's method of attacking such a problem is provided by the following account by Ellsworth Faris:

The quantitative conceptions have entered but slightly into their [the natives'] life. Cloth is measured by fathoms, the outstretched arms of the seller sufficing for a measure, but there is no measure of weight. The volume of oil that is sold is measured by the potful, but there is no rigid standard of size.

There is no formal drill in numbers, as there is no formal drill in anything, but I tried a lad once with the idea of discovering whether he could tell nine times nine. "If nine pieces of cassava cost nine brass rods each, how much would they all cost?" After the inevitable argument that they did not cost nine rods each, but could be bought anywhere at five rods each, he finally yielded the point and agreed for argument's sake, and then set out to try to find the solution. He took nine sticks and placed them on the ground, breaking the last one into nine pieces. He then placed one of

[1] George D. Stoddard, *The Meaning of Intelligence* (New York: The Macmillan Co., 1943), p. 4. By permission of The Macmillan Company.

these pieces on each of the other sticks, and found that he had eight whole sticks and one piece left over, so he announced that the result was—*eighty-one*.[2]

The measurement of intelligence in different cultures is also obstructed by the fact that reasoning is intimately guided by language. A man with a different language conducts his reasoning in different ways, and makes distinctions and generalizations on other bases. Another incident from the Congo will serve as illustration.

I recall a time in the Congo when I had occasion to refer to the tail of a chicken, and had used the word that was in my notes as meaning "tail." I had pointed out the caudal appendage of a dog, and had been told that it was called *bongongo*. This word proved quite intelligible when I applied it to designate the tail of a sheep or a buffalo, but when I said something about the bongongo of a chicken, the whole company burst out into loud laughter. A chicken is not a dog, of course not, and did I not see that a chicken had just feathers sticking out behind and it was not a *bongongo* at all? They called that *mpete*, of course. Was it really true that white people called the feathers of a chicken by the same name that they called the real tail of a dog? Later on I found that the word for tail of a fish is a very different word from either of the other two.

Now the Eskimo psychologist might, on the basis of these facts, write that English-speaking people have such vague, undefined notions of tailhood and of spinality that they cannot distinguish the difference between the feathers of a chicken and the tail of the dog and call both of these by the same name as the steering gear of a fish.[3]

Intelligence, thus, is a part of human functioning, all of which is learned within the frameworks of social organization. Without the social factor, there would be no organized personality nor, for that matter, efficient functioning of a personality at all. The isolation of abilities from the unified organization of the person is an abstraction which has little established value, and possibly is dangerously misleading. A student of the subject has recently stated,

It is important to realize that aptitudes do not exist or operate in splendid isolation from the rest of the personality. Aptitude tests are designed to discover "those who can," but are of negligible value for identifying those who can, but won't.[4]

[2] By permission from *The Nature of Human Nature* by Ellsworth Faris. Copyright 1937 by McGraw-Hill Book Co., Inc. P. 273. The boy mentioned is a member of a forest tribe in the Belgian Congo, and the incident occurred about fifty years ago.

[3] *Ibid.*, pp. 266-67.

[4] Herbert S. Conrad, "Investigating and Appraising Intelligence and Other Aptitudes." Chap. xvii, in T. G. Andrews (ed.), *Methods of Psychology* (New York: John Wiley & Sons, Inc., 1948), p. 536.

Stoddard makes the same conclusion in a more general and vigorous statement concerning the possibility of an I.Q. which is separate from the rest of the organized social personality:

In psychology, disparate levels of discourse on many occasions have been hopelessly intertwined, there being no better illustration of this than the history of the concept of I.Q. constancy: some teachers, believing in it, have marked Johnnie, once and for all, as *dull* or *bright*. Clinical and educational psychologists have called upon everything from genealogy to psychoanalysis to explain, or explain away, radical I.Q. changes, especially if found along a constantly diminishing or accelerating line. *The simple truth is that the I.Q., as frequently envisaged, is a myth:* it is *deus ex machina*—something apart from and independent of actual organic and cultural events. The I.Q., some feel, is fixed: what varies is the relationship of an individual to it, such variation being a product of invalidity in the test and idiosyncrasy in the child—given a perfect test and an ever-normal child, the I.Q. would be constant. This view, as we have seen, is untenable, unrealistic, and unnecessary.[5]

There are of course practical uses of mental tests. The objection here is to their use in supporting an incorrect conclusion. Recent research, using the complex statistical method of factor analysis, has shown certain factors which are independent of one another and related to general efficiency of mental performance. The naming of the factors is itself an act of inference and interpretation, but not necessarily difficult in each case. Thurstone has named seven such factors: verbal ability; facility in simple numerical operations; spatial visualizing in two or three dimensions; fluency in producing unconnected words that meet certain restrictions or requirements; perceptual speed or "facility in perceiving detail that is imbedded in irrelevant material;" rote memory; and inductive reasoning. It is not necessary to regard these factors as "distinct from actual organic and cultural events" in the way Stoddard and others find objectionable.[6]

Aspiration and Competition.—Tests of intelligence must infer what persons can do from what they actually do. Their utility depends to some extent on equalization of motivation, if motivation is a factor in performance. It would be obviously absurd to compare running ability among competitors in a foot race if some were

---

[5] Stoddard, *op. cit.*, p. 258. By permission of The Macmillan Company.

[6] Two important factor analysis studies of intelligence are: Louis Leon Thurstone, "Primary Mental Abilities," *Psychometric Monographs*, No. 1, Chicago, 1930; and War Manpower Commission, Division of Occupation Analysis, "Factor Analysis of Occupational Aptitude Tests," *Educational and Psychological Measurement*, V. (1945), 147-55.

running to reach a desired goal while others ran unwillingly with nothing to be gained by being swift.

There is evidence that motivation is a factor of some importance in performance on tests. It is possible, of course, to find groups of persons like students in schools, in which all members compete with enthusiasm. We live in a society in which competition is valued, and we are trained in games, sports, and school activity to do our best when we know that we are involved in some kind of competition. Most persons thus understand, when taking an intelligence test, that they are to exert themselves. They are also aware of the various rewards of being found bright, and of penalties of being discovered to have low intelligence.

Cultures in which competition is less emphasized may be found in various parts of the world. Where this is so, there is a difficulty in getting persons to try hard on a test, or to work as quickly as possible when speed is a factor. Australian natives have shown resentment at being urged to "hurry up" on a test involving speed, and have been inclined to disregard the wishes of the experimenter in this respect. In some cases there is no concept that a right and exact answer exists, and thus no tendency to pursue it with diligence. Among Mohammedans there has been reported a disposition to take an unenthusiastic view of organized knowledge, with a preference to trust fate and Allah rather than one's own intellectual resources. All such differences interfere with making comparisons of mental abilities across lines of culture.

Research is available to show that some differences within our own competitive culture may importantly affect performance, particularly the speed of work.[7] Furthermore, there is apparently a motivation which depends on "level of aspiration"—a concept which is variously defined but which refers to a conception each person has of what degree of achievement he should be able to reach. It has been shown experimentally that information concerning the abilities or performances of other persons will affect the level of aspiration a person will set for himself.[8] On a literary acquaintance test, four groups were asked to state the scores they thought they could achieve, understanding that test scores would range between 17 and 50. The first group was given no information about the performance of other persons on the test, and set for

[7] John F. Dashiell, "An Experimental Analysis of Some Group Effects," *Journal of Abnormal and Social Psychology*, XXV (1930), 190-99. The article contains references to other studies of the effects of competition.

[8] Dwight W. Chapman and John Volkmann, "A Social Determinant of the Level of Aspiration," *Journal of Abnormal and Social Psychology*, XXXIV (1939), 225-38.

itself an average expectation of 27. The second group was asked to anticipate their grades but also were told that a group of authors and literary critics had been tested and had scored an average of 37.2. This resulted, apparently, in promoting more modest expectations in the second group—their mean expectation of their own scores was only 23, four points lower than that of the first group. The third group was told that a group of psychology students had scored an average of 37.2. Encouraged by this, this group had an average expectation of 31—four points *higher* than the first group. The fourth group was given an even greater reason for expecting to score high; they were told that a group of unselected WPA workers (unemployed men on a government work relief project) had made an average score of 37.2. This last group had the highest expectation of all, with an average of 33.[9] It appears that some of the subjects, when faced with knowledge of the scores of persons who should be experts, had reasoned about as follows: "If they score at that level, I should be much lower," and when comparing themselves with unemployed workers thought, "If they can do it, I should be able to do as well."

Studies have shown a relation of aspiration level to action. In one project, children were allowed to choose pieces of candy having different degrees of availability, some pieces being farther away than others, some even placed up on a ladder.[10] Differences appeared between the tendencies to pursue the more convenient or the more remote pieces. In general, the older children chose the more difficult tasks, and boys exceeded the girls in this respect. The presence of a woman experimenter at the time the choices were made increased the number of choices of remote or difficult pieces.

Fales reports observations of the activity of nursery school children in donning and removing their wraps. The refusal of help in these tasks is considered an index of "rudimentary aspiration." [11] Training in the task increased this level of rudimentary aspiration; the trained children refusing help more often than untrained children, and more often than they themselves had done before train-

[9] Except for the difference between the last two average expectations, both high, all differences of expectations, or "aspiration level," are statistically significant at the 5 per cent level or beyond.

[10] Irvin L. Child, "Children's Preference for Goals Easy or Difficult to Obtain," *Psychological Monographs*, XL, No. 4 (1946).

[11] E. Fales, "Genesis of Level of Aspiration in Children From One and One-half to Three Years of Age." Reported in C. Anderson, "The Development of a Level of Aspiration in Young Children" (Dissertation, University of Iowa, 1940).

ing. Another group given praise for trying was found to take an even higher aspiration level.[12]

Abundant instances from everyday life are available to provide further illustrations of the relation between the goal one sets for himself and the aspiration level, and the amount of effort put forth and the degree of achievement. It often happens that one outstanding sprinter in a high school will lift the performance of fellow members of the track team by showing what is possible and by stimulating the competition among the others. Similarly, the presence of one or more brilliant football players on a team appears to be able to inspire their mates to greater than usual efforts, and to develop additional ability in them as a consequence.

Where public interest rewards success in any sport, it appears that the keenness of competition produces a high standard of performance on the part of the athletes. Players try harder and do better at schools where football fever is strong. A public craze for basketball in some midwestern regions has contributed to a high level of playing ability in the schools and colleges of the area. This principle probably extends into many fields of activity other than sports—writers sometimes develop in small, eagerly competing coteries; traffic skills appear to have a higher development in such competitive street and highway situations as are observable in New York City and in Los Angeles. In fact it is probable that aspiration, resulting from example and from competition, is a general, though not always visible, component in ability of almost every kind.

The Organic Character of Knowledge and Ability.—It has previously been shown that consciousness itself, as well as memory, is related to activity and functions to help activity be efficient. Memory is also preserved in structures of relationships which belong to the general system of organized activity. The kind of knowledge which aids activity and which reveals highly effective intelligence or ability is also related to the whole organization of activity in the person. Information which cannot be related to organized activity normally drops out of the person's fund of knowledge. As Stoddard writes: "The person with a large fund of general knowledge has absorbed it, bound it together, and utilized it in the service of problem-solving situations and adaptations. What he is unable to

---

[12] Other objective research, with theoretical discussion, is presented in K. Lewin, T. Dembo, L. Festinger, and P. S. Sears, "Level of Aspiration," chap. x in J. McV. Hunt, *Personality and the Behavior Disorders* (New York: The Ronald Press Co., 1944), pp. 333-78. The article includes an attempt to reconcile the concept and the observations concerning level of aspiration with the apparently opposite conception of "least effort."

use in this way tends to drop out, to be replaced by other items and clusters that are more functional." [13] Thus the use of such words as "shagreen," "complot," "parterre," and "homonculus" in a vocabulary test do not accurately relate to degree of intelligence in most persons, for even if once learned, these words would not have a function in the conventional life of the ordinary man. The vocabularies we keep alive are those which do function in organized activity, and the general fund of information and techniques which are components of ability have the same dependence on usage.

Just as the organized structure of language possessed by a person is derived from, and always a part of, the language system of a general social organization, so all individual organization of knowledge in the person is derived from organized sources and continuously fed and maintained from these sources. The illusion of discovering much of our knowledge and of making our own decisions often conceals this rich relation we always maintain with the social organization of which we are inextricable parts.

Murphy and his colleagues have reviewed a number of studies which show how groups of people solve problems. In general, where the product of the group process is found to be superior to the problem-solving abilities of its individual members, it is found to be so because of such factors as (a) the larger number of ways of looking at a problem, (b) the larger number of suggestions for a solution, (c) the larger number of effective criticisms of each proposed solution, and (d) the ability of the group to override stubbornness in separate members.[14]

This cooperative approach to problem solving does not, however, contrast sharply with what appears to be individual problem solving. In his solitary attack on a problem, a person with high ability goes through essentially the same kinds of interaction internally. That is, from his memory, derived from participation in organized social life, he examines various ways of looking at his problem, draws suggestions for a solution, finds criticisms of each proposed solution, and, by taking the role of others, achieves objectivity to overcome any personal resistance he may have to the best solution. Here the whole social process is operating within an individual mind.

Cultural Nutrition of Intelligence.—Variations in the richness of personal participation in a culture may affect the development

[13] Stoddard, *op. cit.*, p. 8.
[14] Gardner Murphy, L. Murphy, and T. Newcomb, *Experimental Social Psychology* (New York: Harper & Bros., 1937), p. 738.

of intelligence and ability in persons in numerous ways. The relation of language facility and other types of ability is well known. A student of language development in children has shown that there is a relation between language development and the amount of participation with older persons whose influence might be expected to enlarge the vocabulary.[15] According to this observer there is a relation between the linguistic development of a child and the age of his associates, a particular advantage being involved in much association with adults. Only children have marked language superiority because of this, and children in orphan homes and other institutions are greatly retarded—more so than would be expected by their supposed level of native ability. Furthermore, linguistic development in twins tends to be slower than in singletons, and slower yet in triplets. The Dionne quintuplets are stated to have been extremely slow in language development. In upper economic classes, however, twins were found to catch up in language development by the tenth year.

The relation of language development to richness of association with persons who already have the language well in hand is easy to explain. The only source of growth in this respect is through exposure to someone who knows more than the child does since it appears that the child acquires language by listening to it. As previously shown, all perception seems to require a muscular response of some sort—a tentative action toward the thing perceived—which in the case of language appears to be an actual silent repetition or rehearsal of what is said. When enough practice of this kind has been made for any word or phrase, it is ready to be used by the child in overt speech, and often in fact comes out perfectly the first time that there is an attempt to pronounce it.

Although there is little objective research on the matter, it appears likely that a number of factors involved in effective intelligence are related to cultural opportunity in somewhat the same way as language.[16] The general atmosphere of interest in and respect for learning appears to be an element in motivation of chil-

[15] Dorothea McCarthy, "Language Development in Children." Chapter in Leonard Carmichael (ed.), *Manual of Child Psychology* (New York: John Wiley & Sons, Inc., 1946), pp. 560 f.

[16] See F. Stuart Chapin, "Socio-economic Status: Some Preliminary Results of Measurement," *American Journal of Sociology*, XXXVII, No. 5 (1932), 581-87. Chapin devised an objective scale for rating the quality of homes, and found that intelligence and school grades average somewhat higher in homes with high scores. The well-known findings of lower intelligence scores in orphan homes agree with this result—see the summary of research in George D. Stoddard, *op. cit.*

dren to read, discuss, and inquire, and so to build up a growing structure of organized and consistent knowledge which in time tends to become almost self-nourishing. The amount of reading matter readily available in the home—reading matter of a factual, technical, and scientific character rather than comic books, fantasy, and fiction—appears to be related to intellectual development. An important variable in high school and college success appears to be the sheer amount of reading of this type that the student has done.

Special abilities may also be related to such opportunities for cultural nutrition. Adults who have little appreciation of music, or ability to make it, conventionally account for their lack by assuming some innate defect in ability, or some special handicap as "tone-deafness." Most persons who claim to be tone-deaf can readily be shown to be able to hear sounds all along the normal range of audible pitches; their defect is in lack of understanding of music. They cannot carry a tune accurately, probably because of insufficient exposure to music in childhood. Many such persons have grown up in homes in which there was no music at all, and so have had no opportunity to go through the long process of hearing and learning by responding silently or quietly. The most effective conditions for the production of musical appreciation and ability in a child appear to require not only a large amount of music to be heard, but also a high degree of absorption by the child. An unattended radio, playing by the hour, may be so disregarded that the sound is not perceived at all by the child. On the other hand, exposure to singing or piano-playing on a quiet and cozy evening, by a loved member of the family, may effectively engage the complete attention of the child. Experience of this type over a period of years may be the important factor in producing differences in music appreciation and ability in children.

Socioeconomic Differences in Intelligence.—Since the above opportunities will obviously occur more frequently in the higher economic levels, we should expect to find a general relation of ability to economic class. Referring to observed ability, without reference to a concept of innate capacity, the relationship has been shown many times and may be regarded as a well-established principle. McCarthy, surveying the research literature on language development, reaches the conclusion that "there is considerable evidence in the literature to indicate that there exists a marked relationship between socioeconomic status of the family and the

child's linguistic development." [17]   The relationship involves many
aspects of language, including vocabulary, verbal effectiveness,
length of sentences, maturity of sentence forms, and the like.

The relation of the economic and social level to general intelligence is shown also by many studies of adoptions and placements
in foster homes. For example, a recent report by Skeels and Harms
shows the result of placing 229 children with "inferior social histories" in foster homes.[18]   After a period of residence in their adoptive
homes, the children had less mental retardation and more superior
intelligence than would be expected from a sampling of the child
population of the region, in spite of the fact that 87 of them had
mothers with an I.Q. level of less than 75, and 111 had fathers in
unskilled or slightly skilled occupations. The relation of intelligence to economic level thus appears to be the result of such cultural nutrition as described above, rather than a result of inheritance of the mentality of parents.

Hollingshead has recently shown in some detail a relation of
intelligence test scores by social classes in a small, midwestern
town.[19]   The intelligence test scores of 507 high school students
are classified into four class levels, which for convenience may be
named here, Upper, Middle, Lower, and Isolates, the last being not
only at the bottom in income and prestige, but having the least
tendency to form friendships and to belong to organizations. The
numbers in each class falling in the given test categories are shown
in the accompanying table:

INTELLIGENCE TEST SCORES OF 507 HIGH SCHOOL STUDENTS

I.Q. scores	Classes			
	Upper	Middle	Lower	Isolates
120–139	8	19	11	0
111–119	15	72	82	11
91–110	12	59	128	70
70–90	0	2	8	10
Totals	35	152	229	91

The greater frequency of the lower scores in the lower classes is
conspicuous, and the contrast between the scores of the two extreme classes is particularly marked. Sixty-four per cent of the

---

[17] Dorothea McCarthy, op. cit., pp. 557 ff.

[18] Harold M. Skeels and Irene Harms, "Children with Inferior Social Histories;
Their Mental Development in Adoptive Homes," Journal of Genetic Psychology,
LXXII (1948), 283-94.

[19] August B. Hollingshead, Elmtown's Youth: The Impact of Social Classes on
Adolescents. (New York: John Wiley & Sons, Inc., 1949), p. 175.

upper-class students scored above 110 while only 12 per cent of the isolate group scored above that level.

Social Factors in the Generation of Exceptional Ability.—In general, the more exceptional the ability a person has, the more mysterious it appears, and the less accessible to an obvious explanation for its development. It is always tempting in these cases to employ the somewhat mystical concept of genius, implying abilities of a different order from those of ordinary persons. Such information as is available, incomplete as it is, suggests, however, that the extraordinary performer does not necessarily have any equipment not possessed by other persons except that which he has built up in his experience. There is no direct evidence of an exceptional innate endowment in these persons, but there is much evidence of unusual backgrounds of experience which could make possible the construction of highly efficient mental organization. This kind of organization presumably could have been possessed by any other persons of normal physiological equipment if the latter had spent an equal amount of time in the same activity.[20]

Useful illustration of the hidden tools furnished by mental organization is supplied by observations made on mental calculators. Zerah Colburn, a Vermont farm boy without education, developed such remarkable calculating powers that he was able to extract mentally the cube root of 268,336,125, and on one occasion gave, when requested, the square root of 998,001 in four seconds. In 1833, at the age of twenty-nine, Colburn wrote an autobiography in which he described a feat which he had performed at the age of eight.[21] "It had been asserted... that 4,294,967,297 ... was a prime number. ... Euler detected the error by discovering that it was equal to 641 times 6,700,417. The same number was proposed to [Colburn] who found the factors by the mere operation of his mind."

The literature contains accounts of numerous other such prodigies. Truman Henry Safford, another Vermont farmer's son, at the age of six was reported to have been able to multiply mentally four figures by four figures and to extract square and cube roots of numbers of nine and ten figures. Safford was educated at Harvard and became a professional astronomer. Other scientists, notably

---

[20] Support for this statement, and some amplification of the argument that follows, is available in a paper by the present author, "Sociological Causes of Genius," *American Sociological Review*, V, No. 5 (1940), 689-99.

[21] R. C. Archibald, "Arithmetical Prodigies," *American Mathematical Monthly*, XXV, No. 2 (1918), 92.

Gauss and Ampere, have possessed these superior abilities, as have a number of persons who never did achieve an education. Among the most remarkable of all mental calculators was Zacharias Dase (1824–1861) of Hamburg. Among his feats were the multiplication of two 100-figure numbers in 8¾ hours, and the extraction of the square root of a 100-figure number in 52 minutes.

These and other calculators have been studied by psychologists and by mathematicians who have produced a literature of some size on this phenomenon. In general, the abilities are adequately accounted for without any assumption of special innate abilities or any kind of biological superiority. The mental calculators work with methods which are far more efficient than those used by ordinary persons, so that the number of operations required in computation is greatly reduced. Their speed and ease of calculation are made possible by the possession in their memory of tables, arrangements of numbers, short-cuts, formulas, and tricks which are developed and maintained by virtue of a rich interest in numbers and an immense amount of practice in calculating. A good memory for numbers is required, but there is no reason to believe that this is an innate ability.

The well-known and accomplished mental calculator Salo Finkelstein was investigated by a psychologist at New York University in 1942.[22] It was found that his methods of operation were not unconscious or automatic, nor based on any mysterious capacity unavailable to ordinary persons, but that the impressive memory which was the basis of his ability was explicable in terms of the familiar principles of memory. Finkelstein used methods of active association in observing numbers and maintained these associations by continuous practice. The degree of interest in this memorizing and the long time spent in developing it produced a large number of common associations with three- and four-digit numbers. Because of this he was able to memorize not only large quantities of numbers, but to do it very quickly. Among his reported feats was the memorizing of the number 624,706,845,986,193,261,832 in 4.43 seconds. While this would seem too remarkable to be the result of training, a news report of May, 1936 described an experiment at the Ohio State University in which a graduate student was trained to memorize numbers. After a training and practice period totaling 75 hours, the student was able to memorize the same number in 4.37 seconds.

[22] James D. Weinland, "The Memory of Salo Finkelstein," *Journal of General Psychology*, XXXIX (1948), 243-57.

The circumstances in which the calculating ability is acquired vary, but in general there tends to appear some situation in which an interest in digits is stimulated along with a motive for counting or computing. Four of the well-known calculators were shepherd boys, who had to count sheep frequently. Another requirement appears to be a considerable amount of solitude, during which the preoccupation with numbers is undisturbed by the necessity to be responsive to other persons. Counting and computing develops into a constant silent obsession, with patterns of numbers "running through the mind" in the fashion of a tune which sometimes refuses to depart from our attention even after we make an effort to forget it. One investigator, who himself had developed these abilities in his childhood, describes the process in his case as an elaboration of such silent counting.[23] After ordinary counting failed to maintain his interest, he counted with accents or resting spots at regular intervals, such as 4, 8, 12, 16. Then he counted by thinking only of the resting spots; in effect rehearsing multiplication tables. After thus unintentionally equipping himself with these tables, he built up tables of squares and cubes in similar silent preoccupation and added further tricks as he went along. It is characteristic that he had neither intention nor recognition of what was being developed in this process.

The present author has observed an interesting case of development of some of the well-known calculators' tricks by a person of late maturity. This person, a professor in the social science field, had no previous special interest in or marked ability concerning numbers. At about the age of sixty, however, he became dangerously ill and was confined for several months to a bed. Visitors were forbidden and he was not allowed to move, or read, or converse, and was even advised by his physician not to think about his occupation or any other subject in which there might be reason to worry. Finding himself unable to lie still without thinking at all, he sought mental material which would occupy him and prevent his mind from drifting back to disturbing worries. Remembering advice he had heard years before, he tried the mental division of fractions. Concentrating on the activity hour after hour and day after day, with no purpose other than that of occupying his mind, he built up tables, arrangements, tricks, and formulas which served in his calculations. He discovered, for example, the relation of any two numbers to the square of the number halfway between their

[23] Frank D. Mitchell, "Mathematical Prodigies," *American Journal of Psychology*, XVIII (1907).

magnitudes, and used this relation in making rapid multiplication of two numbers not greatly unequal. When given, for example, two such numbers as 379 and 386 he was able to write the product at once, with no visible delay. He also developed the ability to compute rapidly the day of the week of any date named, and developed algebraic formulas which generalized these procedures. On his recovery and the resumption of his occupation and accustomed life, the discovery process virtually ended, though he did retain by occasional practice some of the abilities he had built up.

The exceptional abilities of the calculators, then, appear to depend on the kind of mental tools they use. Their equipment is far more efficient than the usual methods of computing taught in school, and so makes the task easier. There is nothing to indicate that others could not learn the same tricks, but it seems probable that it would require exceptional conditions for this to take place—particularly with respect to extreme fascination for numbers and a great deal of time alone for practice. Neither of these are actually desirable for the majority of the population and so no proposals for mass education in calculating ability are here implied. This knowledge of the operations of the calculators, however, is an important contribution to the understanding of ability in general, and serves to take most of the mysticism out of the concept of genius. The exceptional abilities clearly arise as a consequence of exceptional experiences, which produce a mental organization of high efficiency for the particular purpose, usually at some sacrifice of other types of knowledge and ability.

There is some similarity to the above account in the explanations of other types of outstanding ability. Masters of the game of chess are able to look ahead and deal swiftly with what appears to be great complexity also by virtue of mental organization acquired by long practice. In planning a move, they do not have to go through the many separate thoughts that would be required of a novice. Their concerns are not with one square and one piece at a time, but with openings, campaigns, traps, end-games, and such conceptions, which are mentally handled as simple units. The eight squares threatened by a knight located in the central area of the chessboard do not have to be observed separately, they appear as a unitary pattern, and the rows and diagonals dominated by a queen make a single pattern as conspicuous in his mind as if they were painted in a separate color. The situation which is hopelessly complex to a beginner is thus perceived far more simply to the advanced player.

A similar principle applies to feats of musical composing. Admirers of Mozart are amazed at the rapidity with which he composed symphonies and overtures of masterwork quality. The achievement is undoubtedly high, but is not to be measured by what the nonmusical person would have to do to produce the same result. The bewildering complexity of notes in a symphony, tens of thousands and sometimes hundreds of thousands, is experienced by the composer as a finite number of organized themes. Some symphonies have two major themes in each of four movements, with a few minor themes and transitions added. Each theme may appear in one or more variations in addition to the original statement, and the variation is only partly a separate act of invention to a veteran composer, who knows before he begins what the promising possibilities of variation are. Once a method of variation is conceived, much of the labor of writing it out is determined and can be done relatively swiftly by an energetic composer. Here again, then, is another illustration of types of mental organization which, as concealed mental tools, enormously speed up the achievements which appear difficult to the uninitiated.

The present author has previously pointed out that a part of our popular admiration of the feats of the composer, the calculator and the chess master is a consequence of the fact that relatively few persons engage seriously in these pursuits and therefore acquire familiarity and contempt for the achievements. Only a handful of chess geniuses stand at the top of the game, but also only a microscopic fraction of the population ever devotes an appreciable amount of attention to the game. On the other hand, a feat which is possibly quite as remarkable objectively is performed as a matter of fact by unknown hundreds of thousands of persons—the feat of rapid reading of printed material. Its commonness distracts our attention from the amount of achievement, which would be taken as marvelous if it were as rare as high chess ability. In rapid reading we take in a large number of symbols in a glance—a good reader may absorb the meaning from 30 to 35 letters in two or three seconds, continuing this speed for hours, at the same time performing the relating operations that bind the material into the memory. It is conceivable that this achievement is as great as those of the famous calculators or composers.[24]

In the study cited above, the organization of case material reveals some factors which are common in the life histories of persons with high ability of various kinds, and which appear to be related

---

[24] R. E. L. Faris, *op. cit.*, pp. 69-70.

to the development of the exceptional ability. These factors are in part accidental circumstances in the lives of the persons, and in part the operation of sociological processes. Sociological processes, in fact, appear to differentiate abilities throughout the whole human range, not only in contributing the production of exceptionally high talent in some, and producing retardation at the other extreme, but also in operating to produce mediocrity in the majority of persons.

Among the most important of these factors is an intensely absorbing, almost obsessive interest in a subject—an interest so dominating that in pursuit of it the person may fail to notice hunger, fatigue, discomfort, and the passage of time. It is this unconventional amount of motivation that has led many of the prolific composers to extreme but productive exertion. For illustration:

Mozart's feat of writing down three of his greatest symphonies in six weeks is an outstanding example. . . . Schubert, assigned by his father to the uncongenial drudgery of teaching school, found time during his sixteenth to nineteenth years to undertake many string quartets, five symphonies, various sonatas for piano and violin, Masses and other church music, eight stage works of varying lengths and intentions, and more than two hundred and fifty songs. Mendelssohn, by his eleventh year, had composed more than sixty separate pieces, and in the following five years showed very great productivity, without the pressure of need or the hunger for applause. Wagner, beginning his real interest in composing at the comparatively late age of eighteen, at once put on the same speed—within a year he completed three overtures, seven scenes from a Faust symphony, and various piano pieces, and was already dreaming along the lines that would lead to the cycle of Ring music dramas. Brahms began composing soon after beginning composition lessons at the age of ten, and was soon nearly wearing himself out by writing great numbers of insignificant works. Such determined interest and absorption is typical of geniuses in other fields. The well known cases of Darwin, Pasteur, Edison, and Curie furnish further examples.

This nearly universal trait of geniuses, however, does not in itself constitute genius. It is in fact not uncommon among children, in the form of interest in Mother Goose rhymes, in Hollywood performers, in gardening, astronomy, and other hobbies, any of which may be acquired or dropped at any age. The interest may be as powerful and time-consuming as those in the lives of geniuses, and yet clearly be seen to be acquired by accident, or produced easily by the intention of parent or friend. The demands of normal social life are such as to destroy or at least limit interests of this type, and consequently most such enthusiasms are merely temporary and lead to no outstanding career.[25]

[25] *Ibid.*, p. 693.

The superiority of the creative determination over fatigue and discomforts is shown by two highly successful contemporary playwrights. George S. Kaufman, author and co-author of a number of outstanding stage successes, worked so intensely on his plays that one collaborator refers to the period of their joint labors as "The Days of the Terror." The working day began at 10 in the morning and continued until the partners were exhausted "which meant starved as well, since Kaufman cares nothing about food." [26] Sometimes two hours would be spent on a single sentence, and an entire day working out an exit. Robert E. Sherwood, another successful author, shows the same disregard of comfort. He works out a play mentally, sometimes over a period of several years, before beginning to write anything down. When he feels ready to write, he applies himself in a concentrated effort, usually getting the play done in a short time by working day and night. Sometimes this requires continuing work during an attack, which he suffers from time to time, of *tic douloureux*, a painful affliction in the sinus region which is pronounced by some physicians to be "one of the most agonizing afflictions known to man." [27]

Even outstanding athletes reflect the same history of fascination by their specialty. Most top baseball players apparently thought of little else during their youth. A news story of a girl figure-skating star showed that a tremendous amount of interest was necessary to sustain the exhausting schedule she usually maintained, a regimen which involved rising at five in the morning, skating for five hours after breakfast, piano practice from one to three o'clock in the afternoon, and ballet lessons for the next two hours.[28]

Perhaps the outstanding billiard player of all time is William F. Hoppe. According to a biographical article, he is said to have begun his interest in the pool table in his seventh year.[29] From that time on he is said to have practiced from four to eight hours a day. He was happy only when engaged in the game, and never showed interest in other standard activities of boys. His own recollection of school is of rows of seats and children, and of books in which he drew diagrams of shots to be tried on the pool table. He remembers that he spent most of his time in school daydreaming about the plays he could make.

Such an interest appears to be an essential type of motivation in

[26] *Time*, November 20, 1939, p. 66.
[27] *New Yorker*, June 1, 1940.
[28] *New York Times Magazine*, February 4, 1940.
[29] From a biographical sketch by Robert L. Taylor in the *New Yorker*, November 16, 1940.

all kinds of exceptional achievement. The interest by itself, however, is insufficient. An abundance of available time for study and
effort is also required, and virtually always observable in the outstanding cases of talent. Practically all violinists of first rank have
spent many hours a day throughout childhood and youth in intensive practice. As previously stated, mental calculators build
their abilities over years of silent preoccupation with the properties
of numbers. But not all the time spent is obvious to others—it is
unlikely, for example, that the teachers in the schools attended by
the young Hoppe were aware that he was applying himself to the
skills of the cue when he was supposed to be working on lessons in
spelling.

The silent and unnoticed practice is in fact a very important
part of the study in some cases of talent. In a study by the present
author, a talented and versatile actor was interviewed on this point
and revealed a lifetime of such concealed study, beginning as far
back as in early childhood. His interest had started after he had
been put in formal clothes to participate in a "Tom Thumb" wedding. Stage-struck from then on, he spent great amounts of time
and attention studying persons and their characteristic mannerisms, trying out their roles in his imagination with the intention
of broadening his repertoire. Similarly, a talented painter revealed
a history of a large amount of study achieved by noticing and
analyzing things about him, while engaged in ordinary routine activity. He saw objects as things to paint, or as problems in composition, or light and shadow, or color. He experienced the furniture
in a room, trees on the street, the faces of friends, as possible material to be employed in a future painting. Such study is not only
inconspicuous to others, but the amount often is not even obvious
to the person engaged in it unless he attempts to become aware
of it.

A factor involved in some types of high achievement is a rich
exposure to predecessors and to the accumulated fund of highest
development in any line up to the time. Originality in most fields
requires a mastery of what has already been done, and this is possible more easily for those students who have a close relation with
adults and teachers, with predecessors and masters. Such a relation is clear in the sequence of German composers—Bach, Haydn,
Mozart, Beethoven, and Brahms. Each takes up the tradition
where the last left it in a way that would have been impossible to
one who had no exposure to such a tradition.

Some child prodigies have been deliberately developed by able parents who lead the child through the existing fields of knowledge so that the frontier can more quickly be crossed. James Mill intentionally reared his son, John Stuart Mill, to be such a prodigy. William Sidis was similarly reared by his psychologist father, Boris Sidis. Edward Hardy was regularly escorted by his mother to the library, where he was made to spend hours daily soaking up knowledge. In other cases, the same advantage has been gained on the child's own initiative, sometimes without even the knowledge of his parents, through self-chosen reading and other rewarding study.

Another factor of importance appears to be a trait of perfectionism. It is characteristic of most outstanding performers that they are highly intolerant of imperfections of a type which would scarcely be noticed by most persons. There is among such persons far greater effort spent to eliminate small flaws—an ambitious singer of this type may spend a month or more working on a single difficult turn of four notes in order that it can be delivered flawlessly. There are many examples in the history of musical composition of composers discarding, revising, endlessly polishing compositions in order to get rid of flaws which most persons would never recognize. The same characteristic is conspicuous in many persons of high achievement in art, literature, and science.

A factor of social interaction appears in a number of cases, in a reciprocal relation between public admiration and the gifted person's desire to have more of it. Public approval is pleasant, and public amazement even more so, and when the latter is produced by an outstanding achievement the tendency often develops to make each future performance or creation even greater than the last, continually to cap the climax. The development is clearly seen in Beethoven, whose First Symphony was good enough to win him lasting fame. The public has received the Third, Fifth, Seventh, and Ninth as surpassing one another in such serial fashion. The use of a vocal chorus in the Ninth was decided on partly because of the difficulty of exceeding the symphonies which preceded it. Brahms, who thought of himself as a successor in the Beethoven tradition, in turn wrote of the difficulty of surpassing Beethoven, while Wagner, who also recognized it, chose to turn to the music drama in the hope of astonishing appreciators of music. The same kind of necessity to make each effort excel the previous ones is seen in the work of Shakespeare, James Joyce, Picasso, and innumerable lesser geniuses.

Another factor of a sociological nature, applying more to creations in the field of knowledge and science than in art, is a kind of confidence in the availability and value of knowledge—a confidence derived in part from association with persons who possess such knowledge and in part from a certain consistency in the culture. There is usually, moreover, a concept of a method, the use of which, it is believed, will secure new knowledge. A child who lives in a family lacking in such conditions, and whose questions are usually answered by evasion, bluffing, or by assertions that the world is too vast and mysterious to be comprehended, is unlikely to have the impulse to try to learn. But if knowledge is defined to the child as highly desirable, and reasonably available, he may at an early age develop the habit of pursuing answers to all his questions and curiosities, and of exploring each new and unfamiliar field of knowledge with which he comes into contact. A study of leading mathematicians reveals that a number of them began the independent study of Euclid, Newton, and other fundamental works at early ages—endeavors which few persons ever have the confidence to undertake unaided.[30] Before he was twelve years old, Thomas Edison, with little formal schooling to his advantage, had read through such solid works as Gibbon's *Decline and Fall* and Hume's *History of England,* and even had made an attempt at Newton's *Principia.* In his newsboy days, he read the contents of whole shelves in the public libraries.

There doubtless is such a thing as a modest genius, particularly if external manners are the mark of modesty.[31] But self-confidence which borders on and sometimes amounts to conceit is a common trait of men of outstanding achievement, often appearing early in life. Wagner furnishes one of the most extreme instances. He completely accepted the social role of the genius, which, as he saw it, included privileges which could not be made available to others. His confidence in himself, moreover, involved a belief that he was exceptional in many ways in addition to his abilities in the field of music. A modern critic writes that Wagner "believed himself to be one of the greatest dramatists in the world, one of the greatest thinkers and one of the greatest composers—Shakespeare, Beethoven, and Plato, rolled into one." [32] Such a self-concept may function as an important aid in motivating a person to attempt confidently where other great persons have failed.

In a number of cases of exceptional ability a certain degree of

[30] E. T. Bell, *Men of Mathematics* (New York: Simon & Schuster, Inc., 1937).

[31] Brahms, for one, affected a degree of modesty, but there are sufficient indications that he accurately knew his ability and his place in the musical world.

[32] Deems Taylor, "A Musical Monster." *Reader's Digest,* April, 1937, p. 56.

isolation appears to be a factor. While it is important in many fields to have the advantages both of contact with what achievements have been made before and of familiarity with methods already worked out, there is also a requirement of a long period of time without distraction, a withdrawal without which creative thought is difficult.

New creation, furthermore, requires some break from convention—a step taken more readily by a person who is able to take a detached view of convention. The maintenance of normal social relations requires a response to a number of different interests, and thereby makes difficult the absorbing concentration on one dominant, and perhaps unconventional, interest. The very act of communication itself, the participation in conversation, necessarily holds thoughts to the conventional, thus discouraging originality. While in the long run the genius will not be recognized if he does not make his contributions communicable to some persons, it is often not possible to progress so far or so rapidly within the frameworks of conventional speech or thought.

In the field of painting, for example, convention interferes with mastery of technique in the use of color. Beginners paint skies blue, grass green, red barns red, white houses white—never perceiving the colors that really enter the eye—and wonder why their pictures fail to look as they had intended. Even the experienced artist must sometimes look at a scene in some strange perspective—in a mirror, for example—in order to break through the paralyzing conventional knowledge of things that interferes with accurate perception of color. In drawing, also, the novice often draws lines parallel because his knowledge that the boundaries being drawn are actually parallel dominates his perception and in spite of the fact that careful and detached attention would discover them to be perceived as convergent. Similar barriers to originality put up by convention are to be found in many fields of activity. The social pressure to be explicable must, in many cases, be resisted during the creative stages of activity.

It is a general tendency, if not a universal one, for primary groups so to emphasize the importance of homogeneity among their members that a social pressure toward mediocrity restricts the development of ability. A contemporary study of the primary relations of children has found that those who are "high communicators" (essentially, thorough members of the primary groups of their own age levels) are subject to this kind of influence. According to the investigators:

We are inclined to sum up these predominant tendencies of the high communicators in the concept of *mediocrity*, as one essential goal of the youth culture, since basically all peer-oriented youth aspire to be like each other, on a level which the majority can reach. Our respondents, when asked what makes a girl or boy popular, describe an all-round youth who above all shuns uniqueness: "smart, but not too smart," "pretty, but not too pretty," "friendly," "gets along well with everybody." Such a goal, for those who are once accepted into the youth culture groups, is relatively easy of achievement. Moreover, the means for arriving at the goal appear, in these findings, to be fairly clearly defined—as just being with the gang, enjoyment of humorous media figures [comic strips] keeping up with the big league games and with the latest tunes, etc. Indeed, satisfactions from goals achieved seem to be common fare, along with satisfaction from the socially accepted means of striving for this achievement. One evidence of such satisfaction lies in the finding that the high communicators, already surrounded as they are by peers, can think of no better companions when asked to imagine ideal conditions.[33]

The foregoing discussion of factors involved in high achievement is not meant to imply that these are the only variables involved. They do appear to show, however, that social processes play an important part in differentiating the population in ability, even at the extremely high levels of ability, and that types of experience are important in the generation of high performances. The role played by differences in innate capacities or by biological differences of any kind is not known. Persons differ in various physiological characteristics such as strength, vigor, and speed of reaction time, but there has been little or no success in linking these variables with differences in actual mental performance.

It is easy to err in studying differences of this type. The famous Seashore music tests were intended as measures of innate and unalterable capacities, and Seashore thought he had succeeded in finding them. In the study of pitch discrimination, for example, the results of his studies appeared to show that the ability is not affected by age or training. He wrote:

It seems probable that just as the physical eye of the child at the age of three is as keen as it ever will be, so the pitch sensitiveness in the ear probably reaches its maximum very early. Development in the use of the sense of pitch with maturation consists in acquiring habits and meanings, interests, desires, and musical knowledge, rather than in the improvement of the sense organ. . . . The physiological limit for hearing pitch does not improve with training. Training, like maturation, results in the conscious recognition of the nature of pitch, its meaning, and the development of habits of use in

[33] Matilda W. Riley and Samuel H. Flowerman, "Group Relations as a Variable in Communications Research." *American Sociological Review,* XVI, No. 2 (1951), p. 176.

musical operations. Training probably does not modify the capacity of the sense organ any more than the playing of the good violin may improve the quality of its tone.[34]

The error turned out to result from inadequate study of the possibilities of training. Later investigators, with more confidence in their ability to train subjects, and perhaps with more understanding of the processes of learning, succeeded in producing marked improvement in pitch discrimination. One of the most decisive studies is that by Wyatt, who trained sixteen university students, most of whom were low or mediocre in this ability.[35] The training consisted of approximately twelve fifty-minute periods of individual training in both pitch intonation and pitch discrimination, with attention centered upon diagnosis of individual difficulties and upon development of the best possible methods of study for each student. The results were almost spectacular—all subjects improved, and the improvement took place in all levels of difficulty. Although their scores were not high to begin with, their improvement on the average was 37 per cent of the maximum possible gain.

Summary

Human activity is organized socially for purposes which are, to a large extent, culturally defined. Persons may differ in their capacities to live up to certain standards of performance because of physiological differences and it is clear that a minimum of physiological capacity is essential to normal performance—severe physical defects can sometimes make speech, reading, and conventional manners impossible. But there is also a great source of variation in abilities which is not connected with any innate or physiological basis. Abilities are acquired in experience, and experiences differ importantly from person to person. Variations in kinds of experiences related to efficiency of performance differentiate mental abilities in ways both obvious and subtle. Such obvious differentiation is illustrated by the contrast in abilities of persons who have the advantages of a college education with those persons who live their lives in isolated mountain valleys where no opportunity for formal schooling exists. The subtle processes of differentiation require

[34] By permission from *Psychology of Music*, by Carl E. Seashore. Copyright 1938 by McGraw-Hill Book Co., Inc., p. 58

[35] Ruth F. Wyatt, "Improvability of Pitch Discrimination," *Psychological Monographs*, Vol. LVIII, No. 2 (1945).

careful study of the relation of experiences to mental organization, as in the illustrations of the mental calculators and similar geniuses.

The high practical value of intelligence tests is not challenged here, but the obsolete concept that they are able to measure an innate capacity entirely apart from the influences of various cultural experiences is rejected. Not only are such factors of general intelligence as verbal ability and facility in simple numerical operations readily shown to be developed by experience and aided by social factors, but, as shown in the final example of the present Chapter, even a trait which has long been assumed to be innately determined —the ability to discriminate musical pitch differences—is greatly modifiable by training when proper skills and instruments are available for the task.

The maximum performance for any person, as well as the ability level in the same person at different times, varies according to how much of an effort he is willing to make. In testing procedure, the attempt is made to minimize this source of variation by urging the subjects to do their best, but this does not even equalize the force of motivation among subjects who believe they are trying as earnestly as possible. Outside the conventional testing situation, variations in performance attributable to differences in strength of motivation are even larger. Some experimental work on the level of aspiration has succeeded in demonstrating the relation of this factor to mental activity in test situations, but of course these results cannot more than hint at the vast differences in interests displayed in music, for example, by the man who, on one hand, does nothing more than carelessly whistle popular tunes and the many top musicians on the other who drive themselves to exhaustion in order to get the last bit of perfection. The former addresses his tune to nobody in particular and cares little about its accuracy or artistic quality, while the latter aims to impress other musical performers and critics whose standards are exacting. The social source of the aspiration level is clearly apparent, even though difficult to measure.

The organization that exists in knowledge in a sense resides in a society. Each person who achieves knowledge does so largely by drawing on the cultural resources and obtains not only the material but most of the organization from the general fund. Just as we, as individuals, speak an organized language by incorporating the collective set of integrated symbols into our own habits, so do we think and solve problems in a methodical way by a similar use of the processes which we absorb from social organization.

The richness of each person's relation to his society is itself a factor in the variations of ability in the population. Isolated persons are in general mentally retarded in direct proportion to the degree of their isolation, and persons who spend their developing years in such inadequate settings as orphan homes have been shown to have deficiencies on that account. On the other hand, children with much exposure to adults have an advantage, as far as the development of ability is concerned, over children who spend most of their time among others of their own ages. Exposure to adults of high qualifications, particularly when the relationship involves close rapport, may be an important factor in the development of knowledge and ability.

Such factors of experience are roughly related to socioeconomic levels, giving an advantage of extra opportunities to participate in the culture to those in the higher classifications and so producing a somewhat higher level of ability there. Research has repeatedly demonstrated such an average difference in school achievement and mental test scores—a developed intelligence is apparently one of the rewards of a high standard of living.

None of these broad influences, however, goes far to explain the performance of persons with exceptional ability, such as the mental calculators, the memory experts, the prolific composers, and the like. These abilities are shown, however, to be acquired in experience. Their rarity is a consequence of the uncommon forms of experience required to generate them—experiences which usually follow from uncommon accidental circumstances, such as fascination with numbers and with the activity of counting, and prolonged isolation, both common elements in the life histories of the calculators. The assumption of any remarkable level of innate capacity in these cases is made to appear unnecessary by indications that the abilities may be acquired late in life in some cases, and by the fact that some efforts at teaching such tricks as digit memory and musical pitch discrimination have been spectacularly successful.

A part of the explanation for the appearance of almost magical inexplicability of the extreme cases of talent also lies in the fact that so much of the development of the mental organization required is done inconspicuously as silent rehearsal over long periods of time. There are indications, in fact, that many persons who are engaged in this kind of preoccupied learning are themselves only partly aware of what they are doing, in the same way that many persons may hum a tune without realizing it.

As shown earlier in the book, man is essentially active and his actions are for the most part guided and organized by the groups to which he belongs. Mental differences, capacities, talents, are, for the most part, acquired in this active and social process, and are not fixed by something apart such as a set of discrete inherited gifts.

SELECTED REFERENCES

FARIS, R. E. L. "Sociological Causes of Genius." *American Sociological Review.* V, No. 5 (1940), 689-99.
STODDARD, GEORGE D. *The Meaning of Intelligence.* New York: The Macmillan Co., 1943. Discusses the relation of ability to social experience.

Chapter 11

THE CHARACTER OF PRIMARY INTERACTION

IT HAS been stated in earlier chapters that human nature is to an important degree a product of society, that is, of organized patterns of interaction. These patterns consist both of complex and formal relations and of relations in small informal groups. The latter, known in sociology as primary groups, are universal in human societies and indispensable. The processes of primary interaction are increasingly recognized as important in the study of social psychology as well as in sociology, and the research on these constitutes the subject matter of the present Chapter.

THE NATURE OF PRIMARY GROUPS

The groups in which men interact vary according to the degree of intimacy of personal contacts and therefore in the influence exerted by the group on the person. The groups with the greater degrees of intimacy and influence are commonly called primary groups—a concept introduced by Cooley.

By primary groups I mean those characterized by intimate face-to-face association and cooperation. They are primary in several senses, but chiefly in that they are fundamental in forming the social nature and ideals of the individual. The result of intimate association, psychologically, is a certain fusion of individualities in a common whole, so that one's very self, for many purposes at least, is the common life and purpose of the group. Perhaps the simplest way of describing this wholeness is by saying that it is a "we"; it involves the sort of sympathy and mutual identification for which "we" is the natural expression. One lives in the feeling of the whole and finds the chief aims of his will in that feeling.[1]

The face-to-face element in the above account is not, of course, an essential feature of the primary group, since there may be very formal and impersonal relations of a face-to-face character, and since intimate and personal relations may be maintained at a dis-

[1] Charles Horton Cooley, *Social Organization* (New York: Chas. Scribner's Sons, 1909), p. 23.

tance by correspondence and other communication.[2] More important is the richness of the sympathy or affection on which the personal interaction is based. It is this feature which gives the primary group its peculiar importance in social life and personality formation, as pointed out in the following well-known passage.

Human life is essentially dramatic. Personality arises as, and because, we play roles in our social intercourse. The process of reflection in which we define for ourselves the meaning of what we have said and what others have said and done to us is also a dramatic event. We become conscious of ourselves when we realize that we are acting like another. Our personality is shaped by the definitions of our acts which we receive from others. We respond to them in our imagination and build up not only our virtues and vices but the awareness of them. And here arises the transcendent importance of the primary group. Only in the primary-group relation is this type of influence directly effected and positively formative. Strictly mechanical relations approximate absent-mindedness, hostile relations tend to generate opposing attitudes, but in the primary group the seeds of a culture live and bear fruit. And the group is a relation between members, not an aggregation of units. The sociological group can be described only by reference to the experiences of its members.[3]

In addition to the features mentioned above, two specific characteristics are apparently required for a group to function as a primary group. These are, first, a feeling of confidence among the members in a structure of mutual affection, and second, a conviction, among the members, of an essential similarity of one to another. The mutual affection appears to be necessary for effective control. We value the good opinion of us others hold and we guide our own behavior to gain and keep it. If we had no affection for the others, and no hope of gaining their affection, their good opinion of us would be of little importance. Some control would still be possible on the basis of threats of punishment and other formal means, but they are less effective, and, in fact, distinctly unfavorable to the maintenance of primary relations—formal controls sometimes even tend to disrupt primary relations. The second characteristic—the conviction of similarity—makes it possible for the members of a group to believe that they understand one another and can therefore cooperate with smooth confidence. Where this is lacking and persons believe that they are not, or cannot be, understood, there is a sense of hopelessness that acts as a barrier to cooperation. The

[2] Ellsworth Faris, *The Nature of Human Nature* (New York: McGraw-Hill Book Co., Inc., 1937), p. 36.

[3] By permission from *The Nature of Human Nature* by Ellsworth Faris. Copyright 1937 by McGraw-Hill Book Co., Inc., p. 43.

relations between boys in a reformatory and the administrative officials of the institution provide an illustration of the lack of both of these essential features of a primary group. The boys, in all but the exceptional type of reformatory, have a strong hostility toward the officials, and care nothing for their good opinion or affection. In general, they assume, perhaps accurately, that no affection is felt for them by the officials and would be disposed to reject any if it were proffered. The sense of similarity is also lacking because of differences in background, age, and responsibility. The boys tend to assume that the officials could not understand them if they tried to, and so make little attempt to keep their own behavior on a basis which would make them intelligible to the officials. Needless to say, in such a situation no primary group relations form between such inmates and officials, and the controls available are of the formal character—specified rules with punishment for infraction.

In the primary group, formal controls are unnecessary and out of place. The control within the primary group operates by causing the person to wish to do what is desired by the others or by the majority of the most influential members. To its members, the primary group becomes a value in itself, and it is more important *how* they behave together than *what* each one does. When the members of a harmonious family, or group of close friends, discuss the matter of what they will do with an available period of time together, the assumption generally is clear that they will arrive informally at some consensus. Often the sentiment is expressed on all sides that it makes little difference which of the various possible activities are undertaken, as long as the members engage in them together. A high-school girl illustrates the point as follows:

I have one very close friend, Joyce Jenson. We met four years ago and we've been going around together since. We plan our clothes, we talk about what we're going to do, and we study together. We come to school together, we take the same courses, we visit each other at home, we go to church together, we plan church parties, and so on. Of course, we don't agree 100 per cent on everything, but we've made up our minds when we don't agree that one is going to dominate the other. Sometimes she dominates me and sometimes I dominate her. If we decide we want to go to a church party, well, maybe I won't want to go, but I'll go because she really wants to go. Then maybe we'll decide to go to a show. Sometimes she won't want to go because she doesn't like the show, but she'll go because I've gone to the church party with her.[4]

[4] Reprinted by permission from August B. Hollingshead, *Elmtown's Youth: The Impact of Social Classes on Adolescents,* published by John Wiley & Sons, Inc., 1949, p. 209.

What takes place in a primary group thus is not a mere sum of individual decisions, but action that emerges out of a process of relations between the persons. It is with this in mind that Harvard investigators have written:

. . . studies here or elsewhere have had little success in predicting from pre-measures of personality variables how persons will behave in a group. It is suggested that the fact that when individuals are put together a *system* is created is the critical fact which cannot be overlooked. For example, if a non-directive leader is put with a group, the end result depends not only on the leader but also on whether somebody else in the group picks up the ball. If somebody does, there will be one result; if not, another.[5]

As indicated in previous chapters, it is in primary groups that personality is acquired and that many satisfactions of life are furnished. It is not surprising, therefore, that persons acquire a general desire for primary group life itself, without explicit calculation of the particular satisfactions that membership in it brings. As products of primary group life, then, human beings continue to seek primary interaction and have a strong acquired disposition both to join and to form primary groups. Such a tendency is universal in human societies, and is present in all but abnormal persons in every society. The absence of such a tendency in the schizoid or schizophrenic personality and defectives of other types is itself generally regarded as an indication of abnormality.

In many of the simple, preliterate societies, systems of kinship designation operate in such fashion as to insure that each person will have membership in primary group life, the value of which is in many instances explicitly recognized by the members of the society. Lowie has written:

In primitive communities . . . a specific mode of behavior may be rigidly determined for each and every possible form of relationship. From the point of view of any individual this means that his tribesmen are classified into certain categories, each one of which implies an altogether special set of social rules to be observed by him. He is bound to render services to an individual of one class; with a member of another he may jest and take liberties: with persons of a third category he must have nothing to do except through intermediaries; and so forth . . . the intensity of the obligation is greater for the nearer relationship.[6]

[5] From the *Report for the Years 1946–1951*, Harvard Laboratory of Social Relations, p. 18.

[6] From *Primitive Society* by Robert H. Lowie, by permission of Liveright Publishing Corporation. Copyright renewed 1948, Robert H. Lowie.

A concrete illustration of this statement is provided by the western Australian Kariera tribe, among whom, according to an investigator:

The recognition of relationships is so extended that everyone with whom an individual comes in contact in the ordinary course of social life is his relative. It is impossible for a man to have any social relation with anyone who is not his relative because there is no standard by which two persons in this position can regulate their conduct towards one another. . . . When [for example] a stranger comes to a camp that he has never visited before, he does not enter the camp, but remains at some distance. A few of the older men, after a while, approach him, and the first thing they proceed to do is to find out who the stranger is. . . . In one case, after a long discussion, they were still unable to discover any traceable relationship between my servant and the men of the camp. That night my "boy" refused to sleep in the native camp . . . he was frightened. These men were not his relatives, and they were therefore his enemies.[7]

The final sentence in the above paragraph provides one explanation of the widespread desire for relatives which is also a desire for a primary group, for these are the persons who can be counted on as friends, not enemies. In civilized societies the suspicion that all strangers may be enemies is not usually as strong, but there is, nevertheless, a general comfort in knowing that one is surrounded by persons whom he can trust and whose affection can be assumed without question.

In Chapter 4 the thesis is presented that the desire for sociability, companionship, and hence primary group membership, is a generalization based on a variety of benefits which are found to result from such experience. Like currency, the benefits may be converted into various concrete forms. But the generalization is not necessarily done separately by each person who desires primary relations; it is, in fact, an aspect of folk knowledge which is a possession of cultures and subcultures. The society instils in its members, in various ways, a sense of appreciation of the value of primary groups. Furthermore, primary groups which are particularly successful may contain in their little subcultures special attitudes which favor the motive. Anderson has shown statistically a tendency for social participation in organizations to be a family characteristic.[8] For a sample of 2041 persons in rural upstate New York,

---

[7] A. R. Radcliffe-Brown, "Three Tribes of Western Australia," *Journal of the Anthropological Institute*, XLIII, 151, 157. Cited in W. I. Thomas, *Primitive Behavior* (1937), p. 99. By permission of McGraw-Hill Book Co., Inc., publishers.

[8] W. A. Anderson, "The Family and Individual Social Participation," *American Sociological Review*, VIII, No. 4 (1943), 420-24.

he finds that "the social participation of an individual is to a considerable degree a function of the social participation of the family ... if husbands participate, wives usually do, and if husbands and wives participate, children usually do ... participation is chiefly a family trait." Figures on membership in organizations, attendance at their meetings, and contributions toward their support, show that in the great majority of families either all members take part or all do not. Only a minority of families participate with a fraction of their membership.

Primary Group Processes

The Tendency to Form Groups.—Because of the strength and near universality of the desire for primary relations it is almost impossible to find individuals in daily proximate association who do not spontaneously form into a number of small primary groups. It is apparently necessary that most persons find at least some groups of very small size. Larger groups may endure for other functions they achieve, but they do not replace the small clique which ranges in size from two or three members to ten or twelve.

Hollingshead has counted the number of cliques among the high school students of Elmtown and tabulated sizes of their membership.[9] These are classified by types. The cliques which formed at the school, 106 in number, varied in size from two to nine members among the boys, and two to twelve members among the girls. The modal size for both sexes was five members. The cliques which were formed after school hours, for recreational activity, 120 in number, averaged slightly smaller. They varied in size from two to seven members, with a modal size of four for both boys and girls. Cliques formed among rural students had a modal size of three.

In an exploratory study, James has attempted to isolate certain aspects of the theory of small group formation.[10] He suggests that there is a kind of opposition between formal internal organization of a group and the primary relationship, so that the latter does not readily survive when the size of the group becomes so large that some formal organization is necessary. In the cases of groups, such as college fraternities, which grow larger than do spontaneous cliques, there is a tendency for subgroups to form within the range of primary group sizes. Field observations of 557 informal groups engaged in conversation, shopping, and children's play, revealed a

[9] Hollingshead, *op. cit.*, pp. 207-8.
[10] John James, "Some Elements in a Theory of Small Groups," *Research Studies, State College of Washington*, XVIII (September, 1950), 144-52.

range of two to six in the size of the group, with an average size of 2.5. Large numbers of observations on other small informal groups showed similar results. The investigator concludes that "this and other evidence . . . suggests that the maximum effective size for un-differentiated action groups, that is, those unproliferated by sub-groupings, is probably somewhere between five and eight, and very unlikely to be above ten." [11]

It is well known that young children of preschool age are not advanced in their ability to form groups and that some appear to be totally incapable. Evidence from the experience of nursery schools indicates that this is one of the abilities that must be learned in ex-perience—children who acquire it either in nursery schools or in directed play appear, in general, to have more tendency to form groups than do children without it. Some attempts have been made to investigate this development. Moreno applied a socio-metric test in an investigation which "disclosed that the child gains, with increase in age, increasing ability to establish mutual relation-ships with other individuals to whom he is drawn." [12] A part of this gain is apparently a result of absorption of a pattern from family activity. An investigator has shown this by means of scales which measure parent behavior and cooperative tendencies of children.[13] The children are found to be more cooperative if: (1) parents have an effective policy of dealing with them; (2) parents have good rapport with children; (3) parents understand the problems of children; (4) there is little disciplinary friction; (5) there is ready criticism within the family; (6) there is a democratic atmosphere in the home; (7) ready explanations of decisions by the parents are given; (8) there are fairly intense contacts between parents and children; (9) children feel accepted; (10) there is little home dis-cord; and (11) there is clarity of policy. The apparent principle that binds these observations together would seem to be the fact that cooperation, the formation of groups and the harmonious be-havior within primary groups require that a number of principles and techniques be learned, and, further, that many of these patterns of behavior may be learned effectively within family life.

Differentiation of Status in Primary Groups.—Although any kind of formal organization appears to be in opposition to primary inter-

[11] *Ibid.*, p. 148.

[12] Cited in Helen H. Jennings, *Leadership and Isolation: A Study of Personality in Inter-personal Relations* (New York: Longmans, Green & Co., Inc., 1950), p. 13.

[13] Charlene T. Meyer, "The Assertive Behavior of Children as Related to Parent Behavior," *Journal of Home Economics*, XXXIX (1947), 77-80.

action, this does not mean that there is no differentiation within the primary group. Normally some persons have more influence and control than do others—some differentiation of status is almost inevitable, even in very small and intimate groups. Although it is difficult to establish the point objectively, it is probable that groups of more than three or four members undifferentiated in status are rare. It is, in fact, not at all uncommon for there to be some differentiation between the members of a pair. Even in sets of identical twins it is not unusual to find one to be dominant and the other submissive.

Status in human groups is not the same phenomenon as the pecking order of hens in the barnyard—it is far more complex as well as functional. It begins to form in early years; children of preschool age develop a significant status in groups of their own making. Not only do personal traits such as size, strength, and aggressiveness enter in, but also general symbolic aspects of each child's background. In an experimental study of preschool children, it was shown that both interpersonal relations within the primary group and such factors as I.Q., family prestige, family income, and the like enter into the determination of the status of each child.[14] Characteristic and persistent status patterns were found.

Within the larger society, status in general is governed by a complex of social attitudes, so that during the years of school attendance children acquire the prevailing patterns and become influenced by them in making their primary group affiliations. By the time they reach high school age there is likely to be a marked tendency to assign status by use of many of the same considerations as are used in adult society and to form primary groups which are fairly homogeneous in this respect. Hollingshead has made some direct observations of this tendency among the high-school youth of Elmtown.[15] Clique membership tends to be homogeneous both for school class, which is essentially age homogeneity, and for membership in the prestige levels of the community. A majority of the clique relations, 54 per cent among the boys and 60 per cent among the girls, obtained within both the same school class level and the same prestige level. Only a very small proportion, 2 per cent among the boys and 1 per cent among the girls, were outside both the common school grade and prestige class. The remaining were homogeneous in one respect and not in the other.

[14] Florence B. Moreno, "Sociometric Status of Children in a Nursery School Group." *Sociometry*, V, No. 4 (1942), 395-411.
[15] *Op. cit.*, p. 211.

To a certain extent, age classifications among school children also constitute prestige levels. Size, strength, knowledge, experience, are all closely related to age during these years of physical growth, and it is inevitable that freshmen will tend to look up to sophomores, and that sophomores will have some preference for members of their own grade over members from the freshman class and will in turn look up to the juniors and seniors. This age prestige, in fact, appears among Elmtown youth to be more important in determining clique membership than are the prestige levels of the community. Among the clique relations of the high school boys there were 32 per cent of such relations within a common school class and outside a common level and only 12 per cent within the prestige levels and outside school class. The same statement applies to clique relations among the girls who had 26 per cent within school class and outside prestige level, and only 13 per cent within a common prestige level and outside their school class. In each case of relationships outside either type of class, most involved only the adjacent prestige class or school grade, indicating that the violation of the homogeneity principle is slight.

The tendency for homogeneity of status among school cliques is similar to the patterns which prevail among older groups in the community where friendship groups, informal clubs, and other primary groups tend to form most readily among persons of nearly equal prestige. The most important primary group which most persons have occasion to form—the married pair—has a well-known tendency to the same sort of homogeneity. Furthermore, the early stages of the process of mate selection—the courtship and dating activity of young people—are also governed by these considerations. In the Elmtown study, the dating relationships of high school students were found, in fact, to be within common prestige levels in 61 per cent of the cases, among members of adjacent prestige classes in 35 per cent of the cases, and separated by one intervening prestige class in only 4 per cent.[16]

Even such heterogeneity as does appear in the latter two findings above is not necessarily of large degree. Not all the clique relations which are judged to cross social class lines involve important differences in prestige, for the division of the town population into such classes is a measure of imperfect reliability—other judges might place some of these couples, which here appear to cross class lines, in the same class. Furthermore, in the dating and even marrying behavior, the tradition of male dominance allows some

[16] *Ibid.*, p. 230.

difference in favor of males, so that it is not regarded as unconventional for a man to date or marry a woman slightly below him in age, income, or prestige level. In the Elmtown cases involving dating across prestige class lines, in fact, in 64 per cent of 107 cases the men involved were in the higher of the two classes.[17]

Functions of Status Differentiation in Primary Relations.—It is highly unlikely that such a universal tendency as status distinction could be accidental. Nor is it likely that it results from a tendency toward cruelty or any other personality characteristic of individuals. It is more reasonable and will be more fruitful of explanation to pursue the question of what functions such distinctions might play in social life.

As previously stated, status is more than a quantitative level of prestige. It is a definition or an organized set of definitions of the kind of actions expected of a person and the kind he is to expect from others. In all but the most relaxed and aimless activities of primary groups there is necessarily a constant question of order of actions, of ranking of influence, and of manner of communication. Where high efficiency is vital, as in a complex business organization or in an army, it is, of course, necessary that not only the duties of each person, but also his rank with respect to all others, be explicitly defined. Even in the more informal groups, however, status considerations enter so thoroughly into the quality of common social interaction that it is a virtual necessity for each member to have a clear understanding of his own status if his actions are to be efficient and without confusion.

Such a clear understanding of status is usually available in most groups. The family system assigns status among the members in a standard fashion, with parents at the top, and, where male dominance is traditional, with the husband and father higher in status than the wife. The children are ordinarily ranked according to their ages. In most other informal groups, status evolves spontaneously in the course of interaction. According to the activities of the groups, and to the traits valued, some persons informally drift into positions of higher status. Seniority, involving as it necessarily does experience and some wisdom, usually contributes to high status and in some groups is an important basis of status selection.

In any stable community in which most members know each other well, status distinctions tend to be based on a fairly accurate

[17] *Ibid.*, p. 321.

knowledge of the character of each person, as his character is collectively known. The whole history of each member is common knowledge and there is abundant material for the evaluation. In a mixed and changing society this kind of knowledge is not available for most persons and there can be no consensus regarding the subtle qualities of each person. Status in this latter situation, then, tends by default to be based on visible indications such as clothing, residence, type of automobile and other conspicuous possessions, and by a general pose. But superficial as it is, even this latter basis of status is related to behavior. In general people will pay some deference to the person who, even though an utter stranger, bears these external indications of high status.

Status is not a general, inherent, and fixed characteristic of a person, but rather a relationship of that person to others, or more exactly, a kind of specification of the appropriate relation of his behavior toward other persons. Because of this relative character and because it is subject to change, status can never be determined with complete accuracy. There is no method of introspection and no adequate psychological instrument which will inform a person of his exact status. As pointed out in Chapter 7, the only mirror in which a person may observe this as well as various other aspects of his social self is through the reaction of others to his behavior. Since this is a variable and distorted mirror, the discovery of a reasonably accurate working knowledge of one's own status is a performance of some skill which requires time and study and becomes increasingly difficult in a heterogeneous and changing social environment.

The difficulty is further complicated by the overlapping of social situations. A person may establish a clear definition of his status and appropriate behavior in each of two types of situations only to encounter confusion when it becomes unclear which of the two he is in at the moment. Two men may meet socially and become friendly on a first-name basis. Later they enter the military forces at different levels. On the next social meeting when both are in uniform there is a conflict between the two status-governing considerations. According to military custom officers and enlisted persons are expected to preserve a clear separation of social status whereas the general mores of a society hold it to be impolite to allow formal rank to create distance between friends. There is usually confusion and embarrassment in such a situation and no standard method of reacting to it.

The Defensive Function of Status Distinction.—Status levels in a community frequently are differentiated by varying degrees of standards of emphasis on folkways and mores. Persons in the higher levels preserve standards of behavior which persons in the lower levels do not fully observe. The selection of informal groups of members from one's own level and the exclusion of persons of lower levels, to some extent functions to protect the behavior standards of the group. The importance of this is shown by the fact that one of the most promising means by which a person can make himself acceptable to persons of a higher level is to adhere carefully to their standards of behavior.

Recent investigations have provided factual support for this relationship between prestige class and behavior standards in a small American community.[18] Members of the community rated one another on five traits—honesty, loyalty, responsibility, moral courage, friendliness. In the responses, all these traits were associated with class level, the upper levels being judged definitely higher than the lower. The authors of the Prairie City study, moreover, state that they suspect that these judgments about traits might have depended less on actual knowledge of specific traits than on some general reputational factor. Such a suspicion derives support from a high degree of agreement between the separate trait scores. But if this is so, it does not mean that the general character superiority of the upper prestige levels is purely imaginary. On scales which objectively measure self-adjustment and social adjustment, the upper levels also had higher average scores.[19] On the other hand, on the basis of the test of personal-social adjustment (California Test of Personality, Secondary Series, Form A) a set of opposite generalizations concerning the character of Prairie City youth of the lower prestige levels was made.[20] In general the low-rating youth: (1) feel that they are not liked or respected by their associates—feel inferior in status; (2) are deficient in social skills which tend to promote harmonious social relations; (3) have not learned or even wished to accept and carry out social responsibilities; (4) are conscious of their personal as well as of their social deficiencies; (5) feel unhappy, discontented, frustrated, and left out of the group; (6) have an assortment of such symptoms as nail biting,

---

[18] Robert J. Havighurst and Hilda Taba, *Adolescent Character and Personality* (New York: John Wiley & Sons, Inc., 1949), pp. 48-49. The study was made in 1942, in a community called Prairie City, which appears to be the same as the Elmtown of the Hollingshead study.

[19] *Ibid.*, p. 107.

[20] *Ibid.*, pp. 103-12.

nightmares, tiredness; (7) tend to regard their condition intolerable and so become self-assertive, defiant, and quarrelsome.

Systematic variation in type of family life in the various prestige levels appears to be causally related to these character traits. A number of aspects of family life in Prairie City are positively correlated with a measure of character reputation of the child.[21] In addition to coefficients of correlation (that is, coefficients which measure degrees of agreement) ranging from .14 to .45 on a number of separate items (interparental relations, regularity in the home, parental attitudes toward children's activities, and so forth), a positive correlation of .45 was found between a general score of family life and a score on the character reputation of the youth. This score represents the measure of relations among thirteen-year-old children only.[22] There is thus a kind of circular process in the status system of such communities. Families differ in standards of behavior, and associate together in cliques and levels according to general similarity of standards, partly for the purpose of protecting the standards from deterioration through common violation. Within their family life processes, they generate characteristic behavior in their children consistent with these standards, and give the children a basis for differentiating each other on similar status and behavior grounds.

Exclusiveness in the Clique

To the extent that we are able to choose our close friends and associates, we tend to choose persons who are interesting, attractive, and essentially similar to us.[23] The choice, however, is never com-

[21] *Ibid.*, p. 240.

[22] The influence of the family on behavior declines during the years of growth, as the youth finds an ever increasing proportion of his activities outside of the home. This fact is clearly shown by the decline in the size of the correlation coefficients (between character traits and family relations scores) with increasing age. Correlation coefficients were computed for ten-, thirteen-, and sixteen-year-old children and show a marked decline in the case of each trait. The correlation of family score with responsibility, for example, falls in the three age periods from .79 to .43 to .34. The correlation with friendliness falls from .71 to .35 to .20. Results of the same magnitude are found for the traits of honesty, loyalty, and moral courage. *Ibid.*, p. 240.

[23] The preference for persons who are interesting may begin in early childhood. One observation finds the principle in operation among four-year-old children whose preferences for one another were systematically recorded. Of fourteen children in the group, one was chosen nine times, and three were never chosen. The children more frequently chosen talked more, contributed more to activity, took initiative more often, and made more attempts to control situations. The differences were not large, but the patterns appeared to be stable. See Mary L. Northway, "Social

pletely free. For one thing, it is circumscribed by space relations. It is awkward to build primary relations over great distances, and so propinquity becomes one of the bases of choice. Within a community, for example, cliques which have no functional basis other than to supply primary relations will usually tend to have a limited spatial range. Within a college student body, moreover, cliques tend to form within dormitories more often than between them. In a small midwestern college, 178 girl students were asked to name their best friends, and 89.5 per cent of the choices made were within the dormitory.[24] A similar finding appears in a study of an eastern women's college in which every student was asked to list which three of her college acquaintances she would most like to keep in touch with. The results indicated a definite tendency to name persons belonging to the same dormitory, the same college class, the same major scholastic interest, and the same socioeconomic status.[25]

The tendency toward small size and homogeneity appears in cliques of factory workers studied by James.[26] The investigator asked 478 employees of a western woolen mill which persons among their fellow workers they liked best. The average number of choices was only 3.8, and 65 per cent of all choices were reciprocal. Of the 178 cliques (groups in which the choices were reciprocal) 157 had two members and 21 had three members. All the cliques showed a marked tendency to be homogeneous with respect to function in the plant, to spatial location of their work, to the shift in which they worked, and to sex. They were not particularly homogeneous with respect to age, perhaps because age differences are less significant in adult groups which are otherwise similar.

The tendency to form cliques with persons nearby probably reflects the opportunity to get acquainted rather than an inevitable link between propinquity and affection since in the Lundberg-Beasley study it is also found that a majority of the persons most disliked are also found within adjacent areas.

While the great majority of persons has the tendency to form friendships and join primary groups, there are differences in the

Relationships Among Preschool Children: Abstracts and Interpretation of Three Studies," *Sociometry*, VI, No. 4 (1943).

[24] John H. Burma, "Cliques and Popularity among Freshman Girls," *Sociology and Social Research*, XXXIV, No. 1 (1949), 21-24.

[25] George A. Lundberg and Virginia Beasley, "'Consciousness of Kind' in a College Population," *Sociometry*, XI, No. 1-2 (1948), 59-74.

[26] John James, "Clique Organization in a Small Industrial Plant." Publication forthcoming.

wish or the ability to do so. Bonney has studied the relationship which exists between success in establishing mutual friendships and general traits of behavior.[27] He found little relationship between mutual friendship and academic achievement, general intelligence, or measures of interest, but substantial correlation with social and emotional adjustment as measured by sections of the Bell Adjustment Inventory. The ability to establish mutual friendships, however, was best related to traits revealed in Bonney's own *Scale for Measuring Capacity to Win Friends*. The skilled in the acquisition of friends were superior to others in praising and complimenting, initiating discussions, display of tolerance and adaptability, group participation, dependability, emotional control, physical vigor, personal appearance, and certain other traits.

The "best friend" choices successfully define the hearts of the cliques both in the Lundberg-Beasley research cited above and in the study of such high school populations as that of Elmtown. Hollingshead asked each student to name his best friend, and found that:

> In every case the listed best friend was known to be a member of the clique of the person who listed him. Furthermore, 78 per cent of the girls and 71 per cent of the boys listed as their best friend a person who belonged to the same prestige class as they did. These figures indicate that these adolescents seek their best friends in their own class oftener than they do their other clique mates; that is, the choice of best friends is associated more closely with class position than the selection of one's other friends.[28]

The failure to include a representative group in each clique is, of course, by no means entirely an effect of the propinquity of the members. Some exclusion is intentional and, as mentioned previously, plays a function in protecting the status of the persons in the clique. Young persons enter a given clique with the prestige qualification of belonging to a family of a certain level, but once in, they tend also to absorb prestige from the other members. Hollingshead observed in Elmtown that "once an adolescent is identified as a member of a particular clique, the reputation of the clique tends to be attached to him by adolescents outside the clique, by teachers, and by other adults who know the youngster and his clique mates." [29]

---

[27] M. E. Bonney, "A Sociometric Study of the Relationship of Some Factors to Mutual Friendships on the Elementary, Secondary, and College Levels," *Sociometry*, IX, No. 1 (1946), 21-47.

[28] Hollingshead, *op. cit.*, p. 215.

[29] *Ibid.*, p. 217.

The students were well aware of this effect, and consciously and deliberately exerted influence on each other to protect this general reputation. An Elmtown girl wrote:

The boys we dated had to meet with each other's approval [i.e., the approval of her girl clique mates]. . . . I easily recall different instances in which some unexpected person asked one of us to some dance. Before we accepted, we usually found out the others' reaction to such a date. It was desirable to be seen with a boy who was liked first by the girls and secondly by the boys themselves. Any divergence from the prescribed list was avoided at all cost.[30]

Students with lower moral standards in general have lower prestige, and therefore threaten group prestige as well as behavior standards. According to an Elmtown girl this behavior is explicitly taken into account.

I don't want to run any of the kids down, but there are certain girls here who are just not my type, and they're not Gladys' type; they'd like to run around with us, but we don't let them. Pauline Tryon [one prestige level lower than the girl writing] and her bunch would like to run around with us, but we turn our backs on them because they run around all night, cut school, and hang out down at the Blue Triangle. There are some kids we'd like to go around with, but they don't want us to go with them. Gladys and I would like to go around with "Cookie" Barnett [one class above the girl who writes] and her bunch, or the G.W.G.'s [a high-level clique], but they snub us if we try to get in on their parties, or dances, or date the boys they go with.[31]

In defense of its collective prestige, a clique may expel a member who fails to take part in the defense. Hollingshead writes of a case of an Elmtown high school freshman girl, of a middle prestige level, who, though popular at the start, was nevertheless dropped from a clique because she started associating with a boy of extremely low status. The girl's mother " . . . summarized the girl's social position first in terms of its effect on her and the father and secondly in terms of its effect on the girl. 'I am disgraced. Her father is brokenhearted. Mabel must be made to see the folly of her foolish actions. She simply must be popular; every girl has to be popular. Now the boys and girls have isolated her.' "[32] Among the penalties the mother must have had in mind is that such isolation restricts the range of choice of marriageable persons—a serious matter for a small-town girl.

[30] *Ibid.*, p. 233.
[31] *Ibid.*, p. 209. The persons quoted, of course, may have emphasized status more than would most Elmtown youth.
[32] *Ibid.*, p. 236.

In order for the separation of prestige levels to be maintained, it is probably necessary for all parties to understand the situation. The avoidance of lower level persons by those above them is not always a matter of functionless cruelty—complications arise when lower prestige persons do not understand their roles. Hollingshead illustrates this with an autobiographical statement of a high-ranking Elmtown girl:

One comical situation which consistently appeared and reappeared in my dating schedule was that of boys not on this preferred list [a list of boys from the high-ranking Cadet Club] asking me for dates. My parents, Mother especially, had pounded into my mind most firmly that I was to be nice to everyone regardless of who they were, socially speaking. Every time I attempted to put this into practice, I ended with a bid for some social event with someone with whom I did not care to go. And it was always these individuals who asked so early that logical excuses were difficult to give. The incongruity of society! *Be nice to people only to a certain restricted degree unless you are anxious to cultivate their friendship.*[33]

The Character of Informal Social Control

In order to maintain the kind of harmony necessary in primary groups, it is essential that the behavior of each member be effectively controlled in the interest of the group. This must be accomplished with little or no formal mechanism of enforcement, and, if disruption is to be avoided, must operate as much as possible in a subtle fashion. The informal social control which governs primary relations operates largely on the basis of careful self-control of each member, who must adapt his behavior to what he believes to be the expectations of others. Rather than make errors and taste the penalties, he must make active efforts to foresee possible errors and avoid them, using the imaginative process of trial and error described in Chapter 7.

Imagination cannot supply all the correct answers, however, and most persons fall well short of perfection in their interaction with others. There is a need for penalties or perceivable consequences of blunders to supply the correction of such errors. These penalties vary with the seriousness of the offense, but occur often enough to be recognized as possible consequences by any person who possesses normal skill in social relations.

The extreme penalty of the primary group is expulsion or avoidance. Frequent use of this would of course destroy any primary

[33] *Ibid.*, p. 233.

group, and this reaction is reserved for the most serious infractions of expectations. When it does occur, it may be crushing in its effect. Among the Mennonites of Pennsylvania and the rural midwest such a device is known as "shunning." A news story of 1948 told of a member who, in an emergency, violated a moral principle of this community by using an automobile to take his sick child to a physician. The shunning penalty was applied; no fellow members of his community would speak to him or have anything to do with him. The effect on him was so severe that he went to court to attempt to force removal of the penalty. Expulsion from certain primary groups may in extreme cases involve a shattering of the whole life organization; it sometimes occurs that banishment from a family or other important group is the occasion for an act of suicide.

A second type of penalty operating in informal social control is the curtailment of intimacy in relations with the offender. Speech and manners become somewhat more formal and association is limited to occasions of a businesslike character, with an avoidance of the more intimate gatherings. Men who have been friendly enough to have a relaxed, bantering relation with one another recognize the disapproval expressed by a pointed suspension of humorous insults. In such cases forgiveness and reinstatement may be symbolized by an undignified gesture such as a dorsal kick.

Another means of control is ridicule of the violator, or of his violations, expressed to his face or behind his back. This method is directly and frankly employed among children and is highly effective. Among polite and sensitive adults it is a drastic penalty to be avoided when possible although, in some cases, it may be used skilfully and somewhat indirectly by ridiculing a violation without acknowledging that the particular offender could actually be guilty of it. By this means it is made impersonal but is still adequate to convey a warning to an intelligent transgressor. In fact, persons normally learn much of what is expected of them by generalizing on the kinds of ridicule and criticism applied to others.

Another means of control, more subtle but important in its effects, is the restrained gesture of disapproval—the lifted eyebrow, the disappointed look, the coolness in the tone of voice, and the like. These are advance warnings of greater penalties to come and are taken seriously by the persons who are skilled enough to perceive them. One aspect of social skill, in fact, involves the sensitivity to interpret such gestures when they are most subtly, perhaps even unintentionally, expressed.

As previously stated, however, the most skilled persons do not have to experience any of these penalties frequently. The most constant process of social control is the avoidance of error through anticipation of the reactions of others. The material from which the ability to make correct anticipations develops does not have to be accumulated from one's own mistakes, but can instead be organized from what we hear people say about others. We know the penalties paid by other offenders more readily than we discover our own. By similar observations of others we also become aware of the many pleasant consequences and rewards of being popular and of being deeply admired.

Almost every kind of relation we have with persons may be affected by this factor. Obtaining a job and earning promotions are supposed to depend on ability; but in most careers opportunities of this sort are a little richer for persons who are liked, and in some cases the personal popularity may be a major factor. Commercial relations between shopper and store clerk would seem to have a minimum of such an element, but during wartime it is a familiar experience to observe clerks holding scarce commodities for favorite customers, sometimes for no more reason than that some housewives smile, converse pleasantly, and generally treat the clerks as human beings. It is probable that social skills are rewarded in a great many ways which could not be noticed or even traced by the person who obtains the benefits and, conversely, the inept person can never know the range and extent of the penalties he pays for his social errors.

To a certain extent young persons may acquire the skills that give success in social relations by generalizing on their own mistakes and successes. To a greater degree, however, such skill may be directly achieved by the normal process of role-taking. Admired persons are emulated in this fashion in an impersonation which is not always deliberately affected, but, to the contrary, is normally unwitting. Each youth may, in fact, combine roles derived from a number of models so that the sources are social but the integration, in his particular case, unique. Havighurst and Taba illustrate this point with their conclusion derived from an inspection of essays written at their request. "The data from the essay on 'The Person I Would Like to Be Like' suggest that the sixteen-year-old is actively integrating the characteristics of a number of people into a composite 'ideal self' . . . different kinds of people are mentioned as outstanding in the community for different desirable characteristics." [34]   In early childhood these models may be taken from members of the family but, according to these investigators, tend during the teen-ages to be taken from attractive and known young adults outside the family, or from successful middle-aged citizens.   In Prairie City it was found that a small number of adults, probably not more than 1 per cent of the adult population, played a large part in the character formation of adolescents in the community.[35]

THE POWER OF INFORMAL SOCIAL CONTROL

At first thought it would not appear that the lifted eyebrow or the threat of ridicule, for example, could be forces of great magnitude.   In certain circumstances, it is true, they may not be, but at best, in a strongly organized primary group within a stable and successful society, these forces may have far more power to govern human behavior than would physical force of any kind.

Probably the greatest force of informal control lies in the fact that in most social situations the conventional way of acting is the easiest and most natural to the persons involved—not because customs are completely adapted to individual dispositions, but because to persons who know no other ways, custom appears in the guise of nature.   Folkways and mores normally provide standard and convenient definitions of the common and recurrent situations of life, and by conforming to them, persons go through their routines with a minimum of frustration.   As previously stated, there is in such a situation no sense of opposition between individual and society, for each individual is to such a large extent a product of a shared society.

It is in the small, isolated, homogeneous society that there exist the conditions most favorable to the most effective informal social control.   Where these conditions are found there is no need for any of the other mechanisms of control—there are no laws, no police, no formal government.   Such a situation is described in an island community inhabited for over a century by a small community of English settlers.[36]   In 1817, three Englishmen settled on Tristan da Cunha and were joined by others from time to time.   They lived in isolation interrupted only by an occasional passing ship.   At the

[34] Havighurst and Taba, *op. cit.*, p. 80.
[35] *Ibid.*, p. 80.
[36] Peter A. Munch, *Sociology of Tristan da Cunha: Results of the Norwegian Scientific Expedition to Tristan da Cunha, 1937–1938, No. 13* (Oslo: I Kommisjon Hos Jacob Dybwad, 1945).

time of the 1938 visit by Norwegian anthropologists they were found to number 103 males and 85 females. They were described as highly moral and deeply religious. They had no institutionalized government; church and school were their only formal organizations. There was no public disorder. It was observed that "what people will think" had the force of law. Persons who quarreled might refrain from speaking to one another, but never engaged in brawling. Violence and bloodshed were unknown. Public teasing constituted the most drastic penalty for infractions of custom.

In the outmoded conception of instinctive regulation of human behavior, the maternal instinct was among those considered to be highly powerful. The defining and controlling power of society, however, is powerful enough to override maternal sentiment, whatever its nature may be. Infanticide is far from uncommon among the various peoples of the world and in some cases is prescribed for a certain situation. Among the peoples of the Niger Delta, for example, the almost general rule is that the mother of twins must be put to death together with her children. But among the Bankundo, less than a thousand miles away, the mother of twins is the object of honor and veneration throughout her life. She wears a special badge, is called "mother of twins" and is given a double greeting, one for each twin. Among other peoples only one of the twins is killed, leaving a proper single child.[37]

In a number of societies the sociological father (the man socially responsible for a woman's children) is not the biological father or the husband of the mother, but rather the mother's brother. It is he who is proud of the children, who teaches them and assumes toward them a relationship essentially the same as that of the father in our system. Rivers, describing such a practice among the Melanesians, wrote:

> If a man imposed on his sister's son a difficult task which resulted in his death or injury, no compensation could be demanded, but if a man put his own son to such a task compensation could be demanded by the mother's brother [the maternal uncle] of the boy. If a man who is fighting is told to stop by his mother's brother he will do so at once, and it is said that if he had refused in the past he would have been killed by his uncle, but a man told by his father to stop would only do so if he felt inclined.[38]

While there may be a tendency in the long run for customs to drift toward technical efficiency, there are always many folkways

---

[37] Thomas, op. cit., pp. 9 f.
[38] W. H. R. Rivers, quoted in Thomas, op. cit., p. 123.

which make demands counter to such considerations. In a stable condition of society these folkways easily prevail, even though at considerable inconvenience to the members. Table manners in present-day society illustrate the point well, but certain preliterate peoples far outdo civilized man in being dominated by considerations of etiquette and sacredness. Among some of the Polynesian peoples such technical processes as house-building and canoe manufacture are richly entangled in nontechnical customs. The particular procedure is such a sacred value in itself that any departure from it could spoil the whole process and cause the house or boat to remain unfinished. According to an observer:

> Every mistake, every awkward move was a bad omen among this people. The priest who made a mistake in the order of the items of his ritual stopped the service at once. A misdirected stroke by a workman, a tool used on the wrong side, a hole bored in the wrong direction, was enough not only to stop an operation instantly but to cause the abandonment of the construction of the house or boat, even if the accident happened at the moment of its completion.[39]

In modern society it is not uncommon to find similar illustrations of the great power of informal control. It is true that in such a period of social change as the present day, many youth disregard the etiquette of their elders. But within their own age groups the informal demands may be precise and powerful. A high school girl who has agreed to go to a formal dance may be desperate if she does not have the right kind of dress to wear. Even the demands of daytime costume fads may drive some girls to unusual efforts to fall in with the expectations of their primary groups in school. In a recent winter period in a western city, an outbreak of shoplifting among high school girls was investigated by the police. It was found that none of the girls had engaged in previous theft, and all were crushed and contrite when caught. It seems that a clothing fad had developed in their school which demanded the wearing of cashmere sweaters more expensive than their parents wished to buy. Driven by the pressure of informal expectations within their age groups, a number of the girls had made trips to the department stores to steal sweaters. When considering styles of women's clothing which emphasize exposure of skin area, it may be difficult to comprehend the strength of the attitude of an earlier day toward modesty, when mention of the world "leg" in the presence of a lady evoked so much blushing that euphemisms like "drumstick" and "joint" were commonly used even for the naming of

[39] J. A. Moerenhout, cited in Thomas, *op. cit.*, p. 43.

meats served at the table. A half-century ago the men who loafed on street corners were stimulated by the sight of a woman's ankle, enclosed though it was in cotton stockings and high leather shoes, as she stepped up on the curb. It was in this atmosphere that there occurred, according to news reports of the day, a choice of death by drowning to avoid being seen in public immodestly clothed. A lady on board the Titanic, the story ran, was offered aid in getting to a lifeboat if she would remove her outer clothing to facilitate swimming. The lady, however, literally preferred to die rather than be seen publicly in her underclothes.

Such is the power of informal social control. Although it guides us most of the time without any awareness on our part, it may, when other forces challenge it, exert an authority superior to any individual kind of interest and exercise even greater power than self-preservation, once widely believed to be the most irresistible instinct.

INFORMAL CONTROL IN OPPOSITION TO FORMAL CONTROL

Where informal controls fail, and successful control still remains important to the group welfare, it is not uncommon for formal controls to be devised to take care of the failure. But formal controls do not work well without the support of informal controls which are integrated with them. In prison, for example, the formal rules are obeyed by the prisoners only in so far as the prison officials enforce them. Beyond that, the only regulation of prisoner behavior is the informal control among the men, operating usually in directions contrary to prison policy. In some prisons this informal and somewhat rebellious process can make administration of the institution exceedingly difficult.

Similarly, in military organizations there is a tendency for informal organization to grow up to control behavior not governed by the formal rules, and to frustrate formal rules which the men believe to be too severe or unjust. According to a participant observer, the army theoretically has a complete formal and rational organization which is supposed to govern every phase of the army life of the enlisted man.[40] The rules specify such details as hours of sleeping and eating, the restriction of social relations between officers and enlisted men, frequency of shaving, selection of seats

---

[40] Anonymous. "Informal Social Organization in the Army," *American Journal of Sociology*, LI, No. 5 (1946), 365-70.

in army theaters, and so forth. Within the organized rules, however, even the nonrebellious soldiers tend to achieve spontaneously some degree of informal organization which supplements, interprets, and in some cases even frustrates the official rules. The anonymous observer writes that in each of the military groups observed by him such an informal voluntary system was found and included almost all the members of the formal unit of men who lived, ate, worked, and trained together. Within the group personal contacts were so intimate and frequent that within a few days of association they came to know one another with a degree of intimacy common only to civilians acquainted for years.

The units of such primary interaction in the military organization were small—twenty members or less. But even in the face of rapid turnover of membership, their continuity was maintained. Newcomers were assimilated within a week's time. When exceptionally large numbers were taken out at one time, of course, there occurred some confusion in the little social organization, but even this was reported to be only temporary.

Independent of the formal military rules and practices there arose in these primary groups of soldiers certain new or partly new mores. The anonymous observer lists five points to illustrate:

1. Any noncommissioned officer who turns an enlisted man in for punishment for any but the gravest offense is an informer and an undesirable member of the group.

2. A man's pass privileges are sacred. Other enlisted men should do everything possible to protect and increase them.

3. Social distinctions between enlisted men by rank are undesirable, and men who claim these distinctions are legitimate targets for abuse.

4. It is not desirable to set too high a standard of work performance. (At another time, exactly the opposite attitude was held.)

5. Men who work together should cooperate in whatever manner necessary to get the job done in the manner easiest for the whole group.[41]

Some of these points have statistical support in recent research among soldiers.[42] The internal loyalty of enlisted men is shown by the overwhelming agreement with the statement, "An enlisted man is usually more concerned with what other enlisted men think of him than with what his officers think." The answers of 89 per cent of the enlisted men and of 78 per cent of the officers were in agreement. Both categories also agreed (87 per cent of the en-

[41] *Ibid.*, p. 367.
[42] Samuel Stouffer, *et al.*, *The American Soldier: Adjustment During Army Life* ("Studies in Social Psychology in World War II," Vol. I [Princeton: Princeton University Press, 1949]), pp. 362 ff.

listed men and 75 per cent of the officers) with the statement that "most soldiers lose respect for a man who is always bucking for a promotion." In similar fashion it is also agreed that "most soldiers usually work just hard enough to get by."

In general, the need for primary relations, and thus for good standing in the only available primary group, is sufficient to motivate the men to conformity with its expectations. For the occasional offender, however there were explicit methods of enforcement.

The informal group had many ways to express . . . its dissatisfaction with . . . regulation, the most effective of these being control of the noncommissioned officer in charge. As a member of the informal group, he was subject to all its pressures. Failure to act in accordance with the interests of the group might subject him to name-calling: "eager beaver," "chicken," "G.I." Even mild social ostracism would bring an offending leader "in line." Failure to be included in the activities and discussions of the group meant isolation and loneliness, because the offending leader had no other social group to which to turn. The whole basis of his social life and status was in this one informal group.[43]

An additional method of punishment sometimes employed was the spontaneous refusal of certain common types of cooperation, such as trading work shifts. For the severe offender in these small primary groups even more drastic expressions of disapproval were employed. The sycophant was held in contempt, and when he disregarded the attitudes of his fellows and sought attention from officers to gain their favor, direct gestures of unmistakable meaning were made in his presence. A soldier's diary cited in Stouffer[44] provides a concrete and vivid illustration of the process.

Stouffer has recently investigated a similar conflict of official rules and informal expectations between a university administration and the student body.[45] A number of hypothetical situations and actions were presented to a sample of 196 students who were then asked to state in each instance both the attitude (favorable or unfavorable) of the students and the attitude they believed would be held by the school officials. Since all the students in the sample did not register the same responses, Stouffer divided them into three types. In Type I he placed those twenty-one students who thought that the attitudes of both school officials and student

[43] *Ibid.*, p. 369.
[44] *Ibid.*, pp. 266-67.
[45] Samuel A. Stouffer, "An Analysis of Conflicting Social Norms," *American Sociological Review*, XIV, No. 6 (1949), 707-17.

body would be in complete agreement on each of the hypothetical situations. Type II was composed of students who thought that the range of acts approved by authorities would not overlap in any way the range of acts approved by the students. For these students, fifty-six in number, simultaneous conformity to both authorities and students was evidently impossible. Most of these, fifty-one out of fifty-six, stated that they would follow the student course of action if their decision was not a matter of public knowledge, and thirty-five claimed they would do so even if it were made public. Presumably the most rebellious students are in this category.

Type III was composed of students who would expect some differences between the attitudes of the authorities and the students, but also believed there would be a certain amount of agreement. This category had the greatest frequency—119 students. If their action were to be a matter of public knowledge, seventy-five of this group would prefer to take an action which is in the range of overlapping approval by both authorities and students—these students seem to be the diplomatic or political type of person. Only thirty-six of this third group would feel it necessary to take action satisfactory to both if their decision would not be public knowledge.

Assimilation to New Primary Relations

An enlisted soldier who becomes an officer becomes obligated in many ways to assume the official point of view even when it conflicts with the expectations of his former comrades who are not officers. The change from one membership to another may have a precise date but the transfer of feelings of allegiance is ordinarily not so abrupt. In most cases, pressures will in time bring about the successful assimilation of the former soldier into the new society of officialdom. While objective research is not abundant on such a process, it appears probable that the process normally is gradual and made possible both by the separation of the new officer from his former primary group and by the forces of the new primary controls on the part of his fellow-officers.

Centers has observed such a transfer of allegiance in an analogous shift of affiliation on the part of industrial workers who when they become foremen are expected by their employers to become a part of management.[46] Here the definition of loyalty is not a mat-

[46] Richard Centers, *The Psychology of Social Classes: A Study of Class Consciousness* (Princeton: Princeton University Press, 1949), p. 194.

ter of complete agreement, however, since some labor unions have taken the stand that foremen should be considered part of the worker organization and members of unions. A sample of 764 foremen were asked questions which were devised to reveal whether the men identified themselves with workers, with management, or with neither. The majority, 59 per cent, considered themselves part of management, a minority of 20 per cent identified themselves with the workers, and another 20 per cent located themselves in between. About 1 per cent did not know what they thought about the matter. A classification of those who identified themselves with management, however, revealed that their numbers increased with time. Of those foremen whose tenure was less than two years, only 49 per cent identified themselves with management. Of those whose tenure was from two to five years, 61 per cent identified themselves with management as did 64 per cent of those with a tenure of more than five years. Thus it apparently took some foremen at least five years to complete the process of transfer of loyalty from one category to the other.

Newcomb has shown that the transfer of political allegiance by college students may be largely a matter of a shift from one primary group to another.[47] At Bennington College it was noted that student political attitudes tended to shift from predominantly conservative toward attitudes of the liberal or radical type. Since most members of the faculty did not hold the latter type of attitude, the formal educational influence apparently could not account for the shift. Furthermore, there was only a slight relation between the amount of shift and the field of study—social science students became on the average a small degree more liberal than students of natural sciences or of music. The investigator's interpretation of the change is that an informal tradition had become established in the student body—a tradition of political liberalism. Each student, entering with the normal desire to be accepted and approved, to achieve some popularity, faced the necessity of gaining the approval of the previously assimilated undergraduates by assimilating, in turn, many of their beliefs.

According to Newcomb:

The conclusion toward which the writer is driven is simply that the histories and personal characteristics of entering freshmen are such that they are impelled, with varying degrees of awareness, toward varying degrees of leadership and prestige. The more they are so impelled, the more it is neces-

[47] Theodore Newcomb, *Personality and Social Change* (New York: Dryden Press, Inc., 1943).

sary for them to fit in to what they believe to be the college pattern. As entering freshmen they are in a particularly weak position to flaunt it. And the less they are so impelled, of course, the less necessary for them to fit the pattern. We may, indeed, go farther than this: the less they are so impelled, the less likely it is that they are even aware of what the pattern is; it is less important for them to know than for those who are so impelled.[48]

A number of objective observations are presented in support of the conclusion that liberal attitudes are developed in this college community primarily by those who desire membership in the network of primary relations. Inspection of degrees of popularity revealed that the more popular students tended to be those with the more liberal political attitudes. Also, the more a student became identified with the college community, the more liberal her attitudes were likely to be. Reputation for active participation in college affairs was associated with liberalism, while reputation for absorption in extracollege social life was associated with conservatism. Furthermore, an abundant amount of autobiographical material collected from the students revealed that many were well aware of the tradition and of the process of transferring their political allegiance by which they gradually conformed in the interests of success in primary interaction.[49]

SUMMARY

Each person begins his life as a member of a primary group, finding his pleasures and satisfactions within a system of intimate, sympathetic, and affectionate interaction. His essentially human character is formed within this process, and, as he grows, his personality development is controlled by it. Each person becomes aware early of the importance of primary relations and thus of the importance of remaining in good standing in primary groups.

It is this fact which is of central importance in the successful

---

[48] *Ibid.*, pp. 58-59.

[49] Such a process has been observed in other situations as well. A study of college students from northern regions attending southern colleges found that over a period of three to four years their attitudes concerning Negroes became progressively less favorable, presumably because of some assimilation into the southern culture of the student body. See Verner M. Sims and James R. Patrick, "Attitude Toward the Negro of Northern and Southern College Students," *Journal of Social Psychology*, VII (1936), 192-204. Lazarsfeld and his coworkers have also found a general tendency for political attitudes to be formed in part by a network of personal influences transmitted through members of families, through relatives and neighbors, and along lines of other informal personal contacts. See Paul F. Lazarsfeld, Bernard Berelson, and Hazel Gaudet, *The People's Choice* (New York: Duell, Sloan & Pearce, Inc., 1944).

operation of a society. Formal controls are necessary in a complex civilization—control through force exerted by officials who apply written rules—but these do not work well, if they work at all, in opposition to the forces of informal social control. In the life of the normal person, the informal forces are of far greater importance in holding behavior within the patterns essential to the successful teamwork of a society.

This necessity and dependence generate the wishes which perpetuate them so that persons normally acquire adequate motivation to form primary groups or to seek membership in those which exist and thereby control their own behavior in such fashion as to keep a good status in the group and to preserve the group solidarity. Thus we have observed a virtually universal and quick-acting tendency to form primary groups. School children, thrown together first as strangers, rapidly form into cliques of which they are highly conscious and which they value intensely. In the more successful groups the members are often aware that the cooperative nature of their activities is more important than the choice of the particular activities they undertake.

Within any social organization there is necessarily some differentiation of status. On the face of it, this differentiation may appear nonfunctional and perhaps even cruel. Within a group of any size, however, coordinated action is difficult unless there is some differentiation of role and consequently some status differences. It is questionable whether any but the smallest of groups, those under five or six in membership, can be undifferentiated in status and it was pointed out that even in the extreme case of identical twins a ranking of status can often be observed.

Homogeneity is a general characteristic of primary groups and is applicable in the matter of the status each member has in his larger community. Within a clique of high school youth there are differences of status, but in general each clique tends to be formed of persons who are in about the same prestige level of the neighborhood or town. It appears likely, moreover, that this tendency toward homogeneous membership in high school cliques is not merely nonfunctional snobbery, but rather a systematic defense of behavior standards instigated in part by families of the youth and in part by the community as a whole. A marriage is more likely to be successful if there are between the partners few contrasts of race, culture, religion, educational level, and social status. A girl learns from her parents to consider her prospects in advance and to control her behavior in her younger ages to maximize the chances of a favorable marriage. Any behavior which threatens her prestige standing is a potential threat to her prospects of marriage to a man of the same level or better. Participation in a clique involves sharing the general reputation and prestige of the clique, and it makes desirable a discriminating choice of companions to protect the clique in general. In the studies of Elmtown and Prairie City it appears that all these considerations are explicitly taken into account by the high school youth in their behavior with reference to primary group membership.

In order to preserve the reputation and in some cases the existence of any primary group, it is necessary to control the actions of members and to have means of preventing destructive violations of behavior standards. In a highly successful primary group each member so understands this necessity that overt penalties are seldom required. Each person checks his potential errors in advance by anticipating the probable reaction to any contemplated action in the previously described process of trial-and-error imagination which constructs the social self. But a range of penalties is available for the person who is insufficiently guided by his own self-consciousness. These sanctions include expulsion, avoidance, restriction of intimacy, open ridicule, restrained gestures of disapproval, and various other means.

There is much reason to hold that the power of this kind of informal social control is, at its best, very great. In the absence of complexity or other interfering circumstances as is the case in some of the small preliterate societies and isolated settlements such as Tristan da Cunha, this kind of control is sufficient by itself to regulate all the behavior of the members. It is also powerful enough to cause people to destroy twins and their mothers, to cause people to sacrifice their own lives when called upon to do so, and to make people conform in their daily behavior to a cumbersome and awkward range of restrictions.

Formal control in such an organization as an army does not work well unless it is supported by a fabric of informal control within the organization. With regard to the principal objectives and rules, most formal organizations can claim this informal support. But, as is shown by the example of army regulations, there is often informal opposition to details and, in many cases, a tendency of informal control to prevail over the formal. Similar observations apply to relations between students and administration in colleges, and to members of various other formal institutions.

The influence of primary group membership is further illustrated by the results of the transfer of membership from one group to another, an event which may also involve an important change in attitudes and behavior.

Selected References

Cooley, Charles H. *Human Nature and the Social Order.* New York: Chas. Scribner's Sons, 1902.

Faris, Ellsworth. *The Nature of Human Nature.* New York: McGraw-Hill Book Co., Inc., 1937. Chap. iv, "The Primary Group: Essence and Accident."

Hollingshead, August B. *Elmtown's Youth: The Impact of Social Classes on Adolescents.* New York: John Wiley & Sons, Inc., 1949. Studies of clique formation in relation to the social organization of a small midwestern town.

Chapter 12

THE DIFFERENTIATION OF PERSONS
BY VARIATIONS OF ROLES

THE DIFFERENTIATION of mental abilities through operations of the social organization has been shown in Chapter 10. In a more obvious and perhaps more important way, society also differentiates personalities through the assignment of various roles to individuals. Personality is in large part built of material derived from social roles. Each person achieves a unique combination of such roles, and creates his own organization of personal character from this and other material, including attitudes and abilities.

THE NATURE OF ROLE AND STATUS

In order to participate effectively in any organized group activity, each person must have some means of knowing what his particular type of action must be, and he must know how to coordinate it with the activity of other persons engaged in the same project. In formal groups this assignment is usually so clearly defined that no special skill is required to know what one is supposed to do. In a factory production line each person has a simple task which is explicitly described for him or for which he is specifically trained and drilled. On a football team, the design of any particular play involves complete specification of the action desired from each member. In a drama, the role is provided by the author and refinements are added by the director. Little or no choice is left to the individual in teamwork of this sort.

In informal and primary groups, however, there is much less explicit specification of the kind of action expected from each member. Etiquette books supply advice on a few minor issues, but complete verbatim knowledge of the contents of an authoritative work on this subject is far from sufficient to guarantee the possessor a high degree of skill in primary interaction. Each person must find his own best role partly by discovering what is expected, and partly by devising a suitable one. There is a range of tolerable variation which permits choices of behavior, and there is a constant shifting of the situation in primary interaction which calls for alertness to the possible desirability of a change in role. For example, a person joining a group of comrades may break out into customary jollification, only to perceive from the reaction that some member has just received bad news and that the role of compassionate friend is at the moment much more appropriate than that of jester.

As indicated in Chapter 7, there is no such thing as perfection in judging one's own status and in devising a role to fit exactly the expectations of others. The problem of conforming to a group cannot be solved once and for all, but requires continuous readjustment. Skill in this activity depends on constant use of the reflexive imagination which tries out actions and inspects possible errors before they are converted into activity.[1]

A rich knowledge of the variety of persons and situations tends to aid in the development of versatility in role-taking. As Cameron has stated:

Any *shift* from one socially defined role to another—whether this occurs in terms of manipulative, verbal, or imaginal operations—necessarily involves a shift in perspective. Clearly the person who is ready and adroit in shifting through a succession of different social roles in his behavior can anticipate the reactions of others and his own reactions with greater success than the person whose shifts are clumsy and reluctant. In short, to have ease and skill in shifting perspectives means to be capable of adapting to a wide range of shifting interpersonal relationships and implies a corresponding immunity from the kind of progressive misinterpretation we encounter in behavior pathology—for example, in paranoid disorders ... the person whose repertory includes a *variety* of well-practiced, realistic social roles is better equipped to meet new and critical situations than the person whose repertory is meager, relatively unpracticed, and socially unrealistic. The skilled role-taker, like the skilled motorist, has a better chance than the unskilled of withstanding the sudden, unforeseen stress and the effects of prolonged, unremitting strain.[2]

Persons who lack the skills and the background of experience which make possible reasonably accurate judgment of the reactions of other persons often misread these by reading their own motives and thoughts into others—a process sometimes referred to as projection. An objective study has succeeded in showing this principle

---

[1] It is shown in Chapter 14 that this is a complex activity which requires an efficient physiological system. Any marked departure from normality in the structure necessary for this activity will reduce its efficiency or prevent it completely.

[2] Norman Cameron, "Role Concepts in Behavior Psychology," *American Journal of Sociology*, V, No. 5 (1950), 465.

in the behavior of college students.[3]   Nearly a hundred fraternity men were asked to rate themselves, and to rate one another, on such traits as stinginess, obstinacy, disorderliness, and bashfulness. The students who rated themselves as others rated them, presumably possessing such social skill or insight, were found to have less tendency to read their own traits (project) into the personality of others.   The differences were not large, but this is hardly to be expected within a group so homogeneous as is constituted by college fraternity men.

Sears has also shown objectively that persons who are uncertain of their own status and thus have feelings of self-criticism also tend to misinterpret the reactions of others, particularly by magnifying in imagination the attention and criticism others accord them. Such persons are said to have ideas of reference.[4]   A questionnaire scale was constructed for ideas of reference, containing such questions as: "Do you sometimes suspect that people on the street are laughing at you?" and "Do other students seem to avoid sitting next to you in class?"   A scale measuring the tendency to feelings of self-criticism was also devised, based on such items as: "Do you often feel that you are a weakling in some ways?" and "Are you worthy of the friendship of your associates?"   The relation of these two personality tendencies is measured by the fairly high correlation—degree of agreement—of .82 (corrected for attenuation) in a group of nearly three hundred college men.   By means of getting objective ratings of the social relations of some of these subjects from their friends, it was shown that there was no objective validity of the ideas of reference; apparently lack of confidence in themselves was alone sufficient to produce the erroneous notions of the thoughts and actions of other persons.

While it is important to each person to know what roles other persons expect of him, the best basis for understanding his own behavior is not the objective situation in which he exists in the group, but rather his role as he conceives it.   The role which guides his behavior is the role he thinks he has.   Others may not consider him unworthy, but if he thinks they do, or knows that there could be reason for them to, his reactions may be guided by a conception of himself as an unworthy person.   The same principle applies to the overconfident or conceited person, who errs in the opposite direction.

[3] Robert R. Sears, *Survey of Objective Studies of Psychoanalytic Concepts.* Social Science Research Council, Bulletin No. 51, New York, 1943, p. 125.

[4] *Ibid.*, p. 123.

Not only is there no objective exactness in the expectations of other persons, and no stability of role within the same group, but there is also the complexity of having membership in various groups and categories, with separate role implications for each. Furthermore, these may overlap and conflict, imposing a necessity of skilful compromise. Thus it is impressively true that the requirement of social life is the possession of a highly active skill in continuous adaptation to an indeterminate, inconsistent, and ever-changing social situation. For normality, there can be no cessation of activity—the adaptive function of consciousness is perpetually indispensable.

It is almost inconceivable, of course, that a person could ever adapt completely to every social influence and expectation—the influences are too varied and inconsistent, too far extended into infinite degrees of complexity and subtleness. Few persons have a problem of overadaptation to social influences, but it appears that such a tendency is possible, and that its effect is to render inadequate the individuality and consistency of character in such persons. In order to conform adequately to our principal primary groups and institutions it is necessary to insulate ourselves, at least in part, from the influence of groups and institutions of a contrasting or hostile character. Otherwise the missionary who goes to convert the heathen would immediately be assimilated into the heathen society; the spy who goes among the enemy would become a traitor to his country; the prison guard would himself become a criminal. These things may occur, but for most persons the greater problem is not how to insulate against the influence of hostile groups, but rather how to gain and preserve adequacy of adaptation to social expectations in general.

Sex Roles.—The behavior of the sexes is not only differentiated in all societies but always to a greater degree than directly required by physiological differences. Most of the personality differentiation between men and women is produced by the social organization which assigns to children from birth onward certain styles of behavior according to their sex. Even before it can begin to have effect, many parents follow the practice of dressing girl babies in pink and boy babies in blue, and by tone of voice and style of approach they assume a femininity or manliness in the respective genders. Part of this treatment of the infant may be intentional, but for most persons the larger part is probably so habitual that it is unrecognized. The character of almost every gesture or action toward a person carries an aspect which is related to the sex of the person, and it is the inescapable cumulative force of this fact, in operation throughout the lifetime of each person, that clearly guides his personality into the appropriate bounds of his or her sex role.[5]

Thus, while physiology differentiates the sexes in certain aspects of mechanism, social organization largely creates the masculine and the feminine personalities. Physiology sets limits to the extent of this differentiation, requiring for example that men have an advantage in the role of athletic and military heroes, and placing women in a position that makes it far easier for them to deal skilfully with small children. Within such broad limits, however, there is room for a great deal of variation that may be somewhat arbitrarily determined by the culture; a fact well illustrated by the variations in the roles of women in the many cultures over the world. In general, the range of variation runs from extreme domination of males and subservience of females to a near-equalitarian status, but it does not extend as far as a clear-cut domination of society by females.

In modern American urban culture, although there is a certain amount of variation in sex roles, some generalizations may fairly be made. In addition to the differentiation by clothing from birth onward there is a visible differentiation by hair style as soon as the girl child has enough hair to differentiate her from male children. The braided pigtails or waved coiffure clearly sets the girl apart from the boy with his crew cut or slicked down trimmed hair, and the result makes it impossible to forget gender whatever the costume worn. In tone of voice, expectation of the future, household routines, toys and gifts, and in many other ways, the members of the family continue to differentiate the sex roles of their children. These separate roles are further fixed by the differential association in play groups and in school of girls with girls, and boys with boys. A social pressure arises to push back into the conventional type of activity any child who tries to take a characteristic role too similar to that of the opposite sex. This is particularly so in the case of

---

[5] A recent text cites a case which involved the requirement of a change of treatment of a child who had formerly and incorrectly been considered to be a boy. Because of a genital anomaly, a five-year-old girl had been mistaken for a boy, called by a boy's name, and given a masculine social role. After a corrective operation the nurses at the hospital were instructed to treat the child as a girl. This turned out to be difficult. It was hard to remember to say "her" and the child did not readily accept the girl role. The nurses declared that they felt "vaguely uneasy as if we had committed an error." See Alfred R. Lindesmith and Anselm Strauss, *Social Psychology* (New York: The Dryden Press, Inc., 1949), pp. 284-85.

boys, since such a departure would be in a downward prestige direction.

There is also apparently a systematic difference in the culture which prepares males for earlier and greater independence and responsibility. This is clearly evident in the formal educational system, which now greatly favors male students in the more advanced and specialized types of training and formerly even excluded females almost completely. A recent student of the matter has found similar consequences to the differential training of the sexes in the parental family.[6] From biographical documents written by women college students, it was shown that in various ways parents "tended to speed up, most often unwittingly, but also deliberately, the emancipation of the boy from the family, while they retarded it in the case of his sister." Boys, for example, were generally provided with earlier and more frequent opportunities for independent action; they were more free to play away from home groups, to choose their own activity, to stay out later. They usually were allowed to initiate certain types of independent behavior earlier than were their sisters—such actions, for example, as walking to school without a parent, going to a movie or athletic contest alone, and later, taking a train trip alone, or accepting a job away from home.

The same documents showed that emancipation for boys tends to be hastened by the fact that they are allowed more privacy in personal affairs than are their sisters. The following three excerpts from the responses of different students are characteristic:

My mother is very hurt if I don't let her read the letters I receive. After a telephone call she expects me to tell her who called and what was said. My brother could say "a friend" and she would not feel insulted.

My brother is fifteen, three years younger than I am. When he goes out after supper mother calls out: "Where are you going, Jimmy?" "Oh, out." Could I get away with this? Not on your life. I would have to tell in detail where to, with whom, and if I am half an hour late mother sits on the edge of the living-room sofa watching the door.

I have a brother of twenty-three, and a sister of twenty-two, and a younger brother who is sixteen. My sister and I had a much more sheltered life than my brothers. My brothers come and go as they please. Even my younger brother feels that his current girl friend is his personal affair. No one knows who she is. But the family wants voluminous files on every boy my sister and I want to date. It is not easy for us to get the complete genealogy of a boy we want to go out with.[7]

[6] Mirra Komarovsky, "Functional Analysis of Sex Roles." *American Sociological Review*, XV, No. 4 (1950), 508-16.
[7] *Ibid.*, p. 511.

It is also found that girls are held to a more exacting standard of filial and kinship obligation. "When the grandmother needs somebody to do an errand for her, or Aunt Jane who doesn't hear well needs help, the girl is more likely to be called upon. The pressure to attend and observe birthdays, anniversaries, and other family festivals is apparently greater upon her than the boy." [8]

The difference of influences of this sort produces a measurable difference in emancipation from parents.[9] From another set of data on 937 students, it was shown that 22 per cent of the females report an extremely close attachment to their fathers, and 36 per cent to their mothers. The corresponding percentages for male students are only 15 and 24. The women reported in 31 per cent of the cases that the principal decisions of their lives had been "very much" in accordance with the wishes of their fathers, and in 34 per cent with the wishes of their mothers. The corresponding percentages for men were only 22 and 21. Women students frequently felt homesick for fathers in 24 per cent of the cases, and for mothers in 32 per cent of the cases. The corresponding percentages for men were only 14 and 19. Other studies of family life have noted and measured the same difference in emancipation between the sexes.[10]

The organized social influences which differentiate the sexes tend to encourage approach toward an ideal type of man or woman, and each person succeeds in conforming to this type in varying degree. Most persons wish to be reasonably representative of their sex, although there are a few atypical women who would prefer to conform to a masculine role and, even more rarely, men who would rather be feminine. To control this kind of deviation, there are various expressions and reactions of disapproval in operation. The masculine woman is penalized in various ways by disapproval and discrimination, and the feminine man even more severely. On the whole, the differential operates successfully and the separate roles of the sexes are generally harmonious with the social organization.[11]

[8] *Ibid.*, p. 511.
[9] *Ibid.*, p. 513.
[10] See E. W. Burgess and L. S. Cottrell, *Predicting Success and Failure in Marriage* (New York: Prentice-Hall, Inc., 1939), and L. M. Terman, *et al.*, *Psychological Factors in Marital Happiness* (New York: McGraw-Hill Book Co., Inc., 1938).

[11] Exceptions are noted in the section of the present Chapter entitled "Contradictions, Inconsistencies, and Dilemmas of Status." In a period of systematic change as experienced in the last century it is inevitable that some inconsistencies of sex roles would be found, and that a certain number of persons would experience a sense of rebellion about them.

Age Roles.—All societies also differentiate the roles of various age groups in their populations. Again, a certain amount of this is physiologically demanded—small children cannot do advanced work and old people cannot bear heavy physical labor—but there is much differentiation in the age standards of behavior in various societies that does not proceed from physiological structure. The age at which one is assumed to pass from the status of dependent child to independent adult varies too much to have detailed dependence on physiological maturity. Capacity to reproduce appears from the ages of twelve to sixteen in most persons, and full height growth from about sixteen to twenty. The adult role, however, may be given to brides as young as twelve in some instances, and may be withheld from dependent college students well into their twenties. In some families, moreover, dependent unmarried daughters living with their parents may be denied the treatment symbolizing adult status for many years more.

In our present-day society the age roles for children are defined fairly explicitly, though in certain areas and on certain status levels the standards have been blurred by rapid changes. The expectation is that each person will conform to his conventional age role, and social pressure is exerted against marked variation in either direction. Ridicule from age mates and concern by parents and other adults bear on the child who holds to interests appropriate to earlier years. Similarly an assortment of disapproving gestures may penalize the child who presumes to a role of one above his age.

The same general principles apply to the whole range of ages. There are subtle and informal social penalties for the schoolboy who tries artificially to gain full adult status, and for the young adult who attempts to look mature by growing a beard or by affecting the clothing and mannerisms of elder statesmen. There is also a pressure against the reverse—the middle-aged man pretending to be a dashing youth, or the young parent who embarrasses his children by publicly joining them in purely child's play. In a stable condition of society there is a variety of pressures which tend to hold each person to the style of behavior appropriate to his own age level.[12] When the time comes to shift to a more advanced age

[12] Because so many privileges and rewards open up during late childhood and teen ages, it is natural that many young persons of our society are eager for the next stage of age development, and, to some extent, that they do what they can to appear to be more advanced than they are in this respect. One reason for beginning the practice of smoking is this kind of eagerness. An objective study of 268 students of ages fourteen to twenty-two, produced a conclusion that smoking is undertaken as a mark of manhood, superiority, and respect, giving the adolescents who take up the practice the feeling of gaining a place among older persons. See A. M. Rizk, "Smok-

status it is normally easy because all supporting influences aid the person in making the change.[13]

Popularity.—A type of status not closely related to any function in group activity, but reflecting a condition of being known and admired in varying degrees is popularity. Although achievement and leadership are often also attributes of those who are popular, these are not identical and it is possible for a person to be popular without any definite leadership role, as it is possible to be elected to responsible positions without being outstandingly popular. Popularity choices, furthermore, go far beyond the small primary clique. While it is true that most young persons would like to share clique membership with those whom they consider popular, they will also readily designate as highly popular some persons who are outside their cliques and for that matter even some with whom they personally are not closely acquainted.

Among children or youth who have not been together long enough to have formed stable cliques, friendly approaches to one another, choices of room-mates, mealtime companions, and the like, may be used as a rough index of popularity. Hunt and Solomon have by this approach investigated certain traits among young boys five to nine years old, in a summer camp.[14] All the twenty-three boys during the camping period of eight weeks stated each week their choices of cabin-mates. In the early weeks, the changes of choices from week to week were frequent—nearly 60 per cent at first—but by the end of the camping period the choices stabilized, with fewer than 20 per cent of the choices changing in the last trial. Boys with previous camping experience were frequently chosen, and at first there was a disposition to choose those boys who already were cabin-mates. Popularity, as measured by fre-

ing Among Adolescents; an Objective Study," *Egyptian Journal of Psychology,* III (1947), 55-67.

[13] Physical development sometimes enters in and provides the cue for the change. Blanchard has cited a case of a girl who took the normal childhood role, playing with dolls, giving little thought to her future and taking no special care of personal appearance until the age of twelve, when menstruation began. Within the next three months, without noticeable pressure from adults, she gave away her dolls, became concerned about vocational preparation, took an interest in her personal appearance, and began to read romantic fiction. Apparently the physiological change gave her a sudden realization that her status was that of a woman rather than that of a child. See Phyllis Blanchard, "Adolescent Experience in Relation to Personality and Behavior." Chap. xxii in J. McV. Hunt, *Personality and the Behavior Disorders* (New York: The Ronald Press Co., 1944), pp. 704-5.

[14] J. McV. Hunt and R. L. Solomon, "The Stability and Some Correlates of Group-Status in a Summer-camp Group of Young Boys," *American Journal of Psychology,* LV (1942), 33-45.

quency of being chosen, was related to various other traits by a measure of correlation (rho). The relation of popularity to athletic ability was at first high (rho=.60) but declined during the period (rho=.25 in the final week). The less visible personality traits began to have effect more slowly, and the relationship of these to popularity increased with the passage of time. The coefficient for generosity, for example, increased during the period from .20 to .34. For ordered activity (as contrasted with restlessness) the relationship increased from .10 to .47; for obedience to counsellors, from .18 to .22, and for lack of egocentricity .45 to .50. In view of this shifting basis of making choices, it might be concluded that the early choices reflected popularity and the later choices indicated actual primary group formation.

A study of choices, expressed as friendship preferences among members of twenty-one fraternities at a college, also indicated that these are not primarily reflections of mutual preferences. Students show a preference for friends they would like to have, apparently desiring to associate with the popular persons in the student body. The most frequently chosen were the upperclass students, presumably because of their greater prestige and familiarity with the college culture (as the popular boys in the camping example were those familiar with the ways of camping).[15]

Actual choices, of course, have to be more realistic than the preferences expressed on a questionnaire. Whatever we would like to do, we actually find our comradeships among those who are available as friends—only a small proportion of those who would like to do so can actually belong to the cliques which include the persons of top popularity.

Leadership and Primary Relationships.—Leadership is not a trait but a relation of the person to others—a relationship which enables him to have more than average control over their behavior by informal means. The relationship, moreover, is to specific persons. There are few if any leaders in general; leaders have influence within specified groups, and the same persons may belong to groups in which they have no leadership role. A conclusion based on an inspection of thirty years of leadership studies is that: (1) leadership is specific to the particular situation under investigation; and (2) leadership involves superiority over the members of the group in at least one of the appropriate abilities. The only common factor in the various studies appeared to be that leaders in a

[15] F. M. Vreeland, "Social Relations in the College Fraternity," *Sociometry*, V (1942), 151-62.

particular field need and tend to possess superior technical competence or knowledge in that area.[16]

In a study of choices made within a population of about four hundred girls at the New York State Training School for Girls, Jennings investigated what she called leadership, but which actually might have been a mixture of leadership and popularity.[17] Among these girls, aged twelve to sixteen, the "leaders" greatly surpassed the "nonleaders" in initiative (making new events happen) and in imagination (enlarging the kind and extent of activity). They also possessed a favorable balance of self-interest and concern for others.[18]

In formal organizations with some definite objectives, such as an army, leadership is far more explicitly conceived. A person achieves his rank as officer by fulfilling formal requirements, which include the achievement of necessary types of knowledge and skill, the accumulation of a certain amount of experience, and the conformity to certain character standards. When by act of Congress he is declared to be an officer, his orders are officially considered to carry force and to require obedience. Actually his leadership is much more effective if he has further unofficial qualifications, such as those of inspiring respect and confidence on the part of his men.

In most formal organizations, and especially in an army, the leadership is partly separated by social distance from those who only take orders. Informal social relations between the two classes of persons is usually sharply restricted. This separation has functions in such an organization although they are not always recognized by the ordinary soldier. Surveys of opinion differences between officers and enlisted men in the U.S. Army during the Second World War reveal a number of ways in which these groups disagree about the proper relation of officers to men.[19] In response to the

[16] From Lindesmith and Strauss, *op. cit.*, p. 75. The generalization is the contribution of W. Jenkins.

[17] Helen H. Jennings, "Leadership and Sociometric Choice," *Sociometry*, 1947, pp. 32-49.

[18] An analysis of the traits of the leader (or popular person), the isolated person, and the rejected person, brings out the following trio of generalizations: (1) the person who can look after his own interests and also those of other persons, with reasonable skill and fairness, is likely to be popular; (2) the person who takes care of his own interests and nothing else is liked by none and disliked by many—a rejected person; (3) the person who takes care of other persons' interests, but not his own, is neither liked nor disliked but treated as a doormat—an isolated person. See Helen H. Jennings, *Leadership and Isolation* (2d. ed.; New York: Longmans, Green & Co., Inc., 1950), pp. 26 ff.

[19] Samuel A. Stouffer, *et al., The American Soldier: Adjustment During Army Life* ("Studies in Social Psychology in World War II," Vol. I [Princeton: Princeton University Press, 1949]), pp. 362 ff.

question concerning whether the soldiers "have good reason to gripe about strict and petty discipline," only a small number of officers (23 per cent) agreed but over half (51 per cent) of the enlisted men agreed. A similar question concerning the way orders are given also produced a sharp difference of opinion with fewer than half of the officers (49 per cent), and a large majority (71 per cent) of enlisted men agreeing that grounds for complaint exist. Concerning the value of neatness and correctness in appearance ("spit and polish") only 40 per cent of the officers considered this overstressed in military life, while 74 per cent of enlisted men thought so. Concerning the necessity of maintaining a degree of social distance between officers and men, opinion differs not only between officers and men, but also according to rank of officers. Concerning the statement that an "officer loses the respect of men if he pals around with them off duty," a great majority of enlisted men (82 per cent) disagreed. But only 54 per cent of second lieutenants, still fewer first lieutenants (39 per cent), and even fewer captains (27 per cent) disagreed.

Enlisted men place greater importance on informal aspects of control, even in the relations of officers to men, than do officers. Asked whether high ability in personal relations—being liked by the men—is important to an officer, only 7 per cent of the officers agreed that it was, whereas 33 per cent of enlisted men and 49 per cent of privates thought so. The officers conceived their roles much more in terms of executive abilities, such as being able to think for themselves. In this respect only 23 per cent of privates agreed, and 44 per cent of noncommissioned officers, but the great majority (75 per cent) of commissioned officers agreed. Because of their greater responsibility, 67 per cent of the officers believed that they also deserved more rights and privileges than enlisted men. Only 23 per cent of the latter group agreed with this. On a particular detail, for example, 84 per cent of the enlisted men, but only 35 per cent of the officers, agreed that officers should observe the same curfews that are required of enlisted men.

Actually the type of work required of an officer would be obstructed if he were to be required to follow all the routines of an enlisted man. Executive functions cannot so easily be reduced to routines, and thus flexibility of action is an essential part of the role. Because of the magnitude of the consequences of his decisions, and other considerations, his time is particularly valuable, and it is in the interest of the whole organization that he use swifter transportation than is available to all, and lose less time in such nonproductive ways as standing in line. Thus the general principle that special privileges be allowed officers is clearly functional, whether or not all the men realize it.

Similarly, the social distance between officers and men, as well as between executives and employees in various other types of organizations, has some useful functions. An executive has to make many decisions which involve choices between persons. In the interest of efficiency, it is required that such choices be made with reference to the general purposes of the organization and not be influenced by personal considerations such as friendship with certain of the men or personal animosity toward others. Any marked departure from this principle not only results in inefficient assignments, but threatens morale when it is perceived by the men that their officers are not providing the most effective organization and teamwork possible.

The role of leader, then, is one which involves a supply of formal power, and therefore requires a certain amount of detachment from personal relations among those on whom the power must be exercised. At the same time, situations are rare in which leaders may totally disregard the factor of personal skill in handling men. A type of role which can successfully combine these apparently contradictory considerations is that of the leader who keeps his social distance from those ranked below him but shows by his actions and words that he has a good understanding of their problems and a sense of affection and pride toward them. For a leader of this type, men will acquire a sense of admiration and loyalty which will motivate them to work more, and with greater application, than they would be impelled to do by formal orders alone.

If descriptive accounts can be trusted, such a relationship has been achieved by most of the highly successful military and political leaders, such as Napoleon, Robert E. Lee, Theodore Roosevelt, and the same relationship has been sought more recently by Patton, Montgomery, and MacArthur. A similar pattern is often achieved in the leadership of a business or industrial organization, a university, a social movement, or even an athletic team. Some football coaches for whom the members of college teams have put forth most devoted efforts, men like Amos Alonzo Stagg and Knute Rockne, have been socially remote, but have possessed the capacity so to inspire deep devotion that a small gesture of approval would produce in a man ecstatic rededication to the collective effort, and a sign of rebuke would move a man to tears. The present author has witnessed both reactions on a number of occasions, as doubtless have many readers.

Contradictions, Inconsistencies, and Dilemmas of Status

Each person in every society inevitably has a number of roles. Some of these roles may differ sharply from others and yet give no occasion for internal conflict. For example, if the occasions for which the various roles are appropriate are clearly specified and kept completely separate, there is no difficulty in making the shift from one to another at the proper time, and no sense of contradiction. A judge may assume a romantic role in connection with an effort to persuade a woman to accept him in marriage. On his bench, however, he readily and completely conforms to the judicial role, even if the woman he is pursuing happens to be in the audience. Both persons understand and accept the fact that the situation is entirely inappropriate for any kind of concession to the romantic role. The same judge, however, in his courtship role normally exhibits no trace of his occupational self—in fact to carry it to any degree into a romantic situation would tend to interfere with his success as a lover.

In a sense then, social life is a drama for each person. On most occasions with which we are familiar, we understand adequately what role is expected. We can also step from one role to another, as the actor leaves the stage and changes back from a despicable villain to a good husband and father. On some occasions, however, two situations which call for clearly different roles will overlap, thus presenting the person with a conflict between the two styles of action expected of him. The child whose role at school is quite different from his role at home may be ill at ease on the occasions when his parents visit the schoolroom. A man whose relation to his wife and children has a different pattern from the home life of his parents may experience a similar discomfort when he takes his family to visit at his parents' home. He finds it difficult to reconcile the simultaneous roles of son and husband and at the moment is unable to escape either one.

Stouffer and Toby have investigated this sort of conflict in a person between the role of the good citizen who lives up to his formal duties and the role of loyal friend.[20] The former is supposed

[20] Samuel A. Stouffer and Jackson Toby, "Role Conflict and Personality," *American Journal of Sociology*, LVI, No. 5 (1951), 395-405.

to conform to general principles of law and custom in a type of response designated "universalistic." The latter is expected to make a "particularistic" response—reacting to the situation on the basis of his relation to his friend even though this may conflict with the generalities of law. Undergraduates at Harvard and Radcliffe Universities were scaled with respect to their tendency to act in a hypothetical conflict situation in one or the other of these ways. The scale was made up from the responses to four dilemmas, of which the following is an example:

You are riding in a car driven by a close friend, and he hits a pedestrian. You know he was going at least 35 miles an hour in a 20-mile-an-hour zone. There are no other witnesses. His lawyer says that if you testify under oath that the speed was only 20 miles an hour, it may save him from serious consequences.

What right has your friend to expect you to protect him?
Check one:
——My friend has a definite right as a friend to expect me to testify to the lower figure.
——He has some right as a friend to expect me to testify to the lower figure.
——He has no right as a friend to expect me to testify to the lower figure.

What do you think you'd probably do in view of the obligations of a sworn witness and the obligation to your friend?
Check one:
——Testify that he was going 20 miles an hour.
——Not testify that he was going 20 miles an hour.

The responses were classified into five general scale types according to a standard method, Type 1 having the most general tendency to make the "universalistic" type of response and Type 5 the most tendency to make the "particularistic" type of response. The latter type included the largest number of students, the former the smallest. The number of statements of Type 5 who would favor their friends against general principles of rules or morality, however, decreased by more than half when the situation was described as involving a fifty-fifty chance that the student himself would be exposed in his improper activity in favor of his friend.

These results, of course, are to be applied to this particular group of students at this particular time, February, 1950. Application of a similar device on other types of persons would doubtless show categories of persons who would face such dilemmas in a manner quite different from the students involved here.

Conflicts in Sex Roles of Women.—Conflicts of this latter sort, however, are avoidable most of the time, and are endurable because of their temporary character.   A more serious conflict of roles results from inescapable contradictions embedded in a culture.   In a complex culture and during a time of rapid change, inconsistencies arise in the social organization and produce role conflicts within persons.   Various observers have pointed out such conflicts concerning the status of women.   The trend toward emancipation of women has affected certain aspects of life more than others.   In a few occupations women have the opportunity of dominating men, although in general the tradition of male dominance is unbroken. A career woman thus in some contexts outranks certain men, and in other situations partakes of the general status of women.   At an office party consisting of both men and women, the female executive has a conflict between being a boss officially and a woman socially—a situation with no standard solution and one which usually involves a certain amount of uneasiness.

An investigator has recently pointed out a similar type of conflicting pressure on young women in school and college.   Having in mind the possibility or even necessity of a career, they are thus subject to the pressure to be superior in their studies.   On the other hand, in the interests of a normal social life and the possibility of marriage, they feel a necessity to make a concession to the tradition of male dominance.   A number of cases are cited in which such women students affect a lower intellectual capacity than they actually have in order to avoid appearing superior to men.[21]

In a number of instances, both types of the conflicting influences come from within the same family or circle of relatives and friends. The following statements by several of the students illustrate the point.

> How am I to pursue any course singlemindedly when some way along the line a person I respect is sure to say, "You are on the wrong track and are wasting your time?"   Uncle John telephones every Sunday morning.   His first question is: "Did you go out last night?"   He would think me a "grind" if I were to stay home Saturday night to finish a term paper.   My father expects me to get an "A" in every subject and is disappointed by a "B."   He says I have plenty of time for social life.   Mother says, "That 'A' in Philosophy is very nice, dear.   But please don't become so deep that no man will be good enough for you."   And, finally, Aunt Mary's line is careers for women.   "Prepare yourself for some profession.   This is the only way to insure yourself independence and an interesting life.   You have plenty of time to marry."

[21] Mirra Komarovsky, "Cultural Contradictions and Sex Roles," *American Journal of Sociology*, LII, No. 3 (1946), pp. 184-89.

I get a letter from my mother at least three times a week. One week her letters will say, "Remember that this is your last year at college. Subordinate everything to your studies. You must have a good record to secure a job." The next week her letters are full of wedding news. This friend of mine got married; that one is engaged; my young cousin's wedding is only a week off. When, my mother wonders, will I make up my mind? Surely I wouldn't want to be the only unmarried one in my group. It is high time, she feels, that I give some thought to it.

All through high school my family urged me to work hard because they wished me to enter a first-rate college. At the same time they were always raving about a girl schoolmate who lived next door to us. How pretty and sweet she was, how popular, and what taste in clothes! Couldn't I also pay more attention to my appearance and to social life? They were overlooking the fact that this carefree friend of mine had little time left for school work and had failed several subjects. It seemed that my family had expected me to become Eve Curie and Hedy Lamarr wrapped up in one.

My mother thinks that it is very nice to be smart in college but only if it doesn't take too much effort. She always tells me not to be too intellectual on dates, to be clever in a light sort of way. My father, on the other hand, wants me to study law. He thinks that if I applied myself I could make an excellent lawyer and keeps telling me that I am better fitted for this profession than my brother.

One of my two brothers writes: "Cover up that high forehead and act a little dumb once in a while"; while the other always urges upon me the importance of rigorous scholarship.[22]

In a number of such cases, the investigator reports indications of a certain amount of bewilderment and confusion of the students in the face of the contradictory influences. In some of the statements they mention hurt feelings, resentment, embarrassment, and worry. About 40 per cent of the students stated that on some occasions they have tried to escape the conflict by concealing the intellectual abilities that threatened their popularity. They "played dumb" on dates, concealed any academic honors, pretended ignorance of some subjects, and allowed the men the last word in any intellectual discussion. Some even deliberately lost games if mental ability was involved. Details of this strategy are revealed in the interviews.

I am engaged to a southern boy who doesn't think too much of the woman's intellect. In spite of myself, I play up to his theories because the less one knows and does, the more he does for you and thinks you "cute" in the bargain. . . . I allow him to explain things to me in great detail and to treat me as a child in financial matters.

One of the nicest techniques is to spell long words incorrectly once in a

22 *Ibid.*, p. 185.

while. My boy friend seems to get a great kick out of it and writes back, "Honey, you certainly don't know how to spell."

When my date said that he considers Ravel's *Bolero* the greatest piece of music ever written, I changed the subject because I knew I would talk down to him.

My fiancé didn't go to college. I intend to finish college and work hard at it, but in talking to him I make college appear a kind of a game.

I sometimes "play dumb" on dates, but it leaves a bad taste. The emotions are complicated. Part of me enjoys "putting something over" on the unsuspecting male. But this sense of superiority over him is mixed with feelings of guilt for my hypocrisy. Toward the "date" I feel some contempt because he is "taken in" by my technique, or if I like the boy, a kind of a maternal condescension. At times I resent him! Why isn't he my superior in all ways in which a man should excel so that I could be my natural self? What am I doing here with him, anyhow? Slumming? [23]

The college from which the above examples were gathered is in New York City where there are large populations in which both the career expectation for women and the tradition of male dominance are strong. Furthermore the women were students in courses in sociology and social psychology in which such issues would be made particularly explicit to them. In another region—the west coast—the same condition was investigated among 163 women undergraduates who, though all unmarried, with few exceptions preferred marriage, a home, and children to a career.[24] In answer to the direct question, "How often have you 'played dumb' on dates because you thought the man preferred you that way?" only 7.5 per cent answered *often* or *very often*. A number of questions were asked concerning what they thought they should be doing in college, and how they should spend their time. The large majority —66 to 89 per cent on the respective questions—gave no indication of experiencing any kind of contradiction. This particular aspect of sex role contradiction is thus found only in particular places, and apparently does not exist throughout the entire United States culture.

Other contradictions in sex roles have also been noted although some of these observations—by Margaret Mead, Pearl Buck, and Florence Kluckhohn, for example—consist of suggestions without supporting research of an objective nature. Komarovsky has published some evidence that the kind of bond between parents and daughters noted earlier in the present Chapter conflicts with the

---

[23] *Ibid.*, pp. 187-88.
[24] Paul Wallin, "Cultural Contradictions and Sex Roles: a Repeat Study," *American Sociological Review*, XV, No. 2 (1950), 288-93.

relationship a wife is expected to maintain with her husband.[25] There is no indication, however, that this difficulty involves more than a small minority of married women.

Jacobson has recently shown a relation between the disparity of attitudes of husbands and wives on the subject of male dominance, and the duration of the marriage.[26] A 28-item attitude scale measuring such attitudes was given to 100 married and 100 divorced couples in Chillicothe, Ohio, the couples having been matched with reference to the date of marriage. By correlation technique it was shown that persons who marry tend to be somewhat similar in attitudes toward male dominance, that couples which remain married display a still closer similarity, and that divorced couples have considerable differences in these attitudes. The attitude related to divorce was shown to be an unwillingness of wives to accept the widespread pattern of male dominance. The average score of the divorced women revealed nonacceptance of this pattern; although none of the divorced women indicated acceptance of the pattern of male dominance, not only the divorced men, but twenty-five per cent of the married women did.

Role Conflicts in a Polygynous Society.—The foregoing treatment of the conflicts which arise for some women because of their dual roles in our society has provided a typical illustration of the nature of role conflicts in general. Roles as a rule are not suddenly invented but evolve out of long collective experience with particular situations of interaction. The adoption of the practice of polygyny among the Mormons, on the other hand, was a sudden occurrence for which the people were not prepared. A number of difficulties were at once encountered, since there was no standard role for the man who had more than one wife, nor for the wife who was not the only spouse of her husband. Some of the consequent confusion in behavior has been described by a student of the Mormon experience.[27]

Among some preliterate peoples who practice polygyny, conflicts among the wives of one man have been reduced by a standard system of ranks among wives, such as a seniority principle in which the first wife holds authority over later wives, with the last wife

[25] Mirra Komarovsky, "Functional Analysis of Sex Roles," *American Sociological Review*, XV, No. 4 (1950), 508-16.

[26] Alver H. Jacobson, "Conflict in Attitudes Toward the Marital Roles of Husband and Wife." Publication forthcoming.

[27] J. E. Hulett, Jr., "The Social Role of the Mormon Polygamous Male," *American Sociological Review*, VIII, No. 3 (1943), 279-87.

subject to control by all the others. Apparently no standard of any kind existed in the Mormon society to regulate matters of this kind, and it was left to the wives within any one family to evolve their own relation to one another, a process which often led to jealousy and overt quarreling. This, of course, also presented a problem to the husband, and again he had to devise his own solution. Various types of approaches were adopted according to the individual ingenuity of the husbands who were involved in such situations. One such effort has been described as follows:

When there was a quarrel between the wives, father would ask one of them to fix supper for the one whom she had quarreled with and then to go and bring the other and they'd all eat together. He would talk it all over with them and wouldn't let them go to bed until everything was all straightened out. It was the same with the children. He would take the ones who had quarreled out riding with him and make them sit together and talk it over. He wouldn't let them separate until they were friends again.[28]

Another reaction, reported in a number of cases, was to turn away, or pretend not to know of the conflict between the wives. One man would claim to be too busy to pay attention to the matter, another would hold that "women's disputes are too trivial," and others would pretend to be ignorant of the trouble, or to be too ill to give any attention to it. Still another solution was to keep the wives apart, or at least never to be present with both at the same time. One Mormon wrote:

Father didn't often appear in public with two wives, except at church parties where he might take all three. He took his wives to concerts and plays by turns. These turns might not coincide with the time of his visits, but they worked out very well. For example, he would announce to Jennie, the first wife, that he was taking Julia, the second, to the concert this evening.[29]

The wives, of course, were subject to strains from the lack of standard roles. In some instances they judged their practical status in the polygynous family by the position they had in the affections of the husband, but this principle did not guarantee either satisfaction or stability.[30]

In one case, the father is reported as having been "very interested in the young girls," and married two when he was 49 and 58 years old respectively. He seems to have transferred his attentions to the youngest wife each time, so that a sort of hierarchy of heart-

[28] *Ibid.*, p. 282.
[29] *Ibid.*, p. 283.
[30] *Ibid.*, p. 284.

break was established in the family. A daughter of the first wife, Annie, reports that his second marriage "nearly killed mother," but after that "she didn't care how many women he married." When he married the third time, it was the second wife, Julia, who was "nearly killed"; she got little comfort from Annie, who took the occasion to remind her that now she knew how *she* felt when he married the second time. But Julia never acted the same toward father again, and besides she always manifested a nasty attitude toward Luella, the third wife who supplanted her.

The jealousy and hurt feelings were also experienced by the children of each wife. According to a daughter of a fifth wife: "Father married my mother on the anniversary of the day Aunt Ida, his first wife, died. I think Ida's children felt pretty badly about that. It was just thoughtless of him." [31]

The investigator found various indications of discomfort and in some cases even guilt concerning the practice of polygyny. When, under pressure from the government, the Mormon officials ordered the custom terminated, there were some who gave every indication of relief. A case is cited which shows how this outcome brought a welcome escape from an awkward arrangement.

Until his first wife rejected him, forcing him to live with his second, the second wife was never publicly recognized although she lived nearby. In his public life he tried to give the appearance of having only one wife, although few if any non-Mormons lived in the community. When he went to parties and to church, he and the first wife went in the buggy, and if Cecelia went, she walked.

But when the church repudiated Plural Marriage in 1890, father fell whole-heartedly in with the officials and deplored marriages made after the Manifesto. A friend of his had four wives and was a fairly old man. Some years after the Manifesto the friend was called on a mission, and married another young woman. Father was scathing in his remarks and said the friend just hadn't waked up to what he had done, marrying this girl illegally and without the authority of the priesthood. He also said that when he waked up to what he had done he would go mad. And the man did go mad and died.[32]

Other Types of Role Conflict.—Similar conflicts exist in various undefined aspects of social life and are particularly common in time of rapid changes. They are also experienced by persons who shift to unfamiliar social situations. Rapid rise or fall in the socio-economic levels may put persons under strains and conflicts of this

[31] *Ibid.*, p. 284.
[32] *Ibid.*, p. 286.

sort. There arises a question of the kind of acceptance that may be found in the new level, and the kind of relation that may be maintained with associates belonging in the former level. This is the role dilemma of the social climber whose embarrassments are often a source of amusement in both the new level to which he aspires and the old level he is deserting.

Heterogeneity of family and community background may also be the source of role difficulties by depriving the person of any consistent standards of behavior. Exposed to many unintegrated roles, he is unable to make a coherent assembly of these influences to build a stable role of his own. The result in some cases is a baffling series of social failures which compounds the confusion. An illustration is provided by the following case, condensed from information supplied by a student:

Philip's parents moved from a distant region to a newly settled area, and took residence in a community in which no stable traditions or organized community life had had time to develop. His father was an outspoken atheist, and his mother was a devout fundamentalist (even to the extent of objecting to Philip's joining the Boy Scouts because an oath is taken by the members). Both parents were highly critical of Philip. His only sister was an enthusiast for astrology, which provided a third philosophical influence on him. Philip never developed a stable character, and even after a period in the armed services and a subsequent period of college study, lacked self-confidence.

In college, at the age of 28, Philip lived with a roommate in a rooming house. He liked dancing, but did not care for athletics. He was self-centered, but imagined many shortcomings and felt a constant need to explain himself. He thought people made fun of him, and interpreted trivial events personally. When a professor asked him not to smoke in the classroom, Philip interpreted it as an intention to humiliate him.

Philip's self-confidence was damaged by low grades in college, and appeared to become generalized. He refused to be taught to drive a car, for example, fearing that he would be unable to succeed.

His confidence in others had been jolted during his experience in military service when he discovered some minor padding of pay claims on the part of certain officers. Ideas of reference began to build up. After becoming intoxicated at a dance he began to suspect that people were looking at him and thinking him "queer." This conviction stayed with him, making it difficult for him to sit still or to concentrate on his studies. He became increasingly nervous and jumpy, but when a friend suggested that he take a job of manual labor in order to relax, he suspected that this was only a trap to test his philosophical sincerity—he had often expressed antagonism to all large companies which he believed to be monopolistic and therefore evil.

Philip was eventually persuaded to seek psychiatric help, and was committed to a mental hospital where electro-shock treatments were administered.

Cases of this sort tend to occur with frequency wherever there has occurred a break in the continuity of culture to the extent that the person is cut off from an adequate fund of organized folk knowledge. He is thus thrown back on his individual resources for obtaining knowledge, judging situations, and making and carrying out a life plan. Such a task is too great for most persons to perform without help from a stable social organization, and the result is usually a series of personal failures, even among persons whose life histories reveal the existence of some outstanding talents. The process is vividly illustrated by the life story of Jack London, the celebrated writer of adventure stories, whose experience was essentially as follows:

From Jack London's boyhood to the end of his life, there persisted a perfect pattern of literary success and personal failure, the latter clearly attributable to the lack of the kind of wisdom in human affairs that is normally derived from folk sources. The explanation of this deprivation is also clearly to be found in the exceptional discontinuity with certain aspects of culture resulting from the circumstances of his birth and childhood life. He had less help in finding his proper roles than most persons get and, as a result, had to find his own roles though not equipped with an adequate wisdom for doing so successfully.

He was separated from contacts of continuity by the triple circumstance of having had no sociological parents (i.e., no adults taking the normal parental role), no conventional neighborhood or community life in childhood, and only a meager school experience. His father, an itinerant astrologer, disappeared before Jack's illegitimate birth, and his mother, who had made one suicidal gesture shortly before Jack was born, had little taste for the role of mother. His nearest substitutes for parents were a stepsister, only eight years older, and a Negro woman who was a wet nurse and friend.

Jack's childhood was spent in a state of chronic poverty, and he began his occupational career at the age of eleven working on newspaper routes, ice delivery, and pin-setting at bowling alleys. By the age of thirteen he had left school, and after holding such jobs as sweeping saloons, he took employment in a cannery in which he worked from ten to eighteen hours a day. This occupation was followed by the more dangerous but profitable pursuit of night theft of oysters from privately owned beds. In the company of fellow oyster pirates he became a convivial, brawling, hard-drinking frequenter of saloons. He later added to this pattern a belligerent, impassioned socialism and a fever for gold and adventure.

Along with all these symptoms of instability he also developed a secret passion for reading, coupled with a determination to excel at everything. On the basis of these trends he exploited his adventures through fiction writing, with great financial success.

The instability and consequent tragedy of errors, however, stayed with him all through his life. He persistently violated the elementary principles of thrift, which appear in the proverbs of many cultures and are deeply embedded in the folk wisdom of this country, and spent far ahead of his earnings. At the peak of his career, for example, when he earned at the rate of $75,000 a year, he spent at the rate of $100,000 a year.

Mature advice concerning the wise choice of friends is on record as far back as the ancient Sanskrit literature, but Jack London persistently blundered by having too many friends too poorly selected. These friends borrowed money continuously, getting about half of his income in his best days when he was supporting, in addition, a large number of relatives, relatives of relatives, friends, friends of friends, charity cases, assorted parasites, and even some persons he had never met. The quality of his estimation of them is indicated by the fact that when a disaster brought on a sudden need of money, London's friends from whom he sought return of loans gave back only fifty dollars of over fifty thousand dollars owed.

Energy and ability are by themselves not sufficient for business success. The heritage of folk wisdom of commerce handed down in the fictional family of *The Late George Apley* would have protected Jack London from an impressive series of financial blunders. He purchased a ranch at first sight, spending all the money he had at the time. He sold one of his best books, *The Call of the Wild,* for two thousand dollars, losing nearly a hundred thousand dollars in royalties. He ordered the construction of a sailboat for seven thousand dollars but had to pay more than twenty-five thousand before it was completed. He plunged impulsively into farming, meeting with total failure because of poor judgment. He lost all his registered pigs and Angora goats by unexplained death, and he planted 140,000 trees to produce "Circassian walnut" (Eucalyptus) lumber only to have them become nearly valueless after a sudden change of fashion.

Blunders of magnitude also occurred concerning his unsuccessful Pacific cruise in his sailboat, particularly in the poor choice of a crew. His choices of wives were badly made. Toward the end of his life, following the destruction by fire of his large dream house on the very date of its completion, London's health broke, alcoholic addiction set in, and not long after, at the age of forty-one, he committed suicide.

SUMMARY

It is the essence of cooperation and teamwork that different persons perform different actions and that these differences are complementary—that is, they fit into a pattern which produces a desired result. It is an error to conceive of heredity as the source of all human differences and to think of social influences as productive only of uniformities. The social process also differentiates persons by assigning them different roles. The differences are valued not merely because variety is the spice of life, but because of the unified organization of action that is produced by such complementary differences. Not all persons in a group can be leaders—some must allow themselves to be led. Nor can each one choose the most pleasant task or role. In the social process, when it is operating ideally, persons are in some way assigned to the kinds of role which best serve the whole group.

The normal social process also gives to each person a sense of appreciation of the value of cooperation and group membership, and thus supplies him with the basic motivation to conform to group expectations. Most persons actively seek to assume the roles in which their actions will have the most harmonious relations to those of other persons in the organizations to which they belong. They find these roles by the skilful use of the trial-and-error process of imagination, aided by the information and standard specifications of roles which is supplied culturally. There is no such thing as perfection in this kind of achievement, but reasonable success can be judged by the degree of harmony each person achieves in the social process.

Certain major differentiations of role—the categorizing of age and sex roles, for example—are standard for a whole society. Physiology requires that both of these differentiations be made, but cultures always add far more than is physiologically necessary. In our society the differentiation of sex roles begins at birth when different kinds of behavior are displayed by other members of a family toward the male and female infants. The separation is carried on by the group by presenting children with different childhood interests according to their sex, by partially segregating them during the growing years and in adult years as well, and by assigning somewhat different major purposes in life to children of each sex. Furthermore, in the dating, courtship, and marriage relations, the sex roles are sharply differentiated by convention. Conspicuous deviations by either sex from conventional styles of behavior are subject to criticism and other sanctions, which in some cases, especially that of the effeminate male, may be extremely harsh.

Age roles are also clearly differentiated by the arbitrary principles of a society. Costumes, styles of behavior, formal privileges, and other indications mark each period of life, and, except where rapid social changes have disorganized standards, there is strong social pressure against any marked departure in either direction from the appropriate age role.

Within any one group further differentiation is made along lines of popularity and of leadership. Persons seek the company of certain types and yield to the influence of other persons because of the characteristic behavior which they value in one another. A leadership role, for example, can usually be won by excelling in one of the principal activities of the group, and by possessing active and imaginative ability to originate and organize activity. In formal organizations there may be, of course, many other requirements and qualifications, but even there the leadership is more effective if the appropriate role is maintained. Social distance may be necessary between leaders and men, but it must be understood as functional, and must not involve antagonism.

In a complex society the members face not only a diversity of roles for various situations, but also a certain amount of contradiction or inconsistency of the demands of different roles. Some may be minimized by avoidance of the situations in which roles conflict, but few persons escape a certain amount of role dilemma. Women, for example, are under some pressure to follow a career, support themselves, and be politically equal with men, and at the same time are expected to conform to the traditions of romance and chivalry by seeming inferior, relatively helpless, and being attractive in appearance and manner. It is in fact possible to make a suitable working combination of roles even in this conflicting set of influences, but the inconsistency in the society is of too recent origin for a standard solution to have evolved. Thus a number of women find the conflict perplexing and troubling in varying degrees.

Similar conflicts may also occur with age roles. In some kinds of situations young persons are given a relatively high amount of responsibility and status, and in others they are treated as juvenile and dependent. The adult veteran who returns from war to resume the status of an undergraduate student often chafes at the assumptions of immaturity under which he is supposed to live at college. A young man who reaches a high position in which he has authority over older men may find himself in a conflicting age role which is uncomfortable both to himself and to those who work under him. Some conflicts of age roles, however, are temporary and require only the passage of time for their solution.

Innovations of customs and institutions may also produce role conflicts, as illustrated by the experience of the Mormon peoples during their trial of polygyny. Roles of marriage partners imply exclusiveness of romantic affection and loyalty, and most polygynous marriages appear to have had some difficulty in finding a compromise with this requirement. Various devices were invented by individual Mormon husbands, but it is not certain that many achieved a comfortable solution for the dilemma, and there are indications that some of these men experienced a sense of relief on the abandonment of the practice.

Role conflicts are also involved in movements of persons from one culture to another, and from one socioeconomic level to another within the same culture. The social climber is often uncomfortably aware that he is not free of the social control of persons in the level which he is attempting to desert, not entirely free of the mannerisms which reflect that background. He may also be aware that many persons in the level to which he aspires recognize his origins, and he may therefore be uncertain of how much affectation he should attempt.

Persons with so little stability in their backgrounds that they have had little opportunity to acquire any consistent set of roles may have a confusing and bewildering social experience wherever they go. In the two illustrative cases cited in the present Chapter, errors of many kinds resulted in virtually complete failure in the whole life experiences and were the result of backgrounds which failed to give them the equipment necessary to find suitable roles.

Persons do not invent many of their actions or styles of behavior individually. These are defined for them, taught to them, and organized for them by the groups to which they belong. Furthermore, organized social pressure is continually exerted to hold persons within their appropriate behavior styles. Each person has his own set of roles; never exactly the same combination possessed by any other, these roles constitute a major aspect of the person as we recognize him.[33]

[33] In present-day civilization there are, of course, great numbers of inconsistencies in society. The above discussion only briefly shows the connection between these and the role differentiations of persons. A considerable literature exists in the fields of sociology, anthropology, psychology, psychiatry, and related fields describing and attempting to analyze the general relations between culture and personality. Among the prominent writers in this field are: Margaret Mead, Ruth Benedict, Clyde Kluckhohn, A. Kardiner, Ralph Linton, Cora DuBois, A. I. Hallowell, John Gillin, Jules and Zunia Henry, Gregory Bateson, Wayne Dennis, E. H. Erikson, Weston LaBarre, Geoffrey Gorer, and others. Representative examples of this literature may be found in C. Kluckhohn and H. A. Murray (eds.), *Personality, In Nature, Society, and Culture* (New York: Alfred A. Knopf, 1948), and in *Culture and Personality,* Proceedings of an Interdisciplinary Conference held under the auspices of the Viking Fund, New York, 1949. On the whole this research trend has been too little influenced by conventional scientific social psychology, and so is not to any great extent based on objective research methods. The field is unsettled and is still in the crude exploratory stages. For a thoughtful criticism of the methods and some of the conclusions of investigators in this field, see A. R. Lindesmith and A. L. Strauss, "A Critique of Culture-Personality Writings," *American Sociological Review,* XV, No. 5 (1950), 587-600.

SELECTED REFERENCES

GUETZKOW, HAROLD (ed.). *Groups, Leadership, and Men.* Pittsburgh: Carnegie
    Press, 1951. Research contributions on various aspects of individual and group
    behavior and leadership.
JENNINGS, HELEN H. *Leadership and Isolation* (2d. ed.). New York: Longmans,
    Green & Co., Inc., 1950. A sociometric study of primary group formation and
    leadership status.

Chapter 13

THE NEUROTIC ROLE

To a certain extent it may be profitable to conceive of some neurotic behavior in terms of special roles or complications of roles.[1] Apart from actual physical defectiveness there occur in many persons a variety of conditions symptomatic of illness and incapacity which have no detectable physiological basis. These neurotic persons may reveal their condition by any of a number of symptoms which appear to be connected with dissatisfaction, unhappiness, and uncertainty. Some feel anxious for no definite reason and have a sense of being small, helpless, inadequate, and deserted in a hostile world. Along with these feelings there may be such symptoms as trembling, nausea, headaches and other pains, nightmares, memory lapses, loss of appetite and weight, dizziness, tension, excessive perspiration, heart palpitations, frequent crying, and fatigue.

The Relation of Neurosis to Conflict

In many cases such symptoms appear to be connected with some sort of chronic problem or crisis the solution of which is beyond the ability of the person involved, and from which open retreat is, for one reason or another, impossible. Thus the neurotic role may be conceived as an indirect and unsatisfactory reaction of the person who can neither surmount his problems nor directly withdraw, but who is suspended in a highly unpleasant state of conflict. A student, for example, who is unable to obtain high grades because of poor preparation and division of interests may be under strong pressure from his family to perform well in college. If

---

[1] It is not the writer's intention in this Chapter to survey the whole literature on neurosis, which is, of course, too large and insufficiently unified to handle here. Some of the behavior which is called neurosis, however, appears to be causally connected with certain defects of social interaction, and there is justification in some cases for the concept of a neurotic role which, poor choice that it may be, nevertheless plays a function in the life of the person who adopts it.

he cannot bring himself to defy the family pressure, he may experience this type of inescapable conflict which he will find highly unpleasant, and perhaps intolerable. A business man whose further advancement is blocked by uncontrolled circumstances may find himself under pressure from his wife to achieve higher rank and income to enable her to keep up with her friends in the competition for status. A housewife may be pulled two ways by her loyalty to her own mother and by her affection for her husband who is antagonistic to the mother. A soldier may experience a conflict between his desire to survive and his wish to maintain his reputation for manliness, courage, and loyalty to his fellow-soldiers. Each of these conflicts has two possible ways out, but for some persons both ways are inacceptable, at least as direct pathways of escape.

The neurotic role offers a possibility of indirect escape from chronic conflicts of this type. A housewife can skip her visits to her mother if she can appear to be ill. Calm, deliberate faking of illness is of course possible and doubtless often tried, but for many it is not a satisfactory device either because of the difficulty of dissembling in a convincing manner and or because for some it involves a troubled conscience. A genuine illness or incapacity may be a welcome relief, providing a means of escape with no accompanying sense of guilt. But such a clear-cut excuse is not always available when needed. What can be done, however, with no great peril to a sense of sincerity, is to watch for emerging symptoms and almost unwittingly nurse them along by overwork, lack of sleep, and the kind of concentration on minor discomforts which magnifies them. By such assumption of a neurotic role it is possible to pursue sincerely and to achieve a useful incapacity which provides a mentally tolerable means of escape from the conflict.

Thus the neurotic can fail in school and not suffer the same degree of reproach from his family, can excuse to his wife his inability to gain promotion and higher income, can fail in a battle without being accused of cowardice, and in various other ways can fail, not make the grade, and still avoid the same degree of guilt which would be inescapable without the symbols of incapacity. In his life the neurotic role thus plays a function. The benefits of this can be exploited in various ways so that the person may become increasingly committed to and dependent on this method of handling difficulties. The neurotic role thus has the possibility of becoming a sort of career.

Animal "Neurosis."—In pursuit of supporting evidence for this conflict basis of neurosis there has been considerable research on the experimental production of "neuroses" in animals by placing them in some conflict situation from which there is no escape. Pavlov himself initiated the investigation by first training dogs to react in different ways to two separate stimuli, then gradually altering the stimuli in the direction of similarity until the dogs could no longer distinguish them. Having an overpowering impulse to choose from previous conditioning, and being completely unable to choose since discrimination was impossible, the dogs trembled, had fits, became immobile, and in other ways showed exceptional discomfort. Variations of this experiment have been tried on rats, pigs, sheep, cats, and other animals, with essentially the same kind of findings.[2]

Apart from minor differences of interpretation of findings, there is little doubt about the objective results of this kind of research. Inescapable conflict clearly causes extreme physical symptoms of an abnormal character in the experimental animals. There is, however, a difference of opinion concerning the use of the term *neurosis* to characterize this reaction. In general, the experimenters appear to have proceeded with the assumption that the animal reaction is the same phenomenon as human neurosis and thereby overlooked the complexity of some forms of human neurotic behavior. As one critic states:

. . . a cat has within its repertoire only a few and relatively primitive patterns even of "normal" behavior; it eats, drinks, copulates, explores, purrs, chases objects or fights; its "neurosis" can therefore consist only of correspondingly simple deviations in the form of self-starvation, sensory hyperaesthesias, rudimentary phobias, compulsions, regressions, fixations, and other relatively elemental behavorial aberrations. Although the pattern of these phenomena are highly suggestive of their more complex symbolic and persistent counterparts in the human, nevertheless, no cat that I have observed thus far has had the imagery to solve its anxiety by, let us say, strutting, growling, or dressing like Mussolini in overreaction to feline feelings of frustration and inferiority. Similarly, a cat will show experimental behavior abnormalities only if a relatively elemental drive, such as hunger, be frustrated or made internally conflictful.[3]

---

[2] For a general review of the experiments, see H. S. Liddell, "Conditioned Reflex Method and Experimental Neurosis." Chap. xii in J. McV. Hunt, *Personality and the Behavior Disorders* (New York: The Ronald Press Co., 1944).

[3] J. H. Masserman, "Psychobiologic Dynamisms in Behavior," *Psychiatry*, V (1942), 341-48.

Another investigator expresses doubt concerning the value of designating these animal reactions as neurosis.[4] Some writers would classify as experimental neurosis any behavior, produced experimentally, which allows the inclusion under this heading of these audiogenic attacks, as well as, presumably, seizures induced by metrazol injection, electro-shock, and dietary deficiency, and any abnormal behavior produced by surgical means which resembles an "abnormal state in man." Without attempting to decide just what behavior of a rat may resemble human behavior it would seem that such a definition strains the meaning of the term confusingly beyond the limits of its original connotation.

The same investigator cites a study in which blasts of air made rats dash about violently, become convulsed, then passive so that they could be molded into almost any position.[5] This study was seized upon as having great significance for "neurotic behavior in human beings." It was soon pointed out, however, that the same response could be elicited in completely untrained rats by a few seconds of simple auditory stimulation. Other reports corroborated both the description of the attacks and the fact that intense auditory stimulation, rather than conflict, was the invariable antecedent of the behavior. The consensus of opinion was that this abnormal response pattern did not fit into the classical category of "experimental neurosis" described by Pavlov and Liddell.

Thus there appears to be much justification for withholding judgment on whether the "neurosis" as produced in the laboratory animal is the same kind of phenomenon connoted by the term applied to human behavior. It seems certain that the far more elaborate nature of the human neuroses is subject to investigation only in the human.

THE RELATION OF NEUROSIS TO FEAR

The common combat neurosis of soldiers is related to fear of injury or death in battle on the one hand, and the conflicting social pressure to appear to be manly, brave, and loyal on the other. Much of what was termed "shell-shock" during the First World War, and "battle fatigue" during the Second World War, actually has turned out to be neither shock nor fatigue but only the reaction of soldiers to this type of conflict.[6] In the descriptions provided in the re-

[4] F. W. Finger, in Hunt, *op. cit.*, p. 416n.

[5] *Ibid.*, pp. 415-16.

[6] Such relatively trivial symptoms as nail biting, restlessness, and enuresis are sometimes considered to reflect neurosis, but these have a function less clear than

search literature the symptoms vary and may include trembling, weakness, crying, nightmares, and even apparent paralysis, but they all have in common the implication of physical disqualification for further combat, for the time being at least, without the penalty of being thought of as a coward and deserter of comrades.

Objective study, based on various types of information, has shown that measured symptoms of neurosis increase with proximity to battle.[7] The number of symptoms is large for men in combat, larger as the length of time in combat increases, and extremely high for combat veterans who are on the way to new battles. Men who were diagnosed as neurotics were found to have shown tendencies in this direction on attitude test performances given at an earlier time. In general, these tests revealed that the incipient neurotic had a greater than average tendency to claim poor physical condition, to report low spirits most of the time, to feel that he was unfairly drafted, to feel that his particular task in the Army was not worth while, and to be unsure of himself. The neurotics also reported with greater than ordinary frequency such reactions as "anxiety symptoms" (nervousness, insomnia, tremors, sweaty hands, stomach disturbances); "psychosomatic symptoms" (including fainting spells, nightmares, shortness of breath, pressure in the head); and "health problems" (dizzy spells, accelerated heartbeat, nail biting, cold sweats, sick headaches).[8]

Although fear is normal and, according to reports, experienced by virtually all soldiers before a battle, there are indications that the fearful state of mind is developed more in those who become neurotic. Soldiers diagnosed as neurotic were found to have had more fears in childhood than did a representative sample of soldiers. In order of frequency, the subject matter of childhood fears remembered and reported by the neurotic soldiers were: high places, being shut up in a room or closet, thunderstorms, falling, sharp knives, being with girls, strangers, walking by a graveyard at midnight, large animals, and the Devil.[9] It is apparent that the tendency to have fears is generalized to a considerable extent; that

---

that of the greater disabilities. It is conceivable that in many children these may be of minor significance, and, in fact, no more than habits which the child never tried to correct. When the incentive is keen, the child may sometimes suddenly take responsibility for self-improvement—high school dating has ended nail biting and electric devices have spectacularly cured enuresis.

[7] Samuel Stouffer, *et al.*, *Studies in Social Psychology During World War II* (Princeton: Princeton University Press, 1949), II, 445 ff.

[8] *Ibid.*, pp. 414 ff.

[9] *Ibid.*, I, 138.

is, persons who fear one or two things tend after a while to fear a range of things.

The neurotic role involves a degree of isolation from group bonds. The neurosis itself is a kind of desertion and it is possible particularly for those persons who have not experienced a full degree of solidarity with a group. To be closely bound in friendship and loyalty is to be unwilling to give in to fear that might involve desertion. Furthermore, fear that is shared is less terrible than fear experienced by one alone. The soldier who knows that his comrades have the same kind of apprehension that he is experiencing, and perceives that they nevertheless maintain an air of calm confidence, knows that he can do the same. He also knows that to quit or desert in any way because of fear would not be justified, since each of his comrades is resisting the same temptation although their situation is as perilous as his.

The neurotic can desert if he can convince others and himself that he is essentially different, or is in different circumstances, from his comrades. By his neurotic symptoms the deserter tries to imply lack of responsibility for the action. He claims loss of control over his actions: "I went haywire," or "I went to pieces." His professions of weakness, loss of memory, and other inabilities which would indicate that he was not well and not himself, imply that he deserves no blame because of his betrayal of his comrades.

It is not always easy to manufacture a fiction and then believe it completely. The neurotic does fairly well at this because he has had, in most cases, a lifetime of practice in the art. By practiced rationalization he achieves a comforting degree of sincerity. But sincerity is not necessarily an "all-or-none" affair. There are indications in a number of cases that despite his insistence on the reality of his condition the self-deception is not as complete as the neurotic would desire. The true casualities may not care to dwell on the circumstances of their becoming wounded, but they do not show the frantic effort of the neurotic to keep the whole matter out of discussion and memory.

As the present author has previously stated:

The claim of amnesia may in some cases be exaggerated. It represents an effort to deny or to forget, but the uneasiness with which a patient approaches the subject of his troubles indicates incompleteness of achievement in forgetting. Organic ailments aid the rationalization and are thus sometimes claimed insistently in the face of denials by medical officers. Some of the neurotics, returned home for a rest, have a guilty sense of being talked about and express envy of those who have lost limbs, implying that the latter had undeniably legitimate reasons for being excused from further fighting.[10]

In spite of the degree of detachment or isolation, the neurotic retains a degree of sociability; otherwise he would experience no conflict. The less sociable schizoid can evade responsibilities with indifference and does not need disability symptoms for excuses. But the responsiveness of the neurotic is a central aspect of his difficulty.

> . . . the conflict that produces the neurosis is a mental torment which reflects the external conflict of social forces. On the one hand there is a social process which, through isolation or other abnormality of social experience during the years of development, left the person in a weak and inadequate condition to meet crises. And on the other hand, there is the present social force of collective expectation which makes it extremely difficult to run away from the crisis, problem, or danger. The pressure is strong to remain loyal to the group, not to let the other men down, nor desert one's friends and comrades and thereby increase the danger to them.[11]

When morale is high, this detachment from the group is reduced, and the response to conditions of hardship and danger is in terms of proud toughness rather than neurotic weakness. During the Second World War the 6,000 American soldiers holding the bleak, storm-swept Aleutian island of Shemya—a barren patch of low tundra two by four miles in extent—had an exceptionally low tendency to neurosis. Their average daily rate of confinement to a hospital or quarters for neuropsychiatric reasons was 0.1 per cent— far lower than the 0.6 per cent for the total Army. Dr. Charles H. Jones, then a major in the Army Medical Corps and the only psychiatrist on the island for eighteen months, accounts for this record on the grounds of high morale among the soldiers. The first landing party lived in tents, and boasted to later arrivals, "You should have been here when it was rough." To have gone through any hardship was the basis of personal prestige. A soldier who struggled through a severe storm only to find his tent leaking would exclaim to his tent mates, "Sure rough, but I made it." Prestige rose with the amount of time spent on the island and the number of harsh experiences. Each member was willing to remain on the island and do his best as long as the others had to do the same. The psychiatrist points out,

[10] R. E. L. Faris, *Social Disorganization* (New York: The Ronald Press Co., 1948), p. 257.
[11] *Ibid.*, p. 257.

In contrast to the point of view prevalent in many training camps in the United States it simply was not socially acceptable to be evacuated from the island with a mental illness . . . this attitude . . . may be regarded as a positive factor in keeping a number of soldiers with minor neurotic symptoms from seeking disposition through neuropsychiatric channels.[12]

NEUROSIS AS A CAREER

A role which is found to play a lasting function in the person's activity may be nurtured and expanded into an enduring organization and in some cases may even become a central aspect of character. The person who discovers early in his life that he can find his way through or around difficulties by neurotic pathways may develop a general and permanent role as a neurotic, and in this sense may make a career out of his neurosis. The longer he keeps the pattern, the more he is committed to it. To escape would require the construction of a complex new set of habits, the building of new relations with other persons, and the loss of the old reputation. Such a change is too great to occur commonly; hence the well-developed neurotic is likely to keep his neurotic role.

Cameron has shown how such a pattern becomes rooted in a system of personal habits and interpersonal relations:

The influence of role-taking is as important in organizing and perpetuating hysterical inactivation as it is in organizing normal behavior. We have seen the effects upon normal behavior of adopting the role of a devoted student or a conventional mother. If circumstances lead a man to adopt the role, let us say, of a disabled person as his own, then the close organization of his behavior into a culturally defined pattern will exclude whatever seems to contradict it. Once he has taken such a role publicly he has committed himself, in others' eyes and in his own, to renounce every inconsistency which he or others recognize. Moreover, if he gains privileges and exemptions in the role of a disabled man, he cannot abandon the role without endangering his community status and his self-respect—unless, of course, he is publicly cured, and this is one of many explar ations for the miraculous public cure.[13]

Cameron has further illustrated the character of two other forms the neurotic role may take—the hysterical seizure and compulsive self-control.

The hysterical seizure itself represents social role-taking which the patient has at one time rejected and disowned but, often because of marked ambivalence, has not successfully repressed. It may be the re-enactment of

[12] Charles H. Jones, forthcoming paper in *Diseases of the Nervous System.*
[13] Norman Cameron, *The Psychology of Behavior Disorders: A Biosocial Interpretation* (Boston: Houghton Mifflin Co., 1947), p. 347.

a role once played in a socially shared context, or it may have been previously elaborated only in fantasy. Its pathological character consists in its intensity, the remarkable exclusion of responsiveness to the immediate social context, and the alteration of the seizure phase with prolonged free intervals which exclude recall of the behavior during the attacks. The whole clinical picture is one of exaggeration and distortion of the contradictions and discrepancies in social role-taking which normal persons exhibit in their everyday life. . . .

A second example is compulsive self-control . . . the patient holding himself in check by formulating unnecessarily strict and meticulous rules for his personal conduct and meting out to himself harsh and humiliating penalties for the slightest infraction. At the same time such a patient may react to this treatment of himself with apprehension and sometimes even with pleading. In other words, he is alternating in his own self-reactions between the culturally defined social role of the hypercritical, vindictive, domineering parent and the reciprocal social role of the anxious, guilty, penitent child.

This alternation of social role-taking does not involve the kind of break in behavioral continuity or the unresponsiveness to the immediate social context so characteristic of the hysterical seizure. Instead, it presents us with the picture of a person who has not succeeded in integrating his reciprocal roles, acquired in childhood, into a unified system of self-regulation such as the average adult exhibits. The roles of unforgiving parent and erring child continue as reciprocal systems of self-reaction which perpetuate in adulthood the expensive fiction of a parent-child struggle, in place of . . . more mature techniques.[14]

In many if not all cases, the neurotic pattern starts in childhood, and grows into a general way of life. The discovery of a role that works is in part an individual act of invention or of generalization from minor incidents. It may thus occur in various types of families, and need not occur to more than one member of a family. In fact the presence of one neurotic in a family may operate as a factor to decrease the possibility of others taking the role since the neurotic unloads a part of his responsibility on the others.

It is therefore not to be expected that a general type of family, like the broken home, would have much relation to the generation of neurosis. In general, the literature on broken homes contains little satisfactory evidence of such a relation, and such crude relationship as does appear in the figures often turns out, on further analysis, to be misleading.[15]

[14] Norman Cameron, "Role Concepts in Behavior Pathology," *American Journal of Sociology*, LV, No. 5 (1950), 464-67.

[15] See R. E. L. Faris, *op. cit.*, pp. 272-74, for an illustration of the disappearance of the apparent relation between broken homes and juvenile delinquency after critical analysis of the statistics. Some other careful and direct studies of behavior of children from broken homes find no significant relationships—see for example B.

Studies of the relationship of birth order to neurotic behavior have been similarly unproductive of useful results. The suspicion that only children or oldest children are more likely to be neurotic finds little support in the figures, and there is little other indication that there is any marked tendency to a particular style of behavior among middle or youngest children. Some apparent, though not large, relationships appear because of factors associated with birth order. First-born children have parents who are younger than those of later-born children. Since in most families the income increases for a time with age of father, later children may have less experience of low income than first-born children. Any general comparison of fourth, fifth, sixth, and later births with only and oldest children is distorted by the fact that large families—large enough to have a sixth-born child—are more common among the poor, the less educated, the foreign-born, and rural populations so that the differences may be due to the latter factors rather than to birth order itself.[16] Furthermore, in the United States there is no uniform standard role for children of first, middle, and last births. It is conceivable that in upper-class nineteenth century England, where such standards did prevail, some behavior differences might have been revealed statistically.

Sears has reported results of a study of birth order and personality traits in a sample of Iowa children and produced some indications of differences between first and second children. Second children were found to be somewhat less dependent and more sociable, possibly because the mothers had the advantage of more experience by the time the second child was born and so treated this child more casually than they had the first. But the relationships shown between birth order and personality traits were small, the number of cases small and therefore of little reliability. The investigators stated that the number of uncontrolled variables was "greater than one might wish," and that the study "was a pilot study, with inevitable inadequacies." [17]

The role of favorite child, a victim of maternal overprotection, is sometimes conceived of as a starting point for neurosis. Objective evidence of the significance of this factor in such developments as the schizoid personality is abundant (see Chapter 14), but a di-

Silverman, "The Behavior of Children from Broken Homes," *American Journal of Orthopsychiatry*, V (1935), 11-18.

[16] For a valuable presentation of such data, see chap. xiii, "Sib Relationships," in Jessie S. Bernard, *American Family Behavior* (New York: Harper & Bros., 1942).

[17] Robert R. Sears, "Ordinal Position in the Family as a Psychological Variable," *American Sociological Review*, XV, No. 3 (1950), 397-401.

rect attempt to observe this factor in the neurotics of the Army failed to show any relationship at all.[18] A large sample of soldiers were given tests to reveal neurotic traits and background factors. Comparisons were made of the psychoneurotic soldiers with a representative sample of soldiers, and also with a selected, "best adjusted" group, with the least tendency to neurosis. To measure the effect of the sense of being a favorite, one item asked, "Were you your mother's favorite child?" The possible replies were listed so that the soldier could check the appropriate one. The results, shown as percentages of each type of soldier giving each answer, are set forth in the following table.

Type of Answer	Best Adjusted Per Cent	Cross Section Per Cent	Psychoneurotics Per Cent
I was an only child in my family	8	8	8
An older brother or sister was the favorite	5	8	8
A younger brother or sister was the favorite	9	9	11
I think I was the favorite	20	17	15
There were no favorites	56	54	51
No answer	2	4	7
	100	100	100

The neurotic soldiers had, in fact, slightly less tendency to believe that they had been especially favored by their mothers, but on the whole the principal conclusion to be drawn from the above table is that in this respect there is little difference between neurotics and other soldiers. A further analysis indicates that there is no important difference in these results when further classified according to age, marital status, or degree of education.

Army research, however, did succeed in showing that there were definite indications in childhood of a neurotic tendency. The soldiers who were classified as psychoneurotics reported in far greater numbers than those classified "best adjusted" a history of having been a sickly child. The neurotic soldiers also reported more of a tendency in childhood to be alone rather than to associate with other children, and during their teen-age and young adult years to have had fewer dates with girls than did others of their age. They also reported in greater than average numbers a dislike of fighting, and an avoidance of bodily contact sports, in childhood years. In short, the evidence from this investigation points to a childhood tendency to partial isolation and to the development of a weak, sickly, cowardly type of personality.[19]

[18] *Studies in Social Psychology During World War II,* Vol. I, pp. 135-36.
[19] *Ibid.,* pp. 133, 142-43.

Weinberg has published a case which appears to illustrate this role in satisfactory detail. The infantryman had been in the army for two and a half years, and had been in or near combat for about three months before experiencing the neurotic breakdown at the age of twenty-three. In his own words:

My father is a welder, and he makes enough money to support us, but he didn't get along so well with my mother. My mother said she was promised to him so she married him. She wasn't in the house very much. She went out with her friends, "women" friends, and drank a lot. They fought a lot, and I didn't like to see them. I went outside and took long walks. When I was fifteen . . . my mother . . . died. I began wandering around and didn't go to school for a week. I wanted to be by myself. I cried, too, but I didn't let anybody else see me.

I've always been alone. I used to play with my sister, but I grew out of that. I stuck around home or went for long walks. There was nobody that I wanted to go with. I never belonged to a club or had a real friend. When I came home from school, I didn't play ball or other sports. I didn't know how. I did little jobs for my father or sat home and listened to the radio. There were three boys who lived on my street, and they wanted to know me. So one day, they started throwing snowballs at me and then tried to make my acquaintance. I got to know them, but didn't have much to do with them. They came around only when they wanted something. Money or something like that. I got onto them, and I wouldn't give them anything. People always wanted something from me.

I quit school in the eighth grade. . . . I got a job through my father in the factory, and the boss let me alone so I could do my work. When anybody lets me alone, I'm all right. When they start to bother me, I feel like fighting. I only know one girl. I got to know her when I was eighteen. She was fourteen, a neighbor.[20]

In this illustration it is evident that there is characteristically no maternal overprotection, but that the other characteristics of the preneurotic child—the partial isolation, the avoidance of violent conflict, the fears are present. In the experience of battle his fears became so overwhelming that other men "got on my nerves." His memories of being under fire consisted largely of being angry and scared, and of wanting to get away. When he was brought wounded to the hospital he woke up shaking and nervous—a condition which could be maintained as a comfortable method of escape from further combat and mental conflict.

[20] S. Kirson Weinberg, "The Combat Neuroses," *American Journal of Sociology,* LI, No. 5 (1946), 465-71.

Character Patterns: Reactions to Crises

The neurotic role is functional in the sense that it provides a means by which the person can escape a type of situation which he finds intolerable. It constitutes one type of reaction to a crisis, a type of reaction which becomes for the person a characteristic way of meeting further crises of the same kind. As long as it provides a reasonably satisfactory route of evasion for him, it is likely to be retained and perhaps extended to an ever increasing range of related crises, and to become a general character trend.

Some attention has been given in recent years to the study of other types of reaction to crisis, and the circumstances in which they become adopted as general patterns of character. One hypothesis which has been popular and influential is the frustration-aggression concept, advanced by Freud and elaborated by Dollard, Miller, and others.[21] In essence, this notion is that the "primary and characteristic" and presumably instinctive reaction to any kind of blocking of activity or interference with the attainment of a goal consists of some kind of effort to injure the person who is believed to be responsible for the frustration, or, if this cannot be done for any reason, to injure someone else as a substitute for the offender. In some statements of the hypothesis there is an assumption of a universal causal relation between frustration and aggression—that is, it is held that all frustration produces aggression and that all aggression results from frustration. Not all persons who find some value in the concept, however, embrace it in this extreme form.[22]

Some experimental research has been attempted in connection with this hypothesis, and has succeeded in producing indications of aggressive thoughts following artificially induced frustrations. In one study, for example, six students were paid to spend a period of twenty-four hours without sleep, undergoing certain tests for part of the time, and being exposed to conditions of frustration which had no apparent connection with the experiences they were

[21] John Dollard, *et al., Frustration and Aggression* (New Haven: Yale University Press, 1939).

[22] In the publication referred to in the previous footnote, there occurs a definition which is sufficiently circular to make the proposition true: aggression is defined as "that response which follows frustration, reduces only the secondary, frustration-produced instigation, and leaves the strength of the original instigation unaffected," and frustration is defined as "that condition which exists when a goal-response suffers interference." By means of such unrestricted tautologies any proposition may be made to seem true, even though it is, at the same time, meaningless and untestable.

supposed to be having.[23]   Certain promises were arbitrarily broken, smoking was abruptly banned, conversation was suddenly forbidden at a time when it was lively and interesting.   Recorded remarks during the experiment and in interviews afterward established that aggressive thoughts occurred, although no actual overt aggression took place and no student even tried to get away from the experiment or to modify its conditions.   Some of the aggression was in the form of jokes, and possibly should not be taken seriously as aggression.   Some of the aggressiveness, moreover, may have been the result, not of the frustration itself, but of unnecessarily tormenting gestures of the experimenter, such as his continuing to smoke in their presence after the students had been forbidden to smoke.[24]

The study thus has its imperfections, but few interpreters would deny that it is reasonable to suppose that some of the feelings of aggression may have been in part the consequences of frustrations during this trial.   Neither this nor any other experiment, however, has shown that aggression is the only or the instinctive or the primary response to frustration.   In fact, it is still more plausible to suppose that there are various possible reactions to frustration and that none of them is instinctive or basic in any ordinary sense but all are instead learned in ordinary conscious experience by persons who are working through their problems of everyday life.[25]

A study by Fredericksen of responses of certain school children to frustration has found that these children do not become aggres-

---

[23] Robert R. Sears, Carl I. Hovland, and Neal E. Miller, "Minor Studies of Aggression: I. Measurement of Aggressive Behavior," *Journal of Psychology*, IX (1940), 277-81.

[24] In the army research on morale previously cited, the investigators found that deprivation *as such* of various comforts and privileges was of much less significance than *relative deprivation*—a concept which they found useful for explaining "a wide variety of otherwise anomalous data relative to attitudes of soldiers toward induction, toward officers, toward promotions, etc.   The point is that a respondent implicitly or explicitly is comparing his own situation to that of others and his responses as to his own situation will vary depending on the reference group or reference category most relevant to him at the time of making this comparison."

[25] It has become in certain quarters a vogue to consider frustration an undesirable aspect of experience and the basis of abnormal complications such as discussed above. Out of this has grown a child-training policy of protecting infants and small children against frustrations.   This notion overlooks the obvious fact that frustration is an utterly inescapable part of life.   Consciousness itself is an aspect of frustration, as shown in Chapter 5, and a completely unfrustrated person would be an automaton without human nature.   The strategy of dealing with frustrations is not a matter of avoiding them, but of selecting the best response in each particular frustrating situation.   Persons who find life insufficiently interesting may devise games to introduce a certain amount of temporary frustration into their experience, and if their skills so build up as to reduce the frustration too much, they may add new ones, such as the traps and bunkers in golf courses and the balk lines on billiard tables.

sive, but rather developed a condition of "submissive negativism"—crying, drawing away, running away, and the like.[26] This was shown in a comparison of children in schoolrooms in which there were different amounts of restriction and dominating control by the teachers. Some interpreters would expect that the children would show displacement of repressed aggression, but there was no evidence of such a reaction—no scapegoat behavior in which innocent persons or objects were made the target of aggressive activities.

Ellsworth Faris has observed, in the course of a study of student autobiographical documents, some sixteen different reactions to frustration: daydreaming, delusion, substitution, sublimation, devaluation, projection (attributing the desire to others), suppression, repression, abandonment, obsession, resignation, despair, suicide, rage, fury, hysteria, and aggression.[27] The list is not necessarily complete nor the categories exclusive, but other investigators have made lists of similar length and character. Cameron lists the following types of reaction to crisis with certain subclasses not included here: direct aggression, simple withdrawal, fear and anxiety, attention-getting, identification, compensation, rationalization, projection, insulation (self-isolation), negativism, regression, repression, and fantasy.[28] A similar attempt at classification is found in another modern text, in which the following types of response to a crisis are presented as having a tendency to be dynamically interrelated, to depend on the severity of frustration, and to be not necessarily bad.[29] In the list are: intensification of effort, reorganization of perception of the problem, substitution of goals, aggression, regression, withdrawal, repression, sublimation, rationalization, projection, autism, and identification.

It appears reasonable that these types of response to a crisis, frustration, or failure may be regarded as devices adopted by the person for the function they play in dealing with the problem. They are learned in experience, in many instances early in life. The young infant, for example, discovers that when certain discomforts become intolerable he may cry and obtain relief through the aid of other persons. He then may generalize this device so that crying becomes employed in a wider variety of difficult situ-

[26] N. Fredericksen, "The Effects of Frustration on Negativistic Behavior of Young Children," *Journal of Genetic Psychology*, LXI (1942), 203-26.

[27] Ellsworth Faris, "Some Results of Frustration," *Sociology and Social Research*, XXXI, No. 2 (1946), 87-92.

[28] Norman Cameron, *The Psychology of Behavior Disorders: a Biosocial Interpretation, op. cit.*, pp. 141-86.

[29] David Krech and Richard S. Crutchfield, *Theory and Problems of Social Psychology* (New York: McGraw-Hill Book Co., Inc., 1948), pp. 53 ff.

ations, and is useful to get out of nearly all his problems. If, in later years, it no longer works as effectively as it did in infancy, he may transform it to such related gestures as sulking or hypochondria. To the extent that he comes to depend on such a method of evading problems, he may weaken his ability to find more direct solutions and may thereby become ever more dependent on the indirect and less satisfactory method.

Investigators at the Iowa Child Welfare Research Station have shown experimentally that such patterns in small children may be altered by skilled training.[30] The subjects consisted of 82 children (38 boys and 44 girls) aged three to six years enrolled in a preschool laboratory. Their average intelligence was high, with a mean I.Q. of 122. Any differences from a representative population of small children were thus probably in the direction of superiority.

Two tests were devised to reveal the characteristic reaction of each child to a problem. The first, the puzzle box test, resembled a jigsaw puzzle problem. The child was shown a small, lidded, colored box in which were fitted ten small colored figures of irregular shape, one-half inch thick, representing such objects as a sailboat and an engine. The experimenter removed these figures and invited the child to put them back into the box so that the lid could be closed again. The task was considered to be difficult even with the time allowance of fifteen minutes.

The second test, the weighted box test, consisted of a five-sided box, heavily encumbered with sixty to ninety pounds of adjustable weights. The box was placed in the middle of a room upside down over a group of attractive toys. The children were shown that the toys lay under the box, and were told that they could play with the toys if they could get them. Ten minutes were allowed for the solution.

During the period of the child's trial concerning these problems, his behavior was classified as mature or immature. Persistent effort in the face of a difficult but not impossible task without requests for help and without loss of composure was considered to indicate a mature type of response. Immature responses were of five types: (1) giving up attempts to solve the puzzle box in less than five minutes or to solve the weighted box in less than two minutes; (2) requesting help during more than one half the total time of the test;

[30] Mary E. Keister and Ruth Updegraff, "A Study of Children's Reactions to Failure and an Experimental Attempt to Modify Them," *Child Development*, VIII (1937), 241-48.

(3) manifesting destructive behavior; (4) making more than two rationalizations; and (5) evidencing exaggerated emotional responses.[31] On the basis of these test records, fifteen children (18 per cent of the group) were classified as immature in type of response.

Twelve of the fifteen immature children were then subjected to a program of training which had the purpose of teaching them to meet difficulty in the more mature ways. They were shown, through carefully arranged experiences, which kinds of responses were most likely to bring success or satisfaction—that is, they were shown the functional value of the mature responses. This was done by means of a series of problems, graded in difficulty, which allowed the children to advance in problem-solving ability and to perceive their own progress. One person conducted the training program in periods which varied from eight to thirty-three minutes according to the difficulty of the problems and the responses of the children. Six weeks were required to subject all twelve children to the training.

Both objective and subjective estimates found that a gradual improvement toward the mature responses took place during the course of the program. At the conclusion of the period the children were again tested on similar, but not identical, puzzles. Their types of responses were compared with those they had used before the training period, and with the types of responses shown on a re-test of an equal number of children, not in the trained group, who during the initial tests had shown some immature responses.

The results indicated marked success of the training effort. On the before-and-after-training comparison, attempts to solve the problem alone rose from an average of about eight and one-half minutes to over eleven minutes, and a show of interest from about six to eleven minutes. Amount of time spent in asking for help declined slightly, and time spent asking for someone else to solve the problem declined from over three and one-half minutes to about one-half minute. Rationalizing and whining declined by

[31] The observations in detail give no support to the notion that aggression is the primary or the most common response to frustration. The major portion of the time spent by the children was devoted to direct attempts to solve the puzzles without aid, and to expressions of interest. For the puzzle box, the mean number of minutes spent in attempts to solve the problem alone was 11.1, and the mean number of minutes spent in showing interest was 10.2. Indications of aggression were much briefer—the average number of minutes spent in destructive behavior was .1, less than one hundredth of the time spent in direct effort. Crying occupied an average of .3, sulking .2, yells .1, and whines .8, and motor manifestations of anger a microscopic .04 of a minute.

about half, and sulking, crying, yelling, destructive behavior, and motor manifestations of anger, which took little time before the training period, now disappeared altogether. No such shift took place in the untrained group of immature children. In this group all changes were slight, but were in the direction of less maturity rather than more. The trained group, in fact, achieved behavior which, by the measurements used, was close to the level of the original group which was judged to be mature.

The fact that the above training effort was neither arduous nor greatly time-consuming, having obtained the results cited in a period of only six weeks, is impressive evidence of the ready modifiability, at this early age, of characteristic approaches to a problem or a crisis. In the course of the experiences of most normal children, there are undoubtedly much the same effects produced, without adult intervention, in the primary group activities in which children see various types of responses and their consequences, and in which they experience the approval and disapproval of the other members of their groups. Anyone who watches children during their preschool and school years is familiar with the frequency with which some of the children abruptly abandon certain rather fundamental ways of response to a crisis, often under the influence of a visible social pressure. Membership in a new group, for example, appears to have this effect in some cases. The boy who discovers his athletic ability and joins a team, gaining a new status and exposing himself to the influence of a coach and of traditions of teamwork, may become greatly transformed in certain of his character tendencies. Some instances of religious conversion, followed by membership in a new kind of group, appear to have an effect as marked. While the possibility of drastic change appears to decline somewhat with advancing age, there is no evidence that character revolutions are completely impossible at any age.

Summary

Persons whose equipment or inclinations are inadequate for the direct solution of the problems they face may discover indirect methods of evasion, such as making the most of a minor illness or disability or constructing some form of weakness which will permit them to escape the degree of responsibility which would otherwise fall on them. The neurotic role, thus, has a function in allowing those who embrace it to withdraw from painful or difficult situations without the full penalty of blame from others or of attacks of conscience.

For such a role to fulfil its function satisfactorily, some kind of concrete evidence is desirable so that the neurotic will not be suspected of malingering. Headaches, fatigue, and such minor symptoms may serve for the housewife, but for the soldier whose fear of battle makes overpowering demands, more crippling and impressive symptoms such as nightmares, loss of memory, and partial paralysis are required. Army research has shown that the tendency to take this latter course has, in most cases, a history extending back to childhood. The essential features appear not to be matters of birth order, nor of maternal overprotection, but rather of circumstances which produce a weak, sickly, cowardly type of personality with a tendency to partial isolation.

The neurotic role is one among many characteristic responses to problems or crises in which a person may find himself. Some attention has been given to the variety of ways in which persons may face crises, and to the circumstances which lead to their becoming habitual. Particular attention has been given to the concept that the primary and natural response to any kind of frustration is some form of aggression. Research indicates that some frustration is followed by aggression, but that this reaction is not necessarily primary, nor even the most common. No uniform list of reactions has become standard since these lists necessarily involve classifications of types of responses, but there appear to be fifteen or twenty common types of reactions to crises of which aggression is only one.

Probably the most common reaction to a problem is to continue to work for a time directly toward a solution. If the solution appears to be impossible or not worth the effort or cost, most normal persons are then capable either of abandoning the effort without conspicuous emotion or of looking for a suitable substitute goal. The "immature" reactions—aggression, rationalization, fits of temper, and the like—probably constitute a very small proportion of the responses of normal persons. Furthermore, as the Iowa experiment cited previously indicates, if skill is applied while the person is in early childhood, habitual responses of the immature sort can readily be removed by training. The immature and the neurotic roles are personal discoveries of inferior ways of meeting a crisis, and may become habitual if depended upon constantly. Circumstances of interaction, in most persons, eliminate these reactions in favor of the more mature and functionally more satisfactory responses to crises.

Selected References

Cameron, Norman. *The Psychology of Behavior Disorders:* a Biosocial Interpretation. Boston: Houghton Mifflin Co., 1947. An important modern work in abnormal psychology, containing interesting observations on the neurotic role.

Maier, Norman R. F. *Frustration: The Study of Behavior Without a Goal.* New York: McGraw-Hill Book Co., Inc., 1949.

Chapter 14

PERSONALITY DISORGANIZATION

NORMAL, ADAPTIVE, and efficient behavior is possible only through a long process of learning in a social organiaztion. By interaction with other persons, each human being actively constructs an organization of his own habits and skills and thus acquires a personality, character, and life organization. Most of the material for his behavior and most of the pattern of the organization is taken directly from the social organizations in which his experience takes place. His selection and combination of the available elements is always unique, but nonetheless socially derived. Personality organization is possible only because of social organization, and thus normal, conventional, cooperative behavior is both cause and effect of society.

An organized personality is one in which the mental content—knowledge, attitudes, habits—are internally consistent to the extent that they provide unity and consistency of character, and are sufficiently consistent with the prevailing standards of conventional behavior to enable the person to behave in harmony with the expectations of the members of the social organizations to which he belongs. Personality disorganization is a certain lack of this consistency and harmony; behavior, no longer having internal consistency and harmony with prevailing standards, becomes unintelligible to other persons and inharmonious to social expectations. The resulting behavior is judged to be eccentric, abnormal, or insane.

Disorganization of the personality occurs when any of the essentials for participation in a social organization are missing or seriously impaired. Knowledge is incomplete concerning what these essentials may be, but it seems clear that they must include: (1) a physiological mechanism of great complexity and without serious neurological or glandular defects; (2) membership in a coherent and functioning social order; and (3) a long history of apprenticeship in primary groups exerting harmonious and consistent influences of informal social control. What the detailed requirements

329

are is a matter for further research—to what extent, for example, can the brain be damaged without effecting personality disorganization? what irregularities of gland functioning are sufficient to impair normality? and how much, and what kind of a family life in infancy and early childhood are indispensable to the acquisition of an adequate personality organization? On such matters there is an amount of useful research information, but the answers are far from final. It is clear, however, that there are a number of times when defects either in the physiological mechanism or in the history of social experience may disorganize the personality and render normal behavior impossible. There is available also a useful amount of information concerning minor defects which appear to cause partial disorganization of the personality; these defects involve behavior which is unconventional or otherwise defective but which does not make the person a complete failure in his actions.

Physiological Defect

In a sense, it may properly be said that the whole mechanism of the body enters into behavior. This is not to say, however, that all parts are of equal importance. Fingernails and hair may function in behavior symbolically to the extent that groups place conventional interpretations on long or colored fingernails, or on scanty hair or the amount of curl in a coiffure. But a broken fingernail or a trimmed scalp does not directly or necessarily impair the efficiency of behavior nor exert any influence toward disorganization except in cases where special and arbitrary significance has been culturally placed on details of these features.[1]

The loss of a few toes may alter certain aspects of personality organization in some instances. An athlete may have to find some new basis of prestige and satisfaction when his running ability is crippled in this manner. Such an experience is ordinarily far from devastating, however, since in most cases the career of an athletic celebrity is a temporary one—a short-distance sprinter might as well give up some toes at the age of twenty-five for his legs are no longer strong enough for championship running anyway. If he holds a record or has a history of famous triumphs, he can and often does reorganize his active athletic role to that of a legendary hero of the past, a remniscing celebrity.

---

[1] Sudden and complete loss of hair by a young woman whose life is built about a role of physical attractiveness and glamour could be somewhat disorganizing. Artificial coiffures, however, constitute an easy method of avoiding such consequences.

Even the loss of arms and legs, which ordinarily enter to a large extent into the actions of the total person, may not in every case fully disorganize the personality. By substitute activities, artificial limbs, and redefinition of roles, the person may compensate to the extent that his actions may continue to be social and normal and in no serious sense disorganized. It is even possible in some cases for a person with amputated hands or with two artificial legs to exploit his condition in such approved ways that it may have certain advantages. By virtue of his artificial hands, a soldier of the Second World War gained fame in a prominent motion picture role and subsequently won national status in a veterans' organization. Also, it is now a familiar fact that the loss of the use of legs is not a serious barrier to obtaining the presidency of the United States. It is virtually a certainty, however, that loss of a nose, without surgical replacement, would constitute a great barrier to political leadership.

Brain Impairment.—The central switchboard and cybernetic mechanism for coordinating the various functions of the body is, of course, of particular importance in the organization and regulation of the personality. Parts of the brain are clearly vital even if other parts appear to be somewhat dispensable. Defects in some of the areas of the brain produce local symptoms such as blindness, inability to speak, or paralysis of certain muscles.

Particular interest has grown during recent years concerning the function of the frontal lobes in the regulation of behavior. Although considerable sections of this brain region can be damaged or removed without loss of life or health, there is evidence to indicate that this part of the brain is required for the most elaborate thought processes—those involved in solving a difficult problem, in planning ahead in situations of uncertainty, in the trial-and-error processes of imagination which seem to be the essence of self-consciousness (see Chapter 7). In many surgical operations involving destruction or severance of tissues in this part of the brain, it has been found that there is no marked loss of intelligence as measured by conventional tests. These tests, however, are largely tests of acquired knowledge and habits which apparently are preserved elsewhere in the central nervous system. Problems which involve novelty appear to require a virtually undamaged frontal region. Goldstein, who has conducted a considerable amount of ingenious research on this point, refers to this function as the "abstract attitude" or the "conceptual attitude."

Analysis has shown that the capacity to assume this abstract attitude, also known as the conceptual attitude, is a prerequisite for normal human behavior: acting voluntarily, taking the initiative, shifting voluntarily from one activity to another, making adequate choices, classifying objects or ideas, grasping the essentials of a complex situation, synthesizing new ideas, reacting correctly to objects or situations with which one is not directly confronted, detaching one's ego from the outer world and reacting in an objectively correct manner. And it is exactly in the problems or tasks which require these abilities that we find patients with gross frontal-lobe lesions defective. Indeed, such a patient may show some peculiarities even in concrete behavior, when the latter becomes dependent on abstract considerations. For example, the patient may be able to recite a series of numbers, but if he is interrupted he cannot continue where he left off; he must start again at the beginning.[2]

Since a considerable proportion of the daily activity of most adults is routine, this problem-solving ability is not constantly used or required and its absence is not always conspicuous. Goldstein describes the experience in connection with neurotic persons and manic-depressives who were normal before the operation with respect to abstract or conceptual thought.

[Patients] are not often confronted with tasks that can be fulfilled only by abstract reasoning. . . .

One patient, who in general seems to live in a normal way, has no relationship with even the closest members of his family; he manifests no interest in his children. Another exists in "a kind of vacuum"; no friendship is possible; one can neither like nor dislike him. Another, a skilled mechanic who is still considered to be an excellent craftsman, has lost the ability to undertake complicated jobs, has stopped studying and seems to have resigned himself to being a routine worker. An unemployed clergyman, who seems to do his work well enough when he occasionally substitutes for a colleague, is not in the least concerned that he is out of work. He is passive, shows poor initiative, depends on his wife to decide everything, does not help at all to plan for the future.[3]

The defects listed above are plausibly connected with a loss of ability for complex imagination. Goldstein studied this loss by means of a test which differs from the conventional intelligence tests by requiring more operation of the active problem-solving imagination employed in situations with a considerable amount of novelty. As he goes on to explain:

[2] Kurt Goldstein, "Prefrontal Lobotomy: Analysis and Warning," *Scientific American*, February, 1950, p. 45.
[3] *Ibid.*, pp. 46-47.

The assumption that lobotomized patients suffered no loss of mental capacity was based on their performance in conventional intelligence tests. Apparently the operation did not reduce their Intelligence Quotient. But is it certain that such tests can reveal the presence of a defect of the kind that might be produced by damage to the frontal lobes? There is good reason to believe that they cannot, for intelligence tests, as usually applied, fail to provide an unambiguous measure of certain important qualities of mind.[4]

In one test, the Goldstein-Scheerer Cubic Test, four colored cubes with diagonal divisions on certain faces were presented to the patient who was instructed to use them to copy a pattern, a simple chevron, for example, which required four diagonal faces to be arranged in a certain way. Normal persons have no trouble doing this, although some of them require some trial-and-error activity. According to Goldstein, however, patients with severe damage of the frontal lobes fail this test. Another test failed by the lobotomy patients is the Goldstein-Stick Test which requires the patient to remember simple geometrical figures outlined with short wooden sticks. According to Goldstein,

> . . . a normal person can reconstruct an open angle with the opening upward just as easily as one with the opening downward; the brain-damaged patient may be able to repeat the latter immediately but be absolutely unable to repeat the former, because, as he explains, the downward angle reminds him of a peaked roof, while the other "is nothing."

In such a case the patient had presumably in his repertoire of habits acquired before the brain damage a concept of the design of a peaked roof, and so required no new problem-solving effort to find this in the pattern of sticks. Having no ready-formed concept for the same design upside-down, however, he was unable to perform even the slight inventive process of finding a conceptualization such as "V for victory" or perhaps "cross-section of a flume" in the simple design.

Hebb, comenting on such findings as these, states:

> The level of intelligence-test performance is a function of the concepts a patient has already developed. Once developed, a concept is retained, despite brain damage that, if it had occurred earlier, would have prevented the development. The patient with brain injury at maturity may continue to think and solve problems normally (in familiar fields), although his intelligence would have been far from normal if a similar injury had happened at birth. The explanation meets the clinical facts and, moreover, is supported

4 *Ibid.*, p. 45.

by the way in which some intellectual capacities are retained in old age when others are disappearing.[5]

Since experiences and requirements for success differ for each person and for each type of life, the loss of this kind of ability does not have the same practical consequences in each case. Cobb illustrates this point with a hypothetical case devised for this purpose:

In understanding such clinical phenomena one must start with the fact that no two human brains are alike. Lesions destroying exactly the same areas in two different brains would not cause exactly similar symptoms. This is because the life experience of each person has conditioned and changed the brain so that it is unique. Take, for example, the effect upon two Swiss brothers of cerebral softenings in the left parieto-temporal regions. One brother lived on the farm in his native valley and carried on with a vocabulary of 2500 words or so. The other became a waiter in hotels, learned five languages, and ended up in a large metropolis. Semantic aphasia in the first would be an inconvenience soon overcome. In the waiter such an aphasia would be an economic catastrophe; he might easily get back enough native German to run a farm, but never could he regain his five learned languages.[6]

It appears proper to conclude from such evidence as the above examples that problem-solving ability requires a fairly undamaged frontal region of the brain, and that persons whose behavior seems little affected by damage in this region are those whose problems have been reduced to routine and who are able to carry on most of their activities on the basis of habit.

Effects of Brain Impairment on Processes of Self-Consciousness. —Since problems of human relations, because of complexity, inadequacy of information, shifting conditions, and other difficulties, are among the most complex that most persons have to face, it is to be expected that skill in this field would require active operation of a fit brain. Evidence from observation of various types of brain damage confirms this. According to Landis and Bolles:

Patients who have undergone this operation [lobotomy] are different from their prepsychotic selves, although sometimes the difference is not immediately recognizable. They are apt to be somewhat indolent; they are often outspoken, saying the first thing that comes into their heads rather than waiting to think what response the remark will produce in others. They are

[5] By permission from D. O. Hebb, *The Organization of Behavior: A Neuropsychological Theory*, published by John Wiley and Sons, Inc., 1949, p. 2.

[6] Stanley Cobb, "Personality as Affected by Lesions of the Brain," chap. xviii in J. McV. Hunt, *Personality and the Behavior Disorders* (New York: The Ronald Press Co., 1944), p. 553.

aware that they are hasty, undiplomatic, and tactless, and often are sorry and apologetic. The emotional reactions are brisk, but shallow and short-lived. They laugh more and are of quicker temper. There is an absence of brooding melancholia, the hurt feelings, the pouting, and the grim silences which marked them before the operations.[7]

Another writer, Gray, mentions "intensified selfishness, indifference to moral obligations, failure to foresee the consequences of acts, gauche manners and emotional instability," as part of post-operative behavior, and furnishes a concrete example in the case of a Vermont quarryman whose frontal lobes were damaged by a crowbar which passed through his cheek into his skull. After the wound healed and the man returned to work, he proved to be capable of physical labor, but could not perform the duties of foreman. His memory appeared to be good, but his behavior was noticeably affected. "He was profane in speech, indifferent to the interests of others, careless of his obligations. . . ."[8]

In the above descriptions, the impairment of the activity of self-conscious trial-and-error imagination is obvious. Bluntness and rudeness in speech and action consist in applying habits and impulses in social interaction without first testing them in imagination and checking those aspects which are found by this cybernetic process to give promise of an unwanted reaction. The brain injuries in these cases have crippled the highly complex mental activity which is required for skillful social interaction. Actions are then not guided by the foresight normally provided by active imagination, and the person is thus partially disconnected from the mechanisms of social control.

Effects of Age, Fatigue, Malnutrition, Alcohol, and Lack of Oxygen on Complex Mental Functions and Personality.—The physiological processes of thought are apparently most efficient in youth. Ability to play championship chess or to make outstanding mathematical discoveries, for example, appears to go into some decline by or before the age of thirty, though the decline is not rapid for many years. In many types of human effort, this decline is concealed by the fact that most persons do not often approach maximum effort in their mental activity. Furthermore, the slight loss of physiological efficiency is often more than compensated for by a gain in the amount of organized knowledge, so that in effective

[7] By permission from C. Landis and M. Bolles, *Textbook of Abnormal Psychology*, published by The Macmillan Co., 1946, pp. 432-33.

[8] George W. Gray, "The Great Raveled Knot," *Scientific American*, October, 1948, p. 37.

ability many men are usually more capable in their fifties than they were in their twenties.

As previously pointed out, some intellectual capacities are retained into old age because they rest on well-established habits, while others deteriorate because they require fresh problem-solving ability. This has ben shown experimentally.[9] Three age groups were tested on certain performances to reveal deterioration due to age; the groups were equated in social background, native ability, and willingness to cooperate, and differed primarily in age. They consisted of a young (twelve to seventeen years), a middle-aged (thirty-four to fifty-nine years), and an old (sixty to eighty-two years) group. Five different learning tasks were assigned which differed in the degree of dependence on established habits. On problems which depended principally on established habits, the three age classes differed only moderately. There was a marked difference, however, in performance on tasks which required new learning which was in conflict with established habits—as in learning false multiplication tables with, for example, the statements $2 \times 4 = 9$, $5 \times 4 = 14$. Apparently the loss of efficiency in the older nervous systems considerably reduces the ability to perform mental operations which involve a large amount of novelty.

Malnutrition may similarly cripple the brain functioning. In some advanced cases of pernicious anemia there is apparently sufficient starvation of the nervous system to produce the same general kind of inability to plan and to be tactful that is observed in many of the lobotomy patients. Routine activity and routine conversation can be carried on from established habit, but any kind of new problem is difficult or impossible to handle. Even short-term starvation may temporarily cripple the problem-solving function of the brain. During the Second World War a famous incident of twenty-one days on a life raft furnished a dramatic illustration. According to Lieutenant James C. Whitaker, one of the survivors of the experience, the simplest kind of solution was beyond his powers when he landed on a beach. During the twenty-one days adrift he had eaten only half an orange and about six raw fish. He could barely walk with the aid of an oar and could think only with great difficulty. One member of the party had trouble keeping his pants on, having lost the fastenings; as he crawled along the beach they kept coming off. Lieutenant Whitaker tried to think what to do

[9] See E. G. Boring, H. S. Langfeld and H. P. Weld, *Foundations of Psychology* (New York: John Wiley & Sons, Inc., 1948), pp. 154-55.

to help. Although he had earlier tied his own pants on with string, neither he nor the man in difficulty could think of doing the same thing in the other case. Even with the example before them, the slight shift in perspective was a mental operation too great for their starved brains.

The same general type of effect on the problem-solving activity of the nervous system is produced by the consumption of alcohol which also operates to depress nervous activity. In spite of the illusion of stimulation and, with moderate doses of alcohol, of increased efficiency, numerous measurements show that from the first observable effect onward, alcohol reduces efficiency. In such measured performances as typewriting, for example, there is a regular reduction in speed, and an increase in the frequency of errors with each additional amount of alcohol consumed.

It is well known to students of alcoholism that the usefulness of alcohol for stimulating the flow of conversation at social gatherings is a result of its influence in reducing the trial-and-error self-critical imagination which in formal situations often tends to make conversation slow, cautious, and uninteresting. So many potential remarks are tried and found doubtful in the imagination that the conversation may be reduced to occasional dull statements separated by embarrassing pauses. The effect of alcohol is to reduce this inhibiting function of imagination by a partial crippling of the nervous system necessary to its functioning. Conversation then flows more readily, though what emerges tends to be based more on habit and impulse than on highly skilled adjustment to the complex social situation.

In more advanced stages of intoxication, the activity of self-critical imagination is so completely suppressed that habits and impulses are carried into action uncriticized and unchecked. If the person has a repertory of polite and considerate habits only, there may be no rudeness at this stage. But if there exist numerous unfriendly attitudes normally checked before expression by cautious inspection of thoughts, they may now form overt rude and belligerent behavior. Not all persons experience a great deal of active hostility of this sort, but there are few who do not have some kinds of thoughts which must be withheld in the interest of tact, and few who lack inappropriate wishes or impulses, whether they be to show off, tell a joke, sing a song, make amorous advances, or interrupt a bore. It is a characteristic feature of drunken behavior that such impulses tend to gain overt expression freely because of the impairment of the self-criticizing function of imagination resulting from the depressing influence of alcohol on the brain.[10]

The effects of lack of oxygen are also similar to those of the various factors discussed above. According to an investigator,

When the amount of oxygen in the inspired air is reduced, a more or less regular progression of psychological events occurs, the first of which is the loss of critical ability, including the capacity for self-criticism. . . . With this loss in judgment and incapacity for self-criticism during anoxia, feelings of exhilaration and of well-being, strikingly similar to the early stages of alcoholic intoxication, are frequently reported.[11]

Here again it is fairly clear that the complex processes of self-critical imagination are delicate and among the first of human abilities to be affected by any factor that slows up the operation of the nervous system.

Skillful participation in social life, therefore, obviously requires a physiological mechanism in excellent order and, in particular, a high degree of efficiency in the brain. Any of a number of factors which slow or block activity in the frontal lobes to that extent slow or block this kind of ability. Established habits apparently are maintained elsewhere and can carry on in spite of this defect, but the kind of novelty which is the essence of both problem solving and complex social interaction cannot be met by habits alone. The physiological machinery for making intelligent choices is an essential for normality of behavior.

ISOLATION AND PERSONALITY DISORGANIZATION

General Effects of Isolation.—A perfect experiment to test the effects of complete isolation on the human is, of course, not available—humane considerations make it impossible to perform. It would require that a number of human infants be separated from other humans at birth, placed in a room apart from all other persons, and fed and attended by mechanisms in such fashion that they would not see other humans or hear their voices. If these infants could survive and grow to adulthood, a comparison between

---

[10] The chronic alcoholic, the confirmed addict, also suffers from impaired reputation and realization of his failures, as well as other factors, and there is some indication that there may be in his case some permanent weakening of the problem-solving imaginative ability. A number of investigators find among addicts such traits as unwillingness or inability to assume responsibility, lack of ambition, restlessness, and the like, all of which may stem from this kind of deficiency.

[11] Nathan W. Shock, "Physiological Factors in Behavior." Chap. xix in Hunt, *op. cit.,* p. 583.

the resulting monstrosities and normal adults could then reveal the contrast between the biological and the social contributions to human nature.[12]

Such information as is available concerning the effects of isolation on the human, fragmentary and inadequate as it is, provides at least a consistent picture and one which is harmonious with the rest of the organized knowledge in the present volume.[13] It points to the general conclusion that, first, virtually all the characteristic behavior which constitutes human nature and personality requires rich and extended social participation for its development and even for its preservation, and, second, that a marked degree of isolation at any time of life results in some deterioration of organized behavior.

The evidence for the above conclusion consists of observations made on various experiences of isolation. These are necessarily scattered and incomplete, for severe isolation of the human is a rare

[12] On the analogous problem in biology, such experiments are possible and have been done with valuable results. An investigator of problems concerning cancer (Philip R. White, "Plant Tissue Cultures," *Scientific American*, March, 1950, pp. 49-51) states: "Every cell of the body has a dual character. First there is a fundamental character which arises from the innate qualities of the cell itself; this cannot be altered without destroying the cell. Then there is a more ephemeral character which arises from the fact that the cell is embedded in a complex environment which includes millions of other body cells; this can be changed without necessarily destroying the cell. The first qualities are personal, so to speak, the second social. So long as a cell remains in its normal place in the body it is difficult or impossible to distinguish between its personal and social qualities. If, however, a cell or group of cells is removed from its usual surroundings and placed in an environment which, though asocial, is sufficient for survival, the social aspects of its character fall away, and we can discover not only what is the real individuality of the cell, but also just how the social factors have affected it."

The results in this field are spectacular enough. Some cells become greatly different in size, form, and behavior, and, in some cases like tumor or cancer cells, they become individualistic or anti-social and a menace to any order which surrounds them.

[13] Unfortunately, the material concerning "feral men"—the occasional and accidental cases of isolated children who survived long enough to be discovered and recorded—is scientifically unsatisfactory. In general the literature indicates what should be expected to occur from such experience, but it is not safe to base conclusions, even those congenial to our own conceptions, on such weak material. Most of the reports are ancient, not drawn from close observation, and fragmentary in character. In some cases the accounts have serious inconsistencies or contain details which are obviously inaccurate and which possibly represent embellishments for dramatic effects. For example, in the relatively recent affair of the Wolf Children of India, said to be found in 1920 in a wolf den, the children were described as going on all fours but are shown in photographs on their hands and knees. Their eyes were said to glow in the dark—an unlikely consequence of life with wolves whose eyes do not glow in the dark. Despite a brief period of partial acceptance of these accounts, the material is not now generally considered sound enough to use. See J. A. L. Singh and R. M. Zingg, *Wolf Children and Feral Man* (New York: Harper & Bros., 1942).

accident, and when it does occur the consequences are seldom methodically described. The strength of this evidence lies in its consistent indication of deterioration.

In earlier periods there have been trials of a method of penology in which prisoners were subjected to long periods of solitude in their cells, sometimes under an enforced rule of silence. One rationalization of this punitive measure was that the prisoner with nothing else to occupy him would be forced to brood on his sins and so would come to see that they were not worth while. The results, however, did not only not support this belief, but rather indicated a tendency for sociability to decline and for various eccentricities to develop with suicide and insanity as final outcomes in many cases. From a review of the somewhat scanty literature on the subject, it appears that it is a common matter for long-term solitary prisoners to be apathetic about release when their terms expire, and in some cases even to show a desire to return to their cells.[14] Some are described as having become thoughtful, subdued, and languid. A woman who spent some months alone in a Russian prison states that her inclination to sociability so deteriorated that she finally lost all desire to have visitors, even her mother, come to see her. She no longer desired to talk, and it required all her resolution to make herself speak on the infrequent occasions of visits from her mother.[15] Students of the prisons of earlier periods in the United States and England report that the effects of solitude and of the silence rule was to bring about a high rate of insanity among the prisoners.[16]

A sociologist of long residence in Texas, W. E. Gettys, states that sheepherders, whose occupations involve long periods of enforced solitude, tend to lose their sociable characteristics. The typical Texas herder avoids companionship and does not like to converse with others, and is generally cross and irritable.[17]

A physiologist who was sent into a jungle in British Honduras for technical research for the chewing gum industry has recorded his experience of being alone for two seasons (June, 1928 to January, 1929, and July to December 1929). In the account, quoted

[14] See this author's article, "Cultural Isolation and the Schizophrenic Personality," *American Journal of Sociology*, XL, No. 2 (1934), pp. 155-64.

[15] Viera N. Figner, *Memoirs of a Revolutionist* (New York: International Publishers Co., Inc., 1927), p. 29.

[16] George Ives, *History of Penal Methods* (New York: F. A. Stokes Co., 1914), pp. 186-87. S. Hobhouse and A. F. Brockway, *English Prisons Today* (London: Longmans, Green & Co., 1922), p. 583.

[17] C. A. Dawson and W. E. Gettys, *An Introduction to Sociology* (New York: The Ronald Press Co., 1929), p. 605.

in full below, he mentions among other effects loneliness, a growing appreciation of animal pets, and a deterioration of sociability and a preference for solitude which remained for a time even after returning home. His fluency of speech was temporarily impaired, and his mental processes, he believed, were somewhat dulled. He feared that further isolation might result in gradual intellectual and mental degeneration.

Honey Camp is situated on the ruins of a Maya village, isolated in the depth of a primeval rain forest. Only two trails lead to the outside world, one to Belize, another to the villages of San Estevan and Orange Walk.

I was the only white person at Honey Camp. Except for my foreman, local laborers were all illiterate Maya Indians who spoke only Spanish and their native Maya language. My foreman, a mestizo, who had a grade school education, spoke English as well as the other two languages. At times British officials from the Forest Trust and the superintendent of the lands made one or two day visits, but these were few and far between. For all purposes it may be said that I was completely isolated. There were no contacts with the civilization in which I had lived. There were no intellectual companions with whom I could talk. There was no social life. There were no amusements. It was necessary to make adjustments to the new environment.

Honey Camp is located on a beautiful small lake known to the Maya as Onha. Here I enjoyed as good fishing as could be desired. On two islands in the lake and on the mainland, there are small Maya ruins which I explored during leisure hours. Game was exceedingly plentiful, so I gave many hours to the pursuit of hunting not only for recreation but to obtain fresh meat. Jaguar, tapir, puma, kinkajou, various birds including wild turkeys, and deer made this an interesting way to break the monotony of the loneliness and incessant work in the jungle. Many dark nights we would go out to hunt deer and kinkajou with miners' lamps in the nearby pine lands or in the forest along the thirty miles of intercrossing trails which had been cut to the thousands of experimental trees.

Although I had some leisure time to spend fishing, hunting, collecting natural history specimens, and exploring, most of my time was devoted to the experimental work. Our routine was invariable when weather conditions permitted. Every morning at four o'clock we went into the bush to tap the sapodilla trees. We tapped until ten o'clock and then returned to camp. I would have breakfast and rest until noon. At twelve the men would collect the latex from the tapped trees, and at one o'clock I would begin the daily laboratory work with the chicle (crude chewing gum). This would last all afternoon and often into the evening. Generally at night I would record data, carry on correspondence, or hunt when the other things became too monotonous. On Sundays and when there was exceptionally bad weather this routine was broken, but the isolation and the nonsocial life remained the same.

Usually in September the trails became closed by fallen trees and impassable swamps filled with water from the incessant rains; the trails remained closed from six weeks to two and a half months, during the severest part of the rainy season. The telephone line would be broken by falling trees, and could not be repaired until the trail was reopened. It was often impossible to send or receive mail. Then I felt the resulting isolation more than ever. There were no letters or newspapers that I could read to keep up contacts. There was no telephone line for emergencies, or for obtaining the local news. A phonograph alone broke the deep quiet of the sleeping jungle at night. In spite of the fact that I had a number of books, I could not interest myself in reading.

I turned to nature, and close contact with nature drew me ever closer. There seemed to be a harmony developing between my nature and nature itself. I did not want to ponder over intellectual matters, and there was no stimulus of intellectual companionship to call for such. I would go out at night and sit under the brilliant stars by the lakeside and forget the outside world. I was drawn by an inward force to harmony with the world about me. My animal pets meant more to me than human contacts. The alligator nearby and the rising palm above the tree tops were nearer than friends. Such times I felt a rapturous joy within.

But there were also hours when I became despondent and longed for civilization. At such times I questioned the reason for existence. Memories of home and friends would haunt me. Any true or imaginary wrong that I thought anyone had ever done me loomed up mentally as a mountain. I could hardly rid myself of it. The only way that I could overcome this lethargy was to go out into the forest or on the lake, and thus bring myself again into close contact with nature. Then I would again reach the other extreme. There seemed to be only extremes of rapture or discouragement and loneliness.

Each time when I left Honey Camp to return home, there was a feeling that I was leaving something behind, for the freedom of communion with nature had given me a strong attachment for the place.

When I reached home after each of the two seasons, I shunned people, and went out of the way to avoid friends. I was chided for not talking and going out and mixing as before. I enjoyed remaining quiet and longed for the lakeside on a quiet jungle night. The effects of the isolation were noticeable even to me. My fluency of speech was temporarily impaired, for words would not flow out as they had done before. My mental processes appeared to be temporarily dulled, and I became convinced that continued isolation in the tropics might result in gradual intellectual and mental degeneration.[18]

Byrd has described somewhat similar deterioration during his period of voluntary isolation in the Antarctic in 1934.[19] His first

[18] C. L. Lundell, "Isolated in a Tropical Forest," *Studies in Sociology*, I, No. 1 (Summer 1936), pp. 10-11.
[19] Richard E. Byrd, *Alone* (New York: G. P. Putnam's Sons, 1938).

reaction after being left by his men at the lonely outpost on March 28th, was a general feeling of peacefulness. Within about ten days he noted a fear of boredom, then of loneliness. By the end of the first month he found that it took some moments after awakening in the morning to collect his wits, and he found himself wondering where he was and what he was doing there. The silence depressed him, and he became irritable and reported that he had difficulty in concentrating. A month and a half after being alone he reported that his table manners had deteriorated to the point where they were atrocious. He also wrote on May 11, after about forty-four days of solitude, that he found it hard to think in words. Further deterioration is mentioned in the weeks that followed, but it is difficult to separate from this time on the effects of isolation from those of a progressive carbon monoxide poisoning from the lamps and motors in his shelter.

In the above illustrations, personalities which were already well organized were threatened with deterioration because of isolation. There is an occasional instance of isolation from birth or early infancy resulting in a consequent failure to develop an organized personality. Although the occurrence of such a case is uncommon, and the opportunity to make scientific observations even more so, competent descriptions are available on two such cases in recent years.[20] In general, as the following condensations from the studies show, the results were as might be expected—the children had developed little or nothing of the characteristically human style of activity and were much like animals although far more helpless than animals at corresponding stages in the life cycle. On being placed in situations of opportunity for social interaction, however, both girls improved in the direction of normality and one became virtually normal within about two years.

The first of these two cases, a girl designated by the pseudonym Anna, was the second illegitimate child born to an uneducated farm girl. Because of the anger of Anna's grandfather, the mother kept the infant confined in an upstairs attic-like room and provided her with only enough care to keep her alive. The infant was given no instruction or friendly attention, was seldom moved from one position to another, apparently was only infrequently cleaned, and was nourished on virtually nothing but cows' milk. She lived in this fashion until her discovery and removal to more favorable environments at the age of nearly six years.

[20] Kingsley Davis, "Final Note on a Case of Extreme Isolation," *American Journal of Sociology*, LII, No. 5 (1947), 432-37.

At the time of her discovery and removal, Anna was unable to walk, talk, or to do anything that indicated intelligence. A description of her mental condition, made shortly afterward when she had learned to walk, by the head of an institution in which she was living, suggests almost total lack of development during her first six years.

Anna walks about aimlessly, makes periodic rhythmic motions of her hands, and, at intervals, makes guttural and sucking noises. She regards her hands as if she had seen them for the first time. It was impossible to hold her attention for more than a few seconds at a time—not because of distraction due to external stimuli but because of her inability to concentrate. She ignores the task in hand to gaze vacantly about the room. Speech is entirely lacking. Numerous unsuccessful attempts have been made with her in the hope of developing initial sounds. I do not believe that this failure is due to negativism or deafness but that she is not sufficiently developed to accept speech at this time. . . . The prognosis is not favorable.[21]

This lack of organization and development, of course, could be a consequence of innate defectiveness as well as of isolation. If marked improvement develops after a reasonable opportunity to participate in social relations, however, it is not reasonable to hold to such an innate determination of the defectiveness. Anna's improvement in the period following her discovery supports the hypothesis that isolation was the cause of the retardation, although malnutrition and illness may also have contributed. About five and a half months after the above description of Anna's behavior, a clinical psychologist found the beginnings of speaking ("in the babbling stage") and decided that there was good promise of her later developing intelligible speech. Anna's vision and hearing were found to be normal and her physical skills had developed to the point of enabling her to climb stairs.

A little over a year later, a report from the school for retarded children indicated that Anna had finally begun to develop true speech at about the level of the average two-year-old child, and had a few complete sentences at her command. She fed herself with a spoon and dressed herself except for fastening her clothes. Her toilet habits were established, and she conformed to group expectations. About a year after that a report indicated further language development together with a development of social skills, though she was far below the expected performances for her age. She was able to follow simple directions, to construct with blocks, to keep clean, to help other children. Her disposition was reported

[21] *Ibid.*, p. 433.

as pleasant, except for a tendency to be easily excited. The question of her future possibilities was ended by her death from hemorrhagic jaundice shortly after this report, at the age of ten and a half years.

The other isolated child, a girl designated Isabelle, was born and discovered at nearly the same time as Anna. Isabelle was also an illegitimate daughter kept in seclusion for the same reason. Her mother was deaf and speechless, so Isabelle had no opportunity to hear speech until her discovery and removal from her mother at the age of six and a half years. At this time she was frightened by the approach of people. She made croaking vocal noises, but had no speech. An observer stated: "She was apparently utterly unaware of relationships of any kind. When presented with a ball for the first time, she held it in the palm of her hand, then reached out and stroked my face with it. Such behavior is comparable to that of a child of six months." [22] She gave the impression of being wholly uneducable.

Isabelle, however, was given a systematic and skillful course of training which produced remarkable improvement and which brought her within about two years to a level of behavior normal for her age. In about a week after beginning the training program she made her first attempts at vocalization, and a little over two months later she was using sentences. Nine months after that she could read and write a little, and could retell a story which had been told to her. Within another seven months she possessed a vocabulary of nearly two thousand words. At the last report when she was a little over fourteen years old, and had passed the sixth grade, she was reported to give the impression of being a bright, cheerful, energetic little girl, participating normally in school activities with other children. In this instance it is clear that the retardation was entirely a result of the isolation. Isabelle, like Anna, had suffered from lack of sunshine and inadequate diet and her legs were severely bowed from rickets, but no apparent retardation is attributed to this malnutrition and its effects.

The above examples show the effects of complete or nearly complete separation from other persons for an extended period of time. In general they support the conception that organized personality is acquired in social interaction and must be maintained by fairly continuous experience in social groups. Such a generalization finds further support in the evidence concerning isolation of other kinds in which the separation is not physical, but is a separation

[22] *Ibid.*, p. 436.

of roles—the case of the migrant, the stranger, the outcast, and others who though spatially near other persons are not engaged in primary interaction with either the persons about them or any others.

Not all mobility isolates persons. It is possible, for instance, to move from a job in one city to another of similar nature in a like locality and find that the new associates and neighbors are so much like those one has just left that it is only a matter of a few weeks before one gains a sense of belonging in the new place. The chronically mobile, though, and those who change from a peasant village in Europe to a metropolitan slum in the United States may for a time be unable to establish effective primary relations and thus be at least partly isolated while surrounded by people. In such a situation they are separated from the forces that normally control behavior and keep it conventional and organized. Unconventionality, irresponsibility, instability of character, and general demoralization can thus develop in this class of persons.[23]

The freedom which results from such detachment from social control may be used for criminality, for personal eccentricities of the bohemian type, or for the pursuit of mildly unconventional ways. A student has described a case of the last type in the behavior of a husband and wife, who, while residing in a small midwestern city, had completely withdrawn from the social relations in the town.[24] The unconventional behavior in this case was in the direction of excessive cleanliness. Such a trait is a virtue which is appreciated up to a certain point, but which, beyond this point, tends to be regarded as queer or abnormal. The couple in this instance inhabited a luxurious and showy residence in a fashionable area of the city and appeared to be determined to keep the shine of newness on the house and its equipment. Shoes were not worn in the house, but were left at the front door. All meals were taken at a restaurant so that the kitchen would not be dulled by cooking; the expensive electric stove was not even connected. The car was left outside the garage to avoid marking the waxed floor. The sewing machine, although not used, was traded in after a year for a newer model. The grounds were kept spotless—the wife was ab-

[23] This statement is supported by a large amount of evidence in the sociological literature. For interesting illustrations see: Norman S. Hayner, *Hotel Life* (Chapel Hill: University of North Carolina Press, 1936); Margaret Mary Wood, *The Stranger* (New York: Columbia University Press, 1934); Everett Stonequist, *The Marginal Man* (New York: Chas. Scribner's Sons, 1937); and any of the modern general sociology texts or studies of urban society.

[24] Alex S. Freedman, "Note on a Case of Mature Social Isolation," *Alpha Kappa Delta Quarterly*, May, 1950, pp. 19-21.

normally irritated when she discovered candy wrappers on the lawn. She even swept the street in front of the house several times each week throughout the year. The couple were, of course, completely withdrawn from social relations in the city.

The isolate role may also be exploited by unconventional methods of gaining a livelihood. The professional beggar furnishes an example of this kind of adaptation. In this case, the relation between the begging and the isolation is reciprocal—begging isolates the person from conventional roles in the community, and the isolation aids in making begging profitable and is thus deliberately sought by various means.[25]

In cases where the satisfactions and welfare of a person depend on particularly close integration with a group, his motivation for activity may be affected by any separation from the group. The soldier's will to fight is said to be threatened by the "isolation of the battlefield." According to a group of civilian psychiatrists who studied combat neuroses, "When an individual member of such a combat group has his emotional bonds of group integration seriously disrupted, then he, *as a person*, is truly disorganized. The disruption of the group unit is, in the main, a primary causal factor, not a secondary effect of personal disorganization."[26] Because of this and other relations between isolation and mental abnormality, there has arisen a strong interest in therapeutic measures involving a reduction of isolation.[27]

In a sense motivation to continue to live is in part connected with social participation. Modern knowledge of suicide shows that isolated persons are much more likely to commit suicide than are persons who are closely integrated in group life.[28] Old persons commit suicide in larger proportions than young, urban populations have higher rates than rural, and such mobile and detached populations as hoboes and roominghouse dwellers have particularly high rates. A study in Vienna of persons who attempted sui-

[25] See Harlan W. Gilmore, *The Beggar* (Chapel Hill: University of North Carolina Press, 1940). Newspaper accounts in February, 1950 told of the death of a professional beggar who left his niece an estate of $15,000. The man had lived well, and had held accounts in forty-three banks throughout the country as well as some life insurance policies. According to his ledger a typical nine-hour day in a metropolis would bring him about $36. He entered the profession in early manhood embittered after losing a leg and experiencing an unhappy love affair.

[26] L. H. Bartemeier, *et al.*, "Combat Exhaustion," *Journal of Nervous and Mental Diseases*, CIV (October, 1946), 370.

[27] See Marshall B. Clinard, "The Group Approach to Social Reintegration," *American Sociological Review*, XIV, No. 2 (1949), 257-62.

[28] The subject is summarized by the author in *Social Disorganization* (New York: The Ronald Press Co., 1948), chap. viii, "Suicide."

cide and failed shows several indications of insufficient social participation on the part of such persons.[29] Of seventy persons interviewed on this point, sixty-one stated that they had no friendships at all. Furthermore, none of the persons belonged "to any community of wider scope than that of the family, love affair, or friendship" with the single exception of a teacher who, in fact, denied having meant to kill himself. None belonged to a political organization, although in some cases their spouses did. Of seventy-eight questioned about love experience, only eleven had normal sexuality. The author believes that subnormal sexuality can exert an influence in two ways—by rendering the person incapable of making lasting attachments and so isolating him, or by making his attachment to one person so strong that he is unable to make other attachments when this one is broken.[30]

It has long been a partially accepted though insufficiently tested belief that mental normality tends, on the average, to occur somewhat less frequently in urban populations than in rural and small-town populations, the hypothesis being that group integration is usually superior in the latter types of area. Such a broad contrast would hardly be expected to yield clear results because of the large amount of variation in types of community life in both small and large towns or cities. There is, in fact, much greater variation within a metropolis than there is between small town and metropolis in these respects. Nevertheless, most statistical comparisons, crude as they are, have shown a general tendency for cities to have higher rates of most kinds of mental abnormality than do small towns and farming regions.[31]

At least one methodical study of the relation between mental abnormality and urban life escaped the difficulties involved in the sampling defectiveness of data from mental hospitals.[32] A satisfactorily large sample of school children of the third and sixth grades of Ohio schools were given tests to reveal variations in degree of departure from normality. Of the 1,229 children studied, 371 lived on farms, 573 were rural but not on farms, and 285 lived

[29] Margarethe Von Andics, *Suicide and the Meaning of Life* (London: William Hodge & Co., Ltd., 1947).

[30] *Ibid.*, p. 125.

[31] For a typical source, see Benjamin Malzberg, *Social and Biological Aspects of Mental Disease* (Utica: State Hospitals Press, 1940). In New York State hospitals, for example, the average annual rates of admission, 1929–1931, was for males 52.7 per 100,000 population in rural areas and 83.4 in cities. The corresponding rates for females were 46.0 and 68.1.

[32] A. R. Mangus, "Personality Adjustment of Rural and Urban Children," *American Sociological Review*, XIII, No. 5 (1948), 566-75.

in a city of 17,000 population. Two tests were used—a test of personal adjustment (involving such matters as self-reliance, personal worth, feeling of belonging, sense of personal freedom, tendency to withdraw, and neurotic symptoms), and a test of social adjustment (attitudes toward social standards, social skills, freedom from antisocial attitudes, family, school, and community relationships). The results indicate a somewhat higher average mental health score for farm and village children than for city children. Statistically significant differences in this direction are found on both types of test between the farm and city children, and between the village and city children. These differences are not of great magnitude, but in each case the farm children have the highest scores, and the city children the lowest. The differences are in the same direction when computed separately for the sexes, but are not in every case statistically significant. Among the prominent differences in detail is that concerning the sense of personal worth and of belonging, in which there is a particularly large contrast between farm and city children, with the greater sense of worth and belonging observed among farm children. These latter also had particularly marked superiority in social skills and in school relations.

There are no doubt a great many more subtle consequences of isolation and of partial isolation of many kinds. In view of the evidence presented in earlier chapters showing how dependent man is on his social organizations, it is to be expected that every degree of variation in the richness of his opportunity for participation should have a variety of consequences. Many of these would not necessarily be obvious, and so it is to be expected that future results will throw much more light on the more subtle consequences of isolation.

Eccentricity Without Dementia.—A considerable proportion of the cases of mental abnormality which are diagnosed as schizophrenia display no physical defectiveness connected in a causal way to the disorder of the mind. It was formerly widely accepted, however, that a progressive neurological deterioration was a feature of this disorder, a theory apparently supported by both the surface behavior of many patients and the results of mental tests. In recent years, however, this conception has been challenged, and the poor test performance of many schizophrenics accounted for on bases other than that of actual deterioration.[33] The observations are consistent with the explanation that the prolonged role of an isolate

[33] Hunt, *op. cit.*, pp. 986 ff.

has allowed the development of considerable eccentricity, which interferes with test performance through such factors as indifference, preoccupation, and unconventional mental associations of ideas.

Performance on tests usually requires social motivation—that is, one submits to the test and applies himself to the difficult work involved because the experimenter asks him to do it. To comply is an act of social responsiveness. The schizophrenic who has experienced an extended period of partial isolation is likely to be somewhat deficient in this kind of responsiveness, and while he may agree to take the test, he has less interest in applying himself wholeheartedly to the work involved. Hunt has pointed out that

. . . the slowness and the excessive variability of the reaction-times of schizophrenics and their failure to maintain a set to react might be taken to indicate a partial extinction of their responses to social stimuli . . . the response used in these studies of reaction-time is motivated by an experimenter's instructions . . . more complete uncooperativeness would represent a more complete extinction of social responses in these patients. Apathy would represent a more generalized extinction or weakening of the interests learned in the course of social interaction.[34]

A task imposed from the outside is likely to be undertaken grudgingly by any person. He will, as shown in Chapter 3, experience less of a completion tendency in an imposed task than in a task which is self-chosen. The test performance of the isolated and therefore inadequately motivated schizophrenic suffers from this fact also. Hunt observed that the majority of schizophrenics fail to sustain a task or topic, and presents evidence that this effect is a consequence of defective motivation rather than of actual dementia. He points out:

. . . the output of schizophrenics on tasks repeated is much more variable than is the output of normal subjects. Hunt and Wittman have secured evidence that intra-individual variability in output is greater in schizophrenia than it is in such an "organic" psychosis as paresis. It has also been shown that the ups and downs of output in individual patients is associated with similar ups and downs in psychiatric ratings of "attitude." . . . Kent and Hunt have found that if one takes the effort to gain the confidence and cooperation of schizophrenic patients, one can frequently get large increases in output without what can be considered practice. So far, Hunt has been unable to find any patient with a typical "organic" disorder in whom such a cultivation of cooperation automatically produces marked improvement in output.[35]

[34] *Ibid.*, p. 995.
[35] *Ibid.*, pp. 1004-5.

Departure from conventionality in speech as a consequence of isolation and indifference to relations with other persons may also produce apparent indications of mental deterioration. Tests of schizophrenics reveal that

. . . they usually fail to see absurdities or to interpret proverbs. . . . They distort the meaning of words, and these distortions of word-meaning and more especially of topical meaning become more and more pronounced with successive requests for clarification by the experimenter. In these distortions, words may take the place of real objects but [the subject may] omit the *as though* and then slip from the figurative to the literal meaning of the words used in the metaphor. Great individual differences among schizophrenics appear in all these performances and in the tendencies indicated here.[36]

Similarly:

Although he did not emphasize the point, Wegrocki described schizophrenics as verbalizing analogies correctly but writing wrong answers because their uncontrolled associative processes had carried them on by the time they got pencil to paper. He also reported that a complex task may serve to control some schizophrenics, for patients who performed his tests without error lapsed into the characteristic jargon in voluntary speech. This agrees with Hunt's finding that schizophrenics who will start usually succeed in doing fairly complex arithmetic progressions. Here the situation continually keeps the task before the subject if he has the capacity to grasp it. On the other hand, in noting absurdities where the instruction to look for them had to be assumed voluntarily or maintained over considerable time while the narrative was being read, they failed miserably.[37]

Commenting on the belief that the schizophrenic has lost actual ability to think abstractly in the same sense as has the lobotomized person, Cameron cites evidence that the apparent loss is actually a result of inadequate rapport and motivation.

Goldstein and Scheerer deny that the schizophrenic can spontaneously evolve groupings according to material, form or color; but Cameron's extremely disorganized schizophrenic patients with marked asyndetic and metonymic thinking, both characteristic schizophrenic disorders, did evolve such groupings using the Ach-Sakharov materials and method, and quite without promptings or suggestions, as the verbatim shorthand records of his transactions plainly show. If one accept Goldstein and Scheerer's criteria for the "abstract capacity level," it is obvious to the writer on the basis not only of test situations but of several years devoted to daily close communication with intelligent schizophrenics of every degree of severity, that the

[36] *Ibid.*, pp. 1014-15.
[37] *Ibid.*, p. 1016.

"abstract capacity level" can be found in most schizophrenics provided the painfully patient technique necessary for effectual rapport with this group is developed.[38]

The above observations point to the conclusion that the kind of long partial isolation, which is the experience of the schizophrenic and the schizoid personality, is capable of producing a sufficient detachment from conventional motivation and meanings so that the behavior *appears* to be indicative of actual deterioration. The observations and test measures which appeared to demonstrate dementia, however, must be reinterpreted in the light of the evidence that in the proper circumstances—in which the motivation and communicability can be maintained—the schizophrenic may perform well on tests on which he had previously failed. Apparently it is easy for a certain degree of unconventionality to be falsely identified as dementia, and for a structural defect to be imagined as accounting for a phenomenon that is actually a consequence of isolation.

Isolation and Mental Disorganization.—It has been shown in Chapter 7 that the organization of mind and behavior which constitutes the normal personality is achieved through experience in a group life of an organized character. Separation from such organized social experience should then result in disorganization of the personality. Such is shown to be the case in the earlier part of the present Chapter. It appears also that partial isolation, of the type as illustrated in the schizophrenic experience, is the cause of a degree of disorganization. In fact, one prominent investigator of abnormal behavior defines schizophrenia as a form of disorganization. He writes:

. . . we may now define the schizophrenic disorders as disorganization and desocialization of the acquired behavior systems constituting personality, and their replacement by behavior dominated or determined by private fantasy, in the absence of organ or tissue pathology adequate to account for the disorder. . . . The normal daydreamer, in returning to socially shared operations, abandons the role-taking that belongs to his private fantasy. The schizophrenic patient, because of his lost social skills, is a daydreamer who cannot completely return.[39]

If, as apparently is so in most cases, the conditions responsible for the partial isolation are always present from infancy or early

[38] Norman Cameron, in Hunt, *op. cit.*, p. 903.
[39] Norman Cameron, *The Psychology of Behavior Disorders* (Boston: Houghton Mifflin Co., 1947), p. 451.

childhood, there is then a perpetual failure to develop a completely satisfactory organization of a conventional sort, and instead the development of a certain amount of a purely personal and virtually incommunicable private mental organization. As Cameron characterizes it:

> The schizophrenic patient is usually a person who has never acquired the degree of social skill he needs for shifting his perspectives through taking successive culturally determined roles when he is under stress. In other words, he has not succeeded in establishing himself firmly in his culture. He does not share his anxieties, conflicts, suspicions or loneliness with others because he lacks the techniques for doing so . . . he is incapable of checking on the validity of his own interpretations by taking the roles of persons whose conduct frightens or puzzles him. Such an individual is left in a personal crisis with only the relatively inept techniques of private fantasy, furtive observation and unwarrantable inference at his disposal. The initial disorganization which develops—as it might in any normal person under critical conditions—renders the socially unskilled and immature person still more inadequate and isolated, while his increasing isolation tends in its turn to reduce yet further his opportunities for the effective personal interaction upon which social adequacy must depend. Thus the patient's behavior may describe a descending spiral from comparative inadequacy to complete ineffectuality, and sometimes to complete inaction.[40]

There are various types of sequences of experiences which may produce such an isolated person—one who, as Cameron says, "has not succeeded in establishing himself firmly in his culture." One process which is common is that which binds a child in extreme dependence on his family, which itself is somewhat out of touch with the surrounding larger society.[41] While any composite case is necessarily an oversimplification, there is some value in describing a typical sequence which resembles a large number of actual cases.

> The process begins in a relation of overprotection by a parent—most frequently the mother. The child is given such special treatment that he conceives of his mother as greatly different from and superior to all other persons. Her authority is thus far greater than that possessed by normal mothers. The child, "spoiled" by this parent, tends to absorb her unconventionally magnified conception of himself. Since by sincere action as well as by words, she shows that she conceives of him as

---

[40] *Ibid.*, p. 486.

[41] Some of the research material out of which this generalization has grown appears in this author's study, "An Ecological Study of Insanity in the City" (Ph.D. dissertation, The University of Chicago, 1931). Also, by the same author, "Cultural Isolation and the Schizophrenic Personality," *American Journal of Sociology*, XL, No. 2 (1934), 155-64, and certain later publications which are referred to in the present Chapter.

far more precious, attractive, moral, and gifted, than are all other children, her compelling authority leads him to see himself in the same light. In the first few years of childhood this conception becomes the pattern about which the whole personality tends to crystallize. The reciprocal process of admiration between mother and child tends to make the conception ever more rigid. By the time the child is ready for school and should be prepared for forced exposure to children of his own age, his personality is sufficiently out of harmony with those of normal school children to obstruct his assimilation into their primary groups.[42]

This "spoiling" process does not by itself destine the child to an irreversible course of isolation—sympathetic children and adults, including skillful teachers, may in time lead the child through a gentle transition toward the conventional roles appropriate to his age. Where such opportunity is lacking, however, the reaction of unsympathetic children such as the tough boys of metropolitan slums, constituting the first exposures of the child to life outside the family, may produce a severe shock. The spoiled child, made conspicuous by his too-elegant grooming and by his egocentric concept of self, is likely to be regarded as legitimate prey by the boys of these districts, and immediate and severe persecution may almost automatically follow. Light hazing may soon be lived down, but harsh treatment may send the child in tears back to his mother, from whom the tender comforting and consoling definitions of the persecutors as unreasonable brutes lead the child even further from the possibility of assimilation into conventional boyhood groups.[43]

At this point a circular process—a "vicious circle"—may start. Rejection by other boys at school and on the streets and playgrounds turns the child increasingly toward his mother and so deprives him of the broader knowledge that would give him the possibility of a conventional social role. The influence of the mother and sometimes of teachers as well operates to keep the child apart from the other children, who are increasingly seen as evil persecutors. The child thus spends the years of youth in separation from normal companionship of his own age groups and thus overinfluenced by the special attitudes and interests of his mother. Since our culture is in part transmitted informally by the mutual interaction of youth, the child so isolated is deprived of much important knowledge of human nature and conven-

[42] A count of the frequency of this factor in a sample of 101 cases, taken consecutively from the records of a mental hospital in Rhode Island, showed that, in those cases which contained sufficient material on the early life of the patient, about 60 per cent had the type of experience described above. See R. E. L. Faris, "An Ecological Study of Insanity in the City," p. 30.

[43] This aspect of the process may account for the fact, noted in a number of cities, that schizophrenia rates are particularly high in the urban slums. See R. E. L. Faris and H. W. Dunham, *Mental Disorders in Urban Areas* (Chicago: University of Chicago Press, 1939), chap. iii, pp. 38-62.

tional behavior. He grows up to lack a context in which to interpret the daily behavior of normal persons. If he derives all his moral ideas from his mother, he may have an impossibly high set of absolute standards, and thus be unduly shocked by both common violations of formal morality and his own temptations in this direction. He may lack the background for interpreting his own status, and thus be unable to realize how unimportant he may seem to persons about him. He may deviate from the conventional in many other ways including vocabulary, interests, and ambitions. As a consequence he has opportunities for endless misunderstandings and failures which can dismay and excite him in such fashion as to compound his difficulties to the point where he develops fully psychotic behavior. Even the experience of hospitalization does not necessarily end this process. In many instances the person is tricked into the commitment to a hospital by relatives, friends, or a trusted physician, who cannot bring themselves to inform the fearful patient that they are planning to take him to be locked up in an insane asylum. The sudden shock of realization produces still another barrier to sociability and conventionality, and the characteristic hospital life with its artificialities and separation from conventional persons further increases the isolation. The most typical course of the schizophrenic in the mental hospital is a lifetime of increasing isolation and deterioration, the consequence of social factors which tended always to separate the person from primary relations in conventional society.

Isolation, Unconventionality, and the Schizophrenic Symptoms. —The picturesque and fantastic behavior which is found in many cases of schizophrenia often has the surface look of extreme defectiveness of a physiological character. Delusions may appear so outlandish that it seems impossible to believe that a person with normal physiological equipment could entertain them. Hallucinations may appear to be too vivid to occur in a system without structural defect. Yet, in the majority of cases, no structural defect is found, and, as shown above, properly motivated tests of ability make it appear unlikely that any serious defect of a physiological nature could be present. It is therefore appropriate to direct attention at the possibility that extreme variations of experience could produce such symptoms. Careful study of cases does, in fact, yield evidence that much of the behavior of the schizophrenic is not actually disorganized, but is organized in a way so unconventional that the sense of it is difficult to grasp without an intimate knowledge of the person's history.

The common delusion of the paranoid schizophrenic, for example—that he is a person of special worth or greatness and that he is being persecuted in a subtle way by persons of great power and prominence—such a notion is not entirely illogical in the light of the special circumstances of his development. If a child is told repeatedly, over the course of years, by his mother who is the dominant authority in his life, that he is far superior in ability to other children, there is no obvious reason for him to question the fact or to reject the role. Since exceptional amounts of interaction with adults are known to be related to the development of certain intellectual abilities (see Chapter 10) he may actually have an advantage at the beginning of school. Lacking the various competing interests and distractions which turn normal boys away from school work, he may earn high grades and strong approval from the teacher. Having more time alone at home, he may further enrich his informational fund by extensive reading. Thus all objective evidence visible to him tends to confirm the maternally-given conception of himself as intellectually superior.

Since most careers require in addition to intellectual ability a sound technique for dealing with people, the isolated person is seriously handicapped in a way which he cannot understand and may know nothing about. He encounters repeated social failures, and in consequence, career failures, with no conception of the actual reasons. In his search for an explanation of how he, a person far superior to those with whom he is competing, is nevertheless unsuccessful in the competition, he turns toward an obvious possibility—one that may in fact have been suggested in earlier years by his mother; certain persons are actively conspiring against him. In the circumstances, it is obvious that the conspirator must be subtle and powerful. Since he produces these results without showing his hand, it is easy to imagine that a number of persons are involved. In order to discover the malefactors, it is necessary to interpret subtle fragments of evidence—hence the devious and suspicious tendency of the paranoiac. Once he decides who his persecutors are, the paranoiac feels justified in making a plan to destroy them for their vicious actions toward a superior and virtuous person. Such a trend, thus, is intelligible as an unfolding of a set of logical attitudes based in part on the ignorance caused by partial isolation, and in part on a maternally-indoctrinated conviction of exceptional superiority. The reasoning is not defective, and in some cases may be of a high order. Nor are the suspicions in every case entirely without grounds, for such an eccentric and conceited person often does actually suffer from some legitimate discrimination and is often, as he suspects, the topic of conversation by others. To persons who have no knowledge of the context and backgrounds of his thoughts and actions, his behavior appears to be crazy, but in the light of the history of his experiences there is no necessity to assume, or evidence for the assumption of, any kind of physiological deficiency. The insanity, a real and dangerous condition, is a product of the unconventional sequence of events.

Another common type of abnormal personality appears to develop from the same kind of isolation coupled with a parental emphasis, not on intellectual superiority, but on religious and moral superiority. To a fanatically religious mother the all-important object of training is to keep her child morally pure and exceptionally pious. In many cases the greatest evil is conceived to be sex, and so the child is brought up in ignorance of objective sex information and only given the vague but powerful notion that sex is a matter which is inexpressibly evil. To yield in any way to sex impulses is, according to this unconventional view, to be hopelessly condemned in this world and in the next.

Because of his isolation from primary groups of his own age during the growing years, this overprotected child lacks the opportunities available to conventional children to gain a more balanced view of sex as a normal part of life.[44] He thus is able to reach adulthood with the belief, or hopeful half-belief, that his human nature and that of the adults he loves and trusts are of the virtuous and nonsexual type. He cannot escape awareness of the general popularity of sex, for the evidence is on every hand—in newspaper and magazine pictures, in movies and stage plays, in fiction, in popular songs, and many other places. But he conceives of the population as divided into two types; those persons who are evil, and those who, like his mother and some others, are good and moral. To lose membership in this latter category appears to him to be an unimaginable catastrophe. For such a person, the time comes eventually when it is difficult to escape indications in his own makeup of an active sexual nature. Often in early adulthood a sexual approach by a member of the opposite sex is sufficiently arousing to produce sensations recognizable as of a sexual character which are immediately interpreted as evidence of an evil nature. The shock is often great, and may produce any of a number of reactions. Some persons appear to lose hope, assuming that nothing can be done to save themselves, and that visible indications of guilt betray them to all other persons. In extreme cases, such discouraged schizophrenics

---

[44] Formal sex education in school may supply the missing knowledge in some cases, but this is a matter of very recent years, and is still not available to the majority of school children.

may abandon all activity, stay at home, and even take to bed and remain mute, face to the wall.

Another common and understandable reaction to the discovery of a sexual nature in oneself is to attempt to deny it, both to self and to others. Just as the paranoid personality tries to find some other agent to blame for his own failures, these shocked persons seek an external cause for their own physiological nature. This is often done by claiming that some sinister persons are producing the unwelcome sexual reaction by means of secretly administered drugs, by poison gas, by telepathy, by electrical or other means. Although the sexual nature of the sensations attributed to the agency of these methods is often not mentioned, sympathetic inquiry usually shows that the subject is aware of it. A patient who believed that scientists at a distant institution were directing brain waves at him was asked what effect these waves had upon him, and explained that they gave him sexual imagery ("dirty pictures"). This notion of being sexually influenced by some external agents has been illustrated by Cameron in the following example:

A young unmarried woman, in an acute schizophrenic episode whose dominant trends were all sexual in character, for several weeks accused one of the staff physicians of controlling her mind electrically by means of a keyboard upstairs. She complained that every now and then she could "feel electrical currents" flow through her body, and sometimes she burst from her room and ran screaming down the corridor to escape their influence. Often the electricity seemed to her to come out of the bedsprings when she was trying to sleep. The patient insisted that a certain staff physician was experimenting on her sexually, and whenever she saw him she demanded that he stop his "electrical experiments." On two occasions she furiously attacked him.[45]

Although the behavior of the person in the above case might be described as the result of hallucinations and delusions, it would not be correct to suppose that she lacked mental organization or objective experiences to support her unconventional interpretations. Cameron points out that she had actually seen a man manipulating a keyboard (for silent piano practice), and that the physician who she believed had been making sexual experiments had lectured on her before interns, manipulating her head in a way that was not comprehensible to her. The false notions were thus not merely the accidental product of a disordered nervous system, but the systematic results of an ignorant person's attempts to explain, in

[45] Cameron, *The Psychology of Behavior Disorders, op. cit.*, p. 400.

acceptable terms, the frightening realization of her own sexuality she was experiencing.

Another reaction to this kind of sexual shock is to compensate by cleaning up, as if "dirty" sex could be conquered by sanitation. Cameron describes a case of a twenty-seven-year-old unmarried woman, an office clerk, who had been trained in childhood to be exceptionally clean and moral.[46] Following a shocking sex experience in early adulthood she became irritable, given to temper outbursts, crying spells, and sleeplessness. She eventually became seclusive and self-deprecatory, stating to her mother that she felt unfit for human company. She mentioned a linkage between pelvic sensations and guilty thoughts. She began to wash her hands excessively, using laundry soap and a strong disinfectant and scrubbing all the way to her elbows. She continued this practice even after a disfiguring dermatitis of the hands and forearms developed, and became acutely anxious if washing was delayed. Her passion for cleanliness was also revealed in her refusal to use a towel or wear a dress more than once after each laundering.

In some similar cases the cleaning urge extends to the whole house, or to the city, and occasionally to the whole world. In one instance a young man of this type began by renouncing tobacco and liquor and attempting to persuade his poker friends to do the same. He followed this with an attempt to stop the use of profanity by his friends. His enthusiasm then developed into plans for a campaign to have the washrooms in public buildings and railroad stations made cleaner, and to have the city streets cleaned up, and quickly expanded into an idea of eliminating all kinds of corruption from the whole world, with perhaps an expedition to Mars after this was accomplished to benefit that planet in the same way.

Occasionally, a particularly active and thoughtful schizophrenic will conceive of eliminating all evil by means of religious revivals, or by founding a new religion and way of life. In one particularly interesting development of this kind, a young man, bothered by a complex of problems involving both sexual and homosexual guilt, alcoholic addiction, and personal failures, produced abruptly what he thought to be a general solution to all of his personal problems and to all the troubles of mankind.[47] He wrote a manuscript for a

---

[46] *Ibid.*, pp. 283 ff.

[47] The case is described more fully in R. E. L. Faris, "Reflections of Social Disorganization in the Behavior of a Schizophrenic Patient," *American Journal of Sociology*, L, No. 2 (1944), 134-41.

book which was to give his system to the world. The essence of the system was that all evil is imaginary, and that "clear and perfect reason," together with love, would make everything right and would eliminate poverty, war, racial antipathies, injustices, disease, and even death. Impressed by his own system, he concluded that he must have been supernaturally destined to save humanity and sometimes expressed the belief that he was Christ returned to earth. The idea so impressed him that he sought communication with prominent persons and with newspapers in order to inform the world, through them, of the coming of the new era to be brought about by his system. On the advice of a physician, his embarrassed family maneuvered him into a mental hospital where his condition was diagnosed as schizophrenia. To his family, and to members of the hospital staff and other patients, his behavior seemed completely crazy and in the violent ward where he was placed he quickly earned the reputation of being the wildest and most unintelligible patient. Nevertheless, a thorough study of his background and his actions revealed that his whole system was logically coherent and that he never lost contact with his actual surroundings except in the temporary fashion in which any preoccupied person does. Further inquiry showed that in his most fantastic claims, such as the possession of superhuman powers, he was speaking in metaphors and always preserved in his own mind a distinction between the extraordinary elements of his new system and the matter-of-fact realities of the world about him. He also was able to refrain from discussing his new system or from taking any roles based on it when there was something to be gained by taking this course; since the savior role was naturally more exciting, however, he assumed it a major part of the time.

In addition to the various reactions to the shock of sex disillusionment described in the above cases, there is a variety of other behavior possibilities, many of which are described in the literature of abnormal behavior. There is also, for example, an occasional person who goes to pieces in a general way, finding no kind of solution and failing to escape the ceaseless torment. Cameron describes a case of such a young woman whose background was typical of the schizophrenic of this type.[48] She was reared by a paternal aunt who treated her with domineering and indulgent overprotection, and thus prevented the attainment of an adequate amount of skill in personal relations. She frightened and repelled other children by her quick temper and her uncompromising de-

---

[48] Cameron, *The Psychology of Behavior Disorders, op. cit.*, pp. 452-56.

mands. Her isolation increased during adolescence as she became ever more involved in preoccupation. From the age of fourteen she began to worry about her autoerotic habit, having heard that it would drive her crazy. She became highly nervous, experienced dreams of terror, and tried to protect herself by keeping a light burning in her bedroom. At times she thrashed about the room with a cane, ostensibly killing snakes. She considered that she deserved great punishment, and on one occasion made an attempt at suicide. After commitment to the hospital she revealed that she expected a life sentence for her "awful thoughts." She considered self-torture, and at times went into stupors. Eventually "her talk began to develop marked disorganization until it became a poor instrument of communication."

In general it may be concluded of the typical schizophrenic that his trouble follows from a long period of partial isolation caused, usually, by the treatment given by a parent and by the reaction of other children to the resulting personality. The isolation prevents the development of familiarity with the conventions and necessary principles of primary social relations, so that he slips into a great number of blunders and failures which he does not understand. The reaction of other persons to these experiences further isolates and confuses him, so that his troubles compound in a reciprocal process. The particular development of the symptoms of the schizophrenic depends on varying circumstances—the common element is an unconventionality so great that other persons can usually perceive no system or order in his behavior, and so judge him to be insane.

A psychologist has, in offering the following generalization on the traits of the psychopath, shown that the essential matter here also is unconventionality of any kind serious enough to appear undesirable and unintelligible to normal persons:

. . . overevaluation of immediate goals as opposed to remote or deferred ones; unconcern over the rights and privileges of others when recognizing them would interfere with personal satisfaction in any way; impulsive behavior or apparent incongruity between the strength of the stimulus and the magnitude of the behavioral response; inability to form deep or persistent attachments to other persons or to identify in interpersonal relationships; poor judgment and planning in attaining defined goals; apparent lack of anxiety and distress over social maladjustment and unwillingness to consider maladjustment *qua* maladjustment; a tendency to project blame onto others and to take no responsibility for failures; meaningless prevarication, often about trivial matters in situations where detection is inevitable; almost complete lack of dependability of and willingness to assume responsibility; and, finally, emotional poverty.[49]

The same investigator has recently devised a scale which has successfuly differentiated between normal school children and behavior problem children, and between Army recruits in general and stockade prisoners.[50] The sixty-four items of the scale appear to involve such general matters as (1) "role-taking deficiencies, insensitivity to interactional cues and the effects of one's own behavior on others ; (2) resentment against family, feelings of having been victimized and exploited in childhood; (3) feelings of despondency and alienation, lack of confidence in self and others; and (4) poor scholastic adjustment, rebelliousness.

The general nature of the type of abnormality brought out by this scale is even more clearly focused in the contrast between those who score very high (abnormal) and those who score very low. Ten high-scoring and ten low-scoring subjects were studied by six members of the Personality Institute staff at the University of California. The traits of the low-scoring normal subjects were: calm, considerate, conventional, dependable, frank, good-natured, helpful, moderate, modest, natural, obliging, patient, peaceable, tactful, and unassuming. The traits of the high-scoring abnormal subjects were: affected, anxious, defensive, dissatisfied, emotional, headstrong, persevering, rebellious, sensitive, tense, wary. Their detachment from smooth-functioning social organization is obvious.

COLLAPSE OF THE LIFE ORGANIZATION

As stated in Chapter 4, each personality acquires organization not only from the general culture and from the groups to which he belongs, but also from the long view of his own future as he imagines and desires it to be. This integrated imagined future is called the life organization. In various ways it affects the integration of the roles a person maintains, guides many decisions he must make, and provides a general stability in his character. It may be illustrated by the view a college student takes of his future—to learn sciences, study medicine, become a physician, marry and have children, live in a comfortable and attractive home, take part in community activities, enjoy hobbies, see his children successful,

[49] Harrison G. Gough, "A Sociological Theory of Psychopathy," *American Journal of Sociology*, LIII, No. 5 (1948), 362.

[50] Harrison G. Gough, "The Identification and Measurement of Predispositional Factors in Crime and Delinquency: A First Report." Publication forthcoming.

and die leaving a good reputation and an estate. As previously explained, this integration, though existing only in the imagination, dominates motives in the normal person throughout the course of his life. Successful progress along the pathway to the goals involved is the principal component of general happiness.

Minor changes are in most cases readily made without disrupting a life organization. The man who finds that he cannot become a physician may change his goal and become a dentist or pharmacist. If the girl who is his first choice does not accept him, he marries another. If his children disappoint him he may compensate by activities with persons outside the family.

But major obstructions may be harder to handle, and in some cases may cause the whole structure to topple. Brittleness in the life organization may exist as a consequence of its extreme integration. A highly specialized person may develop all aspects of his personal skills and his character as well as all his social relations, exclusively with reference to the one principle of his specialty. If this central principle is then removed, virtually everything else is pointless and there is little or no basis on which to rebuild. Such a catastrophe as an extreme physical disability, an unendurable disgrace, or major failure may alone make the whole life organization impossible to fullfil, and thus may deprive the person of a major source of his motivation. Even in such cases it is sometimes possible to rebuild, to work out a structure along different lines, particularly if some relatively unintegrated aspects of the previous personal organization provide a basis for some versatility. In many cases, however, there is no apparent possibility of reconstruction, and so the collapse of the life organization produces a resultant important amount of disorganization of the person.

Among the common responses to failure of this kind is suicide.[51] In many cases the relation is obvious—the person commits suicide on the occasion of a major business failure, the exposure of guilt, the discovery of approaching blindness or painful disease, failure in an examination, the disruption of a marriage. In these cases, the event served to disorganize by removing an essential feature from the structure of the life organization so that a number of unendurable consequences appeared to be inevitable. In extreme cases this event removes all desire to live and in slightly less severe cases it reduces activity to a listless, day-to-day basis. An example of the

[51] See Ruth S. Cavan, *Suicide* (Chicago: University of Chicago Press, 1928), pp. 165 ff.

latter is supplied by a graduate student who was training for a career in a scientific field. His wife died while giving birth to a daughter. The man at once lost interest in his work and in all his plans, took only a mild interest in his infant, lived idly at his parents' home and allowed his mother to care for the child. He ceased to study and made no effort to find a job or even pursue a hobby. His life was reduced to a level of irresponsible idleness which endured for years until circumstances eventually forced him to go to work and support himself.

In some instances there is a similar response of elderly persons to the crisis of retirement. If the whole life organization has been built about the job, the person's character may go to pieces at this time leaving him without interests or satisfactions—a shattered personal organization. It has been plausibly argued that a certain amount of the deterioration associated with old age is not physiological in origin, but rather a consequence of this kind of disorganization. A study of retired professors provides some statistical confirmation of this principle.[52] In answer to mailed questionnaires, these subjects revealed their general reactions to retirement, which were then related to the number and range of their interests. Of the hundred whose reaction was judged "excellent," forty-five had many interests and only twelve had "few" interests. Of those eighty-five whose reactions were "uncertain and dissatisfied," only fifteen had many interests, and twenty-three had few. The figures showing the relationship to the range of interest give about the same results. Of the hundred retired men whose reaction to retirement was classified as "excellent," sixty-four had varied interests and only thirteen had narrow range of interests. Of the eighty-three whose reaction was classified "uncertain and dissatisfied," only twenty-six had varied interests and twenty-four had narrow interests. These interests apparently provided a core which held the life organization together to a satisfactory extent after the shock of termination of the professional occupation.

It appears likely that there occurs, in addition to catastrophic shattering of a life organization, a type of destruction of intermediate degree. In this type of occurrence, the achieved relations do not go to pieces, but the previous image of the future life weakens or disappears and the glittering ambitions once held, which formerly served as important elements in the motivation of general

[52] Elon H. Moore, "Professors in Retirement." Proceedings of a Conference on Research on Aging, August, 1950, Berkeley, California. New York: *Social Science Research Council.* Pp. 17-28.

activity, no longer seem possible. There is no complete collapse and demoralization of the person in consequence of this, but rather a loss of enthusiasm and a tendency to fall back on routines in work and in social life. There is no longer any driving effort to gain promotions or to expand a business, no further effort to improve the abilities, no search for new friends. Habitual activities may be carried on adequately but without enthusiasm. There is a consequent viewing of life as an essentially dull affair, and a tendency to question whether or not it is worth while. As previously pointed out, happiness does not exist solely in a present; if there is no appeal in a future, there is little sense of being involved in a happy life.

SUMMARY

The human personality is an organization of activity produced by experiences of interaction in a social process. The mere fact of interaction with other persons is not sufficient—the social system itself has an organic character. The social organization is brought within the individual to provide a basis for his personal organization, in the same way as the organized language is incorporated into integrated and useful speech habits.

This kind of personal organization is not a matter that is achieved in early life and perpetuated under its own power from then on. It needs to be sustained constantly by the same kind of organized social experience that creates it—constant regeneration is necessary to keep it alive. To behave normally is a highly active process requiring such continuous adaptation that it demands a constant use of skill and energy. A deficiency in any of a number of required conditions may impair the operation of this process and weaken or shatter the organization.

To conform to custom, to adapt to the expectations of others and thereby remain well-integrated in the constantly changing patterns of group life—this requires a complex operation of the central nervous system. Any defect in this physiological essential has immediate and important consequences to personality organization. Slight inhibition of some aspects of brain function due to the influence of alcohol or other drugs, and fatigue or disease, produces slight impairment of all kinds of problem-solving activity, including that related to the problems of adapting to the demands of social groups. More severe damage, such as that resulting from the prefrontal lobotomy operation, may seriously reduce this "abstract capacity," as Goldstein expresses it. The personality consequences are, in general, described as loss of such social skills as tact and consideration for others, apathy toward friendships, and the various kinds of clumsiness that result from inability to make complex judgments concerning the reactions of others toward one's own behavior. The essential skill involved in constructing and reorganizing the self is reduced by this physiological loss. Well-established routines may continue to work successfully, but there is no ability to work out new ways of acting if these older habits are inappropriate.

Since somewhat similar consequences have been observed to follow from such a range of physiological defects as those resulting from age, lack of oxygen, malnutrition, fatigue, and so forth, it appears obvious that an efficient nervous system is a requirement for normal personality, and that personal disorganization may follow from any of a number of kinds of physiological damage. Since the symptoms are often indications of lack of ability to do a certain type of performance, they may be similar in cases of impairment by different agents—that is, at certain stages oxygen lack and alcoholic intoxication may produce somewhat the same defects of functioning.

While physiological functioning of a high order is essential to the normality of a personality, it cannot alone achieve it. The organization of a normal mind is achieved only within the structure of social relations, and a variety of defects in this structure or a separation from the structure itself may also cause deterioration of the personal organization. In cases of total isolation from birth onward, no organization of a conventional personality is possible, as the occasional and accidental cases of such isolation have dramatically illustrated. In the experience of total isolation in adulthood after a fully normal personality has been firmly established, there nevertheless begins a process of disorganization which appears to be continuous with the length of the period of isolation. Such material as is available indicates that the disorganization may become serious and damaging within five months, and possibly totally incapacitating for social normality in something like two years.

A considerable amount of material dealing with partial isolation of various types provides a body of material to give further support to the above generalization. Persons who follow occupations so mobile as to prevent their participation in primary groups or integrated communities tend to show a certain amount of the same kind of disorganization of personality as found among

the spatially isolated. Similar consequences of their partial isolation are found among the unassimilated and solitary migrants from
other cultures, among persons, like the executioner or beggar, with
unconventional occupations, and among persons whose eccentricities or unfavorable reputations have kept them from acceptance
in their communities.

In most of the types of isolation mentioned there occurs, in
addition to a general loss of social skills, a kind of apathy or lack
of ambition for self-development of any kind. Motivation, as
shown in Chapter 4, is largely a matter of social influences. The
isolated person therefore suffers from a deterioration of motivation
and tends to do less planning for his future, to take less responsibility for himself, and in extreme cases, even to lose the will to live.
Research on suicide shows that isolation of one kind or another is
a frequent factor in cases of self-destruction.

A consequence of prolonged partial isolation during childhood
and youth appears to be the development of a kind of eccentricity
such as is characteristic in cases of schizophrenia. Here again, the
loss of conventional motivation has been noted and shown often to
be mistaken for actual deterioration of mental capacity. Mental
test performances of the schizophrenic are often actually inferior,
it is true, but in cases where the skill of the experimenter has been
able to bring out his cooperation, the motivated patient has shown
no inferiority of capacity.

The eccentricity of the schizophrenic is in part a simple consequence of the lack of participation in conventional groups. The
tendency to become preoccupied with unconventional interests,
to devise original figures of speech and employ deceptive metaphors, are examples of this kind of departure.

There is, however, a more fundamental type of deterioration
of the organized personality of the schizophrenic, resulting from
a complex of difficulties arising from the experience of isolation.
In a number of cases the first isolating factor in the experience appears to be the overprotection by a parent, usually the mother.
This produces a special role which makes the child less acceptable
to other children and thus exposes him to a certain amount of rejection and persecution. This leads to even closer attachment to
the mother for consolation, and so the two factors operate recipro-
cally to increase the isolation in a process that is difficult to reverse.
As a consequence, the child grows to adulthood without the advantages of primary interaction in the age groups appropriate to him,
and with a personality seriously distorted by the special influence

of a doting and sometimes culturally unbalanced parent. He lacks an important part of the knowledge of customs, of the subtle ways of people, and of the general principles of human competition and cooperation which are known to normal persons and which make it possible for them to be effective in personal relations.

Lacking this essential familiarity with people and social organization, the schizophrenic can experience a rich variety of difficulties which are essentially mysterious to him. In his attempts to understand and deal with these, he further compounds his troubles and reduces his chances of being understood and accepted by normal people. Because of the particular importance of success in life, the paranoid reaction of conceit and suspicion is a fairly common development. Also, because of the special importance of sex in life, and the special emphasis put upon its control in some subcultures, the psychotic response to discovery of one's sexual nature is common. The individuality of these responses is often so great that, without a full knowledge of the background of each person, the observer interprets them as the disordered product of a defective nervous system. With greater familiarity with the patient's background, he would recognize that the delusions are in fact often fairly reasonable conclusions drawn from experience, erroneous mainly because of the lack of that kind of conventional knowledge which enables normal persons to draw more efficient conclusions. As a consequence of this full acquaintanceship with the background of the patient behavior which appears to be hallucination may be understood in a different light—as having some relation to events as the patient interprets them, and as being in part the result of the habit of using metaphorical styles of expression.

In such fashion, extreme and prolonged social isolation—separation from primary relations which carry the essential content of the culture—so differentiates persons from conventional ways that their actions become so unintelligible that they are judged crazy. This judgment by normal persons further increases the separation of the isolate and therefore renders still more remote the possibility of reassimilation into conventional society.

Personalities may also go to pieces because of a special type of brittleness. Persons who build an organization of activity and attitude entirely upon a consistent life plan in a community may fail to develop adaptability and versatility. Thus, if some accidental event destroys the possibility of the fullfilment of this life organization, all the personality organization upon which it is based is weakened or destroyed. From such a collapse there may result a variety of reactions from light and temporary demoralization to suicide. In general, since motivation of complex activity in the normal life derives from organized social sources, the collapse of the life organization removes an important amount of the motivation to work, plan, or even to continue to live. The various experiences of persons who undergo such a shock illustrate the consequences of such a loss of motivation.

The present Chapter has shown in general that the achieved organization of the personality is the essence of normality of behavior. This organization can only be acquired by an active and undefective organism, and only in a successfully functioning social organization. Defects in either organism or social organization may affect the personal organization in varying degrees and in a number of ways. Our modern society contains large numbers of persons defective for both reasons, but it is probable that at present defects in the social organization are responsible for the greater amount of personal disorganization.

Selected References

Cameron, Norman. *The Psychology of Behavior Disorders.* Boston: Houghton Mifflin Co., 1947.

Faris, R. E. L., and Dunham, H. W. *Mental Disorders in Urban Areas.* Chicago: University of Chicago Press, 1939.

Hunt, J. McVicker (ed.). *Personality and the Behavior Disorders.* New York: The Ronald Press Co., 1944. An important symposium.

Chapter 15

TRENDS AND PROBLEMS IN
SOCIAL PSYCHOLOGY

Backgrounds of Contemporary Social Psychology

Social psychology is a relatively recent development, having had most of its career within the present century, and having entered the objective and scientific stage principally within the last quarter of a century. Thus it is a youthful field of study, and shows the characteristics of its lack of experience. Its advancement was delayed by circumstances which do not affect all other sciences. For one thing, the pursuit of an explanation of human behavior, particularly of complex social conduct, has been believed by many persons to be both useless and immoral, since it implies the operation of causation in what is conceived to be a completely free will. Also, some persons have accepted defeat in advance by supposing that any causation must be so complex that it is forever impossible to analyze the processes of the human mind.

It is easy to see how such discouragement would develop. Proverbs and romances abundantly emphasize the unpredictable character of the human. Men who are bewildered by the conduct of their own children can be excused for failing to see how even a beginning could be made upon the scientific study of the causes of social behavior. Until recently even those investigators who had strong scientific interests had little disposition to risk failure by applying their efforts to this field. Accordingly, it is not inappropriate to give some credit to those who ventured to make a beginning, even if little of value remains from their early findings. The beginners often took what in the end turned out to be an unprofitable road, but a road that had to be tried nonetheless. The fact that the ice was broken in this manner made the task of producing more enduring results easier for those who came along later.

The wrong road referred to above was the application of the principles of individual psychology. All the necessary mainsprings and gears necessary to move man were believed to be internal, and presumably required only a sufficiently penetrating type of physiological inquiry to reveal the formulas of behavior.

Nineteenth-Century Individual Psychology.—In about the middle of the nineteenth century a vigorous experimental movement in Germany laid the foundation for individual psychology. In their laboratories, Fechner, Helmholtz, and Wundt investigated and measured sensations and put their results in organized form so that they could be applied in practical ways. By 1874 Wundt published a general text called physiological psychology and, together with his colleagues, took world leadership in this kind of effort. At about this time William James and other American scholars learned of the movement and transplanted it to this country where the tradition was dominant for the rest of the century and a little longer. During this period it was generally considered desirable for the ambitious psychologist to obtain his graduate training in the German laboratories, acknowledged to be the sources of the best research.

The individualistic and physiological approach also took impetus from the prestige and influence of Darwin, who gave emphasis to the classification of man among the animals and showed the essential mental continuity among them. Pursuing this interest in the levels of mentality, English psychologists, led by Francis Galton, investigated the problems of mental inheritance and founded the practice of measuring mental ability by tests. The mind to be tested was conceived of as internal, physiological, and not importantly changed by experience. The mental test score, if properly computed, was assumed to correspond to a level of capacity fixed by heredity and unalterable by training. This outlook constituted a virtually pure individualistic approach; suggestions of early sociologists concerning the role of social experience in behavior and mentality produced no change of viewpoint.

Both of the above influences gained rapid popularity in the United States where the high standard of living and the rapidly expanding colleges and universities created a great demand for new scientists and new fields of knowledge. Laboratories sprang up all over and were equipped with gadgets for investigating sensations and feelings and for testing intelligence; new departments turned out increasing numbers of doctors in the field. By the early years of the twentieth century, the movement in this country had such impetus that it was no longer required of a man that he obtain his psychological training in Europe—the facilities in the United States had caught up in quality, and greatly surpassed the European in quantity of investigation undertaken. Boring has suggested that this expansion was a kind of frontier, and that the American wave of laboratory foundings was essentially a pioneer movement.[1]

While the air was still full of the Darwinian atmosphere, another influential American psychologist, G. Stanley Hall, spent his life working it into human psychology. To Hall the problem of psychology was to describe the organic unfolding of the mental life in the individual and to relate it to the development of his race and species, and eventually to show its unity with the whole evolutionary history of life. In the process of building this immense and symmetrical structure, Hall and his followers did not allow themselves to be unduly restrained by considerations of careful method. On the fragile basis of observation of a grasping reflex in infants and a small and casual knowledge of the behavior of monkeys, Hall produced a grand observation on the origin of a "climbing power of infants." It involved the assumption that ancestral races were tree-dwellers whose young had to cling, like young apes, to the fur of their mothers, or fall to the ground to be left behind as prey to enemies and thus be eliminated by natural selection. Fear of falling and the effect of falling asleep when being rocked were related to this arboreal period of life. In similar fashion, and at great length, Hall and his evolutionary psychologists interpreted other minor observations. He built his theory, as he said, from the top, and so it is of little surprise that it could not remain standing.

The instinct theory and the related theories putting motivation largely upon a biological foundation have already been discussed (see Chapter 2). It was founded upon the same conviction that the individual organism is all there is to the story, and that a complete inventory of its nature would provide a satisfactory account of behavior of all kinds.

The individualistic approach is still defended by such writers as Floyd Allport, who writes and conducts research in the name of social psychology, but insists that all the reality is within the individual and that the group, the society, the organization, is nothing more than an unreal abstraction. Of this whole movement, Reuter has made the following statement:

---

[1] Edwin G. Boring, "The Influence of Evolutionary Theory upon American Psychological Thought." Chap. vii in Stow Persons (ed.), *Evolutionary Thought in America* (New Haven: Yale University Press, 1950), p. 274.

The great and long-continued vogue of this type of social psychology has been due in considerable part to its quantitative and statistical aspects. It has flourished in the period of the rise of the statistical techniques and in part as a corollary of that development. Its vogue seems to have persisted somewhat beyond the period that would seem to be justified by the scientific fruitfulness of the point of view and the procedures. But work of this order will doubtless continue; probably it will increase as facility in the manipulation of the simpler statistical techniques becomes more general. A growth of this type is determined by facts quite unrelated to the question whether the procedures are to be classed as science.[2]

The above statement was written in 1940. Since that time there has been a perceptible drift further away from the individualistic point of view criticized by Reuter. It may be that the recent development of statistical tools applicable to other than the individualistic point of view has been a factor in making this shift possible. Whatever the causes, the nineteenth-century individualism approach has about reached the end of its vogue.

The Departure from Pure Individualistic Psychology.—It is not possible to furnish an exact origin of the tradition of thought which gave recognition to the role of interaction in organized groups in the formation and control of an organized personality. In a sense, this line of thought may be said to extend back at least as far as the ancient Greeks, but the Platonic reflections are too old and too interwoven with mysticism for most modern tastes. Nevertheless, to the extent that such concepts of society constituted a part of western thought during the centuries that followed, they may have played a part in directing attention to the collective aspects of human life.

Karpf has attempted to show a certain continuity through nineteenth-century European philosophers.[3] Hegel, though far from being adequate in the modern sense, is said to have provided by his concept of "objective mind" an escape from individualism and a route toward some kind of grasp of a collective process. Comte, who offered the word "sociology," more definitely argued for a really social psychology as against the individual psychology of his day which appeared to him little different from phrenology. To Comte, "the scientific spirit forbids us to regard society as composed of individuals" because "the true social unit is certainly the

[2] E. B. Reuter, "The Status of Social Psychology," *American Journal of Sociology,* XLVI, No. 3 (1940), 301.

[3] Fay Berger Karpf, *American Social Psychology* (New York: McGraw-Hill Book Co., Inc., 1932).

family. . . ." The individual in isolation was regarded by him as an abstraction.

In midnineteenth-century Germany there arose a tradition of *Völkerpsychologie,* a word translated in various ways, including "folk psychology" and "social psychology." A journal appeared with this name in its title in 1860, and not long afterward Wundt devoted himself intensively to the field, giving attention to language, customs, and history, and their influence on the behavior of man. He conceived of a "folk mind" which contained elements corresponding to the elements of the individual mind (imagination, feeling, volition) and decided that these elements were language, mythology, and custom. While the methods were naïve and faulty and the conceptions are no longer used, Wundt's prestige kept the focus of attention upon a collective process and upon the inadequacy of a purely individualistic approach. His work, and that of his colleagues and successors, furnished a basis on which later developments of sociology and social psychology in Europe were able to flourish.

Durkheim, whose important publications were issued in the last decade of the nineteenth century, was completely familiar with both the French line of thought from Comte and the German literature of Wundt and his successors. In his statement of sociological method, published in 1895, he succeeded in defining the collective process in such a fashion that it remains generally acceptable today, having been stripped of the mysticism suspected, perhaps with justification, to be in the German tradition.[4] Durkheim elaborated a distinction between actions which have a collective existence (social facts) and purely individual actions like taking a drink of water. A person who is performing his role as husband, brother, or citizen, or any other social role, is carrying out patterns of behavior which in a sense can be said to have an existence in the collective society rather than merely in himself as an individual. These roles are not created by each individual who conforms to them and cannot be explained by any original dispositions within his physiological nature. There is a sense, Durkheim insisted, in which these patterns are external to the individual, since they are there before he appears, and since they act on one in standard ways beyond his field of recognition. Furthermore, the existence of such patterns in the society operates as a force on his behavior—a "constraint." Any mystical meaning in this contention, however, was explicitly renounced by Durkheim—there are no societies without

[4] Emile Durkheim, *Les Regles de la methode sociologique* (Paris, 1895).

individual members, and the activities are performed only by individuals. There is no group mind or consciousness, although inventions and solutions may be reached in a collective process among persons.

Ethnological materials had been used by anthropologists, sociologists, and historians for some time, but Durkheim and his colleague Levy-Bruhl were influential in showing how these could be applied to matters essentially social-psychological. William Graham Sumner, with his influential study *The Folkways*, published in 1906, furnished support to this trend by giving attention to the exteriority and the compulsive character of customs.

The Emphasis on Modifiability Through Environmental and Social Influences.—It is an odd accident that the first books entitled *Social Psychology*, both appearing in 1908, were written by men whose points of view were more in harmony with the individualistic approach than with the organic viewpoint which was in time to become dominant in this field. The two authors, William McDougall and Edward A. Ross, had not much else in common. Both were good writers, however, and were very popular, and made important contributions by influencing many colleges to establish courses in the subject. Ross was a sociologist, a protégé of Lester F. Ward, and to some extent, a follower of the French individualistic school of sociology dominated by Tarde. McDougall was a psychologist and one of the most vigorous of the instinctivists. He made concessions to the collective viewpoint and reinterpreted instinct theory in the direction of flexibility, but never wholeheartedly tore loose from the foundation of individual physiology. Social psychology to him consisted largely of the study of environmental modifications of the individual, with a recognition of the outstanding importance of the social environment. He was capable at times of expressing a thought quite inconsistent with his individualism, such as, " . . . the strictly individual human mind, with which alone the older introspective and descriptive psychology concerned itself, is an abstraction merely and has no real existence." [5]

The major emphasis of McDougall, however, was not on the social aspect of psychology as characterized in the preceding statement, but on such aspects as the following which appeared a few pages later in the same publication:

[5] From *An Introduction to Social Psychology* (2d ed.), by William McDougall. Copyright 1926 by John W. Luce & Co. Reprinted by permission. P. 16.

The human mind has certain innate or inherited tendencies which are the essential springs or motive powers of all thought and action, whether individual or collective, and are the bases from which the character and will of individuals and of nations are gradually developed under the guidance of the intellectual faculties. These primary innate tendencies . . . are probably common to the men of every race and of every age. . . .

The evidence that the native basis of the human mind, constituted by the sum of these innate tendencies, has this stable unchanging character is afforded by comparative psychology. For we find, not only that these tendencies, in stronger or weaker degree, are present in men of all races now living on the earth, but that we may find all of them, or at least the germs of them, in most of the higher animals. Hence, there can be little doubt that they played the same essential part in the minds of the primitive human stock, or stocks, and in the pre-human ancestors that bridged the great gap in the evolutionary series between man and the animal world.[6]

It is this viewpoint which accounts for the fact that the lifework of McDougall did little to advance social psychology, apart from popularizing the title and the course among college students.

The school of psychologists called the "behaviorists" conceived social psychology in terms much similar to those of McDougall— that is, as environmental modification of innate tendencies. They saw the original tendencies, however, as reflexes, similar to but not identical with instincts. And, by the influence of Pavlov's experimentation, they gave their principal attention to one particular type of environmental modification—the process of conditioning. At their most exuberant, they attributed amazing consequences to this process. In spite of its slowness and laboriousness, conditioning was presumed to be the means by which all learning is accomplished. In the highly simplified laboratory situation with animal subjects, the results of the conditioning experiments were so gratifying in their precision and uniformity that there was little disposition to look toward the difficulties ahead. Since research early showed that the same process occurs in the human, it was considered only a matter of time before all elaborate social behavior— language, beliefs, moral standards, institutional behavior—would be interpreted on the basis of the conditioning of responses. For most investigators of this persuasion, however, it was personally preferable to devote the major part of attention to the study of animals, assuring results which could be counted on to be definite and scientific, and leaving the more difficult and uncertain task to others.

The essential failure of this approach has been described in

[6] *Ibid.*, p. 20.

earlier chapters. Even during the period when its popularity was at its height the essential defect was noted:

The exigencies of controversy have forced an interesting extension of the conditioned reflex, which has amounted almost to a repudiation of it. Curiously enough, this has received little attention, yet it seems to be a very vulnerable point. A conditioned reflex is a *movement which remains unmodified,* the "conditioning" consists in producing this movement by simultaneous association with the stimulus of another and irrelevant one. If the reflex is modified or changed the problem of the modification should receive attention. In a "behavioristic" system this is passed over. A "reflex" or "response" is often said to be "conditioned" when it is really modified or changed, that is, when it disappears. A child who learns to repeat what his nurse says to him is said to be conditioned. It is as if Pavlov, in reporting his experiments, would have recorded that the dog secreted saliva in response to a musical note associated with the original stimulus, and then had proceeded to record that in course of time the dog would come to play the violin.[7]

Although research on conditioning, either with animal or human subjects, is by no means at an end, recent years have seen many perceive the difficulty shown above, and the relation of conditioning to learning and other activity become a matter of open controversy. Precisely how learning takes place is not a matter of agreement—a number of theories now compete for a following and there is no certainty that the one that will be victorious has yet entered the arena.

The Emphasis on Interaction.—By the late nineteenth century, there had begun to emerge and compete with the still-expanding systems of individualistic psychology a tendency to consider social psychology as a study of interaction among individuals—sometimes called interpsychology. The conception of individual nature was not much different from that prevailing in other schools, but the attention was upon tides and trends, waves, epidemics, and other phenomena of mass suggestion and imitation. The prominent figure in the early period of this movement was Gabriel Tarde, whose major work, *Les lois d'imitation,* was published in 1890. Finding laws of imitation in the waves and epidemics of crime, he was encouraged to investigate language, art, law, institutions—in fact all the behavior of man, in similar terms. Imitation rose to the position of the distinctive factor in social life and became the basic principle of a system of social psychology and sociology.

[7] By permission from *The Nature of Human Nature* by Ellsworth Faris. Copyright 1937 by McGraw-Hill Book Co., Inc. The statement was written during the latter years of the 1920's, and is reprinted in the above book from a paper published at the earlier period.

Tarde had his followers in France, constituting a somewhat self-conscious school of thought. Prominent among them was Gustave Le Bon, whose *Psychologie des Foules,* published in 1895, gained great influence and had much to do with later interest in crowd psychology.

In the United States, Edward A. Ross, who shares with McDougall the distinction of first publishing a text with *Social Psychology* in the title, was essentially a follower of Tarde although he was also familiar with the contributions of contemporaries of different points of view. In Ross' view, the individual is a biological organism which is dominated and controlled by virtue of the fact that he lives with a great many similar organisms. He early stated that the original social forces were instincts but that these are affected in the interaction of crowds, fashions, convention, custom, and public opinion. In the processes of invention and leadership, great and exceptional men sometimes escaped from this domination of the individual by the currents of social life. Social psychology was in fact defined by Ross as the study of ". . . the psychic planes and currents that come into existence among men in consequence of their association. It seeks to understand and account for those uniformities in feeling, belief, or volition—and hence in action—which are due to the interactions of human beings, i.e. to social causes . . ."[8]

To Ross, some of the content of the minds of men was to be explained by this interpsychology—influences received from one another or from a common human source. A key concept was that of *suggestion*—defined as "the abrupt entrance from without into consciousness of an idea or image which becomes a part of the stream of thought and tends to produce the muscular and volitional effects which ordinarily follow upon its presence . . ."[9] Suggestions are forces which "enact themselves unless they meet resistance." Suggestion and imitation were viewed as two aspects, cause and effect, of the same thing.

The fields opened up by Tarde, Ross and their colleagues have not been overlooked since first being called to attention, but they are no longer conceived of as the main part of social psychology. The attention given to interaction produced results of value, but the full consequences of interaction apparently were not grasped by Ross. His influence, however, was great and valuable because of the vigor of his writing and teaching. He popularized the sub-

[8] From his *Social Psychology* (New York: The Macmillan Co., 1908), p. 1.
[9] *Ibid.,* p. 11.

ject and established it as one of the important inquiries in the field of sociology, not merely a subdivision entirely contained within academic psychology.

Emergence of an Organic Viewpoint.—Around the turn of the century there began to come into view a formulation which constituted a definite advance over anything previously known, approaching, in fact, a revolutionary redefinition of social psychology. The principal contributors were Charles H. Cooley, John Dewey, and George H. Mead. Some foreshadowing had appeared in the writings of J. M. Baldwin and others; later scholars, of course, built upon their contributions.

Dewey's famous paper of 1896 on "The Reflex Arc Concept in Psychology" furnished an important break with prevailing conceptions of the nature of action and was a part of the break with the notions of man as essentially little more than a physiological mechanism. The problem of social psychology became that of showing how the interaction process of a social organization is made internal in the individual so as to give him an organized personality. To do this involved a fairly thorough reinterpretation of the whole field of human psychology—an effort which took some years to develop and which is still in process. The main points, quoted below, of this restatement have been put in capsule form in a recent paper.

> The unit of study is the act. Within the act all the categories of the older psychology can find a place. Attention, perception, imagination, reasoning, and the rest occur, on occasion, when the action takes certain forms or meets certain obstructions. Likewise emotions, the whole gamut of them, can be related to the success, real or imagined, or the failure or frustration of the act or plan or enterprise. Instincts, emotions, imagination, are neither elements, things, nor forces, but are modifications of actions and could be more accurately referred to adverbially, did our idiom permit. But the act is not an isolated occurrence, and all action is, in some sense, interaction. Language distinguishes man from other animals, and language is the unwitting product of collective behavior. Further, the group in which the individual person moves is part of a larger whole, whence come the folkways and the mores, likewise the result of the collective experience which produced the mores without intending to do so.[10]

Cooley's influential *Human Nature and the Social Order*, published in 1902, had great influence in stimulating study of the social self as a consequence of participation in organized group life, particularly in primary groups. Cooley gave the primary group its

[10] Ellsworth Faris, "The Beginnings of Social Psychology," *American Journal of Sociology*, L, No. 6 (1945), 426.

name, and with the aid of his concept of "the looking-glass self" showed that this kind of social group formed the only mirror in which each member may learn what kind of person he is. Each person actively constructs his conception of himself out of the material provided by the reactions of other persons toward him. He must make the best interpretation he can—there is no exactness possible in the process—and the final organization is a matter of his images. But, as Cooley insisted, "the solid facts of social life exist in the imagination" and to know the approximate image a man has of himself provides a better basis of comprehension and prediction of his behavior than was ever given by the possession of a list of instincts or by a theory of conditioned responses.

Mead's contribution to this tradition, shown at some length in Chapters 5 and 7 of the present work, was to show the social process functioning to create the organization of behavior which is called the mind, and in more detail than provided by Cooley, the social origin of the self. His goal was to achieve this with no touch of mysticism, and to emphasize this he referred to his point of view as "behavioristic," although it had no resemblance to the behaviorism of Pavlov, Watson, and their tradition.

Mead's only publication presenting his full thought on this subject appeared after his death and was assembled by friends from notes taken in his course on Advanced Social Psychology. A major part of his influence was exerted through his colleagues and students who absorbed the material from his lectures and made use of it in their own teaching and writings. Since it is natural for knowledge gained in this fashion to appear, after its origins are forgotten, to be original with the user, Mead's influence is partly concealed. But all who have been exposed to his lectures acknowledge the magnitude of his achievement.

In essence, Mead provided an explanation of the origin of the mind in social interaction. The human animal does not begin life with a mind at all; rather, he acquires one. He is able to do this because of his unique ability to let the beginnings of acts function in place of the completed acts, and because of the fact that he lives in organized social relations which he can incorporate into his own repertoire to become his organized reactions. Until this is done his physiological mechanism does not constitute a mind at all—it is no more than an undefined mass of potentialities; without the process of social interaction, it never develops beyond that. Organization is all there is to mind, and Mead indicated how this organization is achieved.

Carrying on from the point to which Cooley developed the concept of the social self, Mead showed in detail how this aspect of mental organization is acquired within the social process. As shown in earlier chapters, the essence of the matter consists of the ability to take the responses of others into one's own activity, thus responding to one's own gestures and so incorporating a social process. By organizing the responses of others and of generalized others the person is able to build an image of his social self and to employ it in the interests of skill in his social relations.

Mead's colleagues and students applied and elaborated his analysis, and continue to do so at the present time. A recent development is the serious attempt to put certain aspects of it to objective experimental and statistical test, but this movement is too new to have gained great headway yet.

William I. Thomas, through his teaching, writing, and research influence, gave support to the general tradition described above even though some of his contributions were inconsistent with it. By urging the importance of life-history studies, and by such concepts as "definition of the situation," he focused the attention of many of his students on that type of approach harmonious with the above formulations of the mind and the self.

Ellsworth Faris contributed to the exploitation of the same line of thought through his teaching, articles, and influence on research. His large course on Social Psychology was for many years designed to prepare students for Mead's advanced course, and the materials of social psychology were here reinterpreted for the students in a way consistent with Mead's formulation. Two of his papers were of particular importance in making the break with the now unnecessary and conflicting instinctivism of the earlier individualistic period. One was, "Are Instincts Data or Hypotheses?" published in 1922 and contributing importantly to the abandonment of instinct theory, and the other was, "Of Psychological Elements," published in 1947,[11] which showed the futility of looking within the physiological mechanism for the elements of motivation. This latter paper in a sense completed the break with the individualistic point of view, and made it clear that the source of motivation as well as of mental organization is social, not biological.

A considerable number of contemporary contributors have acknowledged the influence of the above tradition without necessarily being committed to the kind of loyalty that constitutes a school of thought. Prominent among these are Herbert Blumer, Leonard

[11] *American Journal of Sociology*, XLII, No. 2 (1947), 159-76.

S. Cottrell, Alfred R. Lindesmith, Anselm Strauss, Norman Cameron, and others. It will be obvious to the reader that the present book is essentially based on the same tradition, but also not uninfluenced by the general experimental literature and by contributions from other approaches. It is presumed that this like any such line of thought of a rather distinctive character will, in time, be assimilated into the organized objective literature and undergo a considerable amount of revision and improvement.

The Gestalt and Topological Approaches.—A definite school of thought of German origin was built by Kohler, Koffka, Lewin, and others, based on but giving special emphasis to a few principles recognized by investigators of other traditions. Important among these was the recognition that perception is not a passive and immediate awareness of material entering the mind through sense organs, but is, as has long been recognized and demonstrated, an active process of selection and interpretation. The Gestaltists insisted that, by a sudden kind of apprehension, we create a whole out of inadequate or incomplete perceptions, "seeing," for example, a face in a few scratchy lines on paper or animals, butterflies, and such objects in random inkblots. The total contribution of these researches has provided useful additions to our general knowledge of perception; the main point—that perception is an active organizing process—has stood the tests of time and trial. Some modern investigators have questioned or challenged details of the *Gestalt* explanation—several, for example, have argued for the inadequacy of the learning as a result of a sudden, unanalyzable "insight," and have produced evidence that no such phenomenon takes place (see Chapter 8).

The *Gestalt* school also laid special emphasis on the completion tendency, and produced a number of experimental confirmations of the principle that uncompleted tasks remain to keep memory active. Recent research has altered details of this point also, but it remains as a useful contribution to understanding of human behavior.

Essentially the same sort of holism was applied by the Gestaltists to the personality itself, which was conceived as an irreducible unit. This conception doubtless reflects the dissatisfaction resulting from the earlier and futile search for the elements of behavior in physiology.

Under the leadership of Lewin, a special phase of investigation, called topology, has developed and waned. This inquiry consisted not primarily of new content, but rather of a method of approach to behavior. Its distinguishing characteristics were a wealth of neologisms and a graphic description of persons involved in situations. In the new terminology, wishes were replaced by "valences," environment by "life space," "social field," and "power field," and to some persons, psychology and sociology by "group dynamics." The new terms did not gain wide acceptance, and have declined in their use by those who coined them. In one of his last papers before his death in 1947, for example, Lewin wrote almost entirely in conventional vocabulary.

The graphic diagrams consisted of such patterns as oval lines drawn to encompass life space, smaller segmented ovals with irregular subdivisions to represent the person and some of his characteristics, lines and shaded areas to represent barriers, a cross within a circle to indicate a goal, and a dotted line with an arrowhead to indicate the direction of effort. Some of these patterns suggested to critics a kind of turtle-back design. Little use appears to have been made of such diagrams other than that of translating a verbal concept into spatial imagery, and the device has declined in use in recent years. Although with the death and dispersion of the leading members of the *Gestalt* school the movement itself virtually disappeared as an entity, some of the contributions remain as useful additions to social psychology in general.

Applied Social Psychologies.—Practical applications of social psychology as distinct from other fields of psychology have been of recent and less extensive development than such fields as testing. At the same time, the urgencies for applicable knowledge have been greater in this field than in any other since the most extensive and pressing human behavior problems are those involving the whole personality rather than the minor deficiencies of abilities and traits and other aspects of the individual. Since organized, tested, and applicable knowledge in this field has been slow to develop, applications have grown up somewhat detached from academic social psychology. To meet the insistent public demand, clinical psychologies were built on whatever basis of theory or knowledge was at hand to the practitioner.

By far the most spectacular of all the applications has been that of psychoanalysis, begun by Freud in the early years of the twentieth century. Freud was trained, not in academic psychology, but in medicine. His interest in psychological matters grew out of the popular applications of hypnosis to hysteria and other symptoms of mild abnormality. Freud worked out the searching interview method, encouraging the patient to speak fully and freely about early memories, dreams, present feelings, prohibited subjects, and other material about which persons may ordinarily be reluctant to talk. The method appeared to produce dramatic cures in so many cases that Freud attracted wide attention and eventually drew many students and followers. He became admired and respected as a revolutionary practitioner and widely followed as an authority.

Freud's therapeutic method did not have within it any experimental character that would furnish crucial tests of any theory. Nor was there available in his early productive years any other tested theory which seemed to have any relation to his results. He therefore created out of the medical preconceptions and instinct psychology of his early years a theory of his own. This was elaborated over the course of years but not substantially modified in essentials. Nor did it ever make effective contact with the growing knowledge of academic social psychologies. As a consequence, the theory retained, in Freud's and his most loyal followers' conceptions of it, a considerable burden of obsolete notions of the late nineteenth century—notions of biology, psychology, sociology, and anthropology. In recent years, a number of revisions and interpretations have been proposed, retaining the method and some of the conceptions, but eliminating the instinctivism, the inherited unconscious memory of the Oedipus killing, and other clearly impossible elements. Not all psychoanalysts, however, have embraced such revisions, and in some quarters there is a thought that to do so is to throw out Freud altogether since the whole structure of psychoanalysis as he saw it, and insisted upon, was inseparably bound up with these theoretical points.

Thus it was that the largest and most influential movement of clinical psychology developed in a separate and somewhat hostile setting and has only come to speaking terms with academic psychology in recent years. Problems of cooperation still remain, since in general the psychoanalysts insist upon the necessity of medical training as a qualification for the profession, and as medical doctors they tend to be unwilling for the most part to cooperate with nonmedical psychologists on equal terms—for example, a clinic which contains men of both professions must have a medical man at the head or the medical doctors will not take part at all. Academic psychologists do, however, on many occasions accept this stipulation, and at the present time cooperation and interstimulation are steadily advancing.

The original movement of psychoanalysis has produced related daughter movements under the leadership of men deeply influenced by Freud but differing in aspects they believed essential. Alfred Adler broke away and became the leader of a separate school to which he gave the name "Individual Psychology." As Adler conceived it, the great motivational principle is not sex or libido, but rather an almost desperate desire to overcome or compensate for an inevitable sense of inferiority with which each person starts life. The infant is presumed to feel frustrated by his small size, weakness, and lack of ability and power in comparison to older persons. As Adler saw it, no proof of this proposition was necessary; the infant could not avoid observing the actual situation and logically being outraged. Adler further interpreted most of the behavior of childhood and adult life as a set of attempts to do something about this intolerable inferiority. As he conceived it, every person must drive himself toward superiority of some sort; failure to achieve it satisfactorily results in various complexities and disturbances. The appropriate treatment had less connection with protracted analysis than did the Freudian method and was primarily on the level of consciousness, with interpretations of experiences and life history for the purpose of giving the patient a degree of self-control.

Another outgrowth of the Freudian tradition was the line of inquiry and theory initiated by Jung, who popularized the division of personality types into the categories of introversion and extraversion—terms now assimilated in altered form into the vocabulary of the man on the street. To a considerable extent, Jung made this set of categories the key to his clinical approach. These have been detached from other aspects of his theory to such an extent, however, that there is no longer any general association of them with a particular school of thought. Jung's influence otherwise never extended widely, and a number of brief histories of social psychology have appeared in recent years with no mention of his name. The same is true of various other minor leaders of schisms from the Freudian tradition.

During all the period in which psychoanalysis of various types has been flourishing, there has also been a less doctrinaire pursuit of knowledge of social psychology by clinicians in other fields such as orthopsychiatry, clinical psychology, and clinical sociology. Many of these investigators, particularly in the academic fields, have kept familiar with the literature from every kind of approach and have selected certain useful terms, principles, and findings of each.[12] In the nature of this kind of scientific pursuit, "great men" and "great books" do not stand out. Knowledge is pursued in small amounts, shared by publication and assimilated through cooperative discussion, and is thus a result of a collective process which is entirely lacking in the authoritarian character of those organized schools of thought in which the leader may sometimes be designated "The Master."

While it is difficult to generalize on what the developments in clinical psychology have been, a few trends may be picked out for emphasis. For a time, the emphasis was to a considerable extent on testing of various kinds; a professional operation of which the psychologist had a virtual monopoly. Along with this came an attention to a number of minor behavior problems—nail-biting, enuresis, and the like. Such interest dominated clinical psychology through the 1920's or so.

In the 1930's there developed, no doubt from the example of psychoanalysis, an interest in the use of some of the analytic techniques—free association, the "depth interview," projective techniques, and the like—without commitment to any of the distinctive psychoanalytic theories. The "nondirective" interview technique publicized by Carl Rogers, the Rohrschach tests and related devices, and some of the psychodramatic and group therapy techniques may be mentioned as examples.

A relatively recent development is the attempt to discover principles of social psychology through actual experimentation on small groups. Some of this has been done by the "dynamic" disciples of Lewin, some by persons who designate their research as "sociometry," and some by others belonging to no particular classification. While time has been insufficient for this trend to have made contributions of magnitude, the amount of interest is sufficient to indicate that many persons consider this a promising trend. To some extent, the effort has suffered from an attempt to do too much with an inadequate experiment. For example, in the frequently cited experiment on the reaction of children to different types of leadership, many persons have presumed that the study successfully demonstrated that a "democratic" style of leadership operates with

[12] Leonard S. Cottrell, for example, has recently listed the persons who have been most influential in his particular assembly of knowledge. The list includes G. H. Mead, John Dewey, Sigmund Freud, Kurt Koffka, R. E. Park, E. W. Burgess, H. D. Lasswell, H. S. Sullivan, J. L. Moreno, and Kurt Lewin, and he adds that there are many others. "Some Neglected Problems in Social Psychology," *American Sociological Review*, XV, No. 6 (1950), 705-12.

more efficiency than does an "authoritarian" or a "laissez faire" type of leadership.[13] In view of the excellent discipline, morale, and fighting qualities of some of the fascist organizations, as well of many an "authoritarian-led" football team in the United States, it would appear that such a conclusion is more the product of wishes than of science. As minimum improvement required in a study of this sort, it would be required that some method insure that the leaders involved in the experiment be prevented from loading the results by being more pleasant in the democratic relation and less so in the others, and that subjects be provided who have not been bathed for most of their lives in an atmosphere of freedom, equality, and of dislike for leadership of a military or fascistic character. Both of these conditions would be difficult to accomplish in the United States, but nevertheless some such measures are necessary before the results can be trusted.

Other experiments have been tried to discover the processes by means of which a small group solves a problem, or arrives at a decision, to discover the effects of different types of organization of the behavior of members of a group, to test the effects of discussion and criticism on the phenomenon of emotional catharsis, to test the influence of changes in social atmosphere on the productivity and morale of factory workers, and a variety of similar issues. Not all this research is clinical, nor is it all done by psychologists, but it is an effort in which clinical psychology joins to make its contributions to the general fund of social psychology.

Applications of Social Psychology to "Social Issues."—From time to time a particularly impatient number of investigators has urged the pursuit of solutions to the most pressing problems of the day—war, crime, racial antagonisms, labor conflicts, and the like. Spontaneous efforts in this direction have occasionally been made by individuals, but in 1936 a group was organized to speed the effort—the *Society for the Psychological Study of Social Issues*. Through research promotion and the publication of a journal and yearbooks, this organization has stimulated research in a range of problems and has issued public announcements from time to time concerning issues which it assumed could be illuminated by psychological understanding. Prominent among the present interests of the members of this organization are problems of industrial morale, leadership, social class, race prejudice, mass rioting and mass hysteria, propaganda, and war.

[13] Summarized in Newcomb, Hartley, *et al.*, *Readings in Social Psychology* (New York: Henry Holt & Co., Inc., 1947), pp. 315-30.

It is characteristic of such research to get somewhat ahead of firm knowledge, and a certain amount of the material is frankly presented more in the spirit of hastening improvement and reform rather than in the spirit of objective research. Even where experimental and statistical techniques are employed there is often an appearance of a political or humanitarian attitude which enters into the findings—as illustrated by an emotional flavor shown in some of the studies of the "class system" in the United States by the attempt to show mental or personality abnormality in persons with undemocratic political views or with racial antagonisms, as well as in some of the industrial studies of worker-employer relations. While there is no reason to suppose that unbiased research is impossible in the fields that touch upon "social issues," it is probably true that at present such interests may select a type of investigator whose haste for improvement may interfere with the soundness of findings. This consideration, however, does not by any means prevent such investigators from making useful contributions to organized knowledge, and much of the "social issues" research is in a form that can be used and integrated with knowledge gathered elsewhere.

The Decline of Schools of Thought and Emergence of the Mature Scientific Stage.—Comte once stated that all sciences tend to progress through three stages—theological, metaphysical, and scientific. Park and Burgess restated the general principle by describing the three stages as first essentially metaphysical, then a period of schools of thought, and finally a period of investigation and research—the mature scientific stage.[14] It is a matter of general conviction that the flourishing of a number of rival "schools" in any emerging discipline reflects a scarcity of tested conclusions and a lack of adequate method. Their presence indicates a difference about fundamental matters and an inadequacy of communication. To the extent that a school of thought has a leader—an authority—it indicates that there is no general concept of a research method which can furnish the same result to persons who begin with different expectations.

The "school" phenomenon develops a crippling rigidity in the persons who are members. The leader generally commits himself so publicly, so vigorously, and in such organized fashion that his mind inevitably tends to be closed to contrary findings. In extreme cases, not at all uncommon in the recent history of science, such

[14] R. E. Park and E. W. Burgess, *Introduction to the Science of Sociology* (2d ed.; Chicago: University of Chicago Press, 1924), p. 44.

persons may reject all evidence, however strong, that conflicts with their central notions, as did many a biological authority whose prestige was threatened by the conclusive and revolutionary studies of Darwin and of Pasteur. The followers of any school have their own kind of rigidity, which may match that of the leader. Attitudes of affection, respect, and loyalty toward the leader may make them unable to accept any knowledge which does not have his approval. Experience shows abundantly that the human mind is capable of rationalizing away any kind of experimental finding in such circumstances. The convinced cultist does not ask, "What is the evidence?" but rather, "What is our official attitude on this?" His attention is on the "party line" rather than on scientific method.

Since the early 1920's the development of objective methods has accelerated and penetrated more and more into the various branches of social psychology, thereby weakening the doctrinaire aspects of the rival schools and settling the issues that divided them. Schools disappear, true, with varying speeds of expiration, but today little of the early dogmatism in social psychology survives and some factions as such have virtually vanished. There seems reason to expect the remaining ones to follow the same course and thus soon bring social psychology into its period of maturity.

BASIC RESEARCH PROBLEMS

Social psychology, which is distinct from individual psychology in its concern with the person as a whole and as a product of group life, has most of its triumphs yet ahead of it. The past quarter of a century has seen a gathering momentum of investigation and fruitful conceptualization, but has not brought the solution of all the major issues. Two important achievements were the breaking away from mysticism and the escape from the overly-restrictive conceptions of nineteenth-century biology, but many difficult problems still await solution. It is not possible to formulate all that concerns investigators at the present time; even if this could be done, new difficulties would continue to emerge as the science progressed. Certain major tasks are, however, conspicuous on the present research scene, and it is appropriate in this section to characterize some of them briefly.

The Definition of Physiological Essentials to Normal Behavior.— The abandonment of the instinct theory and of the conceptions of mind as composed of certain "faculties" has set the inquiry free from the domination of biology and physiology. This important advance does not, however, make physiology irrelevant to all aspects of behavior, and no modern investigator proposes to entertain the conception of a mind without an organism. Mind can be thought of as a way in which a physiological mechanism is organized for general functioning as a whole in social life. The mechanism must be present in order to be organized, and although the patterns of organization come into it from the outside, the organized behavior is within the physiological organism itself.

There remains much to be investigated concerning the aspects of the physiological mechanism which constitute the mind and the self. It does not help to dismiss the problem by stating that the mind occupies the whole body. Fingernails and hair can be trimmed with little or no observable alteration of mental organization: in some cases detached objects not actually a part of the body —clothing, possessions, insignia—may function more like elements of the self than do these dispensable parts of the anatomy.

Similarly, toes and fingers, or even larger members, can be removed without essential personal alteration; no one misses his tonsils or appendix after their surgical removal. The loss of arms, legs, eyes, and other instruments of acting and perceiving restricts certain possibilities of functioning, but still does not strike at the physiological center of the self. It is conceivable that research will in time establish the indispensable physiological elements which must all be present and normally functioning in order for mind, self, and normal behavior to be at all possible. This would have to include all the physical processes necessary to preserve life processes, but would not be coterminous with them—a living human organism can exist without mentality or personality. Evidence has been presented (see Chapter 14) to show that the frontal areas of the brain are peculiarly necessary to certain complex mental functioning, but not required for routine human behavior; other parts, however, are crucial for such matter-of-course operations as walking and breathing. Further research will in time define what parts of the brain are necessary for certain functions, and will thus furnish the basis of interpreting many observed defects of behavior. In similar fashion, endocrinology as well as other fields of physiology are expected to define various other types of essentials.

On the other hand, one must not expect too much of physiology. A brain defect may inform us why one man cannot speak at all when others have no difficulty. In such a case physiology may completely settle an issue of behavior. But there will occur other examples of speechlessness in no way connected with physiological defectiveness, and many other issues in speech behavior—fluency, richness of vocabulary, and the like—which can be solved completely only in terms of experience rather than physiology. The biological mechanism is in no way causally related to the problem of explaining why certain persons speak Italian as a native tongue while others speak Chinese.

Much needless controversy will be eliminated when research defines the physiological essentials for normal human behavior and when investigators learn to state the issues in such terms that they can be put to crucial test. The immediate future is highly promising for advances in these respects.

Abilities.—As shown in Chapter 10, physiological research has not been successful in providing the explanation of any large part of the range of human abilities. It appears likely that each person's mechanism does furnish varying upper limits for mental functions of certain types, but there is little final knowledge even in this matter. Marked physiological deficiency is, of course, unmistakably the source of mental incapacity in some cases. But within the normal population it seems highly probable that few persons achieve, or even approach, the upper limit of the physiological possibilities. If every person did in fact reach all his ceilings in this regard, then all variations in ability in the population would be the result of differences in physiological capacity. Otherwise, and this appears far more likely in the present state of our knowledge, most of the variation in the population would be a consequence of factors other than the biological.

Richness of contact with sources of knowledge, motivation, methods of thinking and conceptualization, accumulated and organized mental tools for problem solving (illustrated by the tables and arrangements of numbers employed by the mental calculators), and other unmeasured and relatively inconspicuous factors—present knowledge has shown that all these are important in determining the mental achievements of persons. While there are doubtless unsuspected factors that will be uncovered in time, there is great opportunity for research in the devising of measurement and statistical analysis of those already pointed out.

It is in such a field that there is particularly great promise of practical applications of research knowledge. The mental development in a population is an important aspect of the standard of living, and of the power and safety of the nation, and the development of this type of resource could be more important than new discoveries of oil and coal deposits.[15] There is reason to suppose that the population of this country, high as it may be in comparison with many others, is far short of its actual possibilities in this respect. The educational system has given no great amount of attention to the development of maximum ability, and educational psychology has tended to concentrate more on the measurements of ability and prediction of achievement than on attempts to develop higher abilities.[16]

There are also possibilities in applying the findings of research on abilities to those individual cases where deficiencies of certain types interfere with success and happiness. In recent years it has been found that, contrary to earlier beliefs, many types of reading defects can be overcome by training, and that slow and inefficient readers may learn to become superior in this skill. Recent methods of language training have also revealed the spectacular possibilities of development along this line, in contradiction of a long-followed assumption that each person is endowed with a fixed amount of language ability which can be estimated by scales but not improved by training. There is undoubtedly a great deal of undeveloped

[15] The United States is fortunate to have a wealth of natural resources, an essentially sound (in comparison with other nations) social and political organization, and a high development of ability in the population. To illustrate: During the Second World War there occurred a sudden demand for persons qualified to manufacture, operate, and repair radar equipment. To train persons in electronics theory and mechanical skills from the ground up would be slow and costly. But there existed in the population a stored capital of technical knowledge in the many thousands of amateur radio operators. Many of these were called in for a course of training which had no set time schedule—each person was assigned to a plant for study until it appeared that he was ready for work. In such fashion some were found to be qualified after only two or three weeks, and the nation quickly gained the benefit of this particular resource of ability. This type of story was repeated many times in both military and civilian participation in the war. The same stored ability is also an important part of our productive capacity and inventiveness in peacetime.

[16] The history of psychological interest in musical ability furnishes an illustration of this emphasis. As shown in Chapter 10, recent research proves that one of the presumably basic traits used by musicians—pitch discrimination—is subject to alteration by training. And yet for years such a possibility was denied, and the techniques employed in this matter consisted of tests intended to reveal the fixed amount of discrimination each person possessed. If his score was low on this and other aspects of musical ability, the person was then discouraged from musical study. Some training schools in fact refused admission to those whose scores were low.

Intelligence tests and tests of other abilities have been used for the greater part of the present century in essentially the same spirit. The dominant conception of educational psychology has been that abilities were fixed at a certain level in each child and that nothing could be done to change them. The school systems have much to learn concerning ways to apply the contrasting knowledge now available, and will doubtless be able to make revolutionary changes in policy after further advances in research on abilities.

talent in every person; talent which, when desired, could be brought out by proper methods in the interest of success and happiness. This will very probably constitute the accomplishment of the next half-century.

The Formation and Rigidity of Character.—Conceptions of the degree of stability in the organization of habits and attitudes have varied over the whole conceivable range. An early notion of flexibility is revealed in the concept that a drunkard, a criminal, a despot, could be transformed in a moment by a process of conversion, which gives him a character as new as if he had been reborn. In contrast, there has for some time prevailed in psychology a conception that character is formed within the first few years of life, and can, from then on, be changed only superficially if at all. Neither of these conceptions is based on an adequate method of investigation, and, in fact, there is very little record of direct attempts to make a crucial, statistical test of character rigidity.[17]

Careful organization of what is now known and further research on the stability of habits would permit an assessment of the degree of stability resulting from this factor. There remain, however, various other factors to be investigated. The organization of habits into an interrelated pattern may produce a further reason for their resistance to alteration. These patterns may then be the basis which leads the person to be discriminating in his choice of environments and of social relations and will be further supported by organized group life; a member of a particular religious group, for example, might restrict his primary relations as far as possible to members of his own church, or a golf enthusiast seek the company of other golfers. Further investigation, therefore, of the construction of life organization in the development of each person and of the influence of this on the stability of his behavior should give promising results. Since the life organization is integrated normally with an elaborate social organization, it appears plausible that it is the most important source of character stability. Complex and internal as this phenomenon may be, there is no reason to suppose that it will not yield its characteristics to ingenious statistical inquiry.

---

[17] A careful survey of the literature on this, along with other matters concerning personality traits, was published in 1939. The complete confusion in the literature is well illustrated there. Virtually each one of the whole range of possibilities is supported by a number of authors, and every conceivable explanation is offered for both fixation and mutability of personality traits. See Clarence Schettler, "Topical Summaries of Current Literature: Personality Traits," *American Journal of Sociology*, XLV, No. 2 (1939), 234-59.

Empathy.—As has been shown abundantly throughout the present volume, role-taking is of crucial importance in the organization and control of the person by his social groups. Empathy, or the empathic response as it is sometimes designated, lies at the heart of this process. The concept of an instinct of imitation has long been out of vogue, and for good reason; but there remains a problem of how it is possible for a person to take the role of another and see himself essentially as the other person does. Mead's analysis in terms of inhibited responses to one's initiatory gestures appears highly promising, and deserves further exploration by objective techniques. Furthermore, there is a great need for the investigation of the differences in empathetic skill from person to person, and of the processes by which such skills are acquired. Few persons challenge the practical importance of such a measure of intelligence as the I.Q.—it has been shown to have some relation to the degree of accomplishment in many fields. Personal skill in effective handling of other persons, however, is also generally conceded to be important, although more difficult to measure and explain. It may have a component of factual knowledge—that is, we are more skillful in dealing with persons if we have a good deal of accumulated information about their particular type—but it is also possible that an important factor is the generalized empathetic sense that operates to reorganize activity and the self so that social interaction may proceed smoothly.

Personal Disorganization.—A considerable amount of knowledge is available on the effects on behavior of physiological deficiencies of various kinds and degrees. At certain degrees of seriousness, these may make impossible the normal organization that is personality and character. It is also widely recognized that social organization is necessary to furnish and govern the patterns which become personal organization, and that there are interrelations between social disorganization and personal disorganization. There is considerably less development, however, of this line of research. Some of it has been presented in the present volume, but this amount barely opens up the subject.

It is possible that throughout all the degrees of consistency in behavior of persons, and all the degrees of effectiveness and skill in their dealings with others, there is a relation between the degree of personal effectiveness and the amount and type of participation in social organization. The man who is preferred over a close rival for a promotion in his job may owe his superiority to sense of tact and propriety gained in social relations not available to the other fellow—he may, for example, have spent a few years at a preparatory school where poise and manners constituted a part of the tradition and atmosphere. Similarly the thick-skinned person who offends by his blunt remarks about the persons he is with may encounter repeated social and business disadvantages because of this deficiency in social skill, resulting from lack of experience in sensitive, mannered groups.

There is probably also a variety of mild discontents, restlessness, and vague dissatisfaction with life which could, through adequate analysis, be connected with lesser degrees of social disorganization and inadequate participation by the person in the organized groups of his general society. The person who fails to find a satisfying occupation and moves from job to job and city to city may suffer from the difficulty of building a satisfactory life organization. He may not be disorganized in the ordinary sense, nor even be miserable or bitter, but he may have a disquieting sense that he is not getting anywhere, that life is a generally unsatisfying experience, and that careful work and conforming behavior are unrewarded and scarcely worth while. Since the dissatisfactions of such a person appear relatively trivial in comparison with those of the neurotic or psychotic, little research and clinical attention are given to his problems. If it is recognized that mild discontent exists among many million of persons, however, the importance of the condition will become more obvious.

As shown in Chapter 14, some attention has been given to the relation between severe personality difficulties and social disorganization, but even here only the merest beginning has been made. There is an immense promise in the investigation of the consequences of isolation of every kind and degree. By this means it may eventually be possible to specify the sociological essentials for normal personality in the way that dietary essentials are revealed for the physiological organism. The amount and kind of experiences in social groups of various types, and the consistency of exposure to an integrated social order, may be prescribed in the manner that the various types of foods, minerals, and vitamins are now given in diets. There is already a vague recognition of the general principle, even in folk knowledge; most persons now realize that every child needs a sympathetic family, a good deal of play with persons of his own age group outside the family, a rich exposure, through formal schooling, reading, and general experience, to the general culture, and other such essentials. But this field remains essentially unmeasured and holds its secrets for future research to discover.

Emerging Research Problems.—The issues that make conspicuous appearance are usually those on which substantial investigation is under way. As a science progresses, topics of minor interest which were virtually ignored at one stage may later break into prominence and become major fields of investigation. It is characteristic that many scientists who first notice a new phenomenon do not automatically recognize the significance which in time becomes obvious. Edison could notice a glow on the end of a vacuum cathode tube without recognizing the possibility of the vast and important field of electronics in the same way that many a biologist noticed a clear area about a speck of mold on a slide without at once foreseeing the importance of penicillin and related drugs. Similarly, the future major problems in the field of social psychology at present may be lying inconspicuously in details which may have been observed, but not fully comprehended. The emergence of new issues, new fields, new lines of promising research is one of the few virtually certain aspects of the growing science of social psychology.

CONTEMPORARY RESEARCH METHODS

A considerable proportion of the content of courses and books in the field of social psychology at the present time may be fairly said to rest on no real method at all. Folk knowledge remains as a visible element in this content, and, in fact, is not necessarily the weakest part of it. Many a social psychologist fills in missing links by drawing on his beliefs, absorbed informally during the experiences of his life and untested by any means at all. An additional content of much social psychology is furnished by intentional observations so unchecked and uncontrolled that they can be assured of no uniformity from one investigator to another, and with little cumulative tendency. All this is social psychology without method, and while better than no social psychology at all, it cannot make satisfactory progress without the application of techniques for objectifying, standardizing, measuring, and crucially disposing of issues in the process which transforms informal beliefs into science.

The transformation to the scientific basis is under way, and while its origin cannot be dated precisely, it is essentially a matter of the last quarter of a century with a period of acceleration beginning around the period of the Second World War in the 1940's.

There is little reason to doubt that the acceleration will continue and that each decade to come will yield a larger and more solid amount of tested and organizable knowledge in this field. What new methods will emerge cannot be predicted now—to predict them would be about as difficult as to invent them. In the discussion below is presented a review of some of the instruments in use and under development at present.

The Clinical Method.—The essence of research in the clinic is the intensive and usually somewhat informal analysis of the whole person with some focus on a particular difficulty which provides the reason for his appearance as a patient. The investigator or practitioner applies whatever skills he has acquired in his training and experience and learns what he can by inference, intuition, or insight. Precisely what these latter processes involve and the extent to which they can be trusted are matters in controversy. To the vigorous defenders of the clinical approach it can be granted that such personal judgment is not likely often to be entirely in error, and that some persons may possess an exceptional amount of skill in producing an apparent success of treatment and in offering suggestive hypotheses for research. The clinician is also in a favorable position to observe hitherto unnoticed phenomena and thus bring them to the attention of other researchers, and to see the various aspects of a person and their interrelations in a way which may escape an experimenter or a statistician. For these reasons, the value of clinical study is not questioned here.

There are deficiencies, however, in the clinical type of study if it is conceived of as a complete method in itself. The long-term record of theories based largely on clinical study shows little tendency of such knowledge to converge except as persons tend to adopt allegiance to a common authority. Observers with different conceptions derived from separate schools of thought persistently differ in their observations and interpretations of fact. Defenses and rationalizations of doctrinaire conceptions flourish in such an atmosphere.

The science of medicine took many centuries to learn the penalties of *post hoc* reasoning. It was eventually recognized, however, that it was not enough to treat a person, observe his recovery, and attribute the recovery to the treatment. In the case of many ailments, most persons recover anyway, with or without treatment, and a control group of equally sick and untreated patients is among the requirements for a sound inference about the effects of the

treatment. The mere fact of having a control group does not, however, constitute adequate research techniques. There are important issues in the matter of the equivalence of the two groups
being compared. To assess a treatment of alcoholic addicts, for
example, by giving a cure to those who volunteer for the treatment
and by using those who do not volunteer as a control group, is to
invite serious error.

Even in cases in which an adequate control group is used, there
remains a question of what in the treatment was the effective element in the production of the result. It is well known in medical
research that injections of pure water, administered to a person
who believes he is receiving an effective drug, frequently produce
the same appearance of improvement and recovery that is observable in cases in which the actual drug was used. Thus it is uncertain whether in the latter case the drug or the drama is the effective
element. Similarly, in clinical psychological treatment, it may be
difficult to discriminate, in the absence of elaborate experimental
technique, which of a dozen or more elements involved may have
been the factors producing the change in behavior. In the naïve
use of clinical methods, the procedure has been for the practitioner
to claim that the cause assumed in his theory was the effective
agent, but an examination of the history of clinical work unmistakably reveals the weakness of this policy.

Another common source of error in the clinical practice when
unguided by other methods follows from the natural enthusiasm
and optimism of the practitioner. Hopeful of his method of treatment, he tends to find more success than is really there, or even to
find some success when there may be none at all. This occurs with
no trace of dishonesty, but is the result of a natural bias which is
extremely difficult to avoid and which affects the judgment of the
person under treatment as well as that of the clinical practitioner.
The degree of unreality of such judgment uncontrolled by objective
techniques is shown by the example of the well-known Cambridge-
Somerville Youth Study.[18] A carefully controlled ten-year experiment in the prevention of juvenile delinquency among teen-age
boys found, on the basis of objective evidence, that there was virtually no reduction of delinquency as a result of the treatment.
Nevertheless, the opinions of the trained workers, sought during
the course of the treatment, reflected a strong belief that their
methods were effective. On being asked how many boys they be-

---

[18] Edwin Powers, "An Experiment in Prevention of Delinquency," *Annals of
The American Academy of Political and Social Science,* January, 1949, pp. 77-88.

lieved had been "substantially benefited by their contact with the study," the workers listed about two thirds of the boys being treated, and listed about one half as having received "outstanding" benefits. Among the boys, more than half expressed a belief that the treatment had benefited them. There is little doubt that such an experience is highly typical of informal methods of treatment in many fields.

The optimistic bias of the practitioner is not an insurmountable barrier to research; it merely imposes a technical requirement on the process of judging results of a treatment. The requirement is that the judgment be made by objective methods and by someone other than the hopeful advocate of the treatment, and that, whenever possible, this disinterested observer not know which patients receive the treatment and which ones are in the control group. This method is known and followed in some fields of research, and is often emphasized as an absolute necessity for sound evaluation of any treatment.[19]

The Life-History Method.—For some decades there has been a keen interest in the value of an extensive life-history study of a person as an instrument of research in social psychology. As in the clinical method, the person is seen as a whole and in his social relations, and to a certain degree the patterning of his life history becomes evident. In general, the virtues and deficiencies of this method are similar to those of the clinical method. New possibilities are discovered by this informal type of research, and interrelations become evident which would be difficult to discover in other ways. The person who engages in a large amount of life-history study tends to gain a degree of general insight which may be of value even though it cannot easily be described. He may possess an informal kind of wisdom which will operate to protect against unwarranted conclusions based on more objective methods.

[19] The director of research on the common cold at a laboratory in Salisbury, England, makes reference to this necessity in describing how one must judge the results of efforts to transmit a cold to a sample of patients. "The bacteriologist who has prepared these materials [nasal secretions from persons with colds, a harmless broth or salt solution, or materials of unknown properties] makes the inoculations from numbered bottles taken at random. Neither Smith nor his doctor knows what preparation Smith has received; that will be made known only at the end of the trial, when the clinician has committed himself in writing as to the result. It is not easy to tell just when a person has a mild cold and when he hasn't, and *with the best will in the world an observer cannot make an unbiased judgment* in borderline cases if he has a preconceived idea as to whether the patient ought to be getting a cold or not." Christopher H. Andrewes, "The Common Cold," *Scientific American,* February, 1951, p. 41. (Italics by the present author.)

By itself, however, the life-history method is not an adequate method of discovery. Its value is greatest if used with other more objective methods. Without such support of other methods, it is subject to the same cultish, follow-the-leader tendencies, the *post hoc* fallacy, and the personal biases which are revealed as common in the unguided clinical method.

Testing and Scaling.—Scaling devices perform two important functions in social psychological research. They provide a means of transforming factors of a subjective quality into useful objective material in such a way that other independent observers, using the same devices, can obtain the same results. Ideally they should be able to do so regardless of any differences in point of view, school of thought, or other expectations or states of mind. The best examples of scaling approach this ideal, and, although others are less successful, most scales contain at least some of this type of advantage.

The second function of scaling is to transform qualitative material into quantitative data, thereby putting it into a form available for statistical research. There is a general and growing assumption that all qualities are at least theoretically scalable and that no type of data is necessarily inaccessible to all kinds of mathematical study. To the extent that this is so, the scaling operation is an important step in the transformation of unorganized material into science.

Within the past quarter of a century there has been a rapid growth of appreciation of these devices, which still continues at an accelerated pace. A large literature has accumulated dealing with techniques of scaling, and with various attitudes, opinions, qualities, and relations to which scaling has been applied. The literature is too large to be summarized here; but a few basic approaches may be mentioned.

The technique of equal-appearing intervals, originally devised by Thurstone and Chave, has had much development and use.[20] The original development was made in connection with the scaling of attitudes for or against such subjects as racial groups, religion, or warfare. In essence, the method involves the gathering of a number of statements presumed to reflect different degrees of the attitude under study. These are sorted by judges chosen for competence into categories representing varying degrees of favorableness to the subject, not according to the judge's attitude, but ac-

[20] Louis L. Thurstone, and E. J. Chave, *The Measurement of Attitudes* (Chicago: University of Chicago Press, 1929).

cording to his conception of the meaning of the statement to most persons. Certain statements usually turn out to be too ambiguous to be useful, but others appear to mean about the same to the different judges. These latter are then selected, given a scale value according to where they appeared in the judges' categories, and used for the final version of the scale itself. The typical finished scale contains about fifteen or twenty relevant and relatively unambiguous statements, arranged in random order representing scale values over the entire range of favorableness. It is put in use by allowing a subject to check the statements with which he agrees. The mean or median scale value of these statements constitutes the person's score. The device has proved to be valuable in practice, although it has been pointed out that two persons could have the same score and not agree to the same statements. The necessity of using judges is also conceived as a disadvantage of the method.

A related method, sometimes called the "technique of summated ratings," or the "method of internal consistency," was developed by Likert.[21] The essential difference from the Thurstone method lies in the determination of scale values. The scale allows for five possible responses for each statement, in such grades as "strongly agree," "agree," "undecided," "disagree," and "strongly disagree," which are assigned arbitrary values from 1 to 5 in that order. A large sample of subjects is used for trial checking of the statements. The statements which are found, on analysis, to discriminate between the high-scoring and low-scoring subjects are then chosen for the final test. A statement, or item, is said to discriminate successfully if there is a difference, at a chosen standard of statistical significance, between the responses of the persons whose total scores lie in the highest quartile and the persons whose total scores lie in the lowest quartile. These items are thus most consistent with the total score, and therefore most useful in producing it.

More recently, a different principle of scaling was developed by Guttman, referred to sometimes as the "Cornell technique."[22] It involves a selection of statements which have a virtually invariable order in the judgment of subjects—that is, any person agreeing to a statement in the middle of the series would agree to *all* statements on one side in the order. In practice, a small variation from this perfect standard is possible without destroying the usefulness of the results, but, to the extent that the order is perfect, the scale

[21] Rensis Likert, "A Technique for the Measurement of Attitudes," *Archives of Psychology*, XXII, No. 140 (June, 1932), p. 5-55.

[22] Louis Guttman, "A Basis for Scaling Qualitative Data," *American Sociological Review*, IX, No. 2 (1944), 139-50.

score can be read backward to indicate the attitude—a characteristic not present in other scaling devices.

Certain elaborations of the method have been worked out. An objective method is available to determine the point of neutrality on a given issue. Elaborations of further dimensions of scaling are at present under development, and this particular technique is in a period of rapid growth. The reader who wishes to be current in the modern techniques of scaling would do well to keep watch of the unfolding research literature on this phase of the subject.

A device somewhat similar to a scale—the sociogram—has been in common use in recent years in a special field of interest of sociology and social psychology called "Sociometry." In applying this method, each person in a group or community is asked to make certain choices or rejections of other persons in answer to such questions as: "Whom would you prefer as a roommate?" A chart is then made representing each person by a symbol, such as a circle, and each choice or rejection by a line or an arrow. By this means it can be determined objectively which persons are popular, or leaders, or frequently chosen, and which are isolated. Groups of persons interconnected with lines indicating choices are identifiable as cliques. Ratings for each person may be made based on the numbers of times chosen or rejected by others. Uses of such devices continue to grow in research on the interaction of persons in primary groups.

Statistical and Mathematical Techniques.—The past quarter of a century has witnessed a development of statistical tools and of methods of application that has been of great importance in social psychology. The accomplishment is too great to be summarized briefly. It involves the transformation of subjective material into objective and of qualities into quantities, the precise measurement of variables, the measurement of relations between two or more variables, computations concerning the probability of a decision's being correct, the disentanglement of a set of intertwined causal processes (that is, the discovery and measurement of factors contributing to a phenomenon), and other valuable services to the science.

At the present time the statistical and mathematical developments are far ahead of the applications in social psychology. It is therefore reasonably certain that a rich exploitation of this bag of tools is in prospect in the next few decades. Since there is no sign that the basic mathematical development will slow up, the possibilities are even more attractive for the future. There are more and better statistical methods than social psychology has yet found a use for, and there are calculating machines of incredible refinements available to perform the drudgery at high speeds. The statistical problem consists at the present time of finding the issues that can be handled by these tools, and of putting them into the proper form for treatment. To do this requires understanding of the tools, and involves a considerable knowledge of mathematics. The research social psychologist of the near future will have a great advantage over his colleagues and rivals to the extent that he possesses high qualifications in mathematics as well as mastery of the subject matter of his field.

Although it is often held that the perfect method of science is the laboratory experiment in which the effect of one variable at a time can be isolated, it is often overlooked that essentially the same operation can be performed statistically by calculation of the influences to be varied and the separate measurement of the factor of special interest. Actually, there are some advantages in the latter procedure over the mechanical laboratory experiment. If the data are satisfactorily measurable, it is valuable to compute all the influences in the same operation, rather than to leave some unmeasured and pursue the process of elimination. Furthermore—and this often overlooked point can sometimes be of great importance— the statistical process may reveal some effects of the *interaction* of certain factors in addition to the effects of each of these factors separately. In research involving a small number of observations, it is sometimes impossible to draw a definite conclusion about the results unless the accidental sources of variation in the result are reduced to a minimum by the measurement of the interactions as well as of the separate factors.[23]

Another important promise of modern statistical methods is that of handling what appears at first to be a bewildering complexity. Some persons have in fact retreated from a problem without even attempting a start on the ground that human behavior is obviously so complex that it is futile to attempt an analysis. This impression of hopeless intricacy, however, can be produced by the mixture of a limited number of factors, appearing in different combinations and varying proportions. The untrained investigator, facing the

[23] This point, completely unrecognized by many persons who write on research methods, is clearly presented in R. A. Fisher's *The Design of Experiments* (London: Oliver and Boyd, 1936), and in various other modern texts dealing with analysis of variance.

confusion with no knowledge of how many such factors are involved and no conception of how to begin the process of finding the order in the data, is understandably ready to assume the presence of countless thousands of interacting factors. Such a statistical procedure as factor analysis, however, may reveal that six or eight principal factors can account for most of the phenomenon under investigation.

Factor analysis was developed by Thurstone and others in the quest of the elements of intelligence or ability. While the technique is not yet perfected, it is probably correct in reducing the intelligence test complex to a handful of elementary factors. These may be reclassified and redefined later, but the number of major factors is unlikely to increase to any considerable extent.

In Chapter 4 the research of Winch is cited to show that the courtship behavior of college men is probably reduceable to a set of six or seven factors. Happiness in marriage could be analyzed in the same way, with a not unreasonable amount of research effort. The determinants of status and leadership, as well as many other matters of interest in social psychology, are discoverable by such means.

An interesting illustration of the use of this technique is furnished by a wartime research project of the Office of Strategic Services Assessment Staff, published in *Assessment of Men*, New York, 1948. Candidates for dangerous assignments behind enemy lines were assessed in a set of trials of many kinds, lasting for several days. The trials were physical, mental, organizational, moral, and of other qualities, and yielded measurements or estimates on such variables as motivation for work, energy, initiative, emotional stability, social skills, leadership, ability to assume a false role, persuasiveness, skills in observing and reporting, and others. The factor analysis process, though admittedly incomplete and somewhat defective in this application, simplified these into four principal factors, which were named *adjustment* or *adaptability, effective intelligence, physical energy,* and *authoritative assertion.* What is required for success in such an assignment may turn out to be, if this conclusion is confirmed, an adequate amount of four or five abilities of this general sort.

In a growing field such as this, new developments are always to be expected, and it appears virtually certain that statistical and mathematical methods will be of increasing importance in future research in social psychology.

Experiment.—The popular notion that science can never be applied to human behavior, based on the grounds that one cannot experiment with persons or groups, is overthrown by the fact that there appears increasingly in the research literature a volume of actual experimental results. Certainly the convenience of the laboratory experiment is not comparable; it is not easy to obtain satisfactory conditions for experiments on human behavior, but there is nothing in principle that bars the use of experimental techniques in the full sense of laboratory science.[24]

Throughout the present volume there are cited various examples of attempts at experimental research in social psychology. In the early period of this methodological development, only relatively simple issues were approached in this way. Testing was of such matters as the influence of a competitive situation on the degree of effort expended and the results achieved by persons performing physical and mental tests. More recently, there has developed an interest in the study of interaction processes by such experiment. No large contribution has yet come from this development; the effort is in fact in the ground-breaking stage. As would be expected, the studies which attempt to deal with important issues— the study of democratic and authoritarian leadership mentioned earlier in the Chapter, for example—usually tend to produce inconclusive or controversial findings. The experiments which yield decisive results do so because they are less ambitious projects. Both types of study, however, advance knowledge in one way or another, and both contribute to the experimental habit and frame of mind which is important to maintain in a developing science.

Summary

Social psychology has taken about a century to find its problems, concepts, and methods, and to grow into the stage of mature progressive development in the manner of the more experienced sciences. It took some time, in fact, for the notion to emerge that there is such a field as social psychology; although throughout most

---

[24] The word "experiment" has, of course, a range of meanings in popular and even academic usage. It is sometimes used to designate a policy adopted on trial, without any technical means of assessing the effects of the trial—in the sense that prohibition of liquors or the enrolling of women in the military services is an "experiment." It is commonly used in the social sciences to designate trials of the above sort in which there is a methodical attempt to test the results by some technical, usually statistical, device. In the present discussion, however, the reference is to research which involves some actual manipulation of conditions, often in a laboratory, in such fashion that factors can be separated and observed or measured.

of the nineteenth century the organized nature of life was recognized by some philosophers and sociologists, psychologists conceived of the person mainly in terms of physiological processes and instinctive motives. The outstanding achievement in the early years of the present century was to turn attention to the proper inquiries—to the problem of the organization and control of the behavior of the person by the social relations in which he is enmeshed.

The divorce from the biological dogmas took time. It was an awkward time for a while because there was nothing satisfactory to replace it. The contributions of Dewey, Cooley, Mead, and others of their tradition served to show both the inadequacy of earlier conceptions and a specific and plausible way in which mind and self could be understood as emergents of the social process. Motivation of most behavior is dominated more by these constructed integrations than by any biological drives or needs. More abnormalities of mind and behavior result from inconsistencies and disorganization of these than from physiological defectiveness. The task of recent years has been in part to unify social psychology and to relate its material systematically to these principles.

The unification has been slowed by the separation of certain lines of inquiry. For a time there was insufficient communication between sociological and psychological research and teaching so that each field was slow to profit from the discoveries of the other. Furthermore, not only has clinical study been somewhat separated from main research traditions, but an important part of it has even been inconsistent with academic knowledge until recent years. Regrettable as the fact may be, it is useless to deny that the large and influential field of psychoanalysis was constructed on assumptions independent of and in conflict with the established body of academic social psychology scholarship. In recent years, however, a considerable amount of reinterpretation and reconciliation has been taking place as many followers of the Freudian and related traditions have discarded certain of the instinctive aspects of the theory and replaced them with conceptions which are current in academic social psychology. At the same time, the investigators in the latter field have become conscious of the concepts and methods employed in the clinical approach, and have become interested in testing and putting to use those aspects of it which seem worthy.

The development of research methods has been an important factor in the reduction of rivalries and of schools of thought. A half century ago social psychology had no method which could be designated as scientific. The clinical method by itself, and even the unaided life-history method, did not contain any principles which insured firm advancement. These methods have value, and are, in fact, probably indispensable to social psychology; but unqualified by more objective techniques they are almost as helpless as one blade of a pair of scissors. It is the development of methods of measurement and of the crucial resolution of issues by tests, scales, statistical techniques, and experiments which transforms the inquiry from an aimless drifting of rival schools of thought to a firmly organized and growing body of tested knowledge. This last stage is of such recent development that the mature period can be said to have barely begun. Its prospect within the next few decades is, however, of a progress far more rapid than any previous development.

SELECTED REFERENCES

General works and discussions of method:

ANDREWS, T. G. (ed.). *Methods of Psychology.* New York: John Wiley & Sons, Inc., 1948. Chapters by twenty-two authors, dealing with methods and some recent research results. Fairly representative of modern developments.

HUNT, J. McVICKER (ed.). *Personality and the Behavior Disorders.* New York: The Ronald Press Co., 1944.

LINDESMITH, ALFRED R., and STRAUSS, ANSELM L. *Social Psychology.* New York: Dryden Press, 1949. A modern text with a sociological viewpoint.

McCLELLAND, DAVID C. *Personality.* New York: William Sloane Associates, 1951.

MERTON, ROBERT M., and LAZARSFELD, PAUL F. (eds.). *Continuities in Social Research: Studies in the Scope and Method of "The American Soldier."* Glencoe, Illinois: The Free Press, 1950. Stimulating discussions of theory and method.

MILLER, JAMES GRIER (ed.). *Experiments in Social Process: A Symposium on Social Psychology.* New York: McGraw-Hill Book Co., Inc., 1950.

MURPHY, GARDNER. *Personality: A Biosocial Approach to Origins and Structure.* New York: Harper & Bros., 1947. A systematic modern treatise.

NEWCOMB, THEODORE. *Social Psychology.* New York: Dryden Press, 1950.

NEWCOMB, THEODORE, and HARTLEY, EUGENE L. (eds.). *Readings in Social Psychology.* New York: Henry Holt & Co., Inc., 1947. Many brief items of both research and discussion on assorted aspects of social psychology.

ROHRER, JOHN H., and SHERIF, MUZAFER (eds.). *Social Psychology at the Crossroads.* New York: Harper & Bros., 1951. Seventeen papers by participants in a conference in 1950.

SHERIF, MUZAFER. *An Outline of Social Psychology.* New York: Harper & Bros., 1948.

SHERIF, MUZAFER, and CANTRIL, HADLEY. *The Psychology of Ego-Involvements: Social Attitudes and Identifications.* New York: John Wiley & Sons, Inc., 1947. Deals with the conception of self and its significance to behavior.

YOUNG, KIMBALL. *Personality and Problems of Adjustment.* New York: Appleton-Century-Crofts, Inc., 1947. A recent eclectic text.

History of social psychology:

FARIS, ELLSWORTH. "The Beginnings of Social Psychology," *American Journal of Sociology,* L, No. 6 (1945), 422-28.

KARPF, FAY BERGER. *American Social Psychology: Its Origins, Development and European Background.* New York: McGraw-Hill Book Co., Inc., 1932. A thorough and well organized history.

REUTER, EDWARD B. "The Status of Social Psychology," *American Journal of Sociology,* XLVI, No. 3 (1940), 293-304.

WOODARD, JAMES W. "Social *Psychology.*" Chap. ix in G. Gurvitch and W. E. Moore, *Twentieth Century Sociology.* New York: The Philosophical Library, 1945. Contains a useful bibliography.

INDEX OF NAMES

Adler, A., 385
Allport, F. H., 5, 16, 17, 216, 372
Allport, G. W., 29, 183, 190, 194, 208, 217, 218, 221
Alper, T. G., 43, 131
Alvarez, W. C., 30
Ames, A., Jr., 187, 198
Ampere, A. M., 235
Anderson, C., 228
Anderson, W. A., 254
Andrewes, C. H., 399
Andrews, T. G., 79, 188, 225, 407
Archibald, R. C., 234
Aristotle, 27-28
Asch, S. E., 208

Baldwin, J. M., 150, 153, 379
Bartemeier, L. H., 347
Bartlett, F. C., 182, 190, 194, 195, 198
Bateson, G., 307
Beasley, V., 263, 264
Bell, E. T., 243
Benedict, R., 307
Berelson, B., 206, 277
Bernard, J. S., 318
Bernreuter, R. G., 164
Berreman, J. V., 23
Binet, A., 154
Birch, H., 173
Blanchard, P., 126, 289
Blanton, S. and M. G., 181
Block, H., 208
Blumer, H., 75, 381
Bode, B., 84, 92, 93, 94, 113
Bogardus, E. S., 213
Boldyreff, J. W., 204, 220
Bolles, M., 334, 335
Bonner, J. T., 6
Bonney, M. E., 264
Boring, E. G., 13, 16, 27, 37, 38, 88, 95, 121, 130, 131, 134, 136, 138, 191, 192, 193, 336, 372
Bourne, A., 154

Brockway, A. F., 340
Brooks, F. D., 125
Bruner, J. S., 188, 189, 212
Buck, P., 298
Burgess, E. W., 17, 205, 287, 386, 388
Burma, J. H., 263
Byrd, R. E., 342

Cameron, N., 133, 140, 147, 149, 194, 201, 282, 316, 317, 323, 328, 351-53, 358, 359, 360, 369, 382
Campbell, E. H., 26
Cantril, H., 150, 171, 182, 187, 189, 190, 191, 206, 207, 217, 407
Carmichael, L., 16, 231
Cavan, R. S., 363
Centers, R., 275
Cézanne, P., 202
Chapin, F. S., 231
Chapman, D. W., 227
Chave, E. J., 400
Chertok, E., 164
Child, I. L., 228
Churchill, W. S. L., 209
Clark, G. 96
Clinard, M. B., 347
Cobb, S., 334
Cohen, L. H., 134
Colburn, Z., 234
Coleridge, S. T., 141-44
Comte, A., 373-74, 388
Conn, J. H., 25
Conrad, H. S., 225
Cooley, C. H., 5, 10, 171, 250, 280, 379-81, 406
Cooper, E., 210
Cottrell, L. S., Jr., 171, 180, 287, 382, 386
Cowgill, D. O., 81
Cronkhite, B. B., 160
Crutchfield, R. S., 70, 107, 189, 212, 221, 323
Curie, E., 239, 297

409

Dallenbach, K. M., 130, 131
Darwin, C., 13, 239, 371, 389
Dase, Z., 235
Dashiell, J. F., 227
Davis, C. M., 19
Davis, K., 343
Dawson, C. A., 340
Dembo, T., 106, 107, 229
Dennis, W., 16, 307
Dewey, J., 10, 84, 91, 94, 113, 379, 386, 406
Dollard, J., 85, 321
Dorcus, R. M., 137
DuBois, C., 307
DuBois, P. H., 140
Dunham, H. W., 354, 369
Dunlap, K., 17
Durkheim, E., 374, 375
Duvall, E. M., 28
Dymond, R. F., 171, 180

Ebbinghaus, H., 131
Edison, T., 239, 243, 396
Edwards, A. L., 129
Erikson, E. H., 307
Euclid, 243

Fairbanks, G., 97
Fales, E., 228
Faris, E., 10, 14, 32, 33, 50, 57, 178, 224, 225, 251, 280, 323, 377, 379, 381, 407
Faris, R. E. L., 65, 238, 249, 315, 317, 354, 359, 369
Fernberger, S. W., 211
Festinger, L., 229
Figner, V. N., 340
Finan, J., 69
Finger, F. W., 312
Finkelstein, S., 235
Fisher, R. A., 403
Fitzgerald, A. P., 61
Flanagan, D., 132
Flowerman, S. H., 245
Forbes, T. W., 140
Fowler, R. G., 52
Fredericksen, N., 322, 323
Freedman, A. S., 346
Freud, S., 23-27, 103, 114, 120, 124-25, 128, 132, 321, 383, 386, 406

Gall, C., 133
Galton, F., 371
Gaudet, H., 206, 217, 277
Gauss, K., 235
Gettys, W. E., 340
Gibbon, E., 243

Gibson, J. J., 176, 177, 198
Gillin, J., 307
Gilmore, H. W., 347
Goldsborough, L. S., 28
Goldstein, K., 331-33, 351, 365
Goodman, C. C., 188, 189
Gorer, G., 307
Gough, H. G., 362
Gowin, E. B., 205
Grabbe, P., 212
Graves, R., 141
Gray, G. W., 335
Gross, L., 59
Guetzkow, H., 308
Gurvitch, G., 408
Guthrie, E. R., 199
Guttman, L., 401

Halbwachs, M., 195, 199
Hall, C. S., 104
Hall, G. S., 25, 372
Hallowell, A. I., 307
Harding, T. S., 58
Hardy, E., 242
Harlow, H. F., 39, 173, 174, 175
Harlow, M. K., 173
Harms, I., 233
Hartley, E. L., 194, 207, 387, 407
Hattendorf, K. W., 26
Havighurst, R. J., 261, 268, 269
Haydn, F. J., 241
Hayner, N. S., 346
Heathers, L. B., 129
Hebb, D. O., 83, 96, 182, 185, 199, 333, 334
Hegel, G. W., 373
Helmholtz, H. von, 371
Henry, J. and Z., 307
Herodotus, 143
Herrick, C. J., 83
Hertzman, M., 208
Hertzog, H., 217
Heyer, A. W., Jr., 191
Hilgard, E. R., 80, 134, 199
Hill, R., 28
Hobhouse, S., 340
Hollingshead, A. B., 233, 252, 255, 257, 261, 264, 265, 266, 280
Hollingworth, L., 60
Horowitz, E. L., 150, 207
Horton, L. H., 103
Hovland, C. I., 214, 221, 322
Hughes, E. C., 58
Hulett, J. E., Jr., 299
Hull, C. L., 177, 199
Hume, D., 243

Hunt, J. McV., 19, 24, 126, 229, 289, 311, 312, 334, 338, 349, 350, 351, 352, 369, 407

Ives, G., 340

Jacobson, A. H., 299
Jacobson, E., 39, 95, 179
Jahoda, M., 210
James, J., 255, 263
James, W., 371
Janet, P., 154
Jenkins, J. G., 70, 130, 131
Jenkins, W., 291
Jennings, H. H., 166, 256, 291, 308
Jersild, A. T., 103
Jersild, C. L., 103
Jones, C. H., 315, 316
Joyce, J., 242
Jung, C. G., 385

Kamen, M. D., 7
Kanner, L., 25
Kardiner, A., 307
Karpf, F. B., 373, 408
Kaufman, G. S., 240
Keir, G., 138
Keister, M. E., 324
Kellogg, W. N., 79
Kelly, L. I., 191
Kennard, K. M. S., 96
Keys, A., 21
Kluckhohn, C., 24, 307
Kluckhohn, F., 298
Koch, H. L., 128
Koehler, W., 173, 174, 382
Koffka, K., 382, 386
Komarovsky, M., 286, 296, 298, 299
Kramer, B. M., 190
Krech, D., 70, 107, 189, 212, 221, 323
Kunst, M. S., 26
Kuo, Z. Y., 13

LaBarre, W., 307
Lamarr, H., 297
Landis, C., 334, 335
Langfeld, H. S., 13, 16, 27, 38, 88, 95, 121, 130, 131, 134, 136, 138, 191, 192, 336
Lashley, K., 96
Lasswell, H. D., 386
Lazarsfeld, P. F., 190, 206, 277, 407
LeBon, G., 378
Lepkin, M., 216
Levine, J. M., 127
Lewin, K., 212, 229, 382-83, 386

Liddell, H. S., 311, 312
Likert, R., 401
Lincoln, A., 201
Lind, K. N., 209
Lindesmith, A. R., 22, 121, 285, 291, 308, 382, 407
Lindzey, G. E., 190, 208
Linton, R., 307
Locke, H. J., 17, 205
London, J., 303-4
Lowes, J. L., 141, 142, 144
Lowie, R. H., 253
Luce, A., 121
Lukomnik, M., 44
Lumsdaine, A. A., 214, 221
Lundberg, G. A., 7, 263, 264
Lundell, C. L., 342
Luriĭa, A. R., 134

Mackenzie, C., 20
Maier, N. R. F., 328
Malzberg, B., 348
Mangus, A. R., 348
Markey, F. V., 103
Masserman, J. H., 74, 311
McCarthy, D., 231, 232, 233
McClelland, D. C., 407
McDougall, W., 14, 375, 376, 378
McKinley, D. G., 164
Mead, G. H., 107-9, 113, 150-53, 169, 171, 178, 379-81, 386, 394, 406
Mead, M., 298, 307
Merritt, C. B., 52
Merton, R. M., 407
Meyer, C. T., 256
Meyer, D., 39
Michener, J. A., 54
Mill, J. S., 242
Miller, J. G., 116, 124, 128, 132, 137, 145, 148, 176, 321, 407
Miller, N. E., 322
Mitchell, F. D., 236
Mitra, D. N., 57
Moerenhout, J. A., 271
Moore, E. H., 364
Moore, W. E., 408
Moreno, F. B., 257
Moreno, J. L., 28, 256, 386
Morse, N., 213
Moss, F. A., 199
Mowrer, O. H., 24
Mozart, W. A., 238-39, 241
Munch, P. A., 269
Murphy, G., 7, 10, 13, 33, 36, 37, 39, 44, 45, 48, 50, 76, 81, 105, 127, 139, 140, 154, 230, 407

Murphy, L., 230
Murray, H. A., 19, 131, 307
Mussolini, B., 311

Napoleon, 293
Newcomb, T. M., 194, 207, 222, 230, 276, 287, 407
Newton, I., 243
Nimkoff, M. F., 85
Northway, M. L., 262

Ogburn, W. F., 85
Osler, Sir W., 30

Parfitt, D., 133
Park, R. E., 386, 388
Pasteur, L., 239, 389
Patrick, J. R., 277
Pattie, F. A., 136
Patton, G., 293
Pavlov, I., 78-79, 82, 312, 376-77, 380
Pfeiffer, J. E., 7
Picasso, P., 202, 242
Plato, 243
Posner, B. A., 122
Postman, L. J., 183, 194, 217, 218, 221
Powers, E., 398
Pratt, K. C., 16
Prince, M., 154

Radcliffe-Brown, A. R., 254
Radke, M., 207
Razran, G. H. S., 82
Reuter, E. B., 372, 373, 408
Rice, S., 208
Richards, I. A., 160
Riley, M. W., 245
Rivers, W. H. R., 270
Rizk, A. M., 288
Rogers, C., 386
Rohrer, J. H., 31, 39, 407
Rohrschach, H., 386
Roosevelt, F. D., 209
Roosevelt, T., 63, 293
Rosenzweig, S., 19, 131
Ross, E. A., 375, 378

Safford, T. H., 234
Saul, L. J., 20, 21
Scheerer, 333, 351
Schettler, C., 393
Schindler, J. A., 29, 30
Sears, R. R., 24, 26, 27, 103, 125, 126, 129, 132, 145, 148, 283, 318, 322
Sears, P. S., 229
Seashore, C. E., 245, 246
Senden, M. N., 184
Shaffer, L. F., 125

Shakespeare, W., 46, 242, 243
Sharp, A. A., 128, 129
Sheffield, F. D., 214, 221
Sherif, M., 31, 39, 100, 150, 171, 182, 189, 190, 191, 206, 207, 407
Sherwood, R. E., 240
Shock, N. W., 338
Sidis, B., 242
Sidis, W., 242
Silverman, B., 318
Sims, V. M., 277
Singh, J. A. L., 339
Skeels, H. M., 233
Slight, D. A., 29
Small, A., 17
Smith, M. B., 212
Snyder, F., 185
Solomon, R. L., 51, 189, 289
Sorokin, P. A., 204, 220
Spence, K. W., 199
Spock, B., 28
Stagg, A. A., 293
Stoddard, G. D., 224, 226, 229, 230, 231, 249
Stone, C. P., 12
Stonequist, E., 346
Stouffer, S. A., 31, 53, 70, 71, 76, 107, 210, 273, 274, 291, 294, 313
Strauss, A. L., 285, 291, 308, 382, 407
Sturman-Hulbe, M., 12
Sullivan, H. S., 386
Sumner, W. G., 375
Szent-Gyorgyi, A., 37

Taba, H., 261, 268, 269
Tarde, G., 375, 377, 378
Taylor, D., 243
Taylor, R. L., 240
Taylor, T., 143
Taylor, W. S., 126
Terman, L. M., 287
Thomas, W. I., 17, 62, 64, 76, 254, 270, 271, 381
Thorndike, 14, 199
Thurstone, L. L., 226, 400, 401, 404
Toby, J., 294
Tryon, C. M., 26

Ulio, J. A., 68
Updegraff, R., 324

Valien, P., 61
Van Gogh, V., 202
Volkmann, J., 227
Von Andics, M., 348
Vreeland, F. M., 290

Wagner, R., 203, 239, 242-43
Wallin, P., 298
Ward, L. F., 375
Warden, C. J., 18
Watson, J. B., 15, 16, 77, 380
Weinberg, S. K., 320
Weinland, J. D., 235
Weld, H. P., 13, 16, 27, 38, 88, 95, 121, 130, 131, 134, 136, 138, 191, 192, 336
Welles, O., 217
Wendt, G. R., 134
Whitaker, J. C., 336
White, P. R., 339
White, R. W., 212
Wiener, N., 90-91
Wilson, W., 209

Winch, R. F., 59, 404
Wood, M. M., 346
Woodard, J. W., 408
Wright, Q., 15
Wundt, W., 371, 374
Wyatt, R. F., 246

Young, K., 14, 33, 48, 99, 181, 205, 208, 222, 407
Young, P. C., 137
Young, P. T., 13

Zeigarnik, B., 42, 43
Zillig, M., 127, 189
Zingg, R. M., 339
Zubin, J., 188

INDEX OF SUBJECTS

Ability, 391-93
  chess, 238
  musical, 238-39
  organic character of, 229-30
  social basis of, 223-49
Ability, exceptional
  confidence, factor of, 243
  effects of silent practice, 241
  relation of, to motivation, 240
  relation of, to perfectionism, 242
  retarded by conventionality, 244-45
Abnormality; *see* Disorganization, personality
Act, as unit of study, 379
Activity; *see* General activity
Addiction
  alcohol, 22
  gambling, 23
  miscellaneous, 23
  opiate, 22, 121
  tobacco, 23
Adrenalin, relation to general activity, 38
Age, relation of, to personal disorganization, 335-36
Aggression; *see* Frustration-aggression concept
Alcohol, relation of, to personal disorganization, 337-38
Altruism, 52
Amnesia, 125, 314-15
  false, 133
Applied Social Psychology; *see* Social psychology
Aspiration, relation of, to intelligence measurement, 226-29
Attitude, 16
Attitudes, social, 200-14, 219-20
  alteration of, 209-14
  concept defined, 200-1
  defining function of, 202-5
  derived from reading, 209
  in race relations, 204, 207-8, 210, 212-14
  institutional sources, 209

physical stereotypes, 204-5, 208
  relation of, to authority, 203, 206-9
  relation of, to styles, 202-3
  use of propaganda to influence, 210-14
Authority; *see* Attitudes
Automatic writing, 140-44

Behaviorism, 376, 381
Belief, social basis of, 215-19
Brain
  function of, 38
  impairment, effects of, 331-35

Canalization, 43-47
  destruction of, 45-46
  experiment, 43-44
  relation of, to conditioning, 81
  relation of, to culture, 49-50
Catharsis, 27-32, 387
  relation of, to instincts, 27-32
  research in, 28-32
Character
  formation and rigidity, 293
  patterns of, 321-26
Clinical Psychology; *see* Psychology, clinical
Competition, relation of, to ability, 226-29
Completion tendency, 36, 40-43, 99-100
  in dreams, 101-2
Complexity, relation of, to motivation, 46-47
Conditioned reflex, 377
Conditioning, 16-17, 34
  inadequacy of concept, 78-85
  relation of, to canalization, 81
  relation of, to learning, 78-81
  relation of, to consciousness, 82-85
  relation of, to unconsciousness, 117
Consciousness, 77-113, 115
  as adaptation to crisis, 88-95, 97-98
  exploratory nature of, 94-95
  function of, 83, 85-95
  muscular aspects, 95-96, 178-80

415

Continuity, consequences of break in, 303-4

Cornell scaling method, 401-2

Crisis
relation of, to character patterns, 321-26
relation of, to suicide, 364

Currency aspects of motivation, 51-55

Cybernetics, 90-91

Daydreams, relation of, to consciousness, 99-100

Defect, physiological, effects on behavior, 330-38

Degeneration; see Disorganization, personality

Delinquency, experiment in, 398-99

Desires, 17

Destructiveness, relation of, to low morale, 73

Diet, self-selection of, 19-21

Disorganization, personality, 329-69, 394-96
defined, 329-30

Dissociation of selves, 154-55

Dreads, related to consciousness, 100-1

Dreams
as problem solving, 101-2
fantastic character of, 104
psychoanalytic view of, 103-4
relation of, to consciousness, 101-4

Drives, 17-19, 21, 29
acquired, 22-23
hierarchy of, 13
manipulatory, 39-40
sex, 27, 120; see also Libido
visceral, 38-39
relation to libido concept, 23-25

Divorce, relation of, to role conflict, 299

Eccentricity, 349-50

Ego-involvement, relation of, to completion tendency, 42-43

Einfühlung; see Empathy

Electro-shock therapy, effect of, on orientation, 188

Emancipation, from parents, 287

Emergence, 8

Emotions
defined in experience, 106
defined in imagination, 106
differentiation of, 105
function of, 106
identification of, 16
innate, 15-16
relation of, to action, 104-7

to blocked activity, 16
to emergency response, 105
to institutional roles, 58

Empathy, 177-80, 394

Eroticism, oral, 26-27

Etiquette; see Social control, informal

Exclusiveness; see Primary group

Experiment; see Research methods

Factor analysis, 404

Fatigue, relation of, to personality disorganization, 335

Fear; see Neurosis

Feral men, 339

Forgetting; see Memory

Freedom, relation of, to social organization, 9-10

Frustration-aggression concept, 321-26

Function, as a general human tendency, 35-36

Games, relation to roles and social organization, 152

General activity, physiological basis of, 37-40

Generalized other, concept of, 152-53

Genius; see Ability, exceptional

Gestalt Psychology, 382-83

Gestures, 151-52
conversation of, 109
defined, 108
significant, 108-9

Gregariousness; see Sociability

Group fallacy, 5

Guilt; see Repression

Habit
relation of, to consciousness, 86-87
relation of, to skill, 87
relation of, to unconsciousness, 123

Happiness, 47

Homeostasis, 36

Hypnosis
relation of, to faking, 136n, 138
to repression, 134-39

Hysteria
relation of, to blindness, 134
to malingering, 133

Imagery, relation of, to muscular movements, 95-96

Imitation, relation of, to learning, 177-80

Incest, aversion to, 62

Indecision, relation of, to instability of status, 167

Individual Psychology of Alfred Adler, 385

Infancy, 3
Informal social control; *see* Social control, informal
Insight, 119, 172-74
Instincts, 12-17, 27, 372-76, 381
  defined, 12, 14
  hunting, 14
  limitations of concept of, 12-13
  lists of, 14-15
  relation of, to human behavior, 13-15
    to repression, 124
  substitutes for, 15-22
  overruled by informal social control, 270
Institutional office, defined, 58
Intelligence; *see also* Ability
  defined, 223-24
  difficulties of tests of, 224-26
  nature of, 223-26
  participation with superiors, relation of, 231
  preliterate, 224
  relation of, to linguistic development, 231
  social factors in, 225-26, 230-33
  socioeconomic differences in, 232-34
  tests of, relation to language, 225
  Thurstone factors of, 226
  value, 226
Interaction, 377-78; *see also* Primary interaction
  relation of, to development of mind, 380-81
Interests, 17
Isolation
  relation of, to consistency of self, 168
    to personal disorganization, 338-62
    to concept of self, 163

Kinship; *see* Primary group
Knowledge; *see* Ability

Leadership; *see* Roles
Learning, 172-82
  distinction between "expedient" and "proper" learning, 176-77
  from social patterns, 177-82
  in children, 174
  in monkeys, 40-174
  of speech, 181-82
  relation of, to consciousness, 179-80
    to reward, 39
  sets, 173-75
Least effort, principle of, 36, 63

Libido
  concept of, 23-27
  evidence against, 25-27
  relation of, to object choice, 27
Life history; *see* Research methods
Life organization
  collapse of, 362-65
  defined, 64-65
  relation of, to motivation, 65
Lobotomy, effects of, 332-35
Loneliness; *see* Isolation
Looking-glass self, 380
Love; *see* Romantic love

Malingering; *see* Hysteria
Malnutrition, relation of, to personal disorganization, 336-37
Memory, 190
  dependence on relationships, 191-95
  in early life, 125
  of mental caculators, 235
  rehearsal factor in, 131
  relation of, to context, 129-31
    to lapse of time, 130
    to meaningfulness, 192-95
    to self-esteem, 131
    to social frameworks, 195
  selective, 125, 127-29, 131
  wish and attitude, relation of, 190-91
Mental calculators, 234-37
Mental organization, relation of, to social process, 107-13
Mentality, in infants, 149
Methods; *see* Research methods
Mind; *see also* Mental organization and Unconscious mind
  organization of, 115
Monkeys, abstract thought in, 174
Mood, relation of, to instability of status, 167
Morale, 66-73
  relation of, to neurosis, 315
Motivation; *see also* Morale
  biological, 11-33
  for courtship, 59-60
  individual aspect of, 34-48
  relation of, to ability, 227
    to biological elements, 58-62
    to child-bearing, 60-62
    to marriage, 60
  rigidity of, 63-64
  social character of, 49-76
Motives
  generalization of, 51-55
  institutional integration of, 55-64
  relation of, to general activity, 37

Needs, 17-21
  defined, 19
  relation of, to activity, 36, 39
Negativism, 323
Neurosis; see also Roles
  in animals, research in, 311-12
  career aspect of, 316-20
  case illustration, 320
  childhood tendency, 319-20
  relation of, to birth order, 318
    to conflict, 309-12
    to fear, 312-14
    to isolation, 320, 347-48
    to low morale, 71
    to maternal overprotection, 318-20
Novelty, relation of, to motivation, 46-47

Opiate addiction; see Addiction
Optical illusions; see Perception
Organic social psychology, 379-82
Organism
  characteristics of, 5-7
  defined, 5
  relation of, to society, 7n
Organization, social; see Social organization
Orientation, 96-97, 99, 185-88; see also
    Consciousness and Perception
  in dreams, 102-4
  to a social situation, 188
Oxygen lack, relation of, to personal disorganization, 338

Panic, case of, 217
Perception, 99, 121, 172
  as an active process, 182-85
  as learned behavior, 184-85
  as selection, 183-84
  optical illusions in, 186-87
  relation of, to change, 88
    to orientation, 185-88
  social contexts of, 188-90
Personal disorganization; see Disorganization, personality
Personality, multiple; see Self
Personality organization, defined, 329
Physiological essentials to normality, 389-91
Prestige; see Status
Primary group, 57, 281, 379
  as generator of participation habit, 254-55
  as process, 253
  assimilation into, 275-77
  characteristics of, 250-55
  defined by Cooley, 250

differentiation of status in, 256-62
  homogeneity, 257-58
  in military organizations, 273-74
  motivation for forming, 263-64
  relation of, to formal controls, 252
    to kinship, 253-54
  size of, 255
  tendency to form, 255-56
Primary interaction, 250-80
  defined, 4
Problem solving, 172-76
  affected by brain impairment, 332
  by groups, 230
Prodigies; see Ability, exceptional
Progress, relation of, to motivation, 46-47
Propaganda; see Attitudes, social
Psychoanalysis, 383-85
  example of, in automatic writing, 141-42
Psychology, clinical, 386
Psychology, individual, 371-75
Psychology, social; see Social psychology
Psychopath, traits of, 361-62
Psychosexual development, 25

Race relations; see Attitudes, social
Random activity, 35
Rebelliousness, relation of, to low morale, 73
Recall; see Memory
Recapitulation, 24
Recognition; see Status
Reflex, 34
  prepotent, 16-17
Reflex arc concept, 379
  relation of, to consciousness, 93-94
Regression, 139-40
  in hypnosis experiment, 137
Relaxation, relation of, to consciousness, 179
Repression, 124-25, 127, 134
  experiments in, 128, 132-33
  of early memories, 125
  of guilt feelings, 122
  theory of, 120
Research problems, 389-96
Research methods, 396-407
  clinical, 397-99
  experimental, 403, 405
  life history, 399-400
  mathematical and statistical, 402-4
Restlessness, 39
  relation of, to motivation, 36
Reward, relation of, to motivation, 35
Role of the other; see Empathy

Roles
 age, 288-89
 deficiences of, in psychopaths, 362
 as differentiating factors, 281-308
 deficiencies of, in schizophrenia, 353-55
 institutional, 55-58
 leadership, 290-91, 293
 multiple, 284
 nature of, 281-84
 neurotic, 309-28
 of isolates, 347
 popularity, 289
 relation of, to self, 157
 sex, 284-87, 296-99
Role-taking
 ability in, 282-84
 relation of, to learning, 181-82
  to neurosis, 316-17
Romantic love, 59-60
Rumors, 216-19

Scaling methods, 400-2
Schizoid personality, 318-19
Schizophrenia
 defective motivation and rapport in, 350-51
 paranoid type, 355-57
 regression in, 139-40
 relation of, to isolation, 349-62
Schools of thought, 388-89
Self
 as internalization of social process, 151-55
 conception of, 157-71
 evaluation of, 157-61
 genesis of, 149-53
 integration of, 155
 multiple, 154-55
 organs of, 149-50
 relation of, to isolation, 166, 168
  to primary interaction, 164-66
 revision of, 159-61
 spatial location of, 149-50
 uncertainty and fluctuations in, 161-68
 unstable conceptions of, 167
Self-consciousness, 149-71
 functions of, 155-61
Selfishness, relation to disorganization, 52n
Sex; see also Libido; Roles
 children's interest in, 25-26
Sociability, 51-52
 excessive, 168
Social attitudes; see Attitudes, social

Social control, formal, 272-75
Social control, informal, 156-57
 character of, 266-69
 contrasted with formal control, 272-75
 in military organizations, 272-74, 292
 penalties used in, 266-68
 power of, 269-72
Social order, 5-10
Social organization, 3-4
 dependence of human on, 9-10
 relation of, to human behavior, 8
Social process, relation to self, 150-55
Social psychology, 4; see also Organic social psychology
 applied, 383-88
 backgrounds and trends, 370-89
 research problems in, 389-96
 scientific stage of, 388-89
Society for the Psychological Study of Social Issues, 387
Solitary confinement, effects of, 340
Solitude, relation to ability, 236, 244
Speech learning; see Learning
Statistics; see Research Methods
Status; see also Primary group; Role
 as prescribed activity, 259
 as a relation, 260
 conflicts of, 294-304
 function of, 52n, 259-62, 264
 relation of, to behavior standards, 261-62
 underestimation of, 166
 unstable conceptions of, 167-68
Stereotypes; see Attitudes, social
Stimulus, as initiator of act, 82-83
Stimulus-response theory, 36; see also Conditioning
 relation of, to consciousness, 92-94
Storage aspects of motivation, 51-55
Styles; see Attitudes, social
Sublimation, 126
Suicide
 relation of, to collapse of life organization, 363-64
  to isolation, 347-48
Suppression, 125-26
Symbolization, in monkeys, 174
Symbols, significant, 109

Talent; see Ability, exceptional
Testing methods, 400
Thematic apperception, 99n
Thumb-sucking, 26-27
Topological psychology, 382-83

Unconscious mind, 114-48
  limitations of the concept of, 132-48
  various meanings of, 116-19
Unconsciousness, 178
  psychoanalytic conceptions of, 115, 145
  related to habitual activity, 88, 110
Unconventional behavior; see Disorganization

Unfinished tasks; see Completion tendency

Wish fulfillment in dreams and daydreams, 99-101
Wishes, 17, 43-47; see also Canalization
  relation of, to consciousness, 99
Whole, relation to parts, 5-7

Zeigarnik effect, 42